Singing the Blues

Singing the Blues:

The Conservatives in Saskatchewan

Dick Spencer

2007

Copyright © 2007 Canadian Plains Research Center, University of Regina
Copyright Notice
All rights reserved. No part of this work covered by the copyrights hereon may be reproduced or used in any form or by any means—graphic, electronic, or mechanical—without the prior written permission of the publisher. Any request for photocopying, recording, taping or placement in information storage and retrieval systems of any sort shall be directed in writing to the Canadian Reprography Collective.

Canadian Plains Research Center
University of Regina
Regina, Saskatchewan S4S 0A2
Canada
Tel: (306) 585-4758
Fax: (306) 585-4699
e-mail: canadian.plains@uregina.ca
http://www.cprc.uregina.ca

Library and Archives Canada Cataloguing in Publication

Spencer, Dick, 1931–
Singing the blues : the Conservatives in Saskatchewan / Richard Earle Spencer.

(Canadian plains studies, ISSN 0317-6290 ; 50)
Includes bibliographical references and index.
ISBN 978-0-88977-206-9

1. Progressive Conservative Party of Saskatchewan—History. I. University of Regina. Canadian Plains Research Center. II. Title. III. Series.

JL319.A55S64 2007   324.27124'04
C2006-906317-6

We acknowledge the financial support of the Government of Canada through the Book Publishing Industry Development Program (BPDIP) for our publishing activities.

Cover design: Brian Danchuk Design, Regina
Printed and bound in Canada by Houghton Boston, Saskatoon
Index prepared by Patricia Furdek (www.userfriendlyindexes.com)

Contents

Dedication vi
Acknowledgements vii
Preface viii
Introduction ix
1. Frederick W.G. Haultain: A Man To Remember 1
2. What Might Have Been 13
3. A Doctor in the House 31
4. Bye-Bye Blues 41
5. Against the Storm 51
6. "The Chief" 71
7. The Wilderness 87
8. A Gentleman Player 99
9. The Resistance Fighter 111
10. Singing the Blues 125
11. The Collver File 141
12. Song Sung Blue 151
13. An Emergent Champion 167
14. Blue Skies Smiling? 177
15. Rolling the Dice 187
16. Jailhouse Blues 195
17. Going, Going, Gone 201
18. Saskatchewan Tories and Conservatism in Saskatchewan 213
19. A Summing Up 223
Epilogue 229
Appendix: Provincial Rights Party, Conservative Party and
Progressive Conservative Party Leaders in Saskatchewan, 1905–1997 236
Endnotes 237
Index 251

Dedication

This book is for my grandchildren,
Benjamin and Colette.

My time has been the past:
Theirs is the future.

Acknowledgements

I want to thank the Canadian Plains Research Center, University of Regina, for making possible the publication of *Singing the Blues: The Conservatives in Saskatchewan*. I particularly want to express my gratitude to Dr. Bill Brennan of the History Department at the University of Regina for his scholarship, guidance and counselling during the writing of the book. Dr. Brennan's unwavering support and personal interest in the project were deeply appreciated. I also want to thank Brian Mlazgar, Publications Coordinator of the Canadian Plains Research Center, for his generous and essential encouragement of the undertaking from the beginning.

As well, I am much indebted to a range of Saskatchewan politicians and political associates who willingly shared their knowledge, experiences and insights with me in interviews and correspondence. These were immensely helpful.

Finally, I want to acknowledge the support given me by my wife Lily, who shared my interest in our province's past and encouraged me to write about it. Her love of the people and the politics of Saskatchewan is as deep as my own.

Dick Spencer
Prince Albert, Saskatchewan
December 2006

Preface

This book wasn't written by an academic. It boasts only to have been written by a longtime player and participant in the shifting affairs of Saskatchewan's Conservative Party politics. Adding to the essential studies and expertise of the political scientist and historian, those in this province who actually practise politics, as well as study it, when they write, can help to put a human face on political affairs and offer a little firsthand light and shadow, some touches of narrative and memoir. I've tried to do this.

The impetus for this book has been my interest, a fascination really, in the politics of Saskatchewan and my involvement in it as an observer, commentator and unabashed partisan player over most of my adult life. Much of any insight or perspective I may have to share has grown from direct, "hands on" participation in municipal, provincial and federal political campaigns and in the public service. Years of experience as a city councillor and mayor, three provincial election contests as a Progressive Conservative candidate and five federal campaigns as a party organizer and president of the Right Honourable John Diefenbaker's Prince Albert constituency organization have allowed me many windows on the Saskatchewan political landscape and on the Tory battles fought there.

In writing this book, I'm grateful to have had the benefit of a rich resource of readings from Saskatchewan history and political science publications and from a wide archival print and media reportage. For the last chapters of the book, beginning with the politics of the 1950s, I'm particularly indebted to the players and operatives who have shared their views, interpretations and personal experiences with me. Many of these were and remain valued friends and associates.

My hope for *Singing the Blues* is that it has both enough academic quality to be helpful to students of Saskatchewan politics and sufficient narrative appeal to be interesting to a range of more casual readers.

Singing the Blues is a true story. I've tried conscientiously to be faithful in my telling of it.

Introduction

In the Foreword to his extraordinary book, *The Making of the President, 1964*, Theodore H. White tells us: "Every man who writes of politics, shapes unknowingly in his mind some fanciful metaphor to embrace all the wild, apparently erratic events and personalities in the process he tries to describe."

What "fanciful metaphor" might I have shaped to help me describe nine decades of Conservative Party politics in Saskatchewan? At its darkest my image might be a succession of legions plodding an indefinite, long march from disappointment to disappointment and ending in a last confusion and surrender. Certainly, it could not be some colourful, heroic metaphor of quest, conquest and happy endings. The story of the Saskatchewan Conservative Party has not been a happy one. It's been a tale of Tory blues.

From the party's beginnings in the Territories through its convulsive 1929 campaign and first victory that year under J.T.M. Anderson to its shadowy dissolution nearly 70 years later, the Saskatchewan Conservative Party struggled for relevance and survival. After their 1929 win, Conservatives waited half a century to form their next government, when they won the 1982 election under Grant Devine.

For Saskatchewan Conservatives, later named Progressive Conservatives and often called Tories, the years between the Anderson and Devine governments were confused and troubled times of wandering down a nowhere road. Often Conservatives must have asked themselves, "What's this all about? Where are we going? Where is the promised land?" Tories were always denied government and usually completely shut out of the legislature.

They suffered from soft party loyalties and indefinite, shifting ideological identities. Over the years, the party was weakened by chronic scant funding and lack of patronage leverage. Their organizations, both central and constituency, were small, undisciplined and unreliable, unable to deliver winning numbers. Successive party leaders failed to build majorities. With the exceptions of the young John Diefenbaker and Alvin Hamilton, and in later years, perhaps, Grant Devine, they were earnest but unexceptional men. Most were soon overcome by the seemingly impossible demands and thankless nature of their job.

It wasn't until John G. Diefenbaker's federal Tory resurgence in the late 1950s that provincial Conservative spirits rose. Diefenbaker's populist magic touched the slumping, disconsolate provincial party and stirred some vital signs. However, the party's return to robust health had to wait until the late 1970s with the leadership of Dick Collver. In the early 1980s Grant Devine, building on Collver's work, found that elusive "promised land" and won a dazzling landslide victory in 1982. At last, after 50 years of shadows and blues the Saskatchewan Conservative Party found itself on the sunny uplands. Tories were back on the government benches and seemed poised to remain there a while. Surely they would be powerful players in provincial affairs for years to come!

This didn't happen. Devine's PC government lasted two terms. The first term was stable but troubled; the second term, convulsive and disastrous. After two subsequent routs at the hands of the NDP, the PC Party fell prey to a new right-wing alliance calling itself the Saskatchewan Party and was devoured by it. Whereas conservatism was still alive in Saskatchewan, the Saskatchewan Progressive Conservative Party was not!

Is the Saskatchewan Tory story really over, or just left unfinished? Will there be more story to tell? We don't know.

But what we surely have learned from the adventures of Saskatchewan politics of the past is that nothing in the future should be taken as given. Nothing need surprise us.

1

Frederick W.G. Haultain: A Man To Remember

It's unlikely that today's University of Saskatchewan students, passing to and fro through their Memorial Gates on campus, take notice of a single grave beside these gates. Probably most of them would be surprised to discover the grave and puzzle about the who and the why of it. Yet, buried here are the ashes of the man some believed Saskatchewan's greatest Territorial statesman, the foremost Conservative architect of Saskatchewan's provincial autonomy. Buried here are the remains of Sir Frederick Haultain, a former Conservative Premier of the North-West Territories, Leader of the Opposition in the first Saskatchewan Legislative Assembly, a founder of the University of Saskatchewan, Chancellor of that University and Chief Justice of the province.[1]

Today, F.W.G. Haultain is largely unknown to the general population and much neglected by the few Canadians who have even a vague knowledge of him. This is both surprising and sad. "His was the most remarkable career in public life of any individual in the pioneer period of the Canadian West."[2] Saskatchewan Conservatives today could argue that only Diefenbaker, because of his long federal parliamentary career and incomparable skills as a campaigner, surpasses Haultain in service to the party and the province. Frederick Haultain, Saskatchewan's forgotten Father of Confederation is a man to remember.

In 1887, a redoubtable young lawyer from Fort Macleod, a cattle town in the North-West Territorial District of Alberta, came to Regina, the Territorial capital, to attend his first North-West Council. Frederick William Gordon Haultain was a John A. Macdonald man and destined to become arguably the most distinguished Conservative Party leader in the history of the Canadian North-West and of the province of Saskatchewan. He'd come to the North-West out of Toronto in 1884 at age 27, jolting four days by railway to Calgary, then rolling and bumping two days by stage-coach on to Fort Macleod, there to practise law and politics. He felt not a quiver of doubt or apprehension about his future in the Canadian hinterland.

Young Haultain was a Conservative. Before him his father Colonel F.W. Haultain, a British immigrant, had been active in Canadian politics and in 1864 elected as the Conservative member of the Legislative Assembly for Peterborough in the Province of Canada. The senior Haultain had been a

Frederick W.G. Haultain as Premier of the North-West Territories, c. 1904 (SAB R-B3200).

strong supporter of John A. Macdonald, his Liberal-Conservative Party and the Coalition ministry that would lead to the achievement of Confederation in Canada. John A. Macdonald's Conservative ideology was a skillful blend of toryism and liberalism.[3] Macdonald favoured a conservatism with a wide appeal to an increasingly liberal-minded populace. We can safely assume that young Frederick Haultain carried his father's and Macdonald's political dispositions with him to the Canadian West.

He was eager. He fit right in with life on the frontier. He liked the people and they liked him. Within three years he was their man and on his way to Regina, one of 14 elected members of the Territorial Council and one of its "brightest and most active members."[4] Now he was the Honourable Member for Macleod and from the start a man who wanted change in the North-West. Haultain wanted the Territories to become a province.[5]

In 1887 the North-West Council, provided by the North-West Territories Act of 1875, was a mix of elected and appointed members who advised the Lieutenant-Governor whose administration was directed by Ottawa. Obviously, this was unacceptable in the West. Granted, limited representative government was a step toward the essential goal of responsible government, but this prize was still to be gained. Haultain, as an Advisory Council member and chairman of the Executive Committee of that Council and later as Territorial premier, was always a determined and effective advocate of Territorial self-government. For him, limited representative government was only a tease. His aim and the aim of his Conservative friends was first to achieve responsible cabinet government for the North-West and then push on to autonomy and provincial status.

This ultimate condition was only won after years of hinterland pressuring and petitioning of the federal authority. Haultain and his allies argued a reasoned case in persistent yet cautious presentations. In those early days, politics in the North-West was non-party, non-partisan. Men who were Conservatives or Liberals federally, put aside their party labels and worked together in Territorial affairs. Always, they feared alienating an often indifferent, even hostile Ottawa. At first there was no real widespread people's agitation for Territorial autonomy. The folks at home had other things on their minds. They were poor, and they were few:

> Settlers in the Territories showed scant interest in the question. Their attention was fully occupied with immediate problems of establishing themselves, and the public problems which they saw as pressing were schools, bridges and roads. Constitution matters were remote by comparison.[6]

They had land to clear, bread to earn, houses, schools and churches to build, families to rear, barns to raise, coyotes, gophers, wind, winter and drought to survive. These were hearty, working peoples, a mix of Native and Métis, eastern Canadian homesteaders, European immigrants and American settlers. Their North-West was a far-flung country, its population thin and scattered.[7] Telegraph, railway, newspaper and postal communication was in its infancy. It was inevitable that so much depended on the dogged, talented advocacy of the handful of Territorial representatives from Regina who repeatedly journeyed east to lay their claims before their Dominion governors.

Someone in Ottawa listened. In 1888 Parliament passed a new North-West Territories Act that gave the Territories its first elected Legislative Assembly, an Assembly of 22 elected members and three appointed legal advisors. Significantly, in the Act the Lieutenant-Governor chose an Advisory Council from the elected Assembly to advise him on financial questions. The North-West edged closer to responsible government but not fast enough for some in the Assembly. F.W.G. Haultain spoke eloquently for them, calling the new legislation "only a shadow of self-government."[8]

In 1891, the Dominion Parliament passed a new North-West Territories Act. No longer were any members of the Territorial Assembly appointed. All were elected and their number increased from 22 to 26. The old Advisory Council was replaced by an Executive Committee with Haultain as its head. The Lieutenant-Governor was excluded from this committee. The Assembly assumed a greater control of Territorial finances.

The last nagging question about responsible government was answered in 1897 when Parliament replaced the Executive Committee with an Executive Council made responsible to the Assembly. Here was the Territories' first cabinet. On October 28, 1897, Lieutenant-Governor Mackintosh, delivering the Speech from the Throne in the old Territorial Legislature, congratulated the honourable members "upon the ultimate attainment of a completely responsible system of government."[9] Even though his government still lacked control of its natural resources and remained dependent on Ottawa for essential funding grants, Haultain, now the Territorial premier, must have celebrated into the night with his Conservative and Liberal colleagues and associates. There had been no calling to arms, no mustering of militia, no marching to bugles and drums. All had been accomplished rather neatly in a quiet Canadian way.

How significant was Haultain's contribution to the winning of democratic government on the prairies? It wasn't just considerable, it was crucial.

Grant MacEwan, notable author and student of western Canadian politics and an uncompromising admirer of Haultain argues:

> No student of public affairs in western Canada can review the Haultain years without realizing that the advent of responsible government in the prairie region was mainly his accomplishment.[10]

With responsible government in hand, Premier Haultain could now look ahead with mounting confidence to the next engagement, the struggle for provincial status.

Responsible government had been won, but the victory came with a sizeable price tag. The North-West was growing rapidly, its immigrant numbers swelling and its need for services urgent and constant. Demands for provincial status arose directly out of the Territories' financial problems. The accelerating costs of schools, roads, bridges, public works and public services could no longer be met by the Territorial government. The government's major source of revenue was a federal grant given on a yearly basis at the discretion of Ottawa. What the North-West needed was the more secure financial basis of a negotiated subsidy. Autonomy for the Territories could secure such funding.

Without provincial status, the Territorial government lacked the power to borrow on provincial credit for needed capital funding or raise tax dollars from land sales. Territorial revenue from licences and fees was only minimal. Agitation for provincial status began in earnest in 1900. It was led by the Territorial premier, Frederick Haultain. Haultain and J.H. Ross, a Territorial Liberal, visited Ottawa in 1900 and again in 1901 to express the demands and requirements laid out in a Territorial Assembly resolution calling for provincial autonomy. The case was formally submitted in a draft bill by Premier Haultain to Prime Minister Sir Wilfrid Laurier on December 1, 1901, and called for the creation of one western province made up of the existing four provisional districts of Saskatchewan, Alberta, Athabasca and Assiniboia. By Haultain's own description, offered earlier in an impassioned speech to the 1896 session of the Assembly, "it would be a large province holding its own in Confederation, the most powerful province in Confederation."[11] Later, Haultain suggested "Buffalo" as the name of the new and mighty province. In 1901, in an eloquent appeal to a meeting in Indian Head, he attacked the federal government for wanting to "cut this country up into little pieces." He called for one large province and challenged his listeners:

> Are you afraid of the proposal? Are you afraid to be part of a province exceeding all others in area, in population and in resources? Are you staggered by the realization of your own splendid prospects?[12]

The new province, the submission suggested, should have four members of the Senate and ten in the House of Commons. The new province, Haultain and his colleagues argued, among other benefits "should have the same local constitutional rights and powers as the other provinces and enjoy full control of its Crown lands, natural resources and subsidies."[13]

In a letter, dated March 27, 1902, Clifford Sifton, federal Minister of the Interior, replied to Haultain. Sifton questioned the wisdom of adopting the Haultain proposal to pass legislation forming the North-West into a province or provinces. Sifton argued that the Territorial population had not increased sufficiently for this and "there is considerable divergence of opinion respecting the question of whether there should be one province or more than one province." Sifton concluded, somewhat curtly, "Holding this view, therefore, it will not be necessary for me to discuss the details of the draft bill which you presented as embodying your views."

Haultain protested vigorously in an April 2 reply to Sifton:

> We cannot but regret that the Government has not been able to recognize the urgent necessity for the change that has been asked.

Then, putting aside the issue of constitutional change for the present, he returned to the subject of the financial needs of the North-West:

> While we may, in your opinion, without inconvenience mark time constitutionally, we cannot do without the transportation facilities, the roads, bridges, the schools and the other improvements which our rapidly growing population imperatively requires—and at once.[14]

On April 8, Haultain moved the following resolution in the Territorial Assembly:

> Whereas the larger powers and income incidental to provincial status are urgently and imperatively required to aid the development of the Territories to meet the pressing necessities of a large and rapidly increasing population, be it resolved that this House regrets that the federal government has decided not to introduce legislation at the present session.[15]

Ten days later the subject came up for debate in the House of Commons in connection with a money bill for Territorial schools. Federal Conservative leader Robert Borden entered the fray, declaring existing Territorial federal grants inadequate and supporting Territorial autonomy. Minister of the Interior Clifford Sifton remained unmoved. He told the Commons that while the Liberal government was then considering the financial concerns of the Territories, he thought a settlement of the autonomy question in three or four years would be reasonable. He said the government would not be hurried in so important a matter. And it wasn't.

On May 19, 1904, Haultain wrote to Prime Minister Laurier asking that negotiations be resumed and autonomy legislation introduced in the House of Commons at the earliest possible date. He pointed out that the members of his Territorial Assembly, both Liberal and Conservative, were "absolutely united and representative of the wishes of the people."[16] Four months later, on September 3, Laurier wrote Haultain defending the government's delay in granting autonomy and reassuring him of Ottawa's continuing concern for the North-West. Parliament had just been dissolved and with a federal election imminent, Laurier promised,

> Should the present government be sustained, it would be prepared immediately after the election to enter upon negotiations for arriving at a settlement of the various questions involved in the granting of provincial autonomy with a view of dealing with this problem at the next session of Parliament.[17]

Federal Conservatives, led by Robert Borden, campaigned vigorously for North-West autonomy in the 1904 general election. Frederick Haultain joined the Conservative campaign even though the autonomy question he spoke to seemingly had been lifted from the debate by Laurier's promise to resume the negotiations if re-elected and by Borden's support of provincial status for the Territories. One effect of Haultain's participation in the federal election campaign was to weaken his non-partisan image in Liberal eyes. Both federal and Territorial Liberals were finding his non-partisanship increasingly suspect. Time would tell how this might affect his future relationship with Laurier and the Grits.

The results of the 1904 federal election were decisive. Laurier's Liberals won 52% of the popular vote and 139 of 214 seats in Parliament. Borden carried 75 seats with 47% of the vote.[18] It was evident that the long struggle for autonomy in the Territories was nearly over.

Haultain had hoped for a smooth and rapid transition to provincial status for the prairie West. This hadn't happened. Almost at once the old non-party, non-partisan way of doing politics in the Territories began to change, giving way to increasingly robust Liberal and Conservative allegiances and divisions. Non-partisanship as a regional political movement had weakened as the autonomy negotiations proceeded. With provincial status for the Territories now a certainty, outstanding questions became more and more party issues with inevitable Tory blue and Grit red colours beginning to show. Haultain couldn't control these divisions and, as we will see, began himself to contribute to them.[19]

Haultain was a Conservative, but he really didn't like party politics and wasn't good at it.[20] He had neither the desire nor much talent for partisan politics. He had had little experience fighting at home with Territorial politicians over internal questions. His struggles had been with faraway federal administrations in Ottawa.[21] Partisan politics was a luxury which clashed with the obvious necessity of achieving a united front in the continuous battle with the federal government if any success was to be achieved.[22]

Many thought Haultain more statesman than politician. C.C. Lingard, a recognized authority on the Territorial years, is described as one who thought Haultain rose above the level of politician:

> Lingard's reverent treatment of F.W.G. Haultain's performance during the years of Territorial government involves the elevation of the Territorial premier to the status of statesman.[23]

Whether this was a weakness or a strength is arguable. Territorial Liberals were more aggressive than Haultain and seemingly more natural and skilled in power brokerage. Soon they would outstrip him as the political game got more and more serious.

The Liberal Party leader, Walter Scott, a newspaperman and former Liberal Member of Parliament, was young, energetic and politically astute. His Liberal Party loyalties were lifelong and inextinguishable. He learned his skills as a bare-knuckled political fighter in his early newspaper days in Regina and in the company of Liberal heroes and mentors in Parliament. Scott was a game and scrappy practitioner, comfortable in both Ottawa and hinterland politics. His opponent Frederick Haultain, although a superb debater and parliamentarian, seemed incapable of bloodletting. Haultain was not elusive or disguised in his dealings with others. He was not a Captain General able to arouse party passions in the new partisan politics on the prairies.

In February 1905, Prime Minister Laurier introduced bills granting provincial status to two new provinces to be called Alberta and Saskatchewan. Saskatchewan was to be governed by the Saskatchewan Act. The bills were approved by the House of Commons in July and the new provinces came into existence on September 1, 1905. Ottawa wasn't prepared to yield on the question of resource ownership and management. In Saskatchewan Laurier's friend, The Honourable A.E. Forget, was named the first Lieutenant-Governor of the new province. It was this Lieutenant-Governor's job to name the interim premier of the fledgling province. Would it be Haultain? Conservative voices were raised for him, and expectations of his appointment were high. Such recognition would have been well earned. Haultain had been Territorial premier since 1897 and before that a distinguished member of the Advisory Council and Chairman of the Executive Committee. He had been returned to office in 1902 and had led the struggle for autonomy. "He was thus really the 'Father' of the new province."[24]

There was enthusiasm for him in the West as early as 1903. The *Calgary Herald* in a December 8, 1903, editorial left no doubt about its eagerness that Haultain continue to hold high provincial office. The editorial enthused:

> It is not too much to say that this gentleman who for twelve years has led the Territorial House is the one man signally fitted by experience and attainments to continue to build on the foundation he has so well laid.[25]

But, no, Haultain would be passed over. He would not be appointed interim premier. His supporters in the West and admirers everywhere would think a grave injustice done him, an injustice driven by Liberal Party malice. Even contemporary eastern opinions would express outrage. The *Toronto Saturday Night* would lament that

> This strong, straight, able man who has directed nearly every good thing that has been done for the Territories is to be ousted from any share of the government of either of the two new provinces.[26]

The heavy slamming of these doors should have been anticipated by those attending the Monday, September 4, 1905, inaugural festivities in Regina. On that happy day in what would later be called the "Queen City" the new Province of Saskatchewan was inaugurated in a rousing daylong celebration. From early morning to late at night Regina celebrated, its near 6,000 population swelled by hundreds of visitors brought by excursion trains. Nothing seemed missing, nothing left out! The little city was dolled up in Union Jacks, red, white and blue bunting and arches of wheat sheaves and evergreens. Under these arches passed floats, Mounties, cowboys and Natives with 800 school children singing giddily, sporting commemorative ribbons and clutching bags of hard candy distributed by benign and generous city fathers. A touring circus even provided clowns and elephants.[27] Never before had Regina seen such pageantry nor felt its civic heart pounding and swelling as on that day.[28]

As if the elephants and Mounted Police were not striking enough, the Prime Minister had come to town and the Governor General too. Sir Wilfrid Laurier and the Honourable Earl Grey had come to Regina to proclaim the new province in the name of the Queen and her Canadian Parliament. They had come to make heroic speeches at the fairgrounds and to officiate at the public swearing in of Saskatchewan's first Lieutenant-Governor. After this ceremonial there would be more speeches at a grand luncheon in Government House and in the evening a fireworks display in Victoria Park. What a day to remember!

But something was missing. Someone had been left out! The Prime Minister was there and the Governor General. Of course, the newly installed Lieutenant-Governor, the Honourable A.E. Forget, was front and centre and certainly many provincial Liberal worthy gentlemen attended with radiant smiling faces. But where was the former Premier of the North-West Territories, the Honourable Frederick Haultain? He wasn't invited! There was no place for Haultain! He was not to sit with the dignitaries and be honoured and called upon to speak on an occasion he had laboured so long to bring about. This man, with "the best claim to statesmanship" in all the Territories, was not heard that day.[29] It was an amazing omission! Or was it?

The fact that there was no place on the dais for Haultain on September 4 presaged the events of the very next day. On September 5 the newly installed Lieutenant-Governor appointed his fellow Liberal and former Liberal Member of Parliament, 38-year-old Walter Scott, as interim premier of Saskatchewan. "Laurier had chosen the Liberal he felt would defeat Frederick Haultain, Walter Scott."[30] It would be for Scott to form the province's first government and call Saskatchewan's first election when he deemed it propitious. All the advantages of the premier's office, government patronage and federal support from Laurier were his to call upon.

Haultain could not have been happy with these events of early September 1905. We must assume that he wanted to be premier of Saskatchewan and expected to be named. We must also assume that he believed he had cleared and laid a straight path to his goal and would achieve it. When Haultain was bypassed, federal Conservatives and even national media protested a Liberal plot to deprive him of the provincial premiership. Academic debate of the question continued for years and still remains an interesting topic in undergraduate Political History classes. The constitutional aspects of the matter were argued on both sides. Forget, as Lieutenant-Governor, was the representative of the Crown and as such expected to act independently of the federal authority. Instead, many saw him as a Liberal Party agent when he bypassed the sitting Territorial premier, Conservative Frederick Haultain, for a Liberal Member of Parliament, Walter Scott. Forget

> had left himself open to a charge of being the willing instrument of a federal party machine. The Crown, according to constitutional custom, was above and beyond party politics.[31]

But Liberals argued that westerners in the recent 1904 federal election, having elected seven Grits from the ten Territorial parliamentary seats, had demonstrated overwhelming Liberal Party support, and with the imminent end of non-partisan politics in Saskatchewan they thought a Liberal premier in the new province appropriate. They were eager to see one named, constitutional niceties be damned! As for Forget and his decision to appoint a Liberal to the premiership, either he judged it his personal prerogative to do so or it was Laurier himself who put aside Haultain's considerable claim in a purely political act to give Saskatchewan Liberals a leg up in the two-party struggle for power in Saskatchewan soon to begin.[32]

Federal and provincial events from 1903 through to the 1905 debates on the autonomy bills in Parliament had made it easy to dismiss the constitutional debate as irrelevant. Haultain had himself played both a passive and an active role in the events leading to his removal as a candidate for the Saskatchewan premiership. The decision to bypass Haultain, however sad and unfair it seemed to many, was not an "iffy" constitutional decision, not some institutional failure. Simply put, it was political reality, much of it created by the Territorial premier himself, that took him out of the running. Haultain effectively disqualified himself.

Frederick Haultain (front row, centre) as Premier of the North-West Territories, with a group of civil servants, August 31, 1905, the day before the inauguration of Saskatchewan as a province (SAB R-B3770).

Non-partisanship in the Territories and Frederick Haultain's leadership of it had weakened progressively as the end of the struggle for provincial status neared. It had been that struggle that bound Territorial Conservatives, Liberals and Independents together in a relatively stable non-party association. That time had passed. Trouble for Haultain began to bubble at a March 1903 Territorial Conservative convention in Moose Jaw. Over Haultain's protests the convention passed a resolution to fight the next Territorial election as a Conservative Party. Conservative willingness to toss the no-party label and fight the next election on partisan lines raised suspicions among Haultain's Liberal supporters, while his personal objections to the shift to Tory partisan lines angered some of his Conservative friends:

> Feeling both Liberal and Conservative support slipping away from him and apparently unable to devise an effective strategy to get it back he was forced at last to make a choice between them.[33]

It was not his reluctant shift to the Conservatives in Territorial politics that put him out of the running for the premiership in Saskatchewan. Had he wanted, he might have finessed his way around that. It was his lively participation in the 1904 federal election that disqualified him. In 1904 he openly campaigned for the federal Conservative Party, hoping a Tory federal win would hasten provincial status in the West on terms acceptable to him. The gloves were off! Now the Liberals no longer played "he loves me, he loves me not" with Frederick Haultain. He loved them not!

Later, when Laurier brought the autonomy bills into Parliament, Haultain challenged the "two-province" provision, the government's decision to retain control of public lands and resources and the apparent protection of separate school rights included in the legislation. He would not accept Laurier's terms for autonomy in the Territories. Clearly, Haultain had attacked Laurier, his government and Liberal federal policy. Federal and provincial Liberals alike could now hardly be expected to trust and embrace the Territorial premier in the face of his fierce intransigence. Now they had every reason to do what many of them had always wanted to do and what the traditional political game required. They would secure a sympathetic Liberal government in each of the new provinces beginning with the naming of a Liberal as its first premier.

Frederick Haultain knew politics wasn't a game without rules. Surely, he knew what consequences might follow his attacks on Laurier and the Liberals. He couldn't have been surprised by their disqualification of him. Now he would have to fight to be premier in an election another man would call. If he had regrets about the events of the last year and concerns about his uncompromising part in them, he said nothing.

When Premier Walter Scott was organized, funded and ready for battle on the Saskatchewan hustings, he would make the call and, ready or not, the Conservatives would have to put up their dukes and fight.

2

What Might Have Been

Saskatchewan Conservatives would fight the provincial election as the Provincial Rights Party rather than as the Saskatchewan Conservative Party. Haultain said, "I am a mild type of Conservative."[1] "I stand for a non-party government… ."[2] The party name was an appeal to old Territorial bipartisan loyalties that he hoped were still his to summon. By avoiding a party label he hoped to invoke the spirit of past non-partisan independence and fight a safe and civil campaign. Was this strategy or naïveté? Surely, it was some of each. The Provincial Rights tag also reflected Haultain's sustained protest against federal control of Crown lands and natural resources and his passionate objection to Ottawa's original intrusive guarantees of separate school rights in the new province. He publicly vowed to take the "feds" to court if he won power in Saskatchewan. Haultain called the election of 1905 "a fight for provincial freedom."[3] He appeared to have a "you can run but you can't hide" attitude toward the Grit enemy.

Haultain's belief that party politics was unnecessary at the municipal and provincial level and even somewhat suspect in federal affairs seems unrealistic today.[4] Was he not aware of the strengthening ties between provincial and federal Liberals, and Laurier's work in progress to build Liberal Party satellites in the two new western provinces? Party politics, party organizations, networks, disciplines and brokerage were obviously the order of the day for Laurier and his Saskatchewan lieutenant, Walter Scott. The Liberal hegemony was building. How much of this did Haultain see?

Most Liberals had been preparing themselves since 1903 for their fight to gain power in the new province when its autonomy was declared. The new premier and his party had wasted no time in building constituency organizations, and reminding immigrants of their loyalties to the federal Liberals who had brought them to a promised land, even if many of the promises had been broken.[5] Saskatchewan Liberals not only controlled provincial patronage appointments of party faithful to public service jobs and public works contracts, they had the benefit of patronage available from the federal Liberal government as well.

The game could begin when the Liberal Party team was ready. The warm-up didn't take long! Scott called a winter election for December 13, 1905, a mere three months after his appointment as interim premier. The fledgling province had some 250,000 people. The election was fought in 25 constituencies, 20 of which had old Territorial boundaries with five new ridings added. Scott ran in Lumsden and Haultain left his old southern Alberta Fort Macleod seat behind and stood for election in Saskatchewan's South Qu'Appelle.

Saskatchewan's first provincial election was governed by the rules and procedures of the Territorial election laws already established. Under these laws all male British subjects over 21 years of age who had resided in the Territories for a year were eligible to vote in the constituency in which they had resided for at least three months prior to the election. These provisions were not new to the people of the Territories. In that first election there was no enumeration of voters, but a voter could be sworn in at the polling station. There were no printed ballots carrying the names of candidates or party identifications. In 1905 the voter was given a blank ballot and would simply mark an "X" on the ballot with either a blue or red pencil. Haultain's supporters would use a blue pencil and Scott's Liberals would use a red pencil.

Haultain was at a decided disadvantage in preparing for the 1905 campaign. Premier Scott chose the date of the election, a date he judged the most propitious for himself. In 1905 Scott chose to wait until after November 9 when the Alberta provincial election was held, yielding a generous Liberal victory in the sister province. Alberta Liberals won in 23 of the 25 Alberta constituencies. This was good news for western Liberals everywhere. It certainly didn't lift Haultain's spirits to see the Alberta Conservative Party wreckage.

Haultain was no match for Walter Scott as a political strategist. He was not good at the political game and seemingly not too keen to play it. Scott's election preparations were studied and thorough. In advance of the election Scott arranged for outside speakers to assist in the Liberal campaign if they were needed. Liberal campaign literature was printed in at least one foreign language in order to reach new settlers. Scott and his cabinet ministers contested what were considered the most difficult ridings in order to win or hold them, leaving safer seats to others less known and able. Liberal battle plans were carefully laid. The immigrant vote was assiduously tended and courted. Liberal organizers kept records of new settlers who could be naturalized in time to vote and sent their names to Liberal constituency officers who would make contact with them.[6] This was the poll work, the door-to-door grunt work that in tight races, then as now, can make the difference between a win and a loss.

The education clause of the Saskatchewan Act became an explosive issue in the 1905 election. The school clause had been a bone of contention from the beginning, and arguments over it aroused racial and religious passions, not only in government circles but across the country. In its original form, to some it appeared simply to echo the North-West Territories Act of 1875 with its provision for publicly supported separate schools. However, the Territorial school system had evolved and changed over the years, and the new

Saskatchewan Act's education clause failed to include provisions of later Territorial school legislation, in particular the landmark amendments to the School Act of 1892 sponsored by Haultain. These amendments brought administration of education in the Territories under central control in Regina and reduced the powers of separate school districts.[7] Separate schools in the Territories were still guaranteed, but standards, curriculum, texts and teacher qualifications were to be the same for both Roman Catholic and Protestant schools. The old dual system of school administration with a Board consisting of two sections, one Catholic and one Protestant, was replaced by a Council of Public Instruction responsible for the whole education system. This Council of Public Instruction was the forerunner of the Department of Education. These were important fundamental changes that needed to be recognized in the Saskatchewan Act. Pressure on Laurier to amend the original education clause to reflect these changes resulted in Laurier's amendment of March 22, 1905, which met the demands of most of its critics by including specific reference to relevant Territorial legislation which would keep both public and separate schools under direct control of the government.

The amended Saskatchewan Act school clause did not satisfy Haultain who, even though his Territorial government had passed separate school legislation, did not personally accept the principle of separate schools. He said as much in a January 20, 1891, speech to his own Fort Macleod constituents. He told the meeting:

> Under our present constitution a Protestant or Catholic minority has the right to establish separate schools, but I must confess my opposition to the principle. I see no reason why Protestants should not go to school with Catholics. I believe most people in the country want their children to be educated together without regard to religious differences. I believe the existence of two schools tends to divide children.[8]

Because Haultain, whatever his personal preferences might be, had accepted and enacted educational privileges for minorities, his objection to the amended school clause he submitted was constitutional and had nothing at all to do with public or separate schools. The Conservative opposition argued that inclusion of any school clause in the Saskatchewan Act was an invasion of provincial rights as education was wholly a provincial jurisdiction. By legislating on education, Haultain charged the Dominion government had overstepped its authority and that the education clause and the federal government's refusal to hand over public lands and natural resources to the new province should be challenged in the courts. And so the provincial election battle was joined on at least two highly charged and divisive issues.

The school question in 1905 was almost entirely a religious question. As such, it inevitably drew heated emotional responses. What would Haultain do if the province had the power to legislate for schools, the Liberals asked.

Would he, as he initially suggested, leave the system as he found it in the amended school clause or would he seek to change it to some form of a yet to be fully defined "national" school system? The Liberals pointed out contradictions in Haultain's answers to questions about his plans for school settlement if he gained power. They quoted him refusing to answer questions on the subject in a September 19 meeting in Saskatoon, then telling an October 24 Maple Creek audience that as premier he would "nationalize the schools." Later, on November 22 in Arcola, he was quoted as reversing himself on the nationalization issue, stating that if elected premier he would not change the existing educational system. There was also some question as to whether essential features of a "nationalized school system" had not already been brought into play with Haultain's 1892 School Act amendments.

The school question was made sensational by an intrusion into the issue by the Roman Catholic Archbishop of St. Boniface. Archbishop Langevin, a strong separate school supporter, in a memorandum asked Roman Catholics to support Scott and the Liberal government. He feared that Haultain could not be relied upon to maintain separate schools in the province. "Unite and vote for those who are in favour of the actual system of separate schools," the Archbishop advised.[9] When the Langevin memorandum was made public it caused a firestorm. On November 29 Haultain published an "Address to the Electorate," in which he charged that a conspiracy existed between the Liberal Party and the Roman Catholic Church, a compact he considered a dangerous threat to the school system and to the principles on which it had been built. He went on in the clearest of terms to express his reaction to the memorandum and his now clear desire to see the school system changed. As a result of the threatening compact between the Roman Catholic Church and his Liberal opponents, Haultain told the electorate:

> So long as I was satisfied that the present school system could be worked out satisfactorily, I was personally quite willing to leave it unchanged. But this conspiracy between the Roman Catholic church and a political party I can only look upon as a menace to our school system and to the sound principles upon which it has been established.... As the matter now stands it is clear to me that the only safety for our educational system lies in once and for all establishing it on an absolutely national basis, with equal rights to all and special privileges to none.[10]

Premier Scott denied the existence of such a Liberal-Roman Catholic compact and challenged Haultain to meet him on a public platform and prove his charges. Apparently Haultain had no evidence of conspiracy and was unable to do this. Haultain's allegation, without evidence, was a major misjudgment on his part. Earlier contradictions in his Saskatoon, Maple Creek and Arcola statements on school settlement made him appear uncertain. He seemed unable to clarify his position on separate schools. Later, his emphatic declaration for a national school system coming very near the end of the Provincial Rights' campaign probably attracted less attention than he had hoped, subordinated as it became to his explosive, unproven conspiracy theory of church interference.

Obviously, the constitutional and religious debate over the Saskatchewan Act and the school settlement defined in it were major issues of the campaign and a major factor in the outcome. It was natural that unqualified Liberal support for guaranteed protection for separate schools as embodied in the Saskatchewan Act would attract Roman Catholic voters and that Langevin's unsolicited memorandum would fan anti-Catholic flames and solidify support for Haultain among Protestant voters.

A factor, somewhat undefined and unspoken, that probably influenced the election results was the push-pull contrast of Scott's "peace, progress and prosperity" appeal and its promise of settlement and expansion with Haultain's "fight for provincial freedom" call to arms with its threat of legal challenges to Ottawa, resultant law suits and other religious and political confusions at home. However genuine Haultain was in his determination to achieve what he considered Saskatchewan's constitutional rights, the negative aspects and past tense reference of his campaign did not help create a climate of optimism and victory for him in 1905. If there was some battle fatigue felt in the new province, some yearning for stability, even some desire for reconciliation, these sentiments would surely be helpful to Scott and the Liberals who appeared to be forward looking, with sunny uplands ahead.

The campaign was intense. Walter Scott described the campaign as "the hottest kind of scrimmage."[11] Effective party organization and control of the administration at both the federal and provincial levels gave him an edge from the outset. Scott, with only a Grade 8 formal education, had learned much of politics and communication as a newspaper owner, Regina businessman and Territorial Member of Parliament. On his side throughout this and all of his campaigns was unswerving Liberal Party discipline and loyalty.

Haultain held Arts and Law degrees from the University of Toronto and had more political experience than Scott. He was a deliberate, precise public speaker and a confident campaigner. Haultain's party was more loosely bound than the Grits but loyal to him personally and to his provincial rights cause. The issues were mixed. Predictably, both parties touted ambitious plans for more and improved roads, bridges, schools and railway services. Scott was arguably the more credible messenger of these practical matters, speaking as an incumbent provincial premier with powerful Liberal friends in Ottawa. People thought he could deliver! His sales pitch was positive and optimistic. From meeting to meeting in schools and church halls across the province, he delivered wholesale, sunny promises of "peace, progress and prosperity." Haultain spread less joy. As Leader of the Opposition his battle plan was to attack Liberals wherever he found them. Those in high office in faraway Ottawa were not spared. He had no choice but to launch and pursue a negative campaign that was often more unsettling than reassuring to audiences that may have wanted relief from the enervating constitutional wrangling of the last few years. Perhaps the hinterland longed for good news. Haultain sharpened his attacks on Laurier and the federal Liberals, arguing for complete provincial autonomy, blaming Ottawa for denying Saskatchewan ownership of provincial Crown lands. He continued his warnings against the dangers of federal separate school guarantees apparently imposed on the province, and promoting separation of federal and provincial politics. He attacked the Lieutenant-Governor's recent actions, warning against having a "federal puppet" in Government House in Regina.[12] Haultain called for a review of the tax exemption given the Canadian Pacific Railway in its charter, arguing that the exemption restricted the province's rights of taxation.

Haultain's support came largely from Protestant old settler families and communities. His Provincial Rights Party had less appeal to Catholic and new European immigrant voters. After all, they would "dance with the guy what brung them," and it was the Liberal Party that had brought them to the prairies. This early, carefully cultivated loyalty of pioneer European Roman Catholic immigrant voters to the Liberal Party would continue for years to come in Saskatchewan. And why not? Weren't the "Provincial Righters" and Conservatives mostly Anglo-Saxon Protestants with puzzling signs and passwords? Wasn't it that Tory monster Sir John A. Macdonald who had filched life and treasure from the western half-breed poor and hanged the martyr-saint Louis Riel in vengeful wrath? Certainly, good Liberals didn't discourage any little calumnies helpful to themselves on polling days. The wicked Tories, too, were good at spinning hurtful canards to wound Grit enemies. What about their poisonous whispers about popish plotters in the backroom of the Liberal Party? How better to unsettle the newly come Brits, Scots, Irish and Yanks of Protestant persuasion and enlist them in safe Tory ranks?

On December 13, 1905, Saskatchewan's first legislature was elected from 25 constituencies. The election results were conclusive. Walter Scott's Liberals won 16 of the 25 seats, leaving Haultain and the Provincial Rights Party with the remaining nine seats. Haultain's popular support across the province remained strong. He won 48% of the popular vote to the Liberals' 52%. These numbers reflected both a hotly contested, close-run affair and continuing widespread recognition of Haultain's years of dedicated Territorial leadership. In many senses Haultain was the Provincial Rights Party, and the Provincial Rights campaign was Haultain's campaign.

Haultain's support was concentrated in the southeast of the province, where six of the nine Provincial Rights seats were won in older, settled, predominately Protestant areas. Here Haultain was easily elected in South Qu'Appelle and saw party victories in Wolseley, Grenfell, Whitewood, Moosomin and Souris. Provincial Rights candidates were winners in Moose

Jaw City in the south-centre, and Maple Creek in the far southeast. The only Provincial Rights northern win was in Prince Albert County, one of the oldest settlements in the province.[13] In general, support for Haultain was strongest in the older settled areas along the main line of the Canadian Pacific Railway. The Liberal Party won newly settled areas with populations of mainly differing ethnic groups, predominately Catholic in their religion. Of the 13 constituencies north of the main CPR line, the Liberals won 12, while Scott's Liberals won only four of the 12 southern area constituencies.[14] Premier Walter Scott, as he began in earnest to govern, had a seven-seat lead over Haultain in the legislature. The legislature would meet as it had for the last 15 years in the little Territorial Legislative Building on Regina's Dewdney Avenue. Haultain's new role as Leader of the Opposition would be a less exacting one, but he would play it deliberately and well.

Scott and his Liberal lieutenants must have known then that being the government not only gave them the challenge of providing the promised "peace, progress and prosperity" but the power to build a party organization of such discipline, compass and élan that it would be unbeatable in Saskatchewan for years to come. It would be called a "machine" with all that tough metaphor's suggestions of good and bad in the exercise of domination. And what did Haultain think about all this? Did he rail against the voters and his own candidates because he had lost, or question his own captaincy and threaten to quit the race? Not at all. He seemed to have accepted the election loss without anger or disillusion. Perhaps he felt fated. Yet surely he must have wakened in the far reaches of election night and questioned the organization of his defeated party. Was it inclusive enough, unified and strong enough to stand against the Liberals next time round? Would his own party grow with the burgeoning population, particularly the west and east European immigrant numbers? Had any lessons been learned by Saskatchewan Tories? Wouldn't they, too, like to be a "machine"?

Haultain's failure to win the premier's chair on December 13 was a shock to his Conservative friends and even to some Liberals. To many it seemed inconceivable that this Territorial statesman and champion could lose this one. For 18 years he had served the Territories with distinction and never lost an election. Why now? Why did he lose this most important fight of his life?

There were at least five reasons for the defeat of the Provincial Rights Party and its distinguished leader. The party's five obvious areas of weakness were patronage, party organization, immigrant and settler allegiances, the Roman Catholic vote and the waning appeal of the provincial rights issue.

Patronage first raised its head in the province when Liberal Prime Minister Laurier whispered in the ear of Lieutenant-Governor Forget that he should appoint Walter Scott and not Frederick Haultain as interim premier of Saskatchewan. Who can doubt this or dispute the huge Liberal advantage of having a Liberal as first premier? Gordon L. Barnhart, in his outstanding biography of Walter Scott, puts the matter bluntly:

The federal Liberals believed it was vital to have control of patronage for the first election. To have given Haultain the premiership would have been like giving him the keys to the store."[15]

With Scott and the Liberals calling the signals in Regina, federal and provincial patronage and promises of future patronage were Scott's to command. Politics is about gas and electric power, mining and roads, bridges, schools, hospitals, appointments, jobs and all manner of influences—subtle and otherwise. What would Haultain have done with these "keys to the store"?

Haultain did not have a political organizer like James Calder. Calder was Scott's closest associate in government and a superb organizer of election victories. He mobilized Liberal forces for Scott in the 1905, 1908 and 1912 campaigns. Probably the phrase "on the ground politics" wasn't current in Calder's time, but he understood its meaning and promise.[16] We are not sure that Haultain did.

From the beginning, the enduring allegiance of immigrant settlers to the Liberal Party was beyond Haultain's reach. A vigorous federal Liberal immigration policy peopled the West with largely Catholic eastern European farmers and created a grateful, growing constituency for Laurier and Scott. In contrast, the eastern Canadian Anglo-Saxon Protestant roots of federal and Territorial Conservatives made that party a cold and unwelcoming home for legions of immigrant Canadians. It's doubtful that Haultain's Provincial Righters made much of an effort to befriend these foreign non-English strangers to the hinterland.[17] But from the beginning Scott felt differently and knew better:

> Scott's government drew its electoral strength from immigrant settlers in the province, the largest group being of German and Ukrainian background.[18]

Added to Haultain's difficulties were the ghosts of Batoche and a scaffold in Regina. French Catholics in the new province still felt 20-year-old wounds from the 1885 Riel uprising and the hanging of Louis Riel. Whereas Orange Lodges and Tories in Ontario may have rejoiced at John A. Macdonald's refusal to heed passionate appeals and stop the hanging, Macdonald's ferocious cry, "He shall hang though every dog in Quebec bark in his favour," cost the Conservative Party dearly for years to come.

Haultain's decision to run on a Provincial Rights ticket rather than as a Conservative may have been considerably off the mark. It's probable that he overestimated the anti-Ottawa temper of the electorate. The old hostility was cooling rapidly and Scott, by the end of the 1905 campaign, no longer appeared as an Ottawa "toadie."

Whatever the reasons for the defeat of the Provincial Rights Party in 1905, it wasn't a knock-out blow. Haultain didn't seem beleaguered or threatened. What signs was he reading? He didn't even scramble to change the name of the party to its rightful Conservative label. He went quietly, doggedly on, doing his duty as Leader of the Opposition in the queer, cramped little Legislative Building on Regina's Dewdney Avenue.

Premier Walter Scott called Saskatchewan's second election for August 14, 1908. The election call was preceded by a seat redistribution that increased the number of constituencies in the legislature from 25 to 41. These additional seats were to serve a scattered population with representation in the Assembly and to keep pace with the rapidly expanding settlement of the province. The unexpected dissolution of the legislature and the calling of an election less than three years after the 1905 campaign came as a surprise to Haultain. He believed the early election call was calculated to catch his Provincial Rights opposition off guard. He knew the election announcement made even before the voters' lists were ready would give advantage to the government. Haultain suspected that the early polling in Saskatchewan was instigated by Ottawa to test the federal Liberal Party strength in the West before Laurier called a federal election.[19] Laurier called his federal election two months later and won easily.

The Saskatchewan Liberal Party believed itself ready. It seemed the Liberal organization was, in political science professor David E. Smith's apt phrase, a "well-oiled machine" and was always ready. As in 1905, the Liberal campaign was skilfully managed by Scott and James A. Calder, his director of organization and incomparable campaign strategist. Calder knew that "the lubricant of political machines is patronage."[20] The Liberal Party used public funds and offices to buy and reward its friends. In the early days of the 1908 campaign Haultain charged that the Liberals were using road and bridge gangs for election purposes. Whether he liked it or not Haultain must have known that every party, once in power, was under heavy pressure to use appointments as political rewards. You had to be the government in order to command patronage brokerage. Scott had that advantage.

But Walter Scott had much more than jobs, contracts and perks to trade for victory at the polls. He had an enviable record in office. His Liberals were governing Saskatchewan with assurance, building infrastructure, establishing institutions and structured government, tending to the agricultural and educational needs of a growing population. In 1908 Scott had a program that seemed bound to appeal to Saskatchewan farmers and rural residents, a program to make agriculture the cornerstone of the province's economy, a program with policies to create a good and healthy life in rural Saskatchewan. Among other promises the Liberals offered railway expansion for grain transportation, increased telephone service, the creation of rural municipalities, a rail line to Hudson's Bay, more schools, and free readers in schools. Scott suggested that his warm relationship with Ottawa Liberals would be helpful to Saskatchewan, something Haultain could not boast.

Haultain's Provincial Rights platform was similar in many respects to that of the Liberals. It too placed heavy emphasis on enrichment of life in rural Saskatchewan. Haultain, however, differed significantly with Scott on the question of public ownership. This was not a difference of emphasis as much as a difference of ideology. Haultain advocated public ownership of telephones and government ownership and control of elevators. His Provincial Rights platform called for legislation to protect farmers struggling with powerful combines of grain dealers and lumber interests and construction and operation of a Hudson's Bay rail line by a government commission.[21] This advocacy of direct involvement of government in the provincial economy was an expression of Haultain's conservatism, a blend of western populism and Tory collectivist belief in public policy and state intervention in the economy for the public good.

As in 1905, Walter Scott proved an effective campaigner. He may have surprised some Provincial Righters with his intensity and dash. Haultain's platform skills and public reputation were still formidable, but the angers and rooted indignations of past Territorial autonomy debates had cooled and this time Scott appeared to many provincial voters as a champion of Saskatchewan and not as Laurier's western lieutenant. He and his Liberals easily won their second election, winning 27 of the 41 seats to Haultain's 14. Haultain could not build on the 48% of the popular vote he had won in 1905. Again, in 1908, his Provincial Rights Party took 48% of the vote against 51% tallied by Scott's Liberal's. Haultain remained a strong second-place contender. Was he stalled in second place? Could he break out and win the premiership? He would have to wait for the next election to find out.

In 1911 Haultain's Provincial Rights Party shed that heroic but dubious label and became the Conservative Party of Saskatchewan. Robert Borden, the Conservative federal leader, was soon to be prime minister, having defeated Laurier after fighting a spirited anti-reciprocity campaign. At last, it seemed there was a real friend in Ottawa for Saskatchewan Conservatives! It didn't work out that way.

In the years separating the second and third election faceoffs between Haultain and Scott, a number of issues, some that had already been addressed in the 1905 and 1908 campaigns, continued to engage both men. All of these impacted on the 1912 election campaign and its outcome. Both Haultain and Scott continued to recognize that provincial attention must be given to key questions of telephone service and communications, roads, railway branch lines and grain storage if the quality of rural life in the province was to be sustained and enriched. In particular, two issues were paramount in the run-up to the 1912 campaign. Haultain did not fare well in either debate.

A major question facing farmers was how to escape the growing control of the agricultural industry in Saskatchewan by eastern companies who owned most of the grain elevators in the province. These Saskatchewan farmers wanted more control of the system of storage, loading and selling of their grain. The Saskatchewan Grain Growers Association (SGGA), the dominant voice of the farmers of Saskatchewan, petitioned the Scott government to purchase existing elevators in the province and become directly involved in the grain-handling system. The SGGA believed the government should own the elevators in order to best serve Saskatchewan grain growers. Both Haultain and Scott were sympathetic to the farmers' request for more control, but they differed on the question of ownership of the elevators.

Haultain supported the SGGA in its request for government ownership and operation of the elevators. Such government involvement suited his conservatism and would be in keeping with his personal preference for public delivery of community service, and he would naturally hope to attract some farmer electoral support by siding with them. Scott favoured cooperative ownership of the elevators. Co-operative ownership suited his liberalism with its emphasis on individualism and freedom. He hoped to bring the SGGA over to his viewpoint. What the farmers could do for themselves, they must be allowed to do for themselves. He appointed a Royal Commission to recommend a solution to the ownership problem. In its report the commission eschewed public ownership and favoured a scheme of cooperative elevators owned and operated by the farmers themselves, with financial backing from the provincial government. Scott persuaded the SGGA to support this recommendation of a co-operative venture which he himself had influenced and now welcomed. On March 14, 1911, legislation to establish the Saskatchewan Co-operative Elevator Company was passed by the legislature. The new elevator company, and its branches, was destined to provide Saskatchewan with exemplary service in grain handling and marketing in the years ahead.

And what about Haultain? Having advocated public ownership of the elevator system, Haultain was faced with a dilemma when the SGGA abruptly changed sides on the question of ownership. Now Haultain would either have to abandon support for a public enterprise or, holding to it, vote against the co-operative system and the farmers who now favoured it.[22] He opposed the legislation. He would pay a price at the polls for doing so.

Nothing would prove as damaging to Haultain's hopes of returning to power in 1912 as a looming battle over reciprocity. Freer trade with the United States was much desired by Saskatchewan farmers who sought relief from the cost-price squeeze that tariff protection of eastern manufacturers imposed on primary producers in the West. Walter Scott believed that the question of reciprocity with the United States could be used successfully in securing a resounding victory over Haultain in the 1912 provincial election. As for Haultain, his inconsistency on this emotional issue was certainly bound to hurt him.

In late January 1911 the Laurier government proposed a reciprocity agreement with the United States that would create an expanded market for Canadian primary products and a lowering of Canadian tariffs on goods imported from America. Saskatchewan farmers liked the idea. Such an agreement would reduce their production costs which they believed were much too high. Reciprocity with the United States would, for example, make it less expensive to import farm machinery directly into western Canada from the United States than from Ontario and Quebec. Saskatchewan Liberals saw the tariff as a protection of eastern Canadian manufacturing interests at the expense of the profits of western farmers. In March 1911, Haultain and his Provincial Rights members in the legislature seemed to agree and joined Scott and the Liberal government in approving a resolution supporting Laurier's trade agreement. Haultain spoke glowingly of the prospects of lowering the price tag on important American goods and opening new markets for the province's growing agricultural industry.

But in the following July things abruptly changed when Haultain's Provincial Rights members joined with federal Conservatives at a Moose Jaw convention and created the Conservative Party of Saskatchewan. The party, now aligned with Robert Borden's federal Tories, passed a resolution opposing Laurier's reciprocity proposal. For many observers this was a puzzling reversal by Haultain. How did this happen? It seemed to be an inconsistency that keyed into the conclusion of many that Haultain was not always an effective judge in political battle.[23] Could Haultain have been distracted from a genuine agrarian desire in Saskatchewan for freer trade by emotional attacks on reciprocity sounded by eastern business, banking and industrial powers darkly warning Canadians that annexation by the United States would follow? "Haultain was often forced to abandon his original position and look indecisive, to defend a position that was unacceptable to the people of the province."[24] Did he bow to British heritage values in a Canadian nationalism that obviously appealed across the country and on federal election day, September 21, 1911, swept Laurier from office? Robert Borden's Conservatives won 134 of the 221 parliamentary seats, while Wilfrid Laurier's Liberals were elected in 87 seats. In Saskatchewan things were different. Federal Liberals won nine of the 10 Saskatchewan seats and 60% of the vote. Only one Conservative was elected. This did not bode well for Haultain in the next Saskatchewan provincial election if pro-reciprocity embers still glowed on the prairies.

Scott called a provincial election for July 11, 1912. It would be Haultain's last campaign. He had fought eight others. Again Haultain offered a progressive, populist package including provincial control of natural resources and compensation by the federal government for the revenues raised from this source within the boundaries of the province. His program called for a provincial power policy and the appointment of a freight tariff commissioner to protect consumers from excessive rates. It seemed a lively and attractive manifesto and it would be well presented and defended by Haultain and a full slate of 54 Conservative Party candidates.

Haultain took his campaign across the province by train and buggy. For the first time he campaigned as leader of the Conservative Party of Saskatchewan. Just how comfortable he was wearing that mantle is debatable. Certainly the Conservative Party wanted to claim him as its own, and his relationship with Prime Minister Borden remained warm. Yet Haultain biographer Grant MacEwan wrote that as late as 1911 Haultain still believed that provincial governments "could be more efficient without unproductive party rivalries."[25] MacEwen tells us that Haultain would concede the usefulness of the party system in federal politics but believed there was not that need in provincial or civic politics. It is idle to speculate about how reluctant he may still have been to wear Conservative Party colours in the 1912 provincial election. It would, however, be tempting to do so.

From the outset, Scott and the Liberals and the Liberal press, particularly the *Regina Leader*, summoned 1911 reciprocity election ghosts to haunt Haultain. Voters were relentlessly reminded that it was Haultain's friends—Borden and the federal Tories—who dashed Saskatchewan farm hopes for freer trade. Haultain was one of the bad guys. They mocked him, calling him "Farmer Haultain." "Farmer Haultain," they jibed, was no friend of the farmer. He was a Conservative working for that "eastern gang of Tories."[26] The election of Haultain, they warned, would mean surrender to the eastern trusts. They reminded campaign audiences of Borden's 1911 federal election promises to turn over public lands to the province if he were elected. That promise had not been kept nor, they argued, would Haultain's promise to win provincial control of lands and natural resources be kept.

They flagged him as a federal Tory "toadie," who had turned his back on his own once unassailable reputation as a champion of the West. No matter how he fought back, it seemed Saskatchewan folk were not listening to him as they once had. The Liberal campaign seemed to grow in intensity and confidence as election day neared. Eleven days before the polling, a capricious Mother Nature visited a freakish and terrifying storm upon Regina. In late afternoon on Sunday, June 30, what was later identified as a cyclone roared across Lake Wascana and north into the city, destroying houses, ravaging churches, public buildings and businesses. Hundreds of men, women and children were injured and 28 citizens were killed. The cyclone, which narrowly missed the new Legislative Building, did huge damage to two of Regina's churches, the Metropolitan Methodist church and Knox Presbyterian church in the downtown core. Happily, the storm, which lasted only a few minutes, cut a narrow swath north and northeast through the heart of the city, leaving most of the community untouched.[27] News of this extraordinary calamity was telegraphed throughout the province and beyond, and for a short time the provincial election campaign became a secondary story in Saskatchewan.

Across the province there was enormous sympathy for the people of the Queen City. There was eager, widespread interest in the progress of relief programs and rebuilding efforts in Regina's devastated areas. What could others do to help? What would the Scott government do to help? This was more than a testing of the provincial government. In the midst of an election it was an opportunity for them, however sad. It was unexpected, unwished for political manna for Scott, and he handled it with deft, immediate action.

On July 9, just two days before the provincial vote, the *Regina Leader* recorded that the premier and his cabinet had put at the disposal of the Regina City Council half a million dollars to enable Regina citizens to obtain low-interest, long-term loans to finance the rebuilding of houses and other properties destroyed in the cyclone. "If further assistance is required," the premier had announced, "the government stands ready to furnish it."[28] The government's response to the cyclone calamity could not escape a Regina and indeed a provincewide audience. The people of Saskatchewan could not help but feel a measure of admiration for Scott himself and gratitude for the quick, sure action of his government in coming to the aid of the stricken capital city. Haultain could only stand and watch.

Haultain could not break Scott's hold on public trust and contentment and one wonders how much he enjoyed this last campaign. He was not "an effective political critic."[29] He seemed to lack the raw opposition appetite to "throw the bastards out." He couldn't find or never really sought the Liberal Party jugular! It was not that he wanted to "play nice"; it was just that he didn't know how to play mean. Haultain did not gauge and follow public opinion signs and trends as did Scott, whose "style was pragmatic rather than dogmatic."[30] Walter Scott, canny and sure-footed, would wait for signs of public approval before introducing new legislation. Haultain lacked Scott's patience and prescience. He was never Scott's equal in practising inclusion and outreach in politics. His failure to attract greater farm support in 1912 wasn't just the result of his unpopular positions on elevator ownership and reciprocity. The Conservatives did not craft policies that might have appealed to a growing European immigrant population.[31] Even if Haultain had wanted to show more concern for the non-Anglo Saxon population, he knew that by doing so he would have alienated key elements of his Protestant, English-speaking political base. How much did he personally feel suspicion, even hostility toward Roman Catholic and foreign-born settlers whom he knew had been assiduously courted and won by his Liberal enemies and were not his friends? At all events, this election was not his to win.

Haultain was defeated on July 11, 1912, the third consecutive Conservative loss. It was a shipwreck! Of the 54 seats in the Assembly he won only eight to the Liberal's 46. Haultain's Conservatives suffered a six-seat loss from 1908, and with 42% of the popular vote trailed 15 percentage points behind Scott's Liberals, who won a remarkable 57% of the tally. Three strikes and you're out!

It was time for Haultain to go! He knew it and so did his Conservative friends in Ottawa. The decline of the Conservative Party in Saskatchewan would have to be stopped, the bleeding staunched. Perhaps new leadership would help. Tory Prime Minister Robert Borden had an appropriate job to offer, and Haultain was appointed Chief Justice of Saskatchewan, a prestigious post for which everyone knew he was eminently qualified. It's safe to say that he went willingly to the bench. It would only be four years until Walter Scott too would leave politics, resigning his Liberal leadership a tired and distracted man. Haultain was knighted by the King in June 1916, and as Sir Frederick Haultain he served as Chief Justice of the province and later as Chancellor of the University of Saskatchewan. This gracious, unblemished man, undaunted by political defeat, journeyed on to continued notable service to Saskatchewan.

In politics, a guessing game of "What if?" is often played at the end of a significant career, particularly at the end of an apparently losing career. No early Saskatchewan politician invites the "If only," the

Frederick Haultain, prior to his retirement on October 31, 1938 (SAB R-B277(2)).

"What might have been" game more than Frederick Haultain. What if Haultain had been more strategic and temperate in contesting with Laurier over the terms for provincial status? What if he had compromised and accepted all or most of the settlement proposed by Ottawa while planning to wait and fight another day? Would an appointment to the premiership then have been possible for Haultain, with a win in the province's first election in December following? From that first Conservative government in the province might the party have built political capital and the organization to sustain it in power for many elections to come?

This might have been. But none of it happened!

After politics, Haultain's careers in law as Chief Justice of Saskatchewan and service to the province as Chancellor of the University of Saskatchewan were distinguished. One could fairly conjecture that Haultain's friends in the Conservative Party and beyond might have expected that his long public service to the party and to Saskatchewan would build recognition and reputation for him over the years. In 1944, two years after Haultain's death, the *Canadian Bar Review* published an article entitled "Sir Frederick Haultain."

It was written by H.A. Robson, Chief Justice of Manitoba. In it, speaking of Haultain, the Chief Justice concluded, "If the prairies ever come to the time for monuments to their statesmen, the first choice should be easy to name."[32]

This hasn't happened. There are no monuments to Frederick Haultain. Haultain has faded in reputation even within the Conservative Party, a party that appears to have forgotten him. This is sad. Over the years Canadian political parties at both federal and provincial levels have remembered their beginnings with founding stories of their leaders and heroes. This has not been so much a matter of partisans putting party heroes in the front window for election show as it has been an expression of pride in themselves, their country or their province.

As part of Saskatchewan's millennium celebrations three men were remembered on June 18, 2001, in a memorable ceremony at the Legislative Building in Regina. Her Honour Lieutenant-Governor Lynda Haverstock, Premier Lorne Calvert, the provincial cabinet and all members of the legislature along with special guests from across the province attended. Three monumental busts of former provincial political leaders were unveiled and placed on permanent display in the rotunda of the legislature. The busts, cast in bronze, are mounted on solid marble pedestals weighing 700 pounds each and standing 50 inches high. They are impressive. Those honoured for what Premier Calvert called "vision, leadership and public service in the building of our province" were Walter Scott, T.C. Douglas and John Diefenbaker.[33]

Each of these Saskatchewan statesmen had earned his place of honour in the Legislative Building rotunda. The legendary John G. Diefenbaker ranged beyond political label. He was a Saskatchewan boy who became Prime Minister of Canada. Walter Scott was remembered and honoured as our province's first premier. Saskatchewan had long revered Tommy Douglas, the CCF leader and hero of Medicare. Perhaps only one other Saskatchewan politician might have been judged worthy of joining these three giants, one other Saskatchewan statesman whose "vision, leadership and public service in the building of our province" might have been recognized in bronze that day. Surely that man was Frederick Haultain.

Perhaps had Haultain been unambiguously a Tory party man this honour might have come to him. Although never premier of Saskatchewan he served as the new province's first Leader of the Opposition. Before that, his persistent efforts were widely credited with the achievement of responsible government for the North-West and he served as first premier of the Territories. As premier he fought passionately for autonomy for the North-West and was a foremost founding father of the new province of Saskatchewan. Surely these are valid credentials for inclusion in a list of provincial Tory heroes. Yet, unfortunately, over the years provincial Conservatives have not closely identified with Haultain and have left him largely unsung. This has much to do with Haultain himself. Although he was a Conservative in federal politics, his Conservative image was clouded by his commitment to non-party government in the Territories. His relentless non-partisanship in Territorial affairs, even as partisanship began to grow in the Territories, confused and alienated some Conservatives. As for Haultain himself, it became more and more difficult for him to reconcile the opposing claims of involvement in Territorial Conservative Party organization and leadership of a non-partisan government.

Haultain's Conservative Party affiliation was further confused when Conservatives met in Regina on August 24, 1905, and called for the election "without regard to party names or party affiliation" of candidates pledged to defend provincial rights. Haultain was the driving force behind the resolution and the convention's decision to discard the Conservative label and contest the 1905 election as the Provincial Rights Party. Haultain thought the terms of autonomy an invasion of provincial rights. Rightly or wrongly he did not believe he and his Conservative followers could protest the legislation as Conservatives as well as they could as a Provincial Rights Party. But did he effectively argue and convincingly make the case for discarding the Conservative Party label to enough fellow Conservatives at home and in particular to federal Conservatives looking on? Had he won in 1905, there could be no questioning of his decision. But he lost and that is when hindsight questioning and criticisms inevitably grow in politics.

In 1908 Haultain again fielded candidates calling themselves "Provincial Righters" rather than Conservatives, and it wasn't until the 1912 election that Haultain's party ran under the Conservative Party banner. To what degree this off-again, on-again wearing of the Conservative badge made Haultain appear indecisive, even enigmatic to some Conservatives of his own day and in later years, we can only speculate.

One certainty is that Frederick Haultain was deeply involved with the political life of the new province from the earliest times when its foundations were being designed and laid. His remarkable career in service to Saskatchewan as a frontier statesman has not yet been adequately marked. But there is still room in the rotunda of the legislature for a fourth pedestal and another monumental sculpture cast in bronze.

3
A Doctor in the House

For Saskatchewan Conservatives there was life after Haultain—but not much! The party's health was precarious, its pulse feeble, its condition stable at best for the next three provincial elections. In 1917, 1921 and 1925 the Conservative Party tottered under earnest, luckless leadership, and was overtaken by the drive and muscle of superior Liberal political management.

It was only after Saskatchewan had grown weary of Liberal rule and yearned for change that Saskatchewan Conservatives roused themselves and readied the party for the election of 1929. Faint hopes of Tory recovery, even victory, were building by 1928 as religious and ethnic unrest, ignored or misunderstood by the Liberal government, gathered force and began to shake old values and alignments. The conflagration of 1929 burst from embers smoldering throughout the campaigns of 1917, 1921 and 1925. Surely, it was a measure of Grit arrogance that the Liberal Party took no notice of these dangers.

When Frederick Haultain resigned the Tory leadership after suffering a third defeat in the 1912 provincial election, the Conservative Party chose W.B. Willoughby to replace him. The new leader was elected at a convention in Saskatoon. Willoughby was a Moose Jaw lawyer with some platform talent but a small political reputation. In the legislature seven Conservatives now faced 46 jubilant Liberals led by an assured and jaunty Premier Walter Scott. Prospects for Willoughby and his little Tory band were not good.

Wellington Bartley Willoughby, although a less than dazzling figure, was a capable and conscientious organization man. First elected for Moose Jaw in 1908, he was re-elected in 1912 and again in 1917. As leader he focused on strengthening the party's organizational structure at the constituency level. He was more given perhaps than Haultain had been to establishing riding committees and overseeing membership recruitment and fundraising. Willoughby recognized the fragmented nature of the Tory party he led and the Liberals' immense superiority in party networking and cohesion.[1]

Under Willoughby the Conservatives faced five years of frustrated attempts to build a winning team to fight the next provincial election in 1917. To build that team the Conservatives needed to capture farmer support and capitalize on a simmering Protestant, anti-Catholic temper in the province. They had to harness Anglo-Saxon, "old settler" disdain for east European immigrants without offending the reputed British sense of fair play. Provincial language and ethnic contentions needed sensitive, effective management by both the Willoughby caucus and Conservative Party strategists.

These were tough, nearly, impossible assignments for the Conservative leader.

Willoughby may have thought his hour had come when it appeared his Tories had engulfed the Liberal government in a firestorm of scandal in 1916. In February of that year the Conservative MLA for Prince Albert rose in the legislature and announced to a stunned Assembly that he had evidence of major graft and corruption in the government. He demanded a Royal Commission to examine his charges. Select legislative committees would not satisfy him. He refused to provide details of his evidence until a Royal Commission was established to hear it.

John Ernest Bradshaw, elected in 1908 and re-elected in 1912, had already enjoyed a little brief celebrity in 1912 when he

W.B. Willoughby, leader of the Conservative Party from 1912–18 (SAB R-A28210).

moved a resolution calling for the enfranchisement of women in Saskatchewan, a resolution that won warm, unanimous support from an Assembly that treated the subject of women's rights with some levity. This time the former alderman and mayor of Prince Albert, speaking with an edge and confidence gained from a decade of municipal cut and thrust politics in that northern city, was really in his element. Dropping a partisan bomb on Liberal government benches was a mission any Tory MLA would find satisfying. The government, deeply concerned about critical public opinion, had no choice but to establish the independent enquiry the Tories demanded. The government established three Royal Commissions composed primarily of current and former justices of the Supreme Court of Saskatchewan to examine the allegations.[2]

The Bradshaw allegations were serious. Bradshaw charged that Liberal Party MLAs had been paid to secure liquor licenses for some hotel owners, that liquor interests had offered bribes to Liberal MLAs to defeat legislation designed to bring about prohibition in the province, that liquor interests had contributed to Liberal Party campaign funding, and that prosecution for liquor offenses had in some cases been dropped for political reasons. Among other suggestions of wrongdoing were allegations that public funds had been paid to individuals for construction of roads which were never built.

The first Royal Commission, chaired by former Conservative leader Sir Frederick Haultain, was charged with the investigation of allegations of graft in the construction of the North Battleford asylum, the Regina jail and the Department of Telephones. The second Royal Commission, chaired by Judge Wetmore, examined all road construction contracts from 1913–16 and the construction of a bridge in Saskatoon. The third Royal Commission, the Brown Elwood Commission, was to investigate Bradshaw's charges concerning the acceptance of bribes by certain MLAs over liquor legislation.[3] After sifting the evidence and examining witnesses, the reports of the Royal Commissions cleared Premier Scott and his cabinet of any wrongdoing, but four Liberal MLAs were found guilty of accepting bribes or using their influence to help liquor interests friendly to the Liberal Party. As well, evidence of fraud on the part of civil servants, particularly in the Department of Highways, was uncovered. Penalties for the offending MLAs and civil servants ranged from forced resignations and dismissals to serious jail time. The Chief Clerk of the Board of Highway Commissioners, when found guilty of issuing forged documents, was sentenced to seven years in the Prince Albert Penitentiary.[4] Certainly, in those days not a happy sojourn.

Whatever Willoughby's hopes might have been for the Bradshaw scandals, although titillating for a time, they did not prove disastrous for the government. The odour of corruption did not hang long over the Liberal Party. The Royal Commissions' reports failed to find Premier Scott and members of his cabinet culpable, and others found guilty were charged, tried and punished in quick order. There was never a hint of obstruction or cover-up. There had even been a public call from influential Regina Liberals for a full and proper investigation of the Bradshaw charges.[5] The public seemed satisfied. Even though Willoughby would strive to rekindle the Bradshaw scandal fires in the 1917 provincial election, he would fail. The embers were cold. The case was closed. Willoughby faced a fresh new Liberal leader in the provincial election called for June 1917. Walter Scott, both physically and mentally unable to continue in office, resigned the Liberal leadership in October 1916.[6] He was succeeded by a 40-year-old Regina lawyer and federal Member of Parliament for Regina, W.M. Martin.

After a by-election victory in November 1916, Martin was premier. Premier Martin would prove himself a patient, responsive reader of political winds. Martin knew that the support of the farmers and farm organizations was essential to winning and keeping power in Saskatchewan. Martin and the Liberals were shaken by any show of agrarian discontent. Even rumours of a farmers' revolt and formation of a farmers' political party spooked them. The trick was to prevent farmers, specifically the SGGA, from organizing a political party of their own. They must remain good Liberals. Farmers who had always been generous in their support of the Liberal Party must be charmed and co-opted into staying that way. After all, wasn't it the steadfast Liberals who believed in reciprocity with all their hearts and could not be swayed? And wasn't it the perfidious Tories who could not be faithful to this sacred trust? "We are the farmers' friends," cried the Liberals. Liberal arms embraced them; Liberal ranks engulfed them; Liberal conventions nominated them. And the farmers voted Grit! The Liberal-farmer association was carefully tended and maintained by Saskatchewan Liberals over many years.

Dr. Bill Waiser described the supremacy of the Saskatchewan wheat grower in 1912:

> Over the next three decades the close relationship between the Saskatchewan government and farmers would shape and influence provincial life almost to the exclusion of all other groups, activities and regions. Wheat was king and any provincial government knew better than to dispute it.[7]

Martin also knew that the support of the Roman Catholic church and non-English-speaking immigrants now enjoyed by his Liberals must not be shared with the Willoughby Tories. Liberal spokesmen and propagandists, therefore, didn't hesitate to spread the nasty word that Tories really didn't like "foreigners" who spoke in Slavic and Teutonic tongues and smelled overly of garlic. Perhaps the "nasty word" wasn't all that exaggerated. Saskatchewan Conservatives at the time "showed little concern for the non-Anglo-Saxons and eventually appeared to be hostile to new settlers, their cultures and their languages."[8] After all, men and women who spoke English and had British ways were more comfortably "Canadian," were they not?

In January 1916, Willoughby delighted a Saskatoon Conservative convention by declaring lustily that the English language should be the "sole language of instruction" in the public schools of Saskatchewan.[9] In the June 1917 election campaign these tinder-box issues of language and religion threatened to ignite the province. In the decade to follow they would grow from agitation to conflagration to the convulsions of the 1929 campaign.

The "school question" was never really answered and was filed away. The question debated so vehemently during the 1905 election had become a "language of instruction" issue by 1916, leading up to the 1917 provincial election. Pro-British institutions and anti-foreign, anti-French-Canadian sentiment fanned by the 1914–18 war raised cries of "English first," then of "English only," for instruction in the schools of the province. Conservatives who had forgotten Haultain's more liberal language policies in the Territories now wanted all languages—both French and foreign—gone from provincial schools. The European immigrant numbers in Saskatchewan grew rapidly after 1905, and by 1915 they constituted some 40% of the population.[10] In the eyes of English-speaking citizens the "foreign" population seemed slow to adjust and assimilate as was expected of them. English-speaking people found this immigrant reticence to change disturbing.

In the years between 1916 and 1918 a chorus of opposition to government concessions to foreign- and French-language usage in the schools was raised in the province. In 1916, along with vocal groups from Protestant churches and Orange Lodges, the Saskatchewan Conservative Party, the SGGA, the Saskatchewan School Trustees Association and the Rural Municipalities' Association in various conventions all demanded that English be the sole language of instruction in the public schools of Saskatchewan.[11] In

February 1917, just four months before the June 26 provincial election, the SGGA again passed a resolution asking that English be the sole language of instruction in the public schools. The Grain Growers believed the schools were the chief agents for the promotion of unification of the people of the new province. These resolutions, however, were not all patient and generous invitations to immigrant settlers to join with the establishment majority in a happy homeland. They were not all positive messages of "The more we get together, the happier we'll be." Far from it. In the push for assimilation of the new Canadians there was a scent of intolerance and hostility to immigrant newcomers speaking in foreign tongues. In the war years there were genuine alarmist fears of aliens in our midst, agents of dark powers from across the seas. Anti-foreign prejudice was, as historian Dr. David Smith asserts, "an implacable foe for whom any sign of compromise was abhorrent."[12] The demand for English language instruction to bring about assimilation of the non-English speaking population was unyielding. No government could deny it.

Willoughby's Tories contested 53 of the 59 Assembly seats, but the 1917 election results were decisive. Premier Martin won an easy victory. No one was surprised to see his Liberals win 51 seats in the 59-seat Assembly to the Conservatives' seven. Willoughby's seven-seat total was a loss of one legislative seat and a 6% drop in popular vote from the 1912 returns. The Liberals again won 57% of the vote. Tory times were getting worse. Liberal times were getting better.

What had happened? Conservatives blamed the unsettled times of war, proposed Union Government and conscription passions for much of their loss. Probably Martin's Liberals gained generously from the enfranchisement of women and the government's successful shepherding of prohibition legislation demanded by reformers.[13] Martin seemed able to contain racial antagonisms and disarm or at least postpone a potentially acrimonious school and language debate. The Liberal election machine worked efficiently as usual and, overall, the voters, seeking security and continuity in the uncertainty of the time, stuck with a government they knew and believed to be practical and capable.

A federal election in 1917 followed the June 26 provincial contest. Conservative Prime Minister Robert Borden was returned to power, leading a wartime "Union Government." W.B. Willoughby's provincial career rounded quietly with a Borden appointment to the Senate.

The little rump of six remaining Conservatives in the legislature chose Saskatoon MLA Donald Maclean, a lawyer elected in 1917, to replace the newly minted Senator Willoughby as leader. Maclean served with little distinction in this capacity, resigning his seat and the leadership on the eve of the announcement of the provincial election of 1921 and sending his little ramshackle Tory band into battle leaderless and hopeless. Maclean sensed a groundswell of agrarian unrest in the province and knew that activists in the

Donald Maclean, leader of the Conservative Party from 1918–21 (photo taken from the composite of the Fourth Saskatchewan Legislature).

farm movement were moving closer to independent political action and placing their bets on Progressives and Independents rather than on the opposition Conservative Party. Maclean knew when to leave the game. He disappeared over the hills and far away from politics, accepting an appointment to the bench in 1921 and the safe and ordered life that the job allowed.

The four years leading up to the provincial election in 1921 proved disastrous for the inept Tories. When World War I ended in 1918 with the German and Austrian defeat and the muddied, bloodied trenches of Europe empty at last, there was still much distress far across the sea in Saskatchewan. It was not all jubilation and torch-lit victory parades. In the Queen City, even before 8,000 citizens led by the Regina Salvation Army band marched to Wascana Park to celebrate the armistice, an influenza epidemic had taken a heavy toll, having raged for months in the province. The "flu" would not abate in Saskatchewan until 1920.[14]

The war, with its inevitable, emotional appeal to patriotism and loyalty to King and country, created all manner of tension in the province, casting shadows over immigrant peoples. Some Tories and true-blue Anglos looked with distrust on the foreign-born or even Canadian-born Germans and Austrians. Remember the despised "Hun," the "Boche," Franz Joseph's and Kaiser Wilhelm's black-hearted legions, killers on the ground, on the sea, in the air in Europe. Remember. Could Germans and Austrians on the Canadian prairies be traitors? Some Tories and true-blue Anglos wondered. Was there some political advantage for Tories in these lively suspicions and the unrest they fostered? And what about the east European "foreigners," the Ukrainians, the Russians? Their loyalties, too, were questioned. How Canadian were they? Even the small French-Canadian population in Saskatchewan was suspect. How much real enthusiasm to put on a uniform and fight for Crown and Canada had they shown? Not much! Finally, the old hostility to separate schools and foreign-language instruction raised its head. For the Tories this became a palpable political issue. It gave definition to a growing distemper in the province. Saskatchewan Conservative operatives wanted to fight an election on the anti-foreign, anti-Roman Catholic sentiment in the province. They saw it as a major emotional issue on which Martin and the Liberal government were vulnerable. They were wrong. There wasn't enough meanness in Saskatchewan for such an appeal to succeed. Not yet.

Martin, as shrewd and effective a politician as the early Walter Scott, undercut critics who thought his government soft on the issue of instruction in languages other than English in provincial classrooms. Martin, prompted by political rather than ideological considerations, amended the School Act to prohibit instruction in any language other than English, except for French language instruction to French-speaking Grade 1 pupils. French could also be taught as a subject for one hour a day as part of the curriculum, if a local school board so desired. By doing this, Martin smoothed the choppy waters of school and language debate.

Provincial Conservatives, although happy enough to see the prohibition of foreign-language instruction in Saskatchewan classrooms, were unwilling to accept the limited exceptions granted the French language. The old "English only" cry was again raised, arguing that "schools must serve as a means of unifying the people of the province into one harmonious whole."[15] In the Assembly Maclean's attack on the School Act amendment was ineffective, but with only a handful of Tory votes in the legislature it didn't really matter. It was not Conservative leader Donald Maclean's finest hour in the legislature. Maclean opposed the Martin amendment because he said it didn't go far enough in banishing the French language from Saskatchewan schools. Maclean could not agree to French-language usage even in predominately French-speaking communities and in a highly restricted form. "I stand for one language, the English language," he announced, arguing that even the reduced use of the French language would be "bringing bilingualism into Saskatchewan."[16] He moved a confusing amendment to make English the sole language of instruction during school hours. His amendment left the door open for the use of languages other than English after the 4 p.m. end of the regular school day. This was certainly not his intention but he had ensnared himself. He excused himself by lamely explaining that he "got tangled up" in procedure.[17] This was not a good show for Maclean. One wonders how Premier Martin and his government benches could stifle sniggers all around.

Martin's greatest threat following war's end and the armistice was the resumed agitation for direct political action by Saskatchewan farmers. Martin knew how to meet this challenge; he had done it before. He knew that one way of preventing such direct political action was to make and keep the Liberal Party a farmers' party. Martin had invited prominent farmers and farm leaders into his cabinet, as Scott had done in 1905 when he named W.R. Motherwell, president of the Territorial Grain Growers, as his Minister of Agriculture. Martin had appointed George Langley and C.A. Dunning to his cabinet in 1912 and 1916 respectively. Both men were active in the SGGA and the Saskatchewan Co-operative Elevator Company. Now in 1921 Martin appointed J.A. Maharg, president of the SGGA, to the cabinet. Conservatives watched helpless from the sidelines as the courting and wooing continued.

Conservatives, more than a little breathlessly, watched Martin in quick order publicly loosen his ties with the federal Liberal Party and announce that his provincial followers would campaign under a generic "Government Party" label rather than as the Liberal Party of Saskatchewan.[18] This show of independence from the federal Grits was calculated to provide a signal that Saskatchewan Liberals would welcome, indeed actively court Conservatives, Independents, Progressives, Non-Partisans, all and everyone who would help re-elect the government. A strong pitch would be made for stability, continuity and support for Martin and a trusted "Saskatchewan First" leadership no other leader could provide. Martin gave Tories, farmers and independents little time to prepare by calling an election in June 1921. Some critics in farm circles complained about it being a "snap" election. It was. Certainly, the Tories weren't ready.

The Conservative Party was no threat. It was in serious melt-down. Donald Maclean had retired from the leadership before the election, and the party contested only four ridings out of 63 in the legislature. The governing Liberals nominated 60 candidates. Thirty-five anti-Liberal candidates ran as Independents, seven as Progressives and an assortment of 13 others straggled along. The number of parties contesting the 1921 election showed both dissatisfaction with the Liberals and the pathetic disarray of the opposition, particularly the hapless Tories. The result was a near Tory wipeout. The Conservatives elected two members. The Liberals won 46 seats, 16 of these by acclamation. They faced an opposition of 17, a goulash of the two Conservatives, one Independent Conservative, six Progressives, seven Independents and one Independent Pro-Government member. Martin's Liberals carried 51% of the vote followed by the Independents with 26%, the Progressives with 8% and the Tories with 4% of the tally.

The briefly noted Donald Maclean dropped unlamented from public view to be replaced as leader at a 1924 Tory convention by Dr. J.T.M. Anderson, an educationalist newly come to partisan politics. Anderson's selection as leader of the Conservative Party was made somewhat awkward by suspicions expressed about his loyalty to the Tory party because of a lengthy association with the Liberal provincial government. Some delegates wanted him appointed "field leader and organizer" rather than elected leader.[19] How did the party feel about him? How did Anderson feel about the party? Early perspectives would surely be clouded.

The Saskatchewan farmer see-saw for and against direct political action at the provincial level continued. Agrarian unhappiness in the province was then expressed nationally by the Progressive movement. Various attempts at farmer provincial political organization were made, first by the SGGA and then by provincial members of the federal Progressives. Saskatchewan agriculture was depressed and farmers were deserting the old parties for a new political organization of their own. In 1923 the Saskatchewan Provincial Progressive Association was formed with the promise of better representing the aspirations of the province's agriculture community. The Saskatchewan

Provincial Progressive Association, known as the Progressives, was a few years in the making before its official launch as a political organization in 1923. In the 1921 provincial election a handful of Progressives had run for the legislature, and six of them had won election to the 63-seat Assembly. In 1924, now as a provincial political association, the Progressives met in convention in Saskatoon and adopted an official platform in preparation for the 1925 provincial election. In 1925 the Progressives nominated 40 candidates, gained 23% of the popular vote and again elected six members. Some of the Progressive platform is worth noting here because of its populist and reformist nature and because echoes of the platform would later be found in Conservative Party appeals. In 1925 Progressives urged smaller government for the province, reduction of the number of civil servants, a fixed term for the Legislative Assembly, reduction of the number of members of the legislature from 63 to 42, adoption of the single transferable ballot, completion of the Hudson Bay Railway and assistance to cooperative marketing. The platform also betrayed the lingering influence of federal Progressives by expressing opposition to the party system. Some provincial Progressives still found party politics repugnant. This anti-partisanship ardour would soon cool. The Progressives certainly attracted Grit attention when they put 40 candidates in the field. The prospect of a Saskatchewan farmers' political party was alarming to the Grits, who counted heavily on farmer support and who feared the loss of any of it.

Premier Martin left politics in 1922 and was replaced by C.A. Dunning as leader and premier. Dunning, an SGGA member and former manager of the Co-operative Elevator Company, was a superb choice for leader. Dunning recognized the threat, not only from the provincial Progressives, but from a revitalized Conservative Party that he feared might also "absorb a certain number of the saner and more level-headed farmers and endanger his chances in three-cornered fights."[20]

Dunning was every bit as shrewd and able a politician as Martin and Scott had been before him. He had total control of his party, an organization assembled by the feisty, canny James G. Gardiner, his Minister of Highways and chief political strategist. Soon stories both true and apocryphal about "Jimmy" Gardiner's famed organization would become part of Saskatchewan's political lore. The "Gardiner Machine" would help sweep Dunning and his Liberals to an easy win on June 2, 1925. The threat of the Progressives proved illusory. The Liberals won 50 seats in the Assembly of 63. The Conservatives under Anderson won three seats, the Progressives six seats and four Independents were elected.

The new Conservative chief, Dr. J.T.M. Anderson, one of the three Tories elected in 1925, was MLA for Saskatoon. The Conservatives, after a disconsolate hiatus, now had a leader they thought might have some promise. This proved the case in 1925 when the Anderson Tories took 18% of the popular vote as opposed to 4% in 1921. Considering the party fielded fewer than 20 candidates in 63 constituencies, the 18%, while hardly a confident march to the goal line, was at least a tentative step down the field.

In that 1925 election the Conservative platform was promise-crammed. Unfortunately, they had no daily newspaper to explain their views at a time when the newspaper was the most influential means of campaigning available to a political party. Six daily newspapers supported the Liberals.[21] The Conservatives promised reform of the provincial education system by adopting larger municipal school districts and writing curriculum to help "Canadianize" immigrant children seen stubbornly cleaving to old-country ways. Low farm income and unpopular federal tariff and railway policies were insistent campaign issues, with daily Tory promises that help would come when they formed government. "Vote Conservative!" "It's time for a change!" But there was no change. On election eve, June 2, 1925, Saskatchewan Liberals, serene in the knowledge of their own worthiness and invincibility, celebrated another breezy win.

Anderson, relatively unknown and totally untried in politics, would have to wait for a wave of outrage to carry him into office four years later. For now, he may have thought himself tricked out as a reformer; but fortune didn't beckon him yet, and he was neither brave enough nor gifted enough to make his own luck.

4

Bye-Bye Blues

Who was this new Tory leader, Dr. James Thomas Milton Anderson? How was it that without political credentials and legislative experience this man could spring up from a provincial civil service post in education to the leadership of the Conservative Party? How was it that seven years as a Yorkton district school inspector, a brief stint in the Department of Education and the authorship of a book could lift him quickly to the premiership? Was it that he had personal charm, skill and energy denied his predecessors in the leadership? Not really. Was the party that he led better organized, better financed and better directed than it had been before him? Only somewhat. Was Anderson an outstanding debater, a spellbinding platform performer? He was not so regarded.

Anderson, from the few accounts available to us, was convincing enough on the hustings and in the legislature but hardly dynamic or inspirational. It was as if he were plunging into the sea of politics without first having learned to swim. Certainly, he was not considered a natural, adroit politician in a class with Martin, Dunning or Gardiner.[1] But he could learn politics. And he did!

A star Anderson candidate in the 1929 campaign, John G. Diefenbaker, who proved himself a keen judge in these matters, "never showed great admiration for him."[2] However, in fairness it might be asked, for what Saskatchewan provincial Tory politician did Diefenbaker ever express "great admiration"? As for Anderson, as early as 1927 it was apparent that he was developing some political skills in the give-and-take of partisan exchange and was himself a "work in progress" as a coalition builder and opposition spokesman in the legislature. In 1927, while remaining leader of the Conservatives in the legislature, Anderson retired from the provincial Conservative Party leadership. His withdrawal from the leadership seemed puzzling and may have appeared a sign of timidity and indecision to some observers. A more positive explanation was that the withdrawal was a kind of strategic shading of party colours in order to strengthen Anderson's relationship with the Progressives in the legislature (who may still have been uncomfortable in a partisan role even though the Progressives had been a political organization since 1923). It wasn't until 1928 that the Progressives in convention put these objections to partisanship aside. By early 1928, Anderson had become comfortable in the opposition role and took the offensive against the Gardiner government by effectively attacking its education policies. In the legislature Anderson called for compulsory inspection of private and parochial schools, uniformity of textbooks and elimination of sectarian bias. He called for a Royal Commission to investigate the question of "educational needs and equal educational advantage for all."

He seemed a resourceful, ordinary man who led the party during remarkably resurgent years for Saskatchewan Conservatives, when divisive religious and racial issues were made to order for those hungering to end the 24-year Liberal rule in Regina. Anderson and his Conservatives were able to tap into a rich vein of religious dispute and racism and mine enormous political wealth. Anderson not only gained from these distempered times, in some sense he helped to create them. It was easy for him. He, like American Republican Barry Goldwater in the 1960s, was of the opinion that "In politics you have to hunt where the ducks are." Certainly, in the last 14 fevered months leading up to the election of 1929, Anderson knew where the ducks were.

From the beginning Saskatchewan's predominant Anglo-Saxon Protestant immigrants from Britain, Ontario and the United States were joined by French-Canadian, German, Scandinavian, Russian, Ukrainian, Polish and other non-English-speaking and non-Protestant new Canadians. By and large, eastern Canadians and American immigrants set much of the tone and standards of early Saskatchewan life. "Because of the language barrier and the difference of customs, continental Europeans in general were not included in social and community activities."[3] Many of the non-English-speaking Europeans settled in communities or colonies arranged for them by the federal government and lived apart, maintaining their languages and traditions.

Although the Protestant Anglo-Saxon establishment wanted cultural homogeneity and expected to get it through assimilation and what they called "Canadianization," this homogeneity was resisted by the "foreigners," as they were called, who resented their treatment as aliens and pulled back into themselves to live at ease with remembered ways: the cookery, the costumes and the crafts, the music and the accents of the home country and the past. The dominant "Anglos" grew suspicious of these strangers. They had expected Central and Southeastern non-English-speaking Europeans to blend gratefully into the larger Canadian culture. When this wasn't happening, the English-speaking majority feared that their Anglo-Protestant culture would be enfeebled or plundered as immigrant numbers grew. A climate of suspicion and hostility heightened as the Conservative Party took up its traditional role of prime spokesman for the Anglo-Saxon Protestant population, and the non-English-speaking European Catholic new Canadians remained loyal to the Liberal Party. Anderson and the Conservatives vowed to protect against the perceived threat that non-Anglo-Saxon cultures posed to a united "Canadianized" society in Saskatchewan.

Dr. J.T.M. Anderson was well cast for this role. Born in 1878 in Ontario, he came to Saskatchewan in 1908 to teach school and later to serve as a

Arthur J. McCulloch (left) and J.T.M. Anderson (right) outside Mr. Anderson's bachelor shack. Mr. McCulloch taught at Stowers (later Fair Land) School, and Mr. Anderson taught at Gravel Plains (later Runeberg) School. They lived together in Mr. Anderson's shack. c. 1908 (SAB R-A12057).

school inspector. He earned MA and LLB degrees from Manitoba and a PhD in Pedagogy from Toronto. After working as a school inspector in the Yorkton area among eastern European immigrant folk and attracting attention to his views on the proper education of new Canadians in his book, *The Education of the New Canadian: A Treatise on Canada's Greatest Education Problem*, he was given a significant position in the Saskatchewan Department of Education. In 1918 he was appointed "Director of Education Among New Canadians." What Anderson considered Saskatchewan's (and Canada's) "greatest educational problem" was immigrant resistance to assimilation. The need to "Canadianize" immigrant children and give the "foreign" family the supposed advantages of Anglo-Saxon values was the prime reason for his leaving the civil service to head the Conservatives in the 1925 election, and of his earnest preparation for the crucial drive to complete his mission in 1929.

There was, however, more to his "mission" than bringing Anglo-Saxon sweetness and light to hinterland immigrant settlements. In 1922 the post of "Director of Education Among New Canadians" was abolished by the government, and Anderson went to Saskatoon as a school inspector. He considered this a demotion and blamed Premier Dunning. Anderson's relationship with the Liberals had soured over personal promotion and salary disputes.

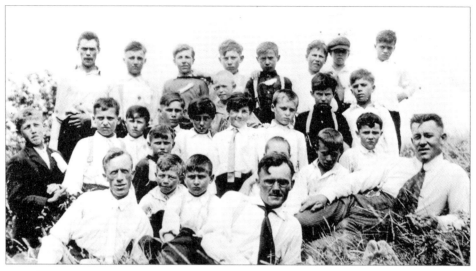

Rev. T.W. Johnson, Dr. J.T.M. Anderson, and and unidentified young teacher, with a group of Ukrainian boys selected for expedition to Lumsden Beach. Insinger District. c. 1925 (SAB R-A3488). Anderson is the furthest to the right.

Dunning and James Gardiner, who succeeded him as premier in 1926, had grown uneasy with Anderson's criticism of immigrant educational policy in Liberal Saskatchewan.[4] Anderson was no longer seen as a well-behaved civil servant standing loyally at the ready to serve the administration. Such men aren't necessarily dangerous, but they are certainly dispensable.

Following his 1925 election as MLA for Saskatoon, J.T.M. Anderson entered the legislature as leader of the three-man Conservative caucus. Anderson was a handsome man, more athletic than debonair. He was distinguished, neat and tailored in appearance. "On the street or hustings he wore a billycock hat and wing collars."[5] Some said he looked like a premier even without being one. He began gathering experience in the political rough-and-tumble of Saskatchewan politics. His academic qualifications in Arts and Law and his work in teaching, school administration and professional authorship gave him valuable credentials. He would need these! He was in tested, able company with Gardiner and his Liberal team sitting opposite in the Assembly. They knew politics. He didn't. Not yet.

But as Anderson got out and around the province he found friends in an aroused electorate, suspicious of the influence of the Catholic Church, uneasy with growing immigrant numbers and threatened, so they thought, by sectarianism in the public schools. It was not just growing immigration numbers that troubled Anderson and the Conservatives in 1928–29. Although he protested that he was not opposed to the immigration of any racial group to the province, few could doubt that he found some new Canadians more desirable than others. In 1928, Anderson proposed the appointment of a Saskatchewan agent-general to promote immigration from Great Britain. Certainly, good British stock would be highly desirable new citizens in the view of many Tories. In 1928, at their provincial convention, Saskatchewan Conservatives endorsed what they called a "selective entry" immigration policy. The convention expressed a desire to attract immigrants "suited to the economic and racial situation" in Saskatchewan so as to ensure "rapid assimilation with the existing population."[6] What about non-English speaking Central and Southeastern Europeans? Where on Anderson's desirability scale would they register? The Liberals accused the Conservatives of appealing to racist prejudices. This was of little concern to Anderson, who believed himself safely in step with the people. Later, in office, he would establish a Royal Commission to study the condition of the immigrant in Saskatchewan.

Sectarianism in the public schools of Saskatchewan became one of the most heated and emotional subjects of the 1929 election. Although the issue was greatly overblown by Protestant zealots, Anderson's Conservatives were able to claim that the Gardiner government was allowing interference with the non-sectarian character of the public school system in the province. No one seriously questioned the rights of Saskatchewan Catholics to separate schools. These were long established. What was at issue was the practice by some Catholic school boards, elected in areas with predominantly Catholic populations, of hiring nuns as teachers and allowing crucifixes and other religious emblems to be displayed in public schools. With Orange Order Protestant passions aroused, the issue was hugely inflated. Anderson recognized the immediate political value of the heated debate over sectarianism and set to work exploiting it. His own strong personal and professional belief in secular public schools made the campaign against sectarianism a mission for him. He promised amendments to the School Act to end the transgressions. He read the public mood correctly. A growing public sentiment wanted the Gardiner government out and the Gardiner machine gone!

In spite of a relatively strong economy, reasonable tax levels, an ambitious road construction and maintenance program, planning for provincewide power production and distribution, a budgetary surplus and a good wheat crop in 1928, social and political uncertainty stirred everywhere in Saskatchewan. Gardiner and his Liberals seemed complacent about the political threat to themselves. Sometime in late 1926 the Ku Klux Klan had come to Saskatchewan. These weren't exactly hokey, American-style, pointy-hooded, slitty-eyed Night Riders burning crosses, plundering treasure, flogging and lynching Blacks and other assorted "sinners" in the name of patriotic, racially pure, good Protestant creed. Not quite. But close. Saskatchewan Klansmen didn't wear hoods and ride horses. They wore business suits and drove into town in new-fangled cars. This less malevolent version of the American Klan flourished for a brief nightmare in the province between the mid 1920s and the early 1930s. They preached Protestantism, patriotism, racial purity, separation of church and state, restrictive and selective immigration, law and order, moral reawakening and one public school for all. Much of this rant was heard at the March 1928 Saskatchewan Conservative convention, a convention attended by a contingent of Klansmen and representatives of the Saskatchewan Progressive Party.[7]

J.F. Bryant, Vice-President of the provincial Conservative Association, member of the Orange Lodge and J.T.M. Anderson's right-hand man, was happy to welcome Klansmen into the Conservative midst as long as they weren't too obtrusive about being there. Bryant was a "fellow traveller" if not an actual member of the Klan. He was "an extreme and public anti-Catholic."[8] This cannot be said of Anderson.

Both Bryant and Anderson believed the Klan could excite apathetic Protestants to vote Conservative. They knew Conservatives could only win the province with a grand alliance of Protestants in Saskatchewan.[9] The size of the Ku Klux Klan in Saskatchewan is difficult to measure. Klansmen boasted a membership of 70,000 at their peak.[10] It is more likely they had about 25,000 members. There are various estimates, but we know the organization grew quickly and by 1929 counted 129 locals spread across the length and breadth of rural and urban Saskatchewan.[11] The Liberal Party was sensitive to the Klan's attack on their Catholic and immigrant supporters and considered the Klan alien and dangerous. The Klan held some appeal to the Progressives and to Independents because of its non-political, non-partisan views. The Conservatives "adopted an attitude that was politically expedient by taking advantage of the emotionalism aroused by the Klan and by secretly obtaining the endorsation of Klan leaders and publicly remaining silent about them."[12]

In 1928 Saskatchewan Tories prepared first for a by-election in the Arm River Constituency and then for the general provincial election expected in 1929. Anderson, still largely underestimated by the veteran, foxy James G. Gardiner, maneuvered deftly before these events to reap the benefits of Ku Klux Klan religious and ethnic agitation. Anderson sensed changes coming to Saskatchewan. His true relationship with the Klan can only be guessed at. The public was never told about any contacts and communications he might have had with the Klan. He certainly was aware of it, listened to it and found it useful in furthering his Protestant, nativist cause. Liberal charges that Anderson helped to make the Klan a political organization were denied by him and never proven.

Premier Gardiner wanted to test the political waters. The redoubtable "Jimmy" was pleased with himself and the apparent prosperity of the province, yet he had phantom misgivings about the health of the Liberal Party and some foreboding about the Klan. Was the Klan a real threat? He wasn't sure. Gardiner called a by-election in the vacant Arm River constituency to find out. He wanted the reassurance that a win in this safe Liberal seat would bring him, and he expected to get it. The by-election was called for October 1928. Arm River, a large rural seat established in 1908, had always been Liberal, and 20 years later appeared safe. It wasn't. The by-election campaign proved a nasty two-way bloodletting between the Gardiner Grits and Anderson's born-again Tories. Arranged "co-operation" from Progressives, Orangemen and independent farmer spokesmen guaranteed the Conservatives the role of anti-government champion. The Conservative candidate, Stuart Adrian, the Grand Master of the Saskatchewan Orange Association, was obviously ideologically suited for the position.

This time the Tories were threatening from the beginning. What made the difference was a newspaper. The *Regina Daily Star*, established just before the by-election, made them serious contenders in Arm River. "We need a paper! We'll never get anywhere until we get one," was Anderson's repeated plea to federal Tories. Finally, they listened and acted. R.B. Bennett, an Alberta millionaire, had deep pockets and as federal Tory leader an election to fight in 1930. He would need Saskatchewan seats in order to form a government. A Conservative daily newspaper in Saskatchewan would help his federal forces as well as Anderson and the provincial party. Bennett arranged a business deal that established the *Regina Daily Star* and ended a Liberal Party daily newspaper monopoly in the province that had existed since 1923. At last, a Tory mouthpiece! The long-desired *Regina Daily Star* began printing on July 16, 1928 and carried the Conservative message in the Arm River by-election. Later, in the 1929 provincial election the newspaper made loud and clear the Tory case against Grit corruption, Gardiner machine politics, sectarian influence in the public school system, unrestricted immigration and a range of other Liberal transgressions that cried out for change in Regina. What a difference a newspaper made! Tory spirits soared. Now all Saskatchewan listened to a Conservative voice. How sweet it was for Anderson.[13]

John G. Diefenbaker, prominent Prince Albert Tory, anticipating his own 1929 candidacy in Prince Albert, entered the by-election fray and publicly debated Premier Gardiner. He charged Gardiner with giving prominence to the Klan by his earlier sustained attacks on it.[14] It's doubtful that the Klan needed Gardiner or anyone else to raise it from obscurity. It was visible and energetic from the beginning and building enough appeal to endanger the Liberals.[15] Anderson and his chief campaign lieutenant and attack dog, J.F. Bryant, were skillful in exploiting the emotionalism and upheaval of the late 1920s in Saskatchewan without appearing to be instruments of the Klan. Bryant was a particularly aggressive campaigner, loud and vehement on the platform, more adversarial, less restrained than Anderson. He dominated the Conservative campaign.[16] Anderson, underestimated by many, was becoming a competitive strategist and performer. He tirelessly travelled the Arm River constituency. He was weary when the campaign ended, but he returned to Saskatoon knowing he'd done well. Well enough, perhaps, to let him dream of someday being "Mr. Premier"!

The Liberals won the Arm River by-election—but just barely! It was a hectic, crowded election day as an astounding 91% of eligible Arm River voters turned out in an incredible march to the polling stations. In 1925 a more normal 50% had voted in the general election, giving the Liberals a comfortable majority of 300 votes. This time the Arm River Liberal machine won by a mere 59 votes. They barely survived the weight of anti-government numbers. In 1928 there was no sophisticated analysis or punditry: no focus groups to consult, opinion polls or exit polls to anticipate or explain election results. But, surely, the on-the-ground eyes and ears of the Liberal organization must have had poll-by-poll intimations of that huge voter turnout and the anti-government passions that excited it. Yet Liberals, while surprised by their near defeat in Arm River, considered it freakish, an accident which they believed could not be repeated provincewide in a general election.[17]

A confident J.T.M. Anderson thought differently. His near-win in Arm River was a beachhead. In the next few months the most determined assault on Liberal power since the days of Haultain was planned. The Tories now had credibility. They were legitimate contenders, a viable alternative government in waiting whether Gardiner and his Liberals knew it or not! The Conservatives attacked what they saw as a criminal patronage system feeding a ruthless Liberal machine and destroying the integrity of the provincial civil service. Whatever role racial and religious issues played in the defeat of the government, this assault on Liberal corruption and dishonesty was certainly significant.[18] The Tory offensive lent palpability and definition to the roiling anti-government emotionalism of the day. Arm River proved that a new alignment of Conservatives, Progressives, Anglo-Scandinavians, American Protestant nativists, Klansmen and closet Klansmen could take on and humble the Gardiner Liberals by stealing usually loyal farmer and immigrant voters away from them. Along with other disaffected folk, these deserters were a mix of voters grown tired of the Liberal Party rule and those denied patronage goodies and grown peevish about a public building not built in their town, a local appointment not granted or a bad stretch of neighbourhood road not repaired. The enduring politics of locality took a toll.

Anderson himself was no bit player in the Conservative management of all of this.[19] He learned politics quickly. Anderson believed in the "Canadianization" of the immigrant, whatever that meant. He believed in public schools free from sectarian influence and may have genuinely feared the Catholic bogeymen his party's spinners had conjured. But he also wanted to win an election. He wasn't all patriot moralist and ideologue. He wanted to be Premier of Saskatchewan and was quickly learning the political trade that could take him there.

On May 11, 1929, Premier Gardiner called a provincial election for June 6. The coalition of Conservatives, Progressives and anti-Liberal Independents that had fought the Arm River by-election again formed ranks. Now, sensing a real win, it was an even more energized and determined collaboration. The goal was to be the government. Good candidates stepped forward. In Prince Albert, John George Diefenbaker eyed the provincial situation and found it promising. After two federal defeats he would try his hand provincially. He was nominated in Prince Albert. On nomination day, in an overwhelming, majority of Saskatchewan's 63 constituencies, there were straight two-way fights between the government and opposition Conservatives, Progressives or Independents. "Saw-Offs" and "understandings" among the opposition parties meant that Conservative candidates were pitted against Progressives or Independents in only a handful of ridings.[20] The opposition concentrated its forces against Gardiner in as many seats as possible.

The general election would not be a kinder, gentler contest than the by-election just ended. The Conservatives would again benefit from a volatile political climate stirred largely by the Klan. In the 1928–29 session of the legislature, the pitch of battle established in Arm River had continued.[21] Contentious matters of sectarian teachers and religious emblems in public school classrooms were again hotly debated. The Tory opposition continued to attack the Liberal "machine" and the participation of paid civil servants in Liberal campaigns. Gardiner's Liberals were put on the defensive again and kept there. When the 1929 battle began in earnest the Anderson Tories returned to some of the old suspicions, warnings and raw nativist appeals of the Arm River by-election struggle. But a Liberal charge that the Tory campaign was centred on anti-Catholic religious bigotry was unfounded. Conservatives may have argued heatedly for secular public schools in the province but such was never an attack on the Catholic Separate School system. It is probable that Gardiner knowingly confused the issue in order to link the Tories with the Klan's anti-Catholic, anti-French-language rant.[22] Grit outrage condemning the exploitation of ethnic and religious differences fell on deaf ears. So did their smug recitations of Liberal virtue and legislative achievements. The Conservative cry, "It's time for a change!" began to resonate in Saskatchewan. After nearly a quarter of a century of Liberal government, people in the province may well have thought it was "time for a change" and may have been a little surprised, but happily so, to see Anderson controlling the issues of this campaign and taking the fight to the enemy.

The Tory campaign wasn't all a negative assault on the Grits. It had positive moments. There were Conservative promises aimed at restoring composure and civility in the Assembly, perhaps even a modicum of trust in government. Anderson proposed legislation to create a non-partisan civil service—a reform long overdue. He promised to establish a Civil Service Commission to oversee the hiring of public servants on merit rather than party affiliation.[23] On the delicate issue of "Canadianization," the Tories advocated a provincial Department of Immigration to work with Ottawa to regulate immigrant selection and numbers to bring them into line with employment opportunities in the province. Anderson vowed to get full control of crown lands and natural resources by negotiating their immediate transfer to the province. Anderson Tories offered Saskatchewan voters not just the defeat of the old bloated regime but the correction of past Liberal wrongs by an uncorrupted new government in Regina. It was an offer Saskatchewan didn't refuse.

J.T.M. Anderson standing on the steps of the Legislative Building with a group of MLAs. First Session of the 7th Legislature, September 4–6, 1929. Anderson is standing immediately to the left of the Speaker, J.F. Bryant (wearing a hat) (SAB R-B8210). A few days later, on September 9, he was sworn in as premier.

On the night of June 6, 1929, Saskatchewan "threw the Liberal rascals out." "Liberalism is dethroned in Saskatchewan after 24 years of uninterrupted sway," lamented the *Prince Albert Daily Herald*, the Grit mouthpiece in northern Saskatchewan. "Local Tories jubilant!"[24] The Liberal numbers in the legislature dropped from their 1925 total of 50 to 28 seats. The Conservatives won 24 seats, up from the three seats won in 1925, the Progressives took five seats and six Independents were elected. Gardiner's government went down even though it had retained the highest percentage of votes and the largest number of seats of any one party in the Assembly. The Grits were out!

Three months later, when the legislature met to debate the Liberal Speech from the Throne, to no one's surprise the Progressives and the Independents joined the Conservatives in defeating the government. A new government with Anderson as premier was in the making. Dr. James Thomas Milton Anderson, composed and sanguine, took the oath of office on September 9. His jubilant Conservatives and their allies had spent a summer of picnics and victory parades celebrating the Gardiner defeat. "Success and long life to a new government," hailed the triumphant Tories. Winners at last! Bye-bye blues!

But in that golden September of 1929 the drought had already begun in Saskatchewan, and the New York stock market crashed in October.[25]

5

Against the Storm

In a patently symbolic song and dance, Anderson resigned the leadership of the Conservative Party and hailed himself leader of the alliance of anti-Liberal members of the legislature. This collaboration called itself the "Co-operative Government" rather than the Conservative government. It was a Conservative government nonetheless and came to be known in the media of the day and in later histories as the "Anderson Government." What's in a name?

Anderson's cabinet, although relatively inexperienced, was keen and eager. One man Anderson particularly wanted didn't make the cut. John Diefenbaker, who expected to be named, Attorney General, was defeated in Prince Albert. He lost by 415 votes. Had Diefenbaker won Prince Albert, he would have added considerable weight to the cabinet.[1] As well as the premiership, Anderson held the portfolios of Natural Resources and Education. The well-known Regina lawyer, M.A. MacPherson, served as Attorney General and J.F. Bryant, the field marshall of the historic Arm River campaign, was named Minister of Public Works. The Liberal opposition considered MacPherson and Bryant their only opponents of cabinet calibre. The rest, they thought feckless. The Liberals found Anderson respectable at best but had "no kind words for him."[2]

The Liberals, hurting from their election beating, could not be expected to heap praise on the victors; but as later events would show, Anderson and his colleagues, at least at the beginning, were comfortably in charge in Regina and could hardly be called "feckless."

As for Anderson's cabinet, recent studies and reappraisals of the Co-operative Government suggest that his cabinet deserves more attention and regard than was given it in the past. Whereas it is natural enough that a province, spooked by a thousand devils of Depression misery, would blame the government in power during those afflicted years and marginalize its accomplishments, it is equally natural that with the passage of time new perspectives might allow a more fair and balanced assessment of things. J.T.M. Anderson's cabinet was not a collection of green slouches and nobodies. Far from it! It was a cabinet with considerable talent. Anderson named 10 men to his cabinet, many of whom had proven appetites for community service and impressive personal and political credentials for public office. The average age of the cabinet was 45, five years younger than Gardiner's cabinet.[3] Four members of the Anderson cabinet had already served in the legislature. Dr. J.T.M. Anderson, MLA for Saskatoon, M.A. MacPherson, MLA for Regina and W.C. Buckle, MLA for Tisdale, all had been elected in 1925. Howard McConnell, MLA for Saskatoon, followed them after winning a 1927 by-election. This was a good beginning for the Co-operative Government's 1929 cabinet.

Anderson served as premier and also held the ministries of Education and Natural Resources. Anderson appointed M.A. MacPherson, a prominent Regina lawyer, as Attorney General, W.C. Buckle, a farm implement dealer and one-time mayor of Tisdale as Minister of Agriculture, Howard McConnell, a lawyer and former mayor of Saskatoon, as Provincial Treasurer and Minister of Municipal Affairs, Dr. Frederick Munroe, a medical doctor and MLA for Moosomin, as Minister of Health, A.C. Stewart, MLA for Yorkton, a lawyer and former mayor of Yorkton, as Minister of Highways, J.F. Bryant, MLA for Lumsden, a teacher and lawyer, as Minister of Public Works and Telephones and J.A. Merkley, MLA for Moose Jaw, a CPR employee and trade unionist, as Minister of Railways, Labour and Industries. W.W. Smith, MLA for Swift Current, and Reginald Stipe, MLA for Hanley were appointed ministers without portfolios. Anderson named Robert (Dinny) Hanbidge, MLA for Kindersley, one-time mayor of Kerrobert and a future Member of Parliament and Lieutenant-Governor of Saskatchewan as government Whip in the Assembly. The cabinet had no farmer members, but W.C. Buckle had served as Tory Agriculture critic in the last Assembly, and his background as a Tisdale area homesteader and farm implement dealer gave him some measure of qualification for the Agriculture posting.

Perhaps to the surprise of some, Anderson had built an able cabinet. It would have to be! His government faced the fierce "take no prisoners" partisanship of the Gardiner Liberals, perhaps "the most formidable opposition in the province's history."[4] They would be hard to match. One thing Anderson and his colleagues had was élan. They had confidence and eagerness to get on with the job of changing Saskatchewan for the better as promised. "It's time for a change," they had shouted. The time was now! The furious dust storms, dried codfish dole and grasshopper plagues of the Depression were not yet even imagined.

Jimmy Gardiner and his Liberal veterans hadn't expected to be turfed. It's doubtful they understood that the 1928 Arm River by-election and the following 1929 general election in Saskatchewan had seen angels and demons at war. They hadn't recognized, nor had they calculated, the emotional upheaval in the province. They had the comfortable belief that good government would be rewarded by a pragmatic, even grateful electorate, that the Saskatchewan Liberal hegemony was indestructible. Hadn't Gardiner told them so? Wasn't one good Liberal worth half a dozen ambiguous Tories in any Saskatchewan market? Things seemed healthy in Saskatchewan when James G. Gardiner left office. Finances appeared sound, crops had been good, credit was readily available. It might not be too much of a reach to say that an almost "boom time" optimism prevailed.[5] The new "Co-operative Government" looked over the prairie scene and smiled. Let's get at it. They began to govern.

First up would be the keeping of key promises in those sensitive areas of non-sectarian public schools, civil service reform, immigration, and Crown lands and resource ownership. Anderson naturally took the education portfolio and moved immediately to honour the Conservative promise to amend the School Act prohibiting the display of religious symbols in the public schools and requiring the use of English as the sole language of instruction. The Conservatives then established the province's first Public Service Commission, promising promotion on the basis of merit and open competition for civil service jobs. What a change this would be! Again, the spirit of the legislation had Anderson's brand on it. He, more than others in the cabinet, knew something of the vagaries and dysfunction of a politics-ridden public service. He had served in one.

The Conservative Party platform in 1929 called for civil service reform which would remove the provincial civil service from partisan politics. In the years 1928 and 1929 serious suspicions and accusations of Liberal corruption and pork-barrel patronage dispensation abounded in Saskatchewan. These were not merely rumours of wrongdoing in high places in far-away government. These were firsthand accounts flagged at the local level in towns and rural districts, of job and promotion favours given to Liberal sympathizers, of public works contracts allotted without public tender and of rewards for government employees doing sundry Liberal Party chores at election time. One wonders how much serious effort the Liberals put into concealing their patronage distribution. It seemed like an exercise in privilege and power that in those times Liberals felt they could practise with considerable impunity. Corruption and patronage became an explosive issue in the 1929 election as passionate outcries against the Gardiner machine were heard and vows to "Break the machine" were made. The patronage system had begun in 1906 when appointments to and in the public service were made by the cabinet, often on the recommendation of government MLAs for appointments from their own ridings. There was no civil service commission until 1913, when a civil service commissioner was appointed to make recommendations to the cabinet. This commissioner was directly responsible to the cabinet and the cabinet retained the final authority in all appointments and dismissals. There were no competitive examinations.

In 1930 the Anderson government passed the Public Service Act following recommendations of a commission of enquiry set up to improve the civil service system in Saskatchewan. The commission of enquiry was chaired by M.J. Coldwell, a Regina alderman and future Member of Parliament and national CCF leader. The Public Service Act called for the appointment by the legislature of a Public Service Commission consisting of one full time chairman who would serve a 10-year term and two others serving five-year terms. The public service was to be graded and classified. Admissions were to be through competitive examinations for positions that required special training and experience. Civil servants were not to take part in politics and could be dismissed for doing so. A joint council made up of government and civil service representatives was given the authority to hear and to adjudicate grievances, appeals and complaints of employees.

Unfortunately, not only were the Anderson innovations in the civil service system discontinued by the Gardiner Liberal government that replaced Anderson and the Conservatives in 1934, several backward steps were taken. No longer was the appointment of the Public Service Commissioners made by the legislature. That power was restored to the cabinet. Now, rather than three public service commissioners, there would be one. This officer would serve for seven years and report directly to the cabinet and be a servant of the cabinet. Competitive examinations were eliminated. In the eyes of many it appeared that the former patronage system was on its way back in Saskatchewan. Gardiner was turning back the clock.

In 1947, what Anderson had begun with his reforms of 1930—reforms later abandoned by Gardiner—was taken up and carried forward by the Douglas CCF government. Douglas enacted civil service legislation that was recognized across the nation as a blueprint for fairness and excellence. After 1947 the public service was to be based on merit and made non-political. Competitive examinations were restored for admission and promotion, and provision for grading and classification of the public service was made. The Public Service Commission appointed by the cabinet would again consist of three persons. Conservative J.T.M. Anderson, who died in 1946, would certainly have approved of Tommy Douglas's 1947 initiatives in civil service reform.

The same Dr. J.T.M. Anderson, former Director of Education among New Canadians, now the premier, set up a Royal Commission to investigate immigration and settlement in Saskatchewan and keep a wary eye on the assimilation of "foreign" settlers and the decline of the rural population in the province. There was more. The long-sought-after provincial ownership of Crown lands and natural resources was now an imperative. Promises to keep.

When J.T.M. Anderson became Premier of Saskatchewan, along with Education he also assumed the Natural Resources portfolio. No one was surprised by his interest in the Education ministry; he had been an educator by profession all his adult life. Nor should they have been puzzled by his taking the Natural Resources portfolio for himself. Anderson wanted to negotiate the return to Saskatchewan of public lands and natural resources denied the province by the federal government since 1905. He wanted to end a 25-year-old, often bitter constitutional dispute, something other premiers, beginning with Scott in 1911 and followed in 1929 by Gardiner, had been unable to do. Anderson remembered Gardiner as premier refusing a federal government

"Completing Confederation." Premier J.T.M. Anderson (front row, fifth from left) and members of his government signing the agreement for the return of natural resources to Saskatchewan. 1930 (SAB R-B459 (4)).

offer to turn over unalienated lands and resources to Saskatchewan because Ottawa would have cut by more than a quarter the federal maximum subsidy originally granted in lieu of the public lands and resources. In opposition, Anderson thought himself made of sterner stuff and chided Gardiner about his failure to negotiate the return of lands and resources belonging to the province. In the legislature he charged,

> Liberal Governments have been "dilly-dallying" to get a return of the resources or an accounting for a quarter of a century. Give us four years and we will get what they have failed to get in twenty-four.[6]

In the 1929 election, Anderson and his redoubtable confederate J.F. Bryant mounted a heated "we were robbed!" campaign across the province, telling audiences that a Conservative government would bring home the long-desired control of Saskatchewan public lands and resources. There would be no more "dilly-dallying." With the election won, the new Co-operative Government kept its promise. M.A. MacPherson, Anderson's outstanding Attorney General, was largely responsible for negotiating the transfer of natural resource rights from Ottawa to Regina. The transfer took place on March 20, 1930. As well as the long-sought-after ownership of its public lands and compensation for lost revenue, the province received the subsidy originally paid in lieu of the lands as compensation for those alienated by the federal government.[7] At last, Saskatchewan was made the constitutional equal of other provinces in Confederation. Anderson, MacPherson and Bryant had reason to smile.

It began to look as if things were brightening in a new Saskatchewan. A Conservative government with ideas and energy brought such promise. And so it might have been, at least for a while, had the "Dirty Thirties" not overcome the province. All the Tory dreams dried up as the decade of the 1930s began.

The "Dirty Thirties" was a decade and more of dreadful economic depression and drought in Saskatchewan. These were years when falling grain prices, trade stagnation, savage unemployment, farm debt foreclosures and small business collapse bred gloom and fear psychology, and paralyzed the province. It was a long drought, a decade of relentless hot, dry winds, drifting precious topsoils, crop failures and endless low, brownish skies heavy and hideous overhead day after day after day. No rain. These were the economic and natural calamities with which Anderson's Conservatives struggled and which brought his reforming efforts in Saskatchewan to a halt. Only months into its term, the "Co-operative Government" found itself less concerned about its agenda for change than with surviving a social and economic disaster overtaking the province.

Anderson looked to federal Tories for help. Liberal Prime Minister Mackenzie King had called a federal election for July 28, 1930, and federal Conservative hopes of beating him and forming a Tory Government were high. The party was led by a westerner, R.B. Bennett, from Calgary. If he were prime minister, Bennett would understand the western plight and come to the rescue. That was the great hope. Alberta's Bennett was a forceful orator and a commanding, emphatic personality. He barnstormed across the country promising to end unemployment by blasting his "way into the markets of the world."[8] He promised prosperity and jobs, jobs, jobs! Westerners desperately wanted to believe him. They flocked to his meetings and huddled by radios listening to his messages. They were cheered and uplifted by his boldness and panache.

Certainly, Saskatchewan Conservatives were captivated. Premier Anderson campaigned earnestly across Saskatchewan for Bennett, allowing that, "It will be my pleasant duty from now on to do all in my power to bring about the defeat of the King government."[9] On election night the federal Conservatives under Bennett handily defeated King. Saskatchewan elected eight Conservatives including the next Minister of Agriculture, Robert Weir of Melfort, Saskatchewan. Now Saskatchewan had only to wait for happy days to come again.

Unfortunately, the Bennett magic didn't work. He couldn't blast his way into world markets to sell Canadian grain and goods. Trade stagnation and unemployment grew and both the federal and provincial Tory governments were forced to concentrate on immediate essentials. Anderson's government turned to finding food for men, feed for livestock, clothing, blankets, heating fuel and debt management for frightened, impoverished Saskatchewan families. The hot winds still blew, and the rains did not come. What did come were Russian thistles, grasshoppers and tramps, bums and drifters begging at back screen-doors for a job or a bite to eat. What also came was a gathering firestorm of bitter human protest.

What would Anderson's government do? First, they would have to look disaster in the eye and accept that a coincidence of economic depression and drought never seen before in Saskatchewan was now upon them. As well, they must recognize that there was no template of policies or planning to consult, no road map, no "paint by numbers" to guide them. The government would have to feel its way along in trial and error, hit and miss, checking out ad hoc solutions and hoping for success. What a challenge for this green new government facing the clutch of unsympathetic Liberal partisans sitting opposite. There could be no soft landing for Anderson.

The responsibility for providing and administering urban relief in Saskatchewan had traditionally belonged to local governments, with the provincial government expected to assist with special grants on a temporary basis only in cases of extraordinary need. As the Depression worsened the federal government, in a series of Unemployment and Farm Relief Acts, began to share relief costs on a temporary basis. Urban municipal governments tried to provide for local needs; but as the costs of direct relief of food, clothing and fuel rose, and bankruptcies and unemployment mounted, local government budgets were overwhelmed. Municipal finances couldn't bear the load, and inevitably government assistance programs became the joint concern of local, provincial and federal administrations: "… relief policies in the 1930s consisted of a veritable patchwork quilt of yearly enactments followed by federal-provincial-municipal agreements at annual or monthly intervals."[10] There was no coordinated national policy in play, and the three levels of government distributed temporary urban relief by adopting and extending whatever current methods were at hand.

For far-flung rural Saskatchewan, in particular, the times demanded a system of planning, a coordinated management of the distribution of government assistance. In August 1931, the Anderson government established a single provincial agency responsible for supervising all rural relief. This agency, The Saskatchewan Relief Commission, at first hired relief officers in each municipality to act as its local administrative officials. These officials were joined by volunteer local relief committees. Later, The Saskatchewan Relief Commission used local municipal councils for field work, assisted by supervisors appointed by the Relief Commission to administer its rural relief programs. The Relief Commission supplied food, clothing, heating fuel, feed, fodder, seed grain, medical and dental care, coal and wood for schools, relief payments for teachers' salaries and funding for repairs of farm machinery. The Commission, using mass buying power, forced down prices in its purchasing of provisions for distribution to the destitute.[11] Shortly after the establishment of the Saskatchewan Relief Commission in August 1931, Premier Anderson declared "No one will starve." This was a promise largely kept by the relief policies of his government administered by the Commission. Rural distress had been contained and kept from worsening, agricultural rehabilitation had been considerably aided in so far as weather conditions would permit. Extreme suffering was averted. The Saskatchewan Relief Commission's record in administering so large a relief program was certainly enviable.[12]

In addition to the Relief Commission's immediate, direct human relief, the Anderson government laboured to stabilize finances, restore balance in the economy, control personal debt and unemployment and establish public confidence in itself as a government in charge and able to cope. The government struggled to maintain work relief programs, particularly in highway construction, trying to provide unemployed, destitute farmers and labourers with work and wages. The withdrawal of the federal government after 1932 from work relief funding, and shrinking provincial budgets, forced the termination of almost all municipal work programs.[13]

At first, apparently believing the drought and depressed economy would be short lived, the Anderson government followed a policy of meeting new public needs with expanded services and no tax increases. But the drought and economic depression worsened. The government faced a money squeeze of declining provincial revenues and rising costs of relief programs. Both the federal government and the provincial business community urged the Anderson government to cut expenditures and raise taxes. The government's limited tax base and difficulty in obtaining loans forced them to adopt the traditional means of retrenchment: tax increases, cutbacks in government departments, particularly Highways, reduction in civil service salaries and personnel, and deficit financing. The government avoided these cutbacks and higher taxes as long as it could.[14]

The Co-operative Government turned its attention to the farmers' plight of falling prices and crop failures and the resulting threats of tax sales and mortgage foreclosures. Saskatchewan farmers' debt load was high and mounting. In 1929 the farmers' marketing agency, the Saskatchewan Wheat Pool, was facing bankruptcy. The Wheat Pool had been established in 1924 to market its members' grain in an orderly way, providing fair prices and dividing the returns from sales among the farm membership. Each farmer received the same price per bushel for the same grade of wheat. This co-operative way of marketing had been highly successful from 1924 to 1928 and had earned the Pool the approval of its farm members. Then came the Depression years and western farmers were caught helpless in falling prices and declining markets. To stay alive they had to borrow. By December 1929 the Saskatchewan Wheat Pool, surprised by the drastic drop in world prices and having borrowed and made a huge overpayment to its members, faced a debt of $15 million. It was forced, as were other Pools in Alberta and

Manitoba facing the same threats of bankruptcy, to appeal to the provincial government for backing to guarantee its bank creditors against loss. To satisfy the banks, provincial bonds were issued to cover the debt. Later, as the Depression dragged on, declining provincial public revenues and increasing relief program costs forced the three western provinces to appeal to Ottawa for help, and federal financial guarantees were given. The 1929 Conservative election platform had promised that a Saskatchewan Conservative government would "give approval and encouragement to cooperative enterprises."[15] Little did Anderson know then how quickly events would require that this promise be kept. The Depression compelled government intervention in the Saskatchewan economy. There was no time then for useless argument about government initiatives versus any Tory philosophy of limited government that Anderson may have held going into the election. The Wheat Pool had to be salvaged and Anderson's Co-operative Government knew it and acted. "The provincial aid in 1929 had kept the Pool from bankruptcy in the initial shock of the 'crash'; provincial lobbying in Ottawa had helped to obtain the federal guarantee that enabled the Pool to survive the long, lean years of the 1930s."[16] More government aid and intervention was critical.

Tax consolidation legislation to prevent foreclosures and provide for orderly means of paying off tax arrears was enacted. It allowed local property owners to defer payment of tax arrears, shifting the debt load forward, hopefully, to more prosperous times when it could be better managed. This had a short-term goal of keeping producers in possession of their means of livelihood.[17] In 1931 the Anderson government also passed legislation for the adjustment of contracted mortgage and bank loan debts. It offered a voluntary conciliation procedure by which farmers' current payments could be postponed. In 1932 this coverage was extended to urban areas. The next year the 1933 Debt Adjustment Bill shifted from mediation of debt adjustment towards government regulation. A Debt Adjustment Board was given the power to review all debts prior to any legal procedure by a creditor against a debtor. If it saw fit, the Board could advise and promote conciliation between the parties. The Board had both the power to arbitrate a settlement if conciliation failed and to rewrite the contracted debt to reduce the interest or principal if they were thought unreasonable. There was much contentious to-and-fro in the legislature and in the media over preserving the sanctity of contractual agreements to maintain confidence in the credit system. By 1934, in spite of furious business community attacks on the Debt Adjustment Act in support of creditor rights and some amendments to the legislation, the Debt Adjustment Act stayed firmly in place. No creditor was allowed to sue for any kind of debt without first securing permission from the Board, and that permission would not be given unless the Board was satisfied the debt was reasonable and the debtor able to pay.[18]

Clearly, Anderson's government was not afraid to weigh the merits of, and place restraints on, creditors' claims in order to ease heavy debtors' loads in

Dedication of the Albert Street Bridge, Regina. Premier J.T.M. Anderson addressing crowd. November 11, 1930 (SAB R-A27549 (1)).

the midst of extreme Depression hardship. In so doing, it introduced a degree of government regulation which was unprecedented in Saskatchewan life:

> In this respect, the imperatives of government reform were neither "capitalist" or "socialist," but derived from efforts to consolidate the agrarian economy as expeditiously as possible.[19]

While the Anderson government had established a system of distribution of rural relief, the problem of urban relief remained serious. Thousands of workers across Canada were thrown into the ranks of the unemployed during the Depression. One group attracted special attention and caused particular anxiety in Saskatchewan. This group was made up of single, homeless, unemployed men who were the responsibility of the federal and provincial governments.

In 1930–31 joint federal-provincial-municipal job creation schemes were begun in Saskatchewan centres to undertake useful public projects and offer some relief to the unemployed. The construction of the Broadway bridge in Saskatoon, the creation of Crescent Park in Moose Jaw and Bryant Park in Prince Albert, construction work on Regina's Albert Street bridge and the draining and deepening of Wascana Lake are among the larger projects initiated by the Anderson government. In 1930, the widening of the Albert Street bridge provided work for 710 unemployed men. In 1931, "the excavation of Wascana Lake employed 2,059 different men for at least a six-day shift."[20]

These men, for a little time at least, were fortunate. Others, without meaningful work and wages, would become trekkers, drifters and bums regarded by governments as potential revolutionaries.

It's probable that people in Saskatchewan today use the term "revolutionaries" only in marketing hyperbole or in jest and taunt. In the 1930s this was not the case. In the first years of the Depression decade "revolutionaries" were real and they were seriously feared. Across Canada the Workers' Unity League, a Communist Party affiliate given the job of organizing and mobilizing the unemployed for political action, was hard at work recruiting workers in urban centres. Agitators and radicals among trekkers and drifters fed the bitterness of the destitute and powerless unemployed. It wasn't long before the Workers' Unity League would come to Saskatchewan. For apprehensive provincial civil authorities, there was a scent of revolution in the air, a hint of drum beat and martial stirring under red banners. Such was certainly the situation in Estevan, a coal-mining town in southeastern Saskatchewan in September 1931.

Lignite coal mining in the Estevan fields was a seasonal operation. Coal miners had to find work on farms to supplement what they could earn in the mines. The introduction of highly mechanized strip mining with its lower costs of production displaced many workers and jobs were lost. As well, a federal coal freight subsidy that had allowed Estevan coal an advantage over Alberta coal in the Winnipeg market ended, and mine operators sought to reduce their costs by lowering the wages of the workers. The miners needed help in resisting the loss of jobs and the reduction of their take-home pay. They called for help from the Workers' Unity League and from the Mine Workers Union of Canada, both of which sent organizers to Estevan. Attempts to bring the mine managers to the bargaining table to negotiate a better deal for the coal miners failed, and the miners went on strike on September 8, 1931. They struck for better wages, better working conditions and recognition of the Mine Workers Union.

On September 29, seeking to generate public sympathy and support, the strikers paraded through Estevan to a proposed protest meeting. Civil authorities, sure that the protest was Communist-inspired and fearing a riot, prohibited both the parade and the meeting. They called the strike illegal. The coal miners marched on. Their protest parade was attacked by the police, and a riot broke out in downtown Estevan. The ensuing violent clash with police killed three strikers and injured 23 others, including bystanders. The police suffered a number of injuries of their own but forced the strikers to retreat, and the strike was broken.

A commission established to study the causes of this appalling event accepted many of the miners' grievances and called for enforcement of safety regulations, improved housing and amendments to the Mines Act. The Anderson government did amend the Mines Act in response to some of the commission's recommendations for changes favourable to workers. For

Anderson the tragic story of Saskatchewan's urban unemployed did not end in Estevan. There was more to come. Relief camps for the unemployed were set up in Regina, Saskatoon and Moose Jaw. These were to provide unemployed men with the necessities of food, clothing and shelter while they waited for placement on farms or in work camps.

On November 7, 1932, in the Saskatoon work camp, as camp numbers steadily increased, living conditions worsened and agitation for better food, healthy air, sanitation, decent housing and more worker control over camp conditions and regulations broke out. Tension in the camp rose day by day, and in February 1933, the situation became acute. Posters urging "Slave Camp Workers Wake Up and Organize" were found at grievance meetings and demonstrations. Workers' Unity League agitators counselled defiance and confrontation with authority. Camp workers were urged to join in the battle to overthrow capitalism or help to establish some new order of revolutionary workers' government.[21] In those increasingly incendiary times the supposed Communist threat to peace, order and good government seemed very real. Anderson's reaction to these threats was tellingly quick and decisive.

In May 1933, the government decided to reduce the size of the Saskatoon camp population by sending 200 men to Regina in groups of 50. The first group was made up of known radicals who on May 8 staged a demonstration when attempts were made to transfer them. The demonstration turned into a small riot which saw mounted RCMP charging and dispersing the demonstrators. When order was restored, one RCMP officer was dead as a result of injuries, and scores of police officers and workers had suffered minor injuries. Twenty-eight workers were arrested. Now in control, the authorities continued their policy of transferring workers out of the relief camp, some to Regina, others to a federal relief camp at Dundurn. The Saskatoon camp was closed on June 30, 1933.

On May 10, two days after the quelling of the so-called riot, Premier Anderson came to Saskatoon to address a Conservative meeting. In a sure-footed, spirited declaration he took full responsibility for the police attack on the workers which saw extra mounted police from Regina brought to Saskatoon. "I made the necessary arrangements," he told an applauding audience. "As long as I live in public or private life I shall do all in my power to drive these disciples of the Red Flag out of Saskatoon and out of the province."[22] For all the heroics of the speech and the undoubted sincerity and probable good intentions of the premier, who saw himself in wildly disjointed times as a protector of civil order, we cannot take our eyes from the faces of the workers caught up in Depression passions and miseries not of their making. We cannot help but look on the riot of 1933 as a sad affair, a struggle of jobless, desperate men against overpowering government authorities.[23] This is not a pretty picture of our past.

And the hardships continued, the stuff of stories and the strategies of survival wrote an unforgetable chapter in Saskatchewan's history. There were

Anderson Cart, made from rear end of an auto, 1932 (SAB R-A42).

"Bennett Buggies" and "Anderson Carts" made from old engineless cars hitched up to a team or a single horse to haul kids to school and folks and necessities about, when there was no longer money to buy gasoline or repairs for the family car or truck. It's doubtful that Bennett in Ottawa or Anderson in Regina were much comforted by having these hybrid—albeit utilitarian— vehicles named for them. The "Bennett Buggy" became part of the idiom of the "Dirty Thirties" in Saskatchewan and is still remembered today. John Diefenbaker, who admired R.B. Bennett, stoutly insisted that had Mackenzie King been elected prime minister in 1930 instead of Bennett, there would have been no "Bennett Buggies," only "King Coupes."[24]

Whereas Premier J.T.M. Anderson's major Saskatchewan opponent, Liberal leader James G. Gardiner, has become the subject of prairie lore with public and personal papers, popular and scholarly biographies, legislative and parliamentary records, and family and collegial testimonies there for our reading, Anderson remains relatively unsung. We know comparatively little about him and his brief adventure in Saskatchewan politics. He may have been a more reluctant political player than was thought at the time. Anderson "revealed an enigmatic personality in his careers as a public servant and as a political leader."[25] He left no personal papers and much of the public record of his five years as Saskatchewan premier was apparently burned behind the Legislative Building after the 1934 defeat of his government.[26] Why, we don't know. We rely on references to him in the correspondence and personal papers of others. Thus, Anderson remains somewhat ambiguous, his story largely untold. The student of the Conservative Party of Saskatchewan is left speculating about the dimensions of the man who was the first Conservative premier of the province.

Dr. Anderson called himself, and liked others to call him, an "educationalist." Perhaps he was always more of an educationalist than a politician. As already noted he was certainly academically accomplished. He was 46 years old when elected Tory leader. He was not a fierce Tory or a lifelong party man. He didn't have to be. He didn't have to work his way up the ranks to the leadership. In 1924 there were only very thin Tory ranks to pass through. The key to Anderson's selection that year as leader was his own celebrity as an author and school administrator and his vigorous advocacy of an educational and social policy catching fire in Saskatchewan at the time.

We do know that the Conservative leader was urbane and self-possessed.[27] He was deliberate and precise, often conciliatory in legislative debate. He didn't shout and thump his desk as some others did in time-worn political theatrics. Anderson was a capable, if not a compelling campaigner, often spirited in his attacks on perceived Liberal wrongdoing. He was genuine, even passionate in his belief that he and his Progressive and Independent confederates could right old wrongs in Liberal educational, public service and immigration policies. In particular, he wanted Liberal Party patronage shut down. He thought it vulgar and criminal. Anderson came late to partisan politics, but after a quick take on the game he played it reasonably well.

We wonder if Anderson, the teacher, the school inspector, the Doctor of Pedagogy, the Director of Education, had to console himself with some pious fibs as he reconciled the meaner aspects of doing politics with his softer self and avowed belief in public decency and transparency. How did this educator balance the raw WASP rant of some in his party against his personal disciplines of professionalism, civility and truth-seeking? How did he reconcile the extreme and public anti-Catholic views of some Tory spokesmen with his own genuine support of the separate school system?[28] How much would winning political office cost him?

Throughout his few years as Tory leader and premier, Anderson's even-handed party leadership was never seriously threatened. There was a little rumbling from time to time when so called "True Blue" Conservatives expressed suspicions about the rightist loyalties of the Progressive and Independent components of the "Co-operative Government." They were also uneasy with Anderson's views on debt relief, which were seen as a bit too reformist for "True Blue" comfort. Many "True Blue" Tories were also creditors and looked for a fair return on loan investments. The "True Blues" were led by Dr. D.S. Johnstone of Regina, who served as president of the Saskatchewan Conservative Party from 1930 to 1932, when he was replaced after attacking Premier Anderson at a 1932 party convention. Johnstone and the "True Blues" thought Anderson a pale blue Tory who had abandoned what Johnstone saw as the rightist principles of true Toryism in return for cooperation with enemies on the left. To add to the heresy, Johnstone charged that Anderson had not done enough to reward party supporters and workers with patronage benefits. One wonders what form such rewards could have taken during the catastrophic Depression years. Johnstone's "True Blues" continued their attacks on the Anderson moderates up to and during the 1934 provincial election.[29] Their relentless agitation was a vexing problem for Anderson and it would continue into the Diefenbaker years.

Anderson held his "Co-operative Government" together during the high-pressured Depression years under relentless Liberal opposition attack. He was good at building coalitions. It may be that some of his human resource management skills as an educationalist rubbed off on Anderson the politician. He managed well without a big stick! Even after he was booted out of office in the 1934 election disaster there was no spate of recriminations from sulking contenders to replace him. Had he wanted the leadership, the job would have stayed his. He didn't want it.

Dr. Anderson's struggle was nearly over when the legislature met in February 1934. This would be the last session of the "Co-operative Government." Anderson's five-year wrestle with Depression politics had taken a toll on him. The man was worn out by unemployment, dust, rust, grasshoppers, crop failures and the partisan rancour of the gladiatorial Jimmy Gardiner in the legislature. Anderson may have felt relief when on April 7 the legislature finished its last sitting and prepared for dissolution and a June election in a province blanketed by despair.

The Liberals, although invited, had steered wide of any alliance with Anderson, leaving themselves free to blame the government for all the misfortunes of the day. In 1932 and 1933 Anderson promoted the idea of a coalition government with a "Provincial Union Cabinet," a non-partisan administration to govern the province during the time of crisis. A wily Jimmy Gardiner called for the "best brains and best thought to be brought together in a spirit of co-operation and helpfulness,"[30] but he didn't mean it. It's likely that this relentless partisan believed all or most of the best brains and best thoughts in the legislature already sat on Liberal benches. Gardiner knew he had only to wait for the bad times to overtake and defeat a reasonably good Conservative government. The people had suffered. Someone had to pay. "Throw the bastards out!"

"Liberal Ways Bring Better Days!" sang out the glad Liberal election chorus. Anderson called the 1934 election for June 19. He knew he couldn't win it.

Instead of making the election announcement with appropriate fanfare from his own Saskatoon riding, staging an event from the Legislative Building or on a radio hook-up from Regina, he casually made the election call in Chaplin, then a little way station village west of the capital. Certainly, there was no sense of moment in the announcement. Nor was there meant to be.

In this rather modest setting the premier, with more spirit than he may really have possessed, told a clutch of supporters, "There is no doubt whatever but that the government will be returned with a substantial majority."[31]

Jimmy Gardiner's Liberals, with a well-greased, smoothly running provincial machine, waited for the flag to fall and were off in a roar. Gardiner opened in Prince Albert on May 16 for incumbent T.C. Davis, who had defeated John Diefenbaker in 1929. It was a big, noisy Prince Albert rally with Gardiner excitedly predicting "Better Days" for all Saskatchewan. Any prospect of "better days" in Saskatchewan was promising and eagerly welcomed by town and country folk alike. Most believed they were then living in some of the worst.

This time most of the two-way battles that had concentrated anti-Liberal sentiments and helped the Conservatives gain power in 1929 were gone. In their place were three- and four-way contests. The 1934 battle lines were changed. There were some new kids on the block joining in the gang fights. The Farmer-Labour Party was the one to watch. Led by British-born Major James Coldwell, a Regina alderman and school teacher, it had nominated 53 candidates for the 55-seat Assembly. An attempt by Liberal spokesmen to wound both Anderson and Coldwell was a charge of collusion between them to defeat Gardiner and form another cooperative government.[32] The Farmer-Labour Party had grown out of the Saskatchewan section of the United Farmers of Canada and the Independent Labour Party and was the Saskatchewan arm of the federal Co-operative Commonwealth Federation. Coldwell was a gifted campaign orator, precise, vigorous and eloquent on the platform. To both Anderson and Gardiner, Coldwell's party was a dangerous left-wing agitation. They dismissed the new party as the "Socialist Party" or, when the socialist appellation failed to generate enough fear and loathing, they called it "Communist" or "Red." In the fevered 1930s that was a sure bogeyman's kiss. It hurt the new party but not mortally, as election night results would demonstrate.

Dr. Anderson and his Depression-weary Conservatives knew the odds were against them. They fought a relatively lacklustre campaign, a "we stood by you now you stand by us" defense.[33] Again and again Tory speakers asked, "What would they have done?" Anderson hoped a generous electorate would conclude that neither Liberals nor socialists could have done more or better in government. The Tories knew they entered the 1934 campaign seriously wounded, hurt not so much by fair-ball analyses of the government's response to the Depression crisis as by a stubborn public association of them with bad times they did not create and could not control. This association, perhaps largely subliminal, followed the Conservative Party like a dark cloud for years to come. What about the condition of the party war machine. Was it ready to meet the Liberal challenge? Perhaps not. It was thought by some that Anderson showed weakness as a captain general in not preparing adequately for the 1934 campaign. Some believed "he had been preoccupied with solving the province's economic problems and had neglected Conservative Party constituency organizations."[34] Anderson and Bryant certainly knew that 1934 struggle with Gardener's Grits would be a tough one. Gardiner was a fighter who believed in battle red in tooth and claw and never took his eyes off his troops in the field. He and they would be ready for combat.

Why would Anderson fail to maintain and strengthen his constituency organizations before the 1934 campaign? Was such a failing a factor of his own softer cooperative nature, or was it caused by weakening cohesion in his coalition? Was he all knocked out by five years of woeful times and unable to muster the needed energy and will to fight on? Did he resign himself to defeat or even inwardly long for release? Good questions for which there can be no conclusive answers.

Anderson put 53 candidates in the field and fought back. Cabinet heavyweights J.F. Bryant and M.A. MacPherson joined the premier in exhausting speaking tours across the province. John Diefenbaker from Prince Albert, although not a candidate this time, delivered some good sonorous stuff on the campaign trail. He was a young Tory to watch, a man on the way up if the party could open a corridor for him.

He and others fought on the Anderson record. It was a reasonably good one, but would anybody listen? Conservative campaigners praised Anderson, their leader. A sterling man, they called. him, a faithful Saskatchewan son who had governed under appalling economic conditions. Conservatives knew the Liberals' greatest weapon was the Depression. Diefenbaker told audiences, "The Liberal Party in this province has been stirring up trouble and searching for something to criticize for months but had to resort finally to a world condition and blame that on the present government."[35] Diefenbaker was right.

From the start a predictable Liberal campaign run by veterans of the political game assailed Anderson's caucus as incompetent, inadequate bunglers unable to protect the people and direct a provincial recovery. Throughout the campaign Anderson was also harassed by dissension in his own party ranks. As noted, he was attacked by the petulant "True Blues" who had never really accepted him as party leader and now accused him, as they had done before, of betraying Tory principles by taking Progressives and Independents into the government.[36] The "True Blue" leadership actively urged Conservatives to purge their party by voting Liberal, however bizarre such advice must have sounded. Provincial voters were constantly reminded of the sins of the federal Conservative government under the millionaire Prime Minister, R.B. Bennett. Remember the lines of unemployed, the flour-sack dresses, rabbit stews and empty lunch buckets Liberal speakers taunted: "Remember Bennett's high tariff policies! Remember 'Liberal Ways Bring Better Days!'"

The Tory party with its 1934 platform, "Something of the Achievements of the Anderson Government," its leader's tour, radio broadcasts, public meetings and newspaper advertisements reminded the voter of the government's immigration and public school policies, the snaring of Crown lands and natural resources for the province, the Cancer Commission, the new School for the Deaf and particularly the Public Service Commission and key Depression legislation, the Saskatchewan Relief Commission and the Debt Adjustment Act. They reminded the voter of the government's establishment of a psychopathic ward in the Regina General Hospital and its labour-friendly amendments to the provincial Workmen's Compensation and Minimum Wage Acts. They reminded the electorate of the government's creation of a superannuation fund for retired teachers, provision for high school correspondence courses for rural students and expansion of vocational education in the province. They boasted of the Tory government's multimillion-dollar highway program and construction of a system of numbered highways that served the settled areas of the province.

The Tory slogan, "Don't swap horses while crossing a stream," was sounded by the Anderson and McConnell campaigns in Saskatoon and picked up and used across the province. It seemed sensible, prudent advice. After all, the Depression wasn't over in Saskatchewan. The question, of course, was whether or not the voters considered the Tory horse capable of crossing the stream with its rider still safely upright in the saddle. The 1934 party platform included

> provision for a Commission to administer all aspects of education in the province; a minimum salary for teachers; additional provincial parks; more new highway construction when finances permitted; a province-wide service for agricultural representatives to assist farmers; water conservation through government-sponsored irrigation projects and support for national unemployment and health insurance schemes.[37]

They touted two new boards, an Advisory Economic Council and a Health Service Board. The party's campaign scare tactics included the charge that Liberals, if allowed back in office, would revive sectarianism in provincial schools by repealing amendments to the School Act and abolish the Relief Commission. Anderson reminded the voters of the earlier Liberal scandals revealed by Royal Commissions in 1931, suggesting that the Grits could not yet be trusted with power. A disillusioned Saskatchewan electorate was told, "We've rounded the corner, the Depression's worst is over." Help was on the way! "Vote Conservative." But Saskatchewan wasn't listening.

The Liberal reply can be summarized in one of its more creative and alliterative slogans: "A Merciless Mess of Mismanagement and the Way Out."[38] On June 19, for better or worse, the Saskatchewan electorate took the way out. They elected James G. Gardiner with 50 Liberal seats. They elected five Farmer-Labour members. They defeated all Conservative candidates. In spite of a thin second-place finish in the popular vote, not a Tory was left standing!

The Gardiner Liberals, with a popular vote of 206,191, had 48% of the total. Anderson's Tories tallied 114,973 votes and 27% of the popular total. The opposition Farmer-Labour Party, with 103,582 votes, won 24% of the total votes cast.[39] M.J. Coldwell, the Farmer-Labour leader, was defeated in his own Regina riding, as was Anderson in Saskatoon.

At 8:30 p.m. election night Premier Anderson conceded from his Saskatoon headquarters. His statement to the Canadian Press read:

> The electors have decisively spoken and decided to place the Liberals in power. I trust the new government will experience less difficult times than those faced by the government during the last five years of unprecedented adversity."[40]

There was more resignation than fortitude in this concession statement. Where was the usual gallant stuff about "I'll lay me down and bleed awhile and then I'll rise and fight again"? Obviously, Anderson didn't feel that heroic. Also, his expression of satisfaction that the voters who that day defeated him "had just as decisively rejected socialism" may have been considerably misplaced.[41] It's not clear how decisively the voters had rejected socialism, given the rather generous numbers garnered by the young Farmer-Labour Party in its first election bid!

Premier-elect Jimmy Gardiner and his jubilant Liberals celebrated across the province and long into the night. In Regina, after arriving by plane from Melville, Gardiner was cheered by hundreds lining Albert Street and Albert Memorial bridge as his motorcade, preceded by a pipe band, brought him to the steps of the Legislative Building. James G. Gardiner, surely one of the most colourful and enduring political brawlers ever to serve as Saskatchewan premier, was back on the job.

Dr. J.T.M. Anderson was out of a job. He hadn't even been able to hold his own Saskatoon riding. To Conservatives, all their struggles to ameliorate the troubled Depression years must then have seemed curiously pointless. Yet their struggles were hardly that. Instead, the Conservative government's labour to lessen the distress and hardships of the ravaged province was remarkable. Much credit was due the Anderson government, but only with the passage of time and the advantage of perspective would such recognition be given them.

What more can be said of Anderson? Surely, he was raised to politics and carried forward in it more by chance and the peculiar passions of the times than by any huge ambition, power of character or *kismet* of his own. When he found himself in the premier's chair he served responsibly and usefully for a short and difficult tour of duty. In those stormy years he was more good housekeeper than statesman, but he was principled, courageous and steady when that kind of management was essential.

As with Haultain before him, the old question of circumstance and potential occurs: "What might have been?" Had it not been for drought and

Depression, Anderson's Conservatives might have built on a few good works in their first term and won again in 1934, securely establishing the Conservative Party in Saskatchewan. Anderson himself might have spent longer in command, grown more proficient in the office and carried more reputation with him at the leaving of it. In 1936, at a provincial convention of the party in Regina, he resigned the leadership and took a job as manager of a Saskatoon insurance agency. Anderson supported Diefenbaker in the 1938 provincial campaign and later stood for the federal Conservatives in 1940, running against M.J. Coldwell in Rosetown-Biggar. He lost both battles.

After his last defeat, seemingly without struggle or regret, the former premier slipped into the shadows of private life. For a time the Saskatchewan Conservative Party faded with him. It wasn't until the early 1970s that a provincial Tory revival began. By then, Dr. J.T.M. Anderson was long gone from the scene, either forgotten or ignored. But are "forgotten or ignored" fair enough deserts for Saskatchewan's first Conservative premier? There are Tories today, this writer among them, who believe that Anderson has been significantly undervalued in the past and deserves a more prominent place in Saskatchewan's political history than he has been given, and a rank closer to the top among Conservative Party leaders than even Tories themselves have allowed him. Saskatchewan Conservatives should take a new, long look at Anderson. They might find a hero.

In 1961 Saskatchewan-born Ralph Allen, celebrated journalist and sometime editor of *Maclean's* magazine, expressed an honest concern that Sir Robert Borden, Conservative World War I Canadian Prime Minister, had been short-changed by Canadians in their judgment of his 11 years in office. Allen wrote:

> Whether time will revise this judgment upward, no one can say. But if a public servant's net worth is the sum of his useful actions, minus his mistakes, multiplied by his difficulties, then Borden deserves his country's gratitude.[42]

Surely, this must also be said of Saskatchewan's Conservative premier, J.T.M. Anderson.

6

"The Chief"

After the debacle of its 1934 defeat the Saskatchewan Conservative Party was like an accident victim pulled from a wrecked car, bruised and dazed but still breathing. The party survived with 27% of the popular vote. It registered a significant number of second-place finishes across the province and remained competitive in the cities. But it had been booted out of the legislature. Not a Tory left in sight.

The lack of representation in the Assembly was deadly. You don't get your message out if you're not in the forum to speak. Out of sight, out of mind! It was a politician's nightmare! But after this provincial wipe-out and the R.B. Bennett federal loss that followed in October 1935, there weren't many Tories left in Saskatchewan to suffer the frights.

John G. Diefenbaker, a Prince Albert lawyer, was then the party's provincial president. With Dr. Anderson's expressed intention to step down as leader, the party waited on Diefenbaker to call a leadership convention to replace him. There were rumours that Diefenbaker wanted the job. He had already served the Conservative Party in a number of capacities. He knew from early years that he wanted to be a lawyer, and his heroes were Abraham Lincoln, John A. Macdonald and R.B. Bennett. Later, to that celebrated company he would add Winston Churchill. A political career for him seemed inevitable.[1]

From his youthful University of Saskatchewan debating and Mock Parliament days Diefenbaker knew he had extraordinary oratorical and debating skills which would serve him well, first in the courtroom and then on the political platform. Early in his career he joined the Conservative Party, at that time a road less taken in Prince Albert, Saskatchewan, but he chose to wear Tory blue.

Long before he was "Dief" or the "Chief" he was Mr. J.G. Diefenbaker, a fascinating young bachelor lawyer in Prince Albert. There was something special about him. The piercing eyes, the timbre of his voice, the commanding mannerisms and pent-up energy in the courtroom or on the public platform, all begged notice. John Diefenbaker was different and he was showy.

He first ran for the Conservative Party in the federal election of 1925, when he was 30 years old. He lost to the Liberal candidate. The very next year he boldly took on the Right Honourable William Lyon Mackenzie King, Prime Minister of Canada, and lost. He was gaining a reputation not only in Conservative politics but as a successful and sought-after courtroom defence lawyer. There was more than a little Clarence Darrow in this prairie criminal lawyer, including perseverance. Diefenbaker campaigned for the provincial Conservatives in the 1928 Arm River by-election. Here in debate he was a match for Premier James Gardiner in one memorable encounter and proved himself one of his party's most effective champions.² The next year, in the 1929 provincial election, he ran in Prince Albert as a Conservative against T.C. Davis, Liberal Attorney General. He lost a close race.

This third defeat on the Tory ticket was disappointing but didn't destroy his enthusiasm for the party. In 1933 he sought and on a third ballot won the vice-presidency of the Saskatchewan Conservative Party at its October 11 convention in Saskatoon. In November of the same year he ran for mayor of Prince Albert. He lost narrowly to Hal Fraser, a fellow Prince Albert lawyer who had Liberal Party credentials and generous local newspaper support.³ In the 1934 provincial election, although not a candidate himself, as provincial vice-president of the party he campaigned for Conservative candidates across Saskatchewan. In August 1935 he replaced J.A.M. Patrick as provincial Tory president when Patrick was named a District Court judge by Prime Minister R.B. Bennett.

With a disconsolate J.T.M. Anderson waiting to be relieved of his Tory command, it was Diefenbaker's job as party president to call a leadership convention to replace him, if and when aspirants to that hollow crown could be found. At that time, the Saskatchewan Conservative leadership role was hardly enticing. In his memoirs Diefenbaker says he did not hanker for the leadership of the shadowy and exhausted party: "I did not have it in mind to become Party Leader, nor did I campaign in any way for the office."⁴ Yet he did encourage his own candidacy while avowing preference for others he knew were more experienced and more sought-after than himself but unlikely to run. Robert Weir, former federal Minister of Agriculture in the Bennett government, and M.A. MacPherson, Anderson's Attorney General, were thought the most desired candidates.⁵ Anderson himself was not ruled out as a candidate, if he had wanted to stay at the helm. He didn't.

Diefenbaker called a leadership convention for October 28, 1936, more than a year after assuming the provincial presidency. In the weeks leading up to the convention he openly solicited support for a leadership run from prominent Tory delegates. In particular, he asked for the support of H.E. Keown, a prominent Melfort lawyer, a Diefenbaker friend and legal associate. "Bert" Keown would, in time, succeed Diefenbaker, first as party president and then as party leader. It is safe to say that in the Saskatchewan politics of the late1920s through to the early 1940s, Bert Keown shared a collegial relationship and a political camaraderie with Diefenbaker that was unequalled by any other Conservative politician in those early years of Diefenbaker's career. Even R.L. (Dinny) Hanbidge, who was to become a close personal friend in later years in federal politics, or the young Alvin Hamilton, who joined Diefenbaker in the 1938 provincial campaign, did not enjoy the degree of comradeship with Diefenbaker that was, for a time, accorded to Keown.

Diefenbaker and Keown met early in Diefenbaker's career. In 1927 he and Keown attended the Winnipeg Conservative leadership convention that chose R.B. Bennett as federal Tory leader. Diefenbaker attended as the whip of the Saskatchewan delegation. Bert Keown was Saskatchewan's representative on the party's national executive. In 1928, at the request of J.T.M. Anderson, Diefenbaker and Keown campaigned together in the Arm River by-election. They spoke at a packed meeting in Bladworth for Stuart Adrian, the Conservative candidate. In his memoirs Diefenbaker describes Keown's easy handling of obstreperous hecklers and his amusement at Keown's cavalier quotations of public-debt figures.[6] Diefenbaker thought he and Keown were a good team:

John Diefenbaker, upon election as leader of the Conservatives in 1936. Diefenbaker led the party until 1940 (SAB R-A78).

> I have known a number of men who have been exceptionally good stump speakers. Gardiner was one, another was my friend Bert Keown. He had a magnificent, voice and a dry wit.[7]

At the 1936 leadership convention in Regina Keown was nominated for the provincial leadership of the party but withdrew his name in favour of Diefenbaker. Later, in 1942, he supported Diefenbaker's national leadership bid at the convention in Winnipeg that elected John Bracken. In the 1938 provincial election with Diefenbaker as provincial leader and Keown as President of the Saskatchewan Conservative Party, they were a small and lonely team in the battle to keep the Tory party alive. "Bert Keown did a good deal for me over the years," Diefenbaker said in his memoirs.[8] At no time was Diefenbaker in greater need of a friend. Denis Smith, in his extraordinary biography, *Rogue Tory*, describes Keown as "Diefenbaker's only active companion in the discouraging struggle of 1938."[9]

The discrepancy between Diefenbaker's claim of indifference to the leadership and his apparent efforts to secure it shouldn't confuse us. Probably

Diefenbaker wanted the top job but hesitated to publicly reach for it for fear of suffering rebuff. Four past defeats had made him cautious. He was gun shy. He wanted a sure thing and hoped for a popular draft. That draft didn't come either before or at the leadership convention. He was not the roaring toast of 600 Conservatives gathered in Regina's City Hall auditorium on October 28, 1936, but he was an acceptable candidate, and he was available. When 10 others, including Weir, MacPherson, Keown and J.T.M. Anderson, were nominated for leader but withdrew from the race, only J.G. Diefenbaker of Prince Albert was left standing. He was declared the new leader of the Saskatchewan Conservative Party, elected by acclamation. He made a good acceptance speech, well received by the convention. The provincial news media were also impressed, noting his youth, conviction and debating skills. Would these be enough? The Conservative *Regina Daily Star* called the young Diefenbaker, "One of Saskatchewan's most able criminal lawyers."[10]

He had about 18 months to prepare for the next provincial election expected in the spring of 1938. His place as party president was taken by H.E. Keown, who would prove a much-needed good right arm for his leader. Only Alvin Hamilton and Diefenbaker's wife, Edna, his driver and cheerful companion on miles and miles of potted gravel roads, would equal Keown's loyalty and tenacity in the desperate campaign to follow.

The Saskatchewan Liberal government was no longer led by the redoubtable Jimmy Gardiner. Gardiner had been summoned to Ottawa by Mackenzie King to serve as federal Minister of Agriculture. He had been replaced as premier and Liberal leader in Saskatchewan by W.J. Patterson, who had served as Minister of Highways and of Natural Resources in the Gardiner government. Patterson had been chosen for the leadership by his Liberal caucus and Liberal council colleagues because of his administrative abilities and his affability and popularity. He was a "good ol' boy" in the Liberal ranks. Patterson seemed sluggish on the campaign trail. He was only an adequate public speaker, certainly no match for Diefenbaker or Co-operative Commonwealth Federation (CCF) leader George Williams.[11] No matter. Patterson inherited a disciplined, fully manned, well-financed provincewide organization assisted by deep federal pockets and patronage leverage. As well, Saskatchewan Liberals had escaped much of the Depression calumny and remained robust and spirited.

The anti-Liberal vote could not be gathered up by the Conservatives. This election it would be split three ways, shared by Tory, CCF and Social Credit candidates. Unlike 1929, there seemed no possibility of an anti-government coalition under Conservative leadership. Diefenbaker began his leadership with a degree of optimism. "I thought we had a chance," he wrote in his memoirs.[12] Premier Patterson called a provincial election for June 8, 1938. Four parties—the Liberals, Conservatives, CCF and Social Credit—would fight it out. Diefenbaker's attempts to organize constituencies, line up potential candidates and raise necessary funding had been less than promising. At one point he thought he had 40 ridings manned, but many of these were paper candidates who lost heart and withdrew: "One by one my candidates drifted away."[13] With only 24 candidates to contest Saskatchewan's 52 legislative seats, he knew from the outset that his Tories could not win government and would be lucky to take even a handful of seats.

Where would John Diefenbaker run? He wanted Prince Albert. It was home. But Prince Albert had rebuffed him four times in the past. He'd lost Prince Albert in two federal campaigns, one provincial campaign and in a mayoral contest. Each time, he had lost to the Liberal Party; if he stayed at home, he would lose again. Diefenbaker chose Arm River, a seat then held by the Liberals by fewer than 300 votes. In 1934, the Conservative candidate had garnered 38% of the vote. He had campaigned extensively there in the 1928 Arm River by-election. He knew the area and its Conservative Party operatives who wanted him to leave ungrateful Prince Albert and come south to them. "You can win Arm River," they told him.

Premier Patterson lacked the versatility of Dunning and Martin and certainly the force and creativity of Gardiner.[14] Even so, Patterson led his Liberals well enough and was able to deploy a full slate of 52 seasoned candidates in a strong if somewhat uneven and defensive campaign. He was well funded and strengthened by the participation of that incomparable partisan Jimmy Gardiner, on loan from Ottawa for campaign appearances on his home turf. The Liberals defended their record in office, fending off traditional attacks on the "machine" and characterizations of a somnolent status quo government out of touch with a new world.

The Liberal platform offered predictable, motherhood programs of highway construction, health services, industrial development and debt relief. "This is a government you can trust. Vote Liberal." To elect the tainted, inept Tories would be foolhardy. Forget them. To experiment with the radical protest movements such as the CCF and especially Social Credit would be egregious voter folly. Liberal Party broadsides, delivered with evangelical zeal, warned against the dangers of socialist or Alberta-exported Social Credit attacks on British heritage values and institutions.

The CCF, formerly the Farmer-Labour Party, fought to increase its five-man membership in the legislature and establish a legitimate and lasting political presence. To do this, they needed to shift the sands of politics in Saskatchewan, challenging both the Liberals and Conservatives and taking second place from one of them. Obviously, the Tories were most threatened. The CCF platform and rhetoric had been cooled considerably from the Farmer-Labour 1934 edition, which was a touch too Red, hot and spicy even for a volatile Depression-beleaguered province. The flagship of the Farmer-Labour platform in 1934 had been their "use-lease" land policy. It was supposed to have been a new and sound approach to landholding in Saskatchewan and a boon to farmers facing debt problems, foreclosures and mortgage companies threatening the family farm and the province's cherished rural way of life. Farmer-Labour leader M.J. Coldwell had been confident the land policy was a winner. He cheerfully allowed that the policy was "the best thing we have in our platform."[15] He would be greatly surprised. The "use-lease" land policy would, in fact, prove a dead-weight clunker in Coldwell's 1934 election appeals and put the Farmer-Labour Party on the defensive throughout the campaign.

The "use-lease" policy had seemed a practical way to provide indebted farmers with security of tenure and thus preserve the family farm. Its principles were clear enough. The debt-ridden farmer would surrender title to his land to the government and would be given a "use-lease" on the land. The government would deal with the mortgage company and the farmer would have security of tenure on the land for as long as he wanted to farm it. He could not sell the land, but he could pass the lease on to his family. The problem in 1934 was to sell the "use-lease" proposal. Would Saskatchewan farm folk buy this? The Liberal and Conservative parties attacked the policy, calling it Soviet-style nationalization of the land. This, they argued, was not the Canadian way; it was a wicked socialist scheme, foreign in the eyes of independent prairie homesteaders and their descendents. This proved a telling, emotional argument against the Farmer-Labour land policy. Various answers were heard to questions about whether the farmer could sell his lease, borrow money against it, or scrap it and buy back his title after yielding it. Even Farmer-Labour candidates themselves had difficulty understanding their own "use-lease" policy, and certainly presenting it to dubious—even hostile—audiences was difficult. This flawed land policy and some serious rough-housing with the Roman Catholic hierarchy over statism and social ownership had put victory in 1934 out of reach for the Farmer-Labour Party. In 1938 the CCF jettisoned the unpopular "use-lease" policy in favour of a much more voter-friendly one. This policy favoured the retention of title by the farmer and renegotiation and possible amortization of his debt. With this there might be solace for both the debt-laden farmer and his anxious creditors.

The wild card in the 1938 election was the new—and in Saskatchewan largely unknown—Social Credit Party, an oddball import from Alberta. Not only was Social Credit, as a purported right-of-centre movement, a challenge to Diefenbaker's Conservatives, it also threatened the CCF as a fellow protest party apparently questioning all the political, social and economic structures of the province. Social Credit was radical and throbbing with fundamentalist certitudes. Its founder and leader, Alberta Premier William Aberhart, who had been a radio evangelist and founder of the Prophetic Bible Institute, invaded Saskatchewan, nominating 41 candidates—all approved, if not chosen, by the Alberta Social Credit League out of Edmonton.[16] With a well-oiled mix of demagoguery and showmanship Social Credit showed itself from the first as a serious threat to Patterson's Liberals. Aberhart's platform was an ambiguous litany of negatives.[17] His core attack was against the financial system. He stormed against powerful eastern money barons, promising to end their enslavement of the West. A Social Credit victory would provide social "credits" or social "dividends" to all Saskatchewan citizens and bring their purchasing power into line with their production costs. It sounded good—but how was this done?

Unworkable and unconstitutional as it proved to be, it had a tantalizing buzz to it, and "Bible Bill" Aberhart fascinated huge Saskatchewan audiences with razzmatazz and snake-oil salesmanship. They flocked by the thousands to his meetings across the province and listened to his fervent radio appeals. The Prince Albert Armouries overflowed with 3,500 people at an Aberhart rally there. Not until John Diefenbaker was elected national PC leader in 1956 and returned home was such a crowd gathered in Prince Albert.[18] In 1938 "it was certainly Aberhart who benefited most from the fact that politics provided the pre-eminent diversion during the Depression."[19] Aberhart spent three weeks in Saskatchewan travelling in multi-car cavalcades to over 40 meetings. It is difficult today to know how to characterize these events. They seemed a mix of fervent "Praise the Lord" revival meetings and "Send in the Clowns" circus entertainment. Inevitably, Aberhart's rallies were the best show in town. On election eve Aberhart addressed over 5,000 supporters in Melville, a crowd that rocked the rafters of the town's hockey arena. The Aberhart campaign was puzzling to Tory, CCF and Liberal organizers who had not seen such a whirlwind before and watched with apprehension. Melville was won by the Social Credit in 1938. Aberhart was able to coalesce with CCF and Conservative forces in a co-operative effort that defeated Liberal C.M. Dunn, Minister of Highways in the Patterson government. Melville being Jimmy Gardiner country, this was a signal Social Credit win. Aberhart's audiences looked for sunbeams and silver linings. Years of hopelessness during the Depression had made them vulnerable to scam, and they listened intently, wanting to believe. He promised to rid them of old politics, old bureaucracy and old debt. Were these sound economic prescriptions or just malarky? People didn't know, but what had they to lose!

Premier Patterson's Liberals fought back, likening the Social Credit invasion to German and Italian Fascist party tactics. British democracy was endangered, they warned, matching Social Credit hyperbole with hot jingoist gusts of their own. The CCF, led by feisty farm leader George Williams and joined by former provincial leader M.J. Coldwell and Saskatchewan CCF Member of Parliament T.C. Douglas, put 31 candidates in the field and mounted an effective attack on the Patterson government, branding it inept in dispelling the economic woes of the province—if not in fact causing some of them. Whereas the CCF was still weak in the larger cities (it ran no candidates in Regina, Saskatoon, Prince Albert and Moose Jaw), it campaigned earnestly in small-town and rural Saskatchewan, legitimized and emboldened by the impressive performance of its five members in the last Assembly.

What about the Conservatives? What called itself the Saskatchewan

Conservative Party was really only pretending. Its few riding associations were skeletal, manned for the most part by tired, old family loyalists and hungry young lawyers waiting to prosper in better times. Diefenbaker Tories were still grotesquely handicapped with "Dirty Thirties" stink and blame. The party was queasy with self-doubt and fading ideological conviction, plagued by desertions to the Liberals to stop the dreaded Social Credit and desertions to Social Credit to stop the dreaded socialist CCF. Once again the whining cries of conflicted "True Blue" Tories were heard questioning the party's right-wing credentials.[20] The "True Blues" complained of "leftist" control of the Conservative Party and sniffed the scent of betrayal on every wind. These mainly Regina-based critics yearned for the safe old WASP days of small business-directed government. The hostile Dr. D.S. Johnstone had not gone away after being turfed from the party presidency in 1932, as had been hoped. Johnstone and a remnant of his "True Blues" were still around for Diefenbaker to suffer. They viewed Diefenbaker as no better than J.T.M. Anderson and described the little rump of Diefenbaker candidates as "our left wing" Conservatives. Johnstone charged that 10 years of leftist control of the Conservative Party had caused it to disappear.[21] Other Tory dissenters ran as Independents, supported saw-offs with the CCF or proposed CCF-Conservative coalition candidates to defeat the Liberals. The Diefenbaker party ran in many directions when it moved at all.

Undoubtedly, Diefenbaker wanted to enter the 1938 campaign leading a party seen as the clear alternative to the Patterson Liberal government, a Tory party most likely and best able to gather up the anti-Liberal vote. But he knew this wasn't the case. The traditional two-party system was gone from Saskatchewan. Diefenbaker knew there were three parties now, battling the Grits for power. He also knew his Conservatives were far from the leading contender among them. The CCF, now the official opposition in the legislature, and the strange and feared Alberta Social Credit newcomers threatened Diefenbaker from the left and from the right.

For months before the election there was recognition at the constituency level that a divided anti-Liberal vote could result in a sweeping Liberal win. None of the opposition parties alone could bell the cat. Conservative, CCF and even Social Credit Party constituency members sought ways to unite behind a single opposition candidate. These "arrangements" were supported by both provincial and federal leaders in the Tory and CCF parties, for whom the prospects of defeating the Liberals in Saskatchewan seemed an attractive strategy. Much of this cooperative inclination had begun with Anderson. Anderson had not only set a progressive direction for the Conservative Party, he had begun cooling its partisan zeal and promoting cooperative endeavours with other political groups, first in the 1929 campaign and later in the Co-operative Government. It is little wonder that in 1938 John Diefenbaker found many Tory local associations weak in both organization and partisan allegiance and eager to join with other parties if they were to fight at all. The Tories were fast losing identity and it would be folly to believe they did not know it and suffer helplessness in the face of realities seemingly beyond their control. John Diefenbaker could only stand and watch. Diefenbaker believed the Conservative vote, particularly in rural seats, was volatile and likely to swing to other opposition parties thought to have a better chance of defeating the Grits. Both he and H.E. Keown knew

> the Conservative organization was a hollow shell, an organization which existed on paper only. That the party kept going at all is a tribute to the dedication of a few determined men such as Diefenbaker and Keown who spent much time and money trying to breathe some life into it.[22]

Diefenbaker's Tories could easily become the major casualties of a four-party provincial contest.

In at least 16 rural constituencies Conservative Party organizers supported political cooperation in one form or the other.[23] The most extensive and strategic co-operation between Conservative and CCF parties was negotiated at both the provincial and federal levels and saw Conservative and CCF candidates opposing each other in only 15 of the 53 provincial seats.[24] By mid March 1938, Tory and CCF negotiators had drawn up a list of constituencies which gave 18 seats to the Conservatives, 21 to the CCF and the remaining 13 yet to be allocated.[25] Although the Social Credit leadership officially opposed any trade with the socialist enemy, Social Credit constituency level officers, by the election of 1938, had entered into tentative agreements to cooperate with the CCF in at least 10 ridings.[26] At the core of the movement to achieve these arrangements among the three opposition parties was both their determination to defeat the hated Grits and a desire by all of them to win seats for themselves. In the context of the appalling Depression experience not yet ended, the ease with which all three opposition parties embraced a pragmatic cooperation in selected constituencies can be explained.

Everyone in Saskatchewan in some measure had shared the stark privations of the Depression years. The struggle to survive had taught hard lessons and created progressives and reformists at every level of government and in every political party. The need for social and agrarian reforms and the use of government to bring this about was paramount and put ideological differences aside. Urgent personal and community needs and the struggle to meet them had united people in the constituencies during tough times and now made their cooperative political activity possible and comfortable.

The time was "out of joint" for the new Conservative leader, John George Diefenbaker, who was bravely optimistic at the beginning of the campaign but soon must have noticed that no one in Saskatchewan was paying much attention to him. Nor was anyone in Ontario paying attention. The ruling federal Tories weren't sending care packages. No speakers, organizers or even lines of credit were loaned or gifted. Ottawa turned a deaf ear to appeal after appeal for financial help and left Diefenbaker and a clutch of dispirited loyalists to manage as best they could. In his memoirs Diefenbaker complained bitterly that provincial Tories had been abandoned by the national party, which thought his chances hopeless.[27] He also suspected that "established economic interests" that might have helped him financially were frightened by the prospect of a Social Credit victory and had poured money into the Liberal Party and left his Conservatives desolate.[28]

The Saskatchewan Conservative Party was virtually bankrupt when the June 8, 1938, election was called. In 1937 the party was forced to close its central office. It couldn't pay for rent and staffing. The provincial Tory president, H.E. Keown, wrote Diefenbaker in January 1938 that he was forced to miss meetings of the party because he couldn't afford "the costs of travel, food and lodging." According to Keown, Diefenbaker himself was under heavy expense and carrying a financial burden. Diefenbaker was later to take out a personal bank loan to pay the election deposits of some of his candidates.[29] Keown, Diefenbaker and other prominent Conservatives were so desperate for money they constantly implored Ottawa for help, warning of a collapse of the Saskatchewan Tory wing if it wasn't given. After the election Keown estimated the party had been forced to fight the entire election on less that $5,000, and was left with a debt of $2,500 with no way of repaying it.[30] It wasn't just the provincial cupboard that was bare. The constituency coffers were empty as well. The lean Depression years had left most everyone too poor to buy party memberships or contribute to party campaign fundraising. Tories, now out of office, had neither patronage leverage to provide funding, sources outside the province to tap, or committed constituency members and workers willing to dig deep. In all these particulars the Liberals, CCF and Social Credit would prove better off. Morale at all levels of the provincial Conservative party was at an all-time low.[31]

Without money, no political campaign can get off the ground and into the air. In 1938 Diefenbaker's Conservatives had only a limited budget for printing and distribution of party platform and election pamphlets. There was no budget for newspaper or radio advertising, and with no such funding Diefenbaker was unable to muster an effective campaign for his little roster of candidates. Without money there would be no paid organizers in the field to commit and motivate the relatively small base of Conservative Party supporters who were expected to structure local campaigns. Campaign headquarters and town and rural polling divisions had to be manned and activated, ready for the election call. By the end of 1937 Diefenbaker and Bert Keown knew this was not happening. Correspondences reaching them from the Battleford, Bengough and Torch River constituency associations were typical in their expressions of despair. They all reported no funding, no organization, no candidates in sight, mounting desertions to other parties and no real will to stagger on. Even communications between the party Central Office and the ridings was breaking down. By the end of 1937 Keown had to admit to Diefenbaker that "we have not got a full list of officers in the various constituencies."[32] Not only was there no activity to recruit new members, the old members were dropping out of the game. Even Melfort, Keown's own home constituency, a riding that contained districts that in 1930 had sent Conservative Robert Weir to Ottawa to become R.B. Bennett's Minister of Agriculture, was now in serious difficulty. Historian Patrick Kyba concludes, "It is perhaps not surprising that in 1938 Conservatives at all levels of the party sought alliances with anyone and everyone who could help defeat the hated Liberals."[33]

Gamely, the Conservatives touted their election package as an expression of "common sense." Diefenbaker boasted that his program could be financed and delivered. It wasn't, he said, a "pie in the sky" purchase of the voter with his own money. The Tory spin was that Diefenbaker's Conservatives were cautious custodians of the public purse, their platform pragmatic and responsible, nothing too exciting, nothing high risk. It was, however, far more lively than that!

While the Conservative campaign, lacking adequate advertising, was "submerged and, virtually invisible, Diefenbaker's program in 1938 was worthy of considerably more attention than it received."[34] It had some remarkable progressive planks. The platform called for adjustment of farm debt, protection against unfair mortgage foreclosure, re-establishment of a Wheat Board, a study of crop insurance or guaranteed acreage payments, and implementation of public health insurance and hospitalization. The Conservative platform called for enforcement of the Minimum Wage Act to ensure fair wages for labour. Saskatchewan teachers were told that arrears on their salaries suffered during the Depression hard times would be paid within a year of Diefenbaker's taking office. The Tory platform promised to abolish the 2% sales tax. The platform called for an end to "machine politics" and promised electoral reform in the form of

> revision of the B.N.A. Act to meet present day needs, the establishment of the single transferable ballot, reduction of the size of the legislature and replacement of the existing three provinces [Alberta, Saskatchewan and Manitoba] with one province.[35]

The platform recognized the sad plight of many ex-soldiers in the province who were unemployed. It deplored the Liberal government's abolishing of the provincial Relief Commission and adopting a policy that lent itself to political influence. It promised to reinstate all ex-servicemen who had been unjustly dismissed by the Liberals. The platform promised to provide an economical system of highway construction and maintenance designed to permit the fullest possible use of farm teams and manual labour instead of machinery, and with particular regard to construction of market roads to serve the farming population. The platform called for the development of a pulp and lumber industry in the province, the building of a hydroelectric power facility on the Saskatchewan River, the establishing of reforestation and afforestation policies and development of electric power from the Estevan coal mines.

This was a platform that Diefenbaker later described as "moderate" and "progressive." It was more than that. It was a platform that even a CCF partisan could find attractive. R.M. Balfour, President of the Regina Conservative Association, when presented with the party's 1938 platform, commented, "A few years ago you and I may have thought this platform a bit radical, but Conservatism is not opposed to advancement with the time."[36] Balfour must have thought it a shame that such a platform could not be carried across the province by Diefenbaker and a full slate of Conservative candidates with the money, organization and talent to market it. Tory campaign pamphlets proclaimed "Liberal Promises Have Gone With the Wind, Restore Dignity and Decency in the Conduct of Public Affairs."[37] Party literature touted Diefenbaker as the man supremely able to bring about this restoration.

John George Diefenbaker in his great federal campaigns "single handedly transformed Canadian politics into a 'spectator sport'."[38] But in the 1938 provincial election, although he was "the consumate partisan actor of the campaign," there was no such power yet.[39] That would build gradually. Diefenbaker, with his wife Edna at his side, campaigned tirelessly day by day in 1938, practising the blending of his courtroom deconstructive talents with his favourite populist themes. He attacked the Liberal government's failure to reduce farm debt in a bankrupt province. He ridiculed the Gardiner legacy of patronage and machine politics still cheerfully operating in provincial licensing and inspection. Major rallies in Regina and Saskatoon were attempted but with small success.

A young man named Alvin Hamilton joined Diefenbaker in this campaign and became a friend and protégé. Hamilton, a farmhand who worked on his uncle's farm near Delisle, felt the Depression pain of the little people of Saskatchewan—the farmer, the immigrant and the laboring poor. He became a lifelong Conservative and a follower of John Diefenbaker. Hamilton would himself become leader of the Saskatchewan Conservative Party and later a devoted, perhaps somewhat unsung, lieutenant and federal cabinet minister under "The Chief." In the 1938 campaign the 26-year-old Hamilton, with no resources of his own, did what he could to support his hero and the Tory cause. His assistance was mostly that of an organizer and cheerleader. The young Hamilton would spell Edna off driving Diefenbaker to meetings and undertook the desperate chore of collecting campaign funds. It was "Buddy, can you spare a dime?" Few could! Hamilton was a frequent visitor to John and Edna Diefenbaker's small bungalow home at 22–20th Street West in Prince Albert. He was a friend and admirer of the warm and loquacious

Edna, whom he credited with much of her husband's later blossoming and success in politics.[40] Certainly, Edna's campaign days in 1938 were as arduous, long and driven as those of her indefatigable husband.

On June 8, 1938, both the Diefenbakers, Bert Keown and their faithful young friend Alvin Hamilton were stunned by Diefenbaker's personal defeat in Arm River and a humiliating Conservative rejection everywhere in the province. All three expected to see at least a few Conservatives elected to the legislature. First among these they hoped would be the leader, John George Diefenbaker, who had the field to himself against the Liberals in Arm River. But no! The Saskatchewan Conservative Party again failed to win a single seat!

The Tory defeat was devastating, though hardly unexpected. That the powerful Liberal "machine" would defend the Patterson government and re-elect it was never in doubt. As already noted, efforts by Diefenbaker and Keown to beg, borrow or steal a campaign budget failed. The CCF, with five members already in the legislature and good on-the-ground constituency organizations in place, made it impossible for Diefenbaker to claim his Tories were a logical alternative to the Liberals, a government in waiting. Finally, the intervention of Social Credit with 41 candidates robbed Diefenbaker, not so much of so-called right wing voters as of anti-Liberal reformists looking for expression and finding excitement and promise in the new protest party. Diefenbaker later said, "Social Credit delivered a knock out blow to all 23 Conservative candidates."[41] As for the wisdom of Diefenbaker's accepting and promoting "saw-offs" with other parties to beat the Liberals, it is probably fair to judge that he had no option. He was under pressure from both provincial and federal Conservatives to do so and unable to control widespread Tory opinion at the constituency level that favoured cooperative arrangements with others. Politics in Depression-stricken Saskatchewan had become complicated in the 1930s, particularly in the last half of it. Partisan party lines, especially in rural constituencies, had gradually grown more and more amorphous. Because all parties had some progressive elements seeking agrarian relief, and had developed similar reformist programs, it was inevitable that partisan allegiances would weaken. It is now obvious these accords and "saw-offs" with the CCF and Social Credit did his party little good in 1938 and may have diminished the Conservative Party and contributed to the subsequent ascendancy of the CCF.

In his memoirs and personal correspondence and conversations Diefenbaker did not dwell long on his few years as provincial party leader. His tenure in that office lasted only a few months beyond three years and was a mere footnote in the remarkable story of his lifelong career. After the 1938 defeat, Diefenbaker was immediately swept up in national and personal politics. His experience as Saskatchewan Conservative leader was brief, unhappy and largely out of his control. Later, looking back on those years he may well have found them painful, marginal and irrelevant, perhaps better forgotten than remembered.[42]

In 1938 the Tories won no seats in the legislature and tumbled to fourth place in party standing, far behind the winning Liberals, well behind the second-place CCF and trailing even the third-place Social Credit. Saskatchewan Conservatives dropped to 12% from their respectable 27% of the 1934 popular vote. The Liberals led with 45% of the popular vote and 38 seats. The CCF won 10 seats with 19% of the vote. With 16% of the vote Social Credit elected two members to the legislature. A mixed grill of unity candidates, Independents, Independent Labour and Labour Progressives won two seats with a combined 8% of the provincial vote. John Diefenbaker lost Arm River by 190 votes to his Liberal opponent. The vote was 3,295 for the incumbent Liberal to 3,105 for Diefenbaker in a tight two-way contest. This was Diefenbaker's fifth personal defeat. But this was a different loss. This time he was the leader of the party, and he had led his party into oblivion. He was humiliated and inconsolable. He had hopes for a win in Arm River. There he had a two-way fight with the Liberal Party and should have garnered all of the anti-Liberal votes. In particular, he expected to receive CCF support. He was known in the riding, having campaigned there in the 1928 by-election. He lost Arm River after spending only three days in the constituency when he should have spent longer. He had no heavyweight surrogates either in the riding or sent into the riding to help. Like all the other 23 Conservative candidates, he had little or no money to finance an adequate campaign. The prestige of the leadership was supposed to take up the slack. Apparently it didn't. He could not gauge the number of Conservative voters who by 1938 were still beset by Depression woes and unhappy with both the Anderson and Bennett governments.

Diefenbaker believed that extraordinary measures were taken by the Liberals to defeat him. What he called the Patterson-Gardiner machine sent in an army of government inspectors to work against him, arguing that with such a puny slate of candidates he had no hope of forming a government, and Arm River would be better served by a government member. Certainly the Liberals would work hard to defeat the Conservative leader, a man they would not want to meet in the legislature.

George Williams, the CCF leader, told Diefenbaker after his defeat that the CCF had honoured the saw-off arrangement: "I know that in Arm River our people played the game very, very well and had hoped for a different result."[43] This may or may not have been true. His old nemesis, T.C. Davis, again won Prince Albert, and a huge picture of the winner with a giddy account of wild Liberal celebrations in downtown Prince Albert filled the front page of the local newspaper. There was no mention of Diefenbaker except of his loss in Arm River.[44]

There were those who thought he might leave politics.[45] It's probable that both Diefenbakers were exhausted and needed to rest and refuel, but neither John nor Edna ever lost sight of John's goal of fame and power. For Diefenbaker, there could be no stopping now!

John Diefenbaker (right) during the 1958 federal election. Although he left provincial politics in 1940, Diefenbaker would be a dominant figure in the Progressive Conservative Party in Saskatchewan for decades to come (The Right Honourable John G. Diefenbaker Centre, MG01 XVII JGD 481a).

The Social Credit scare was over in Saskatchewan. Now the "funny money" invasion from Alberta seemed an extravagant stunt. The Patterson Liberals did not have to look over their shoulders, watching apprehensively for advancing "Wild Bill" Aberhart and his "Socreds." What some wise Liberal elders might have noted with concern was the rising appeal and legitimacy of the CCF. That young party had grown out of Saskatchewan's traditional agrarian and farmer-labour movement and was fast becoming more partisan and more passionate than any other political party in the province. The CCF was here to stay.[46] Significant political realignment was under way in Saskatchewan. The Saskatchewan Conservative Party, long a force in the province, no longer held second rank. It no longer held any rank! The CCF was now the real alternative to the Liberals. It was a government in waiting. The waiting would not be long.

Saskatchewan Tories reacted stoically to the 1938 defeat. Where there's little life, there is little feeling. As with Anderson in 1934, the party didn't seem to blame John Diefenbaker for the 1938 decimation. They held a provincial convention in Moose Jaw on October 26 and refused Diefenbaker's offer to resign the leadership, insisting that he labour on.

It was obvious to both John and Edna Diefenbaker that no chance existed for him in provincial Conservative politics. Their conclusion was both sober and plaintive. As he had in 1925 and 1926, Diefenbaker looked eastward to Ottawa for opportunity. On June 15, 1939, he was nominated as a federal candidate in the Lake Centre constituency. The election call came for March 26, 1940. This was Diefenbaker's sixth campaign. This campaign might have been his last kick at the can had he lost. But he won. He took Lake Centre by a spare 280 votes and was now a Member of Parliament. Thus Diefenbaker began a remarkable federal career that would bring him fame and power as leader of his party and Prime Minister of Canada. He wasn't reluctant to lay down the mantle of provincial leadership. It's true it had been a useful apprenticeship, but it had also been a hard and cheerless haul. That dreary job now fell to the Conservative provincial president, H.E. Keown of Melfort, Saskatchewan.

Throughout nearly four decades to follow, John Diefenbaker grew in power in his home province, ranging and hovering over Saskatchewan politics like some Dickensian Spirit or Shakespearian Ghost warning and chiding Conservatives to action or to caution. He was not always helpful or even consistent, but "The Chief," as he was later called, continued to influence affairs in Saskatchewan until his death in 1979.

7

The Wilderness

Bert Keown, the new Conservative Party leader, had been both a party man and a professional associate of Diefenbaker's. Keown lived in Melfort, Saskatchewan, where he practised law from offices in the old landmark, red-brick, downtown post office. The print on the door's frosted glass window read: "H.E. Keown and Co., Barristers, Walk In." He was a successful and much sought after advocate. Keown was a large, expansive and confident man, perhaps a little intimidating to some townsfolk. In the courtroom and on the political platform he was a comfortable performer. Keown was charming in masculine company and enjoyed an occasional drink and a game of cards with Melfort's prominent, preferably prosperous, business and professional citizens.[1] John Diefenbaker was a frequent and welcome visitor at the Keown home.[2] Keown's ideological commitment to the Conservative Party was deep and certainly his loyalty to John Diefenbaker was real and unfailing. In the context of his time, Keown's service to the party was considerable.[3]

Keown, even more so than Diefenbaker in 1936, was doomed to a failed leadership. He led a scattered, wraith-like party, abandoned by eastern federal Tory officers, press and bagmen, a party facing the inexorable rise of the CCF. Clearly, the next provincial election would be fought by only two major parties. The governing Liberals and the ascending Co-operative Commonwealth Federation would square off. The once formidable Conservative Party of Haultain was out of all contention and well on its way to becoming a pathetic irrelevancy.

Bert Keown was helpless in the face of these shifting times and the CCF challenge. So were the Patterson Liberals, but they didn't know it. In 1940, when John Diefenbaker left Saskatchewan for a career in federal politics, Bert Keown took his place as provincial party leader and, with World War II raging in Europe, declared that partisan politics in Saskatchewan should cease for the duration of the war. The Saskatchewan Tory party engine idled in hiatus until the approach of the 1944 provincial election, when a new Conservative leader had to be named. Keown did not want the job. He was aware of the wretched condition of the party. He remembered the accumulated frustrations of the desperate struggle of 1938 and had no heart to continue in a seemingly hopeless quest. Keown returned to his law practice and a career that later culminated in an appointment to the bench. He would remain a Tory party man and a friend and mentor to both Rupert Ramsay and Alvin Hamilton, both of whom would follow him as Tory party leader.

It's uncertain how seriously either the ruling Liberals or expiring Tory remnants took the CCF. How well did they know or understand them? While there was some Liberal Party concern before the 1944 election about possible loss of government seats, there was no panic or extraordinary preparation for the battle. Why was the Liberal collapse in 1944 so startling to so many? The CCF wasn't newly minted. It had been around awhile and was obviously pumping up muscle and gathering speed. This socialist-turned-social democratic party had healthy roots in the protest movements and agrarian politics of the province. The CCF sprang from the earlier Progressives, the cooperatives, the United Farmers of Canada and the Saskatchewan Farmer-Labour Party.[4] Its 1934 and 1938 electoral successes were substantial and encouraging. Its leadership was impressive. The party articulated the westerners' old complaints about eastern control of the financial and marketing levers that directed their lives and eastern advantages from tariffs and freight rates.

H.E. (Bert) Keown, Provincial Conservative Party leader, 1940 (courtesy of the Keown family).

From the beginning the CCF was superbly led. British-born, erudite Major James Coldwell was its first leader when it was called the Farmer-Labour Party. He was steady and capable, a keen debater and a passionate partisan. Coldwell led the new protest party from 1932 to 1935. He fought a vigorous campaign in the 1934 provincial election but failed to win a seat for himself. In 1935 he contested and won a federal seat and resigned the provincial leadership. He was succeeded by George Williams, a buoyant and aggressive farmer and long-time agrarian political activist who led the CCF in the campaign of 1938, winning 10 seats in the legislature and setting the stage for the CCF takeover soon to follow. Williams resigned the leadership in 1941 when he joined the armed forces for overseas service. His leaving the leadership was more of a boon than a setback for the party. Williams was "assertively opinionated and his greatest weakness was his capacity for making abrupt changes in policy."[5] With Williams gone, a brilliant, combative Baptist minister, T.C. Douglas, the federal member for Weyburn, was chosen Saskatchewan CCF leader in 1942 and led the party to a resounding victory in 1944. Douglas headed a social democratic government in Saskatchewan for the next 20 years. It was a remarkable two-decade show!

In 1942 the federal Conservative Party, only somewhat more robust than its ailing Saskatchewan provincial wing, at a December 11 Winnipeg Convention elected Manitoba Premier John Bracken, leader of that province's Liberal-Progressive government, as its new national leader. Bracken wanted the word Progressive added to the party's designation. With considerable reluctance, the party changed its name to suit him. The "True Blues" were not impressed! They did not like Progressives. Now the party of Macdonald, the historic Conservative Party of Canada, became the Progressive Conservative Party of Canada. Bert Keown found himself leader of the Progressive Conservative Party of Saskatchewan. Not that it made much difference to anyone. Certainly, it made little difference to Keown, who was replaced in the provincial leadership by Rupert Ramsay of Saskatoon shortly before the 1944 provincial election. Keown was spared the bumps and jolts of leading a campaign and the slings and arrows that follow defeat.

The 1944 convention to elect the new Progressive Conservative provincial leader was called for February 15–16 in Saskatoon. Federal Progressive Conservative leader John Bracken was scheduled to address the convention. Bracken was facing a federal election in 1945 and was eager to introduce and test-run some aspects of his developing PC manifesto, particularly its agricultural policy. Bracken, as a former Progressive Party member and Liberal-Progressive Party Premier of Manitoba, was certainly at home in Saskatchewan, where as a young man he had taught in the College of Agriculture at the University of Saskatchewan before moving to Manitoba.

M.A. MacPherson of Regina, a former Saskatchewan Attorney General in the Anderson government, had chaired the party's nomination search committee which had interviewed several prospective candidates for the Tory leadership. On Tuesday, February 15, H.E. Keown officially resigned the provincial leadership, clearing the way for the election of a new Tory leader in Saskatchewan. Keown delivered a farewell message to the party on Tuesday night and told the convention, "I want my successor as leader to be a man closely identified with agriculture." He concluded by assuring the convention, "I am not severing my connection with the party. I will seek the party's nomination in the provincial constituency of Last Mountain and continue to work for the party with all the power at my command."[6] The next day the convention chose Rupert David Ramsay, a 44-year-old professor in the Agricultural Extension Branch of the University of Saskatchewan, as Bert Keown's successor. The new leader had the support of Keown and M.A. MacPherson. Alvin Hamilton also expressed his approval of the Ramsay candidacy. Rupert Ramsay had been the clear and easy choice by both provincial and federal Tory authorities. Not only did Ramsay fill the bill as Keown's

Rupert Ramsay (left), leader of the Progressive Conservative Party from 1944–48 (SAB S-B2658, Progressive Conservative Party Fonds).

desired agriculturalist, he lived in Saskatoon where the provincial Tory headquarters were located and would soon serve as federal director of organization in Saskatchewan as well as leading the provincial party. As federal director of organization he would be paid a salary by the national office, a much-needed remuneration the provincial coffers could not provide the leader on a sustainable basis.

Tory leader Rupert Ramsay had few enemies. He was a quiet man, accounted decent and sincere in his relationships with political friends and foes.[7] He seemed an enduringly composed and tidy man. He was not a natural or even a comfortable politician.[8] Ramsay had left a satisfying teaching job in the College of Agriculture at the University of Saskatchewan to lead the Progressive Conservatives. He began with some optimism about rebuilding the party but left perplexed and deeply disappointed that Tory politics in Saskatchewan proved a thankless pursuit for him.

When Premier William Patterson called an election for June 15, 1944, it came at the end of a six-year term. Because of World War II exigencies, Patterson was able to extend his government's mandate an extra year with the passage of special legislation. It is unclear whether this extension was to his advantage politically because the CCF, and particularly its leader, Tommy Douglas, used the extra months strategically in fundraising, membership drives and candidate searches. As well, governments postpone elections at the risk of raising suspicions that they fear taking their case for re-election to the people and have failures and dark secrets to conceal. Patterson put a full slate of 52 candidates in the field. So did Tommy Douglas.

Progressive Conservatives surprised many with the number if not the calibre of their 39 candidates. The 1944 Progressive Conservative election manifesto began with a comprehensive agricultural policy statement that clearly carried Rupert Ramsay's stamp. It opened with a call for

> fair prices for farm products by expanding trade by progressively lowering the barriers to trade and for equality for agriculture in Saskatchewan to ensure prosperity for all other groups in the province since urban prosperity is inseparable from rural prosperity.

Vocational training for farm youth/extension of agricultural education and research were called for:

> Progressive Conservatives believe that the best kind of programs to assist farmers can best be provided by the Agricultural Extension Department and the Department of Women's Work at the University of Saskatchewan. A Progressive Conservative government would raise the level of living on the farms of this province to a basis comparable with that of urban People.

The manifesto promised Saskatchewan farmers all the benefits of a rural electrification system:

> We recognize that because of the sparseness of our farm population, farmers cannot bear the full costs of rural electrification and that some share of the cost must be borne by the provincial and federal governments.

The platform promised that a Progressive Conservative government would cooperate with the federal government in providing for low-interest rehabilitation loans, repayable on a crop share or other flexible basis for farm building repairs and maintenance, and that development loans supervised by trained personnel repayable on a crop share basis would be made available to northern settlers so that they could increase their area of cultivation and enjoy a decent level of living. The manifesto called for the removal of the Agricultural Field Man Service from the provincial Department of Agriculture and its placement under the administration of the University of Saskatchewan, where it would be permanently free from all political influence.

The educational planks in the 1944 platform included the introductory statement that "all children must have the same opportunities for free education" and a promise to introduce a system of equalization of grants so that all children in all school districts would have equal access to grade and high school education. A Progressive Conservative government would introduce a system of university scholarships. The platform called for

> a system of pay scales for teachers with a higher minimum than at present so that all school districts have equal opportunity to attract the best qualified men and women into the teaching profession.

As a post-war reconstruction measure, a Progressive Conservative government would assist needy school districts in the reconditioning and modernizing of their buildings.

Under the heading "Social Welfare and Income Security," the Tory platform called for the creation of "strong completely staffed and separate provincial departments of Social Welfare and of Health." It further committed to the reorganization of child services in the province to deal with child neglect and protection. Progressive Conservatives would press the federal government to increase old age pension benefits and lower the age of recipients to 65. A Tory government would "re-organize the system of aid to needy mothers with dependent children and put it on a basis of actual need." A Progressive Conservative government would seek closer cooperation with municipalities to encourage combined "welfare districts," such as union hospitals for rural areas and organized welfare departments in cities.

The platform advocated the development of a strong and effective health program, free from political influence and the provision of extended health services for all people, regardless of income, through adequate diagnostic and treatment centres. It promised hospital accommodation to an agreed suitable level and provision for nursing care in the home of those needing it.

In the field of natural resources, among other measures the Tory program promised more funding of forest research and conservation and planning of the utilization of natural resources. The platform called for government support for local industries and long-term loans for the establishment of machine and repair depots.

On the labour front the Tory platform committed a Tory government to the establishment of a sound and cooperative relationship and partnership between the Saskatchewan agriculture industry and Saskatchewan labour. It enunciated a policy of uniform labour relations in Saskatchewan, stating the Progressive Conservative belief in the principle of collective bargaining as a desirable instrument to promote the interests of labour, industry and the people in general. Adequate labour representation on government boards and committees would be encouraged. A Tory government would support the principle of preferment of ex-service men and women for employment and their rehabilitation in civilian life would receive the very first consideration of a Progressive Conservative government.

The Public Service plank of the 1944 Progressive Conservative manifesto echoed the enlightened civil service reforms of the Anderson government in 1930. In 1944 the party manifesto put the Tory case bluntly:

> Employment in the public service must be removed from the sphere of patronage. We shall establish a Civil Service Commission that will see that appointments to the public service are competitive and made on the basis of merit.[9]

Unquestionably this was a comprehensive, well-crafted platform that deserved attention. But no one noticed. All eyes were on the sizzling Liberal-CCF two-party contest.

The 1944 campaign was arguably the nastiest since the ugly pyrotechnics of 1929. The CCF published an extensive election manifesto promising policies to strengthen agriculture, secure the family farm with management of farm debt, and programs for improved highways, health and education. The party proposed a range of economic policies for post-war rehabilitation. It promised protection of collective bargaining and launched a spirited attack on Liberal patronage in all its crafty forms.[10] The CCF, then campaigning as a "movement" or a righteous "crusade" rather than a party, would later learn the many meanings and uses of patronage. CCF leader T.C. Douglas charged that the Liberal Party was an old party totally out of touch with a post-Depression, postwar electorate now looking with new confidence for golden days in Saskatchewan. The CCF would build a new Jerusalem, a cooperative commonwealth of sweetness and light! "Humanity First!"[11]

The Liberals spent most of their time abusing their CCF rivals in vicious, fear-mongering diatribes rather than in defense of their record or current manifesto. They warned Catholics and eastern Europeans against godless socialism. They warned farmers against eastern power-grabbing big labour. They warned citizens against the stifling authoritarianism and regimentation of doctrinaire, collectivist planners.[12] Such men are dangerous! The Liberal Party was the protector of the liberties and freedoms of the people, and the people would be saved if they recognized, in time, the dangers on the left. So said the Grits.

The party leaderships were uneven in the campaign. On the left was Tommy Douglas, recalled to Saskatchewan from Parliament in 1941 to lead the CCF, first as president, then as party leader. Douglas was a peerless debater, fervent in his advocacy of social democracy. On the platform he was a spellbinder. His passionate campaign appeals were ornamented with poetry and social gospel. His clipped, staccato, rapid-fire assaults on soulless Grits were delivered with fiery clarity. Douglas had humour and the comedic talent to use it with devastating effect, tormenting his adversaries and drawing loud, rolling whoops of laughter from partisan audiences. It wasn't all sparkling platform performance for Tommy Douglas, however:

> The personality and activities of the CCF leader were a major factor in the campaign. Douglas worked night and day, travelling, speaking at numberless meetings and picnics, organizing, encouraging his candidates and preparing and delivering radio addresses.[13]

He led by example.

The lumbered and plodding Liberal campaign led by Premier Patterson was no match for Douglas and the CCF. Patterson had the affection and trust of his party and some degree of respect across the province. He was a familiar figure. Many called him "Billy." But he was not a gifted meeting hall or radio performer. He had no public humour, flair or panache.

Douglas and the CCF won a decisive victory on June 15, 1944. The Liberal Party was blown away. Whereas a Liberal defeat was not totally unexpected, the June 15 demolition staggered not only the decimated Liberals themselves but the media, the public and CCF victors as well. When all the ballots were counted, all the tears dried, the shouting stilled, the coffee cups and beer glasses emptied and party committee rooms across the province closed, the CCF had won 47 of the 52 seats and a whopping 53% of the popular vote. The Liberals were reduced to five seats from the 38 they held at the election call. They garnered 35% of the vote. Rupert Ramsay's Progressive Conservatives were erased from the charts, winning only 12% of the popular vote and no seats. All 39 PC candidates lost their deposits.

There was no doubt that Saskatchewan was sticking with its favoured two-party politics, with 88% of the popular vote cast on June 15 divided between the new CCF government and the Liberal opposition. Twenty years of left-of-centre rule had begun in the province. The Saskatchewan Progressive Conservative Party, like the ghostly *Mary Celeste*, would sail on without crew or destination, battered and listing but still afloat and still remembered.

The philosopher Havelock Ellis writes in *The Dance of Life*, "The Promised Land always lies on the other side of a wilderness."[14] So it proved for Saskatchewan Tories, who could only reach their electoral promised land by crossing a daunting sprawl of wilderness which probably seemed endless to them. When Saskatchewan Progressive Conservatives suffered a third consecutive defeat in 1944, they knew they were deep in the wilderness. Tory elders and chroniclers must have reflected fondly on happier, earlier years, when the Provincial Rights and Conservative parties gained large or at least respectable percentages of the popular vote and won government in 1929, after many years as a credible alternative to the ruling Liberal Party. But the arrival of the CCF, shifting party bases and the blurring of ideological lines changed the game. In the elections of 1934 and 1938 the CCF displaced the Tories as official opposition and became the new alternative to the Liberal government. The CCF victory in 1944 pushed the Liberals back into second place, and the Tories continued to slide deeper into third-party status. Rupert Ramsay remained as PC leader, a leader with no seat himself and no members in the legislature. A narrowly re-elected Billy Patterson would serve briefly at the head of an enfeebled five-member Liberal rump. The new Douglas government had clear skies and smooth sailing. It wasted no time enacting programs and policies long envisioned and charted by party leaders. It settled in for a long, sweet haul of power and office.

Ramsay's Tories spent the next four years in fitful attempts to build some semblance of a provincial organization, but they knew their prospects for the next election were hopeless. They had no appetite for the fight. But ready or not they were made to fight when Premier T.C. Douglas called a provincial election for June 24, 1948. Ramsay would not only face the nimble and witty Douglas leading an experienced cabinet and a veteran slate of CCF candidates, he would now contend with a new Liberal leader, Rosthern Member of Parliament Walter A. Tucker. Tucker had succeeded Patterson in an August 1946 leadership convention. Tucker's Liberals were energized by the change in leadership and a platform that hardened and narrowed their 1944 stock attacks on collectivism and left-wing intellectualism.[15] The Liberals were hopeful that the province had recovered from its flirtation with socialism and, with reason returned, would correct the errors of the last election. Tucker was a big man, a hearty campaigner, perhaps given to more bluster than was helpful. His Liberals would fight for individual initiative and against what he saw as increasing, dangerous government activity and control in the lives of the people. The Liberal battle cry was "Tucker or Tyranny!" As the battle cry suggested, the theme of the 1948 Liberal campaign had an anti-Communist smell to it. Tucker warned that if re-elected the CCF would "gobble up land, confiscate savings and restrict personal freedoms." It was a Red scare.[16] Walter Tucker believed the CCF could only be defeated by the combined efforts of non-socialist parties and worked hard to convince local Conservative associations not to run against Liberal candidates. Ramsay had little or no control over constituency politics and had to leave decisions regarding "saw-offs" to local riding executives, although he did not approve of any. Tucker was not satisfied with scattered riding level cooperative agreements, and wanted a formal coalition of Liberal and Conservative forces. He offered terms for such an organized alliance to Ramsay, who refused even to discuss them. Obviously Ramsay had little or nothing to contribute to such a coalition even if he had favoured it.[17]

Rupert Ramsay was correct in an earlier 1946 assessment of Progressive Conservative Party fervour: "They will not fight!" The party could field only nine candidates to contest 52 legislative seats. Seven of the nine candidates ran in rural seats and two contested city ridings in "saw-off" arrangements with the Liberals. Elsewhere in the province PC voters either supported coalition candidates jointly nominated by Liberals and Conservatives, voted for Independent anti-government candidates, chose among Liberal, CCF or Social Credit candidates, or just stayed home. There were only four joint candidatures in the province, and only one of these, A.H. McDonald, was a Conservative. He won his seat in 1948 but joined the Liberal Party soon after the election.

In 1948 Rupert Ramsay again faced organizational anemia and political squeeze. This time his little slate of nine candidates was an accurate representation of the Tories' third-party weakness. Ramsay pushed on gamely, publishing a detailed manifesto promising practical governance. This program was largely drafted by himself and his 36-year-old lieutenant and friend, Alvin Hamilton, his PC candidate in Rosetown. They called the program "The PC Plan for Saskatchewan." Stripped of much of the usual ornamentation and rhetorical flourish of election publications, the manifesto dealt with nine major areas of concern: agriculture, health care, highways, education, labour, taxation, pensions, industry, and natural resources in direct, unadorned, pragmatic terms. For agriculture the platform promised a wheat stabilization fund to provide security for farm income. The platform's health plank called for provincial cooperation with federal authorities in the planning of a national health plan and the provision of health care programs in the province. The Tories promised a highway program that would feature the construction of one north-south and two east-west paved provincial highways. The PC program proposed abolishing the provincial education tax and reducing local school taxes. The labour plank provided for two weeks of paid vacation per year for all workers. Old age pensions were to be raised to $40 per month. A PC government would sell all public utilities deemed not suited to government ownership. A PC government would press for the building of the South Saskatchewan River dam and speed power development from all sources within the province. A Ramsay Tory government would assist development of the prairie's natural resources, particularly those in northern Saskatchewan.[18] The emphasis on northern development foreshadowed Alvin Hamilton's later deep and lasting concerns for the Saskatchewan and Canadian north.[19]

In an early 1948 election radio address, Alvin Hamilton, speaking in support of Ramsay, described the party's philosophy as "progressive capitalism." He argued that Tory progressive capitalism would promote equal opportunities for all and that it was synonymous with liberty. Private enterprise, he maintained, will solve social and economic problems by providing opportunities to independent-minded citizens. "There need be no more jumping back and forth from the Gardiner frying pan into the C.C.F. fire." He told his radio audience that the machine politics of Jimmy Gardiner and the controls of state compulsion were equally threatening and that a middle way for liberal-minded, progressive people must be found.[20] The democratic leadership of Rupert Ramsay and the Progressive Conservative Party was that middle way in Saskatchewan.

Ramsay fought a ghostly campaign with only a handful of candidates and no funding for them or for himself. He filled the dual position of provincial party leader and Director of Organization in Saskatchewan for the federal Progressive Conservative Party. The latter office, whether active or not, paid him a salary which allowed a modest personal livelihood. He was fortunate to have this national party salary as there were few Saskatchewan sources of funding available. It was a hand-to-mouth subsistence for the party and for its leader.

The CCF was re-elected on June 24, 1948. The government, with 48% of the popular vote, won 31 seats to the Liberals' 19 seats and 31% of the votes. Ramsay's Tories, contesting only nine seats, garnered 8% of the popular vote and were again shut out of the legislature. Social Credit, although fielding 31 candidates, also gained only 8% of the vote and failed to elect a single member. The Liberal-Conservative coalition candidate, A.H. McDonald, won election as did one Independent. There had been some faint hope in Liberal bosoms that the "Tucker or Tyranny" campaign might overcome the CCF and bring down the government. But on election night in 1948 the Liberals knew that in spite of a 5% drop in its popular vote, a loss of 16 seats and the defeat of two cabinet ministers, the Douglas government was alive and well and the CCF there to stay awhile. Whether the Saskatchewan Tory party was alive and there to stay awhile seemed anybody's guess.

A weary Rupert Ramsay wanted out. He resigned the leadership in the fall of 1948. The party executive delayed calling a convention to replace him, hoping he might "reconsider his decision."[21] But he wanted to go. In his last report to the provincial executive following the 1948 election defeat he wrote:

> I am forced to believe that Progressive Conservatives are through provincially in Saskatchewan. There will always be Conservatives here but not enough and too widely scattered to be effective politically."[22]

He was shrewd enough to know that a new leader had to be chosen, and chosen quickly, to give that leader time to prepare himself and the party for the tough rebuilding job ahead. Ramsay wanted Alvin Hamilton, and he set out to persuade a reluctant Hamilton to seek the provincial leadership. When Hamilton finally contested and won the post Rupert Ramsay wrote the new leader, telling him, "Many times it will seem to you a thankless job, uphill and in second gear."[23] For Rupert Ramsay it had all been "uphill and in second, gear," and he was glad to see the end of the ride.

However thankless Ramsay may have thought the job of Tory leadership, his contribution to the party and to the province was considerable. He kept the party alive and breathing and his own authorship of ideas for the party platforms of 1944 and 1948 was significant.

It is clear from those party platforms that Rupert Ramsay believed the PCs occupied the political centre in Saskatchewan and were as close to the Saskatchewan values of the 1940s as any political party could be. In the 1940s he was more interested in proposing practical programs for enhancing Saskatchewan living than joining in the rancorous socialist-anti-socialist ideological debates argued at the time by CCF and Liberal campaigns. He called his Progressive Conservative Party a "people's party" and indeed the progressive nature of the party's 1944 and 1948 platforms lent some legitimacy to the claim. Ramsay's call for a mix of government involvements, social programs and private initiatives certainly had a red-Tory ring to it.

Even his opponents recognized the quality of the man. When Rupert Ramsay was elected PC leader, a scant four months before the 1944 provincial election, the rabid Liberal-supporting *Regina Leader-Post*, in an editorial, welcomed his entry into provincial politics. The editorial read, in part:

> Rupert Ramsay's long service as head of the agricultural extension department of the University of Saskatchewan brought him into close contact with the rural population, especially the younger people. His association with education and farming gives him unusual status. His entry into politics as a party chief gives him a unique opportunity to guide political effort and political method in this province into new and better channels.[24]

That Ramsay sought those "new and better channels" cannot be questioned.

A Gentleman Player

8

Alvin Hamilton was a lifelong career politician. Along the way he worked as a farm labourer, a high school teacher, basketball coach and World War II RCAF navigator, but his passion was always politics. Tory politics. For 60 years he was active in the Saskatchewan Conservative Party. He served it provincially and federally as organizer, candidate, provincial leader, Member of Parliament and federal cabinet minister. In his last years he remained a mentor, an advisor and a friend to young Conservatives across the country who sought him out.

He began as an earnest 17-year-old attending a Conservative meeting in tiny Bounty, Saskatchewan, in 1929. A young John Diefenbaker had come to town to campaign for the Tories in the provincial election. Diefenbaker fascinated the boy with his spirited attack on James Gardiner's "machine" politics and other assorted, perceived Liberal follies and corruptions. From an early age Hamilton disliked and distrusted Liberals, admired John Diefenbaker and found a lifelong home in the Conservative Party. He paid a price for his Tory allegiance and candidacies, losing three provincial and three federal elections before winning election to Parliament in 1957. He suffered an additional federal defeat in 1968.[1] Hamilton's pay back was the satisfaction of 10 federal victories and an outstanding parliamentary career.

Alvin Hamilton, one of five orphaned brothers, was born in Kenora, Ontario, in 1912 and at the age of 15 shipped out west to live with an aunt and uncle who farmed near Delisle, Saskatchewan. Young Alvin worked on the farm for his uncle, took his early education in Delisle and went on to teacher training at the Normal School and a BA degree from the University of Saskatchewan. He became a popular history teacher and basketball coach at Saskatoon's Nutana Collegiate. When war broke out, he joined the armed forces and served as a flight lieutenant in the RCAF.

Alvin Hamilton's choice of the Conservative Party was made at a young age. His interest in politics began early and developed quickly. In 1929, as a 17-year-old high school student, he worked for the Conservative candidate in the Rosetown provincial riding. The candidate was Nathaniel Given, the mayor of Delisle and the young Hamilton's Sunday school teacher. Aside from his admiration for his teacher and mentor, Hamilton was repelled by what he saw as abuses by the Gardiner machine in dispensing contracts for road work and other patronage favours, vigorously attacked by Given in the campaign. Nathaniel Given won Rosetown in 1929. In 1930 Hamilton again joined a Conservative campaign. This time he worked for William Loucks, a Delisle area farmer and Superintendent of the Delisle United Church Sunday School, who stood for the Conservative Party in the Rosetown-Biggar federal riding. Hamilton knew and admired Loucks and wanted to help him. William Loucks won the Rosetown-Biggar federal seat. After these two successful ventures in Tory ranks, Hamilton's commitment to the Conservative Party grew. His antagonism to the provincial Liberal government and to the patronage corruption of the Gardiner machine made a Liberal membership impossible for him. He rejected the Farmer-Labour movement for what he suspected was its statist obsession. By 1934, when he worked for Given's re-election in Rosetown, and by 1935, when he managed Loucks's campaign for re-election in Rosetown-Biggar, Alvin Hamilton was a tried and true Conservative. When both men were defeated his commitment to the Conservative Party never weakened.

When John Diefenbaker sought and won the leadership of the Saskatchewan Conservative Party at its 1936 convention, he was enthusiastically supported by Alvin Hamilton, then a university student and a representative of the Rosetown constituency. Diefenbaker would lead the Tories in the upcoming provincial election. In 1938 Saskatchewan Conservatives seemed confused and turning in several directions at once, unsure of how best to defeat the Liberal Party. Should they join in some kind of alliance with the rightist Social Credit, negotiate agreements with the left-of-centre CCF, or stand alone and fight? Pressures for agreements with other parties came from both federal Tory sources and from provincial constituency associations. The anti-Liberal animus in Tory ranks, the compulsion to defeat the hated Liberals at any cost, was everywhere and seemed certain to prevail. Alvin Hamilton was a victim of these uncertainties. At 26 years of age Hamilton had won his party's provincial nomination in Biggar, but at the last minute, when he brought his nominations papers to be signed by party executives, he was dismayed to find himself deserted even by his friends Given and Loucks, to whom he had been so helpful. Both Given and Loucks told their young friend that they now believed the Social Credit candidate in Biggar had a better chance than any Tory of beating the Liberal incumbent. Loucks himself ran as a Social Credit candidate in nearby Rosetown. Hamilton experienced, for the first time, a Tory proclivity to abandon the party ship in stormy waters, a frailty that to his deep chagrin he would witness in the years ahead with Rupert Ramsay as party leader and throughout his own years at the Tory helm. Apparently, in 1938, agreements negotiated by Conservative organizer and fundraiser F.W. Turnbull and George Williams, provincial CCF leader, called for "saw-offs" in a number of constituencies. It was agreed that Biggar was one of the ridings which would not be contested by the Conservatives, just as the CCF would not oppose John Diefenbaker in Arm River. Diefenbaker must have known about the "saw-off" in Biggar but was unwilling or unable to manage events. Apparently, he had no control over the local executive's decision to support the Social Credit candidate in Biggar. Diefenbaker suggested that Hamilton run in Tisdale instead. Hamilton declined the Tisdale offer and returned to the Tory campaign as an organizer in northern Saskatchewan. There can be no doubt that Hamilton's disappointment in Biggar led to his later opposition to so called strategic arrangements and "saw-offs" with other parties.

One wonders to what degree J.T.M. Anderson's initiatives in building the 1928–29 coalition of Conservatives, Progressives and anti-Liberal Independents compromised future Tory party sense of identity and weakened bonds of loyalty and commitment to party principles and leadership. In the post-1934 election disaster years, what exactly were those Tory principles? What essentially was a Conservative in Saskatchewan? These were questions with which Alvin Hamilton would grapple, although his own commitment to the Conservative Party was never shaken.

In the 1938 provincial election Hamilton served as the northern organizer for the Conservatives and drove John and Edna Diefenbaker to and from meetings over miles of gravel roads. He wrote speeches for Diefenbaker, which may or may not have been solicited or used by the leader.[2] Diefenbaker ran in Arm River and lost there by a scant 190 votes after spending only three campaign days in the constituency. How much attention Hamilton gave to Arm River and the leader's personal campaign there cannot be known for sure, but probably it was considerable. The next Diefenbaker-Hamilton collaboration was in Diefenbaker's successful 1940 federal campaign in Lake Centre. Hamilton campaigned extensively in Lake Centre for Diefenbaker and in Rosetown-Biggar for Dr. J.T.M. Anderson, whom he had persuaded to take a run at M.J. Coldwell, the CCF sitting member.[3] The 28-year-old Hamilton was flush with pleasure when his hero Diefenbaker finally won election to Parliament. Diefenbaker joined Ernest Perley as the second of two Saskatchewan Tories in Parliament. Alvin Hamilton looked on and wondered when his own time might come.

In 1945 Flight Lieutenant Alvin Hamilton, on leave from RCAF duty, came home to run federally as a Progressive Conservative in the Rosetown-Biggar constituency. He faced the formidable M.J. Coldwell, now the national leader of the CCF. Hamilton, an attractive 33-year-old, campaigned in uniform. He travelled the length and breadth of the constituency, speaking every day, attracting good crowds and favorable media notices. But Coldwell was a national figure, a powerful speaker, well organized and financed and a local hero to boot. Coldwell lived in Rosetown and was unbeatable. On June 11, Hamilton ran third. He returned to the RCAF and then back to his teaching duties. There would be other elections, and he would be a candidate. And he would be ready.

Three years later, after much personal field and leg work, Hamilton was nominated PC candidate for the Rosetown provincial constituency. His contesting of the spirited 1948 election was better planned and better financed than most PC campaigns in the province. Hamilton's personal appeal gathered new money and new recruits in the Rosetown riding. From the start the campaign had energy and optimism. He campaigned by airplane, a strategy that gave him speed and a touch of drama and also reminded constituency folk of his recent war service.

The Saskatchewan CCF government had been in office for one term and was about to be tested. Hopes were rising in Liberal and Conservative hearts that the socialists might be defeated this time. From the opening bell of a nasty slug fest the government was under Liberal attack. In some constituencies Tories refused to run candidates, leaving the field open to Liberal challengers. There were a number of these "saw-offs" and one such arrangement was in Rosetown, where the Liberals stepped aside and did not nominate against Alvin Hamilton. Even so, Hamilton faced a hard battle. The seat was held by the Honourable J.T. Douglas, Minister of Highways in the CCF government. His patronage leverage as highways minister obviously made him a tough competitor. Reportedly, there was a lot of building and maintenance activity on the roads and highways in the Rosetown constituency during the weeks leading up to the provincial vote. J.T. Douglas was strengthened by the participation of federal leader M.J. Coldwell, who came home to Saskatchewan and visited Rosetown, which was in his federal Rosetown-Biggar seat.

Hamilton was fortunate in having a sound, ready-made provincial program to espouse. He campaigned on Rupert Ramsay's immensely practical platform, "The P.C. Plan for Saskatchewan," a plan which Hamilton had helped to craft.[4] Its theme of resource development was flogged across the constituency. "Saskatchewan is a rich province waiting for development! Saskatchewan has yet to be discovered!" Hamilton preached to attentive audiences, but on June 24, 1948, he didn't win. Douglas defeated Hamilton by 450 votes.

Rupert Ramsay resigned as Tory party leader and federal Director of Organization in Saskatchewan in October 1948. Alvin Hamilton succeeded him as a salaried federal Director of Organization. Hamilton's immediate job was to ready the party for the federal election expected in 1949. He also directed whatever provincial affairs needed attention until a new Saskatchewan PC leader could be put in place. He knew that he was the choice of the retiring leader for that job, but he wasn't chasing it.[5] He was engulfed in preparations for the next federal election and already searching for suitable candidates to provide the new national leader, George Drew, with a full Tory slate in Saskatchewan. When that federal election was called for June 27, 1949, Alvin Hamilton needed a candidate in Rosetown-Biggar, a constituency he knew well. Someone had to run against M.J. Coldwell. It didn't take a soothsayer to know that there was little hope of anyone defeating Coldwell, particularly a Tory, but someone had to run. Hamilton gamely stepped into the breach and took the nomination himself.

Again, he was soundly beaten by Coldwell. He ran a poor third with fewer votes than he had garnered in 1945. Hamilton could not have been too stricken by the defeat. The Canadian PC Party was then led by the Toronto patrician, George Drew, remote and unloved in the Canadian west. Drew was what Hamilton later liked to call a "General Bull Moose Tory."[6] Under Drew's somewhat quirky direction the party lurched to a 26-seat loss across the country, electing only 41 members to the Liberals' 193. In Saskatchewan, as in 1945, only Diefenbaker was a winner. For now, distant federal grass seemed not so green to Alvin Hamilton.

Undated formal signed portrait of Alvin Hamilton, for Robert Leith (Dinny) Hanbidge. Hamilton led the Saskatchewan Progressive Conservatives from 1949–57 (SAB R-B9362).

Pressure mounted on him to seek the provincial PC leadership. Three former Saskatchewan party leaders—Diefenbaker, Keown and Ramsay—urged him to take up the burden they had themselves with much relief put down.[7] National office spokesmen explained that he could serve his party best in the dual function of provincial leader and federal Director of Organization in Saskatchewan. They were well aware of Hamilton's energy and persistence as an organizer. They offered him a salary and an office in Saskatoon.[8]

On October 12, 1949, shortly after his federal defeat, a 37-year-old Alvin Hamilton easily won the leadership of the Saskatchewan Progressive Conservative Party. The convention, which was held in Regina's commodious Hotel Saskatchewan, could have been convened in any small-town school auditorium or Legion Hall. Only 98 voting delegates and a smattering of visitors and press attended. It was a subdued little gathering. They gave Hamilton the job and praised him as a leader sensitive to farm and labour problems, a young man suffused with the confidence and purpose of a visionary. Much of this oratory was required convention applesauce, but there was genuine affection for the new leader. He was seen as a politician who valued public service for its own rewards and not for its sometime celebrity. They knew him as a patient, tenacious competitor who would stay the course.

John Diefenbaker used to say, "Age is just a chronological distinction!" The 37-year-old Alvin Hamilton was young by chronological measurement, but already a veteran well-seasoned in Tory politics. He had campaigned for John Diefenbaker provincially in 1938 and federally in 1940. He had already lost three elections himself, one provincial and two federal. He knew the cities, towns and villages, the highways and byways of Saskatchewan. He had visited and travelled them. He knew the need for money and organization to build winning campaigns. He knew good men and good ideas were not enough. It's doubtful he began his leadership with much genuine optimism, although his public face would never betray him. At the university his football teammates called him "Happy." They found him genial and hopeful, winning or losing, and "admired his enthusiasm for the fight."[9]

Hamilton began immediately to prepare for the next Saskatchewan provincial election. This was grunt work, hard work! He was still relatively unknown. The media ignored him, and commentators referred to him as an "organizer" for the federal Conservatives for months after his election as leader of the Conservative Party.[10] He planned monthly schedules of travel, visiting ridings, huddling with remnants of constituency executives when he could find them, organizing new ones where none existed. He sought out opportunities and invitations to speak. He sold memberships, planned programs and wrote political copy. He had minimal support staff in the Saskatoon office and no official Regina party headquarters. With no elected members in the legislature he had no accommodation in the Legislative Building. He was, to use his own expression, "pretty well the chief cook and bottle washer" of the Saskatchewan party.[11]

Premier T.C. Douglas dissolved the legislature and called a provincial election for June 11, 1952. He and his ministers were confident. They had reason to be. The provincial economy was healthy, some said buoyant. The province was making a good recovery from the strains and pangs of drought and war.[12] Government promises of economic and social change were, for the most part, being kept. Government attempts to keep those promises were manifest. Liberal Party boasting that it could "do better" fell on deaf ears. Apparently the CCF was not a dangerous, collectivist conspiracy after all, and Saskatchewan felt reasonably safe. Certainly, the Progressive Conservative Party was a threat to no one.

After eight years in government the CCF was taking on respectability. Whatever happened to the "Tucker or Tyranny" threat? In 1952 no one was talking about tyranny. No one was talking much about Tucker! Unlike 1948, when there were signs of Liberal recovery from their 1944 trashing, there were no rosy prospects for them this time. In 1952 Tucker, at best, hoped to keep his 1948 winnings or gain a seat or two, but certainly not win government. In a wholly CCF-Liberal two-party contest the CCF was favoured to win. As in the Diefenbaker, Keown and Ramsay years, the Conservative Party was a distant, third-rank obscurity, its leader and platform ignored.

Although Tory leader Hamilton had polled well in Rosetown in 1948, he did not seek a return bout. His reasonably good numbers against J.T. Douglas had been gained in a two-way contest. No such "saw-off" with the Liberals was offered in 1952. Hamilton decided to try his luck in Lumsden. Lumsden was part of the old Lake Centre federal riding where John Diefenbaker had won three elections. Perhaps some of Diefenbaker's Lumsden friends would lend a hand. Perhaps not. It was a lonely campaign for Hamilton. He was able to field only eight candidates to contest 53 ridings. One candidate ran as an Independent Progressive Conservative.[13] Obviously, Hamilton's candidate search had come up near empty. The CCF and Liberal parties each ran full slates, and even Social Credit fielded 24 candidates.

It was no secret in the Conservative Party that Hamilton was forced to spend significant sums of his own federal Director of Organization salary on travel and assorted other election expenses in 1952. To what extent Tory federal officers shared his conviction that a strong provincial organization can help elect a national government, and needs to be valued and nurtured by the federal party, is debatable. National headquarters did pay Hamilton's salary for both federal and provincial services, and it can be argued that "during Hamilton's years as leader the provincial party owed its very existence to its federal counterpart."[14]

While Saskatchewan Tories lacked money and candidates in 1952, they didn't lack ideas and a lively platform. It was a plain-spoken document with little fuzzy ambiguity and ideological slant. First off was the usual third-party cry that the two major parties were bully boys, squandering precious time in meanspirited bickering. Vintage stuff! The platform argued that even a handful of Conservatives in the legislature would bring much-needed decorum and substance to Assembly debates. The party's 1952 election platform was a natural continuation of the party's earlier 1948 election manifesto. The principal author of the 1952 manifesto was Alvin Hamilton. Hamilton had set out to distinguish the PCs from the CCF and the Liberals with a bold program of provincial development that he hoped would attract attention and new voter support. He called the platform the "Ten Point Program of Development."

The program promised to set up a "Saskatchewan Valley Authority" to start immediate work on the South Saskatchewan River Dam and to open up three million acres of valuable agricultural land in the Carrot River Valley. Hamilton pledged to start a Soil Conservation and Utilization Program to put agriculture on a more secure economic basis, and to inaugurate a five-year program to build 2,000 miles of hard-surfaced highways. The program would provide for the building of a $50 million tourist industry over a 10-year period by the use of such devices as the Recreation Homestead. The Tories promised cheap electrical power for industries by using natural gas, and guaranteed economic transmission of natural gas by allowing no gas pipeline monopolies. A new oil policy was touted that would encourage large-scale scientific development of oil resources in the province. Surface right holders would be given a percentage royalty on all oil and minerals found on their lands. The provincial government was to assume 50% of the costs of local education. Hamilton's government would concentrate on job creation for

Saskatchewan young people. This latter cry became an opposition refrain in Saskatchewan heard each election time as the provincial population refused to grow.[15]

Hamilton did what he could to market the program and cheerlead his little band of candidates. He was a good public speaker, usually serious and ardent, with more than a little of the sports coach and school teacher in his instructional tone and exhortations from the platform. He wanted people to listen to his ideas and understand them. He had genuine respect for his audiences and they for him. Those few who came to hear Hamilton were attentive and responded warmly to the man. Away from the platform Hamilton moved comfortably among farmers and townfolk at farmgates, in Red and White and Co-op stores, in the cafés and hockey rinks of the small centres he visited. Like Diefenbaker, he "mainstreeted." He was unhurried and responsive, never showy or conspicuous. Folks listened to him, shook his hand and wished him luck, but they didn't vote Progressive Conservative.

From the start the 1952 PC campaign had little chance of success. Tories had only one, faint hope—to elect Hamilton in Lumsden and maybe a couple of others somewhere. This didn't happen. On election night the CCF won 42 seats with 54% of the vote. Theirs was an 11-seat gain over 1948. Tucker's Liberals, with 39% of the vote, dropped eight seats from 1948, electing 11 members. All 24 Social Credit candidates were defeated. The Tories were wiped out. With only 2% of the popular vote, Hamilton and all his candidates were defeated. All ran third. All lost their deposits.

For Alvin Hamilton, the distress of the Conservative defeat was particularly deep because he was now the leader of the party. He could feel the pain of his defeated candidates. This would be especially true of young candidates he had recruited, who followed him into the fray and suffered humiliating losses. One such young follower was Martin Pederson, Hamilton's candidate in Hanley. More would be heard from him. Hamilton could not sift the ashes of the 1952 defeat for long. He was still the Progressive Conservative federal Director of Organization in Saskatchewan and the 1953 federal election was fast approaching. He had to earn his bread and butter. He had to see that candidates were in place and federal organizations readied for an election call.

John Diefenbaker was fussing about the recently gerrymandered Lake Centre riding and preparing to run in Prince Albert. The old Lake Centre riding was deliberately cut, merged and fitted to remove blocks of Diefenbaker supporters, add Liberal and CCF voting strength, and rid the House of Commons of the Conservative star.[16] Who would run in the new Lake Centre seat? Would Alvin Hamilton, the federal director, have to step in and take a nomination himself as he'd done in 1949 in Rosetown-Biggar? These questions were answered when both Hamilton and Martin Pederson ran as federal Tory candidates, Pederson in Lake Centre and Hamilton in Qu'Appelle. Both were defeated, but Hamilton doubled the previous PC vote in the

Qu'Appelle constituency and established a strong foundation for a victory there in 1957, when he would leave provincial politics and begin a long, prestigious career in Ottawa.

Hamilton had one last job to do as provincial leader. He had to prepare his shattered Tory band for the 1956 provincial election. He had no reason for optimism. The old hobgoblins of a troubled leadership still hovered round. The party had no money, little organization, ghostly membership and sagging morale. Its prospects for any recovery in 1956 were nil. What made the sad state of the provincial party particularly frustrating for Hamilton was the slow but palpable strengthening of the federal party and a probable Diefenbaker leadership of it. He yearned to be in Ottawa with Diefenbaker but that, if it happened at all, would have to wait.

During lonely times at provincial headquarters in the Royal Bank building in downtown Saskatoon, Hamilton was visited and encouraged by young Martin Pederson. When the provincial legislature was in session Hamilton would visit Regina to coach and confer with Robert Kohaly, a 32-year-old Tory MLA elected from Estevan in a 1953 by-election, the second Tory elected to the legislature between 1929 and 1975. The Liberal Party did not oppose Kohaly in the Estevan by-election, allowing him a relatively easy win. Kohaly, a World War II Canadian army veteran wounded in the raid on Dieppe and then an Estevan lawyer, was an exciting possible successor to Hamilton. Robert Kohaly was a dark-haired, handsome young man, popular in Estevan and quick and effective in the legislature where he "distinguished himself as a vocal and prominent critic of the government."[17] It was hardly surprising that this lone Tory MLA would be noticed and courted.

In 1954 Social Credit, then powerful in Alberta and British Columbia, was eager to establish itself in Saskatchewan. It wanted Robert Kohaly. Agents of the Alberta and British Columbia parties met with him and offered him the leadership of a coalition of PC and Social Credit forces to be called the Saskatchewan Social Credit. A half-million dollar war chest would be provided by deep Alberta and British Columbia pockets to finance the 1956 campaign. Kohaly refused to abandon Alvin Hamilton and the Progressive Conservative Party. In 1956, whereas cash-strapped Alvin Hamilton could field only nine candidates for Saskatchewan's 53 seats, the well-oiled Social Credit nominated everywhere including Estevan, where they cut so deeply into Kohaly's Tory vote that he suffered defeat.[18] Kohaly thought Saskatchewan a wasteland for the Tory party and for himself. He ended his political career and returned to his legal practice. He was 35 years of age. Perhaps he was a little sad and a little resentful, but it didn't show. Hamilton was a friend and mentor to both Kohaly and Pederson. The three of them had much in common, including their World War II overseas war service. When Kohaly was defeated in 1956, Hamilton called his loss a "tragic blow" to the Progressive Conservatives.[19]

T.C. Douglas called the election for June 20, 1956. Douglas approached his fourth election confidently. The Saskatchewan political scene had changed somewhat since 1952. The Liberal Party had a new leader, A.H. McDonald, who succeeded Walter Tucker. Tucker, probably with considerable relief, returned to federal politics after two provincial defeats. A.H. McDonald was first elected from Moosomin as a Conservative-Liberal coalition candidate in 1948. He ran and won Moosomin as a Liberal in 1952 and was elected Liberal leader at the party's convention in November 1954. "Hammy" McDonald was a widely liked, conciliatory leader, a centrist in political disposition. He believed his "middle of the road" approach to politics and subdued campaign style was right for the Liberal Party in 1956. It wasn't. The acceptance of CCF government programs, stable to good economic times, a continuing love-hate fascination with Tommy Douglas and above all Social Credit, a new kid on the block who wanted to play rough, demanded a sharply profiled Liberal platform and an attack-dog leadership.

Social Credit, led by Premier Bennett of British Columbia and Alberta's Premier Manning, fielded a full slate of candidates in Saskatchewan and mounted a significant campaign that left everyone guessing. Social Credit recruiters made Conservatives a main target for enlistment. Theirs was the largest and most effective Social Credit invasion since the Aberhart hordes of 1938. Their solicitations and conversions made it difficult for Hamilton to raise money and attract candidates. He could no longer claim to be the only alternative to voters who favoured neither the Liberals nor the CCF. Now they had a fourth party to consider.[20] How would this fourth party affect the outcome of the vote? Could the McDonald Liberals hang on to second spot and official opposition status?

Hamilton was hurt by Regina Tory indifference to him and the party's refusal to run candidates. Even in Prince Albert, fast becoming Diefenbaker country, no PC candidate was nominated. Hamilton feared that the noisy, free-spending Social Credit campaign for "good business government" would sap what little strength the Tories had left. Where would Alvin Hamilton run? Provincially, in the past he had tried his luck in Rosetown and in Lumsden and lost both times. This election he would run in his home city, Saskatoon. He and his family lived in "The City of Bridges." His party's provincial office was downtown in the heart of the city. He had taught school and coached basketball in Saskatoon. Here, he had served in a number of community services. He was a graduate of the University of Saskatchewan in Saskatoon, and it was from this city that he had gone off to war. Saskatoon might bring him luck.

With only nine candidates nominated to contest 53 seats, there was no hope of any real success. However, as in 1952 the Tories presented a strong, practical platform that again had Alvin Hamilton's prints all over it. The "Development Program" again called for a Soil Conservation and Utilization Program to put Saskatchewan agriculture on a more secure economic basis, a five-year program to build more hard-surfaced highways, the provision of cheap electrical power to industries by using natural gas, the building of a $50 million tourist industry over a 10-year period and assumption by the province of 50% of the cost of local education. The key policy of the 1956 platform was the establishment of a Development Fund to finance large-scale capital projects from provincial resource revenues. Clearly, this expressed Hamilton's core belief in the economic development of Saskatchewan through both private enterprise initiatives and state participation. Add cooperative enterprise to the mix and we have the warm and fuzzy "Saskatchewan Way" touted by politicians of all stripes in later years. Hamilton's 1956 platform was appreciated by those who took time to read it. The Tory leader's home-town newspaper called it "one of the best thought-out programs" of the campaign, and praised its revolving development fund financed from resource revenues as "an example of the party's generally sound approach to Saskatchewan needs."[21] Once again that old faint hope stirred. If he could win Saskatoon and Kohaly hold onto Estevan, there could be two PCs in the legislature and the beginning of recovery at last.

But there was no Tory recovery. Tommy Douglas and the CCF won again on June 20, 1956. The CCF numbers were reduced from 42 seats to 36, with a drop of 9% in the popular vote. Hammy McDonald's Liberals increased their numbers from 11 to 14 seats in the Assembly but also lost 9% of the popular vote. The big winner was Social Credit with a surprising 22% of the vote and three seats. They entered the legislature for the first time since 1938. In 1952 Social Credit had nominated in only 24 of the 53 seats, winning 4% of the vote and electing no one. This time, running a full slate, they took Nipawin, Rosthern and Meadow Lake from the Liberals and were now the third party in the legislature. Hamilton lamented that the Conservatives got fooled once again and voted Social Credit in over two- thirds of the province.

Alvin Hamilton's little band of nine candidates struggled to win 2% of the popular vote and elected no one. Now they were deep down in fourth place in Saskatchewan politics. Their one MLA, Robert Kohaly, was beaten in Estevan. Hamilton's own bid for a Saskatoon seat proved a disaster. He ran seventh in a field of eight candidates vying for the city's two seats. Hamilton's Saskatoon defeat was humiliating. He felt destroyed as provincial leader. Not only did he know he must step down, for the first time in his eight years as leader he wanted to go. With the 1952 and 1956 election defeats he'd had two strikes and was out! He told John Diefenbaker after the Saskatoon defeat, "I've been defeated several times before, but this is the first time that I was left so completely numb."[22]

Alvin Hamilton knew why Saskatchewan Tories couldn't win! He knew the party lacked material firepower and psychological fibre. Tories weren't believers. After the 1956 defeat Hamilton lamented to friends, "If our fellows could only learn to stand fast and vote for what they believe!"[23] He knew that Saskatchewan politics, from Haultain and Scott to the present, had been a highly competitive two-party system with periodic long stretches of one-party rule. His Saskatchewan Tories had been off the radar screen for two decades and now appeared weaker than ever. How could they get back into Saskatchewan's traditional two-party game?

Perhaps a little help was on the way. John Diefenbaker's election as PC national leader set federal Tories building muscle in the west. As Diefenbaker's popularity rose in Saskatchewan, federal constituency organizations grew in preparation for a 1957 assault on the St. Laurent Liberal government. The Tories campaigned under a new slogan, "It's Time for a Diefenbaker Government."[24] Federal PC victories in 1957 and 1958 had a sanguine effect on the ailing provincial party, providing both psychological and organizational uplifts.

Hamilton continued as provincial leader for another year, but he was only marking time. In a few months he would be deeply into a do-or-die struggle to win a federal seat and be a winner at last. His June 10, 1957, second candidacy in Qu'Appelle seemed a now-or-never leap, a last chance for life in politics. He had been defeated in three provincial and three federal elections leading into this run. He had to win Qu'Appelle! It would take hard work, and there wasn't much time for provincial caretaking.

Alvin Hamilton left behind a larger legacy than he knew. Most of it was personal. He left a reputation for persistence and civility in public advocacy. Because people remembered Alvin Hamilton, the Conservative Party always seemed to them a sane and safe option. He was a gentleman player, a principled, honourable man. He left his provincial successor a network of his own personal friends and admirers to lend a hand in keeping the Saskatchewan Tory ship afloat. He also left a legacy of sound and appealing Tory party platforms on which others could build in later years. Hamilton was himself the principal author of these. In his eight years as provincial Progressive Conservative leader he was denied office and the power to implement these policies, but he knew as no one knew better the inevitable struggle of a third party fighting to be government in Saskatchewan's traditional two-party system. It took a special cut of man to hold fast and carry on.

On June 10, 1957, Alvin Hamilton won Qu'Appelle with 6,217 votes to the Liberal's 5,512 second-place finish in a four-way contest including CCF and Social Credit opponents. Victory at last! He resigned as provincial PC leader and entered the Diefenbaker cabinet, first as Minister of Northern Affairs and Natural Resources and then as Minister of Agriculture.

Hamilton never lost sight of provincial politics in Saskatchewan and the struggle of his own party to survive there.

9

The Resistance Fighter

When Alvin Hamilton marched off to political wars in Ottawa he left behind a valued comrade, Martin Pederson. Theirs was a relationship of personal friendship and common cause, relatively unsung publicly but recognized in Tory ranks by those who knew both men.[1] From their early years Hamilton and Pederson had been active in both provincial and federal PC politics. Both were Saskatchewan farm boys. Both served overseas in the RCAF in World War II. Both were elected leader of the Saskatchewan Progressive Conservative Party at the relatively young age of 37.

Hamilton and Pederson each spent troubling leadership watches resisting Liberal efforts to absorb the PC Party in order to dominate the right-of-centre in Saskatchewan and win two-party faceoffs with the CCF. The Liberal call was to "Unite the Right." Both men knew there were Tories whose dislike and distrust of the Liberals was such that they would abandon their own party and vote CCF to defeat a Liberal, if they thought they could not do that job themselves. In these Hamilton-Pederson years, keeping Tories together and on task was a slippery pursuit.

Martin Pederson's parents farmed near Hawarden, Saskatchewan. A young John Diefenbaker, provincial Tory leader in the late 1930s, was a frequent visitor at the farm. The Pederson family was one of very few Tory families in the district, and Diefenbaker was made welcome and was glad of it. Young Martin joined his parents around the kitchen table listening to Diefenbaker. He was captivated by the intensity of the Tory leader's personality and by his fierce attacks on the Patterson Liberals at home and the King Liberals in Ottawa. Diefenbaker found the teenager a lively boy, eager to hear political talk and already keenly anti-Liberal. Hawarden was a Liberal stronghold and at school young Pederson, a lone Tory defender, was often involved in playground scuffles over political differences.[2] He was a scrapper!

At 18, just out of high school, Pederson was quick to join the air force and ship overseas to fly Hurricanes, American Tomahawks and Typhoon fighters. He survived several plane crashes and came home in 1945, a 24-year-old, battle-tested veteran. Soon his battles would be political, and he would fight them with the same courage and intensity he took into the skies over France and Holland. After moving to Saskatoon he was soon back into Progressive Conservative politics. He met and liked Alvin Hamilton and helped him organize a Young PC Association in Saskatoon, which sent him on to the provincial YPC leadership in 1949. In 1952 he was one of the eight Tory candidates nominated and mowed down in the CCF onslaught. He ran third in neighbouring Hanley, garnering only a miserable 450 votes. Certainly this was not a happy occasion, but Pederson had seen worse. He expected and would wait for better. He didn't bruise easily.

When Pederson heard that his boyhood hero John Diefenbaker was going north to contest Prince Albert in the 1953 federal election, and that his friend and provincial leader Alvin Hamilton was running in Qu'Appelle, Pederson decided to join them in the federal contest. He sought and won the Progressive Conservative federal nomination in Diefenbaker's old riding of Lake Centre. Of the three, only Diefenbaker won. Although Pederson was again badly beaten, he remained active in both provincial and federal party affairs, and three years later, in 1956, he was elected president of the Saskatchewan federal PC Association.

Both Alvin Hamilton and Martin Pederson supported John George Diefenbaker's successful 1956 run for the national leadership of the PCs. Both looked hopefully for Tory power-building in the west. In June 1956 the luckless Hamilton led the provincial Tories into one more futile battle in Saskatchewan, fielding only nine candidates, all of whom were butchered without a squeal. Hamilton's later 1957 federal win in Qu'Appelle left the provincial leadership open.

There was no rush to grab the reins, but the obvious successor was Martin Pederson. He was elected leader of the party in October 1958. He had been around PC politics long enough to recognize the enormity of the odds against him in spite of the good name, thoughtful programs and skeletal organization left him by Hamilton. He appreciated what little he had. "My job was enormous but Alvin gave me a good start," he acknowledged.[3] He eagerly watched the rising federal Tory prairie tide.

In 1957, with Diefenbaker leading the national party, there were glimmers of hope for Saskatchewan Progressive Conservatives. Federal nominating conventions were well attended, good candidates were selected, election machinery was set in place and three MPs, including Diefenbaker and Alvin Hamilton, were elected to a minority PC government. Tory advertisements proclaimed, "It's time for a Diefenbaker government!" It was! Diefenbaker's magic had begun to work. It was obvious that the canny "Chief" would soon call for a majority mandate and be back on the campaign trail to fight for it. He called an election for March 31, 1958. With federal numbers swelling, federal coffers filling, federal organizations burgeoning, it wasn't surprising to see Diefenbaker's forces under the "Follow John" banner win 51% of the Saskatchewan vote and all but one of Saskatchewan's 17 seats in a stunning national victory.[4] Saskatchewan followed John!

Martin Pederson was elected provincial PC leader six months after the Diefenbaker landslide and waited to learn how the new federal power might affect his provincial party. Could any of the Diefenbaker star dust rub off on him. He faced a provincial election in 1960. In the glow of the federal party's

Martin Pederson upon his election as Progressive Conservative Party leader, October 1958 (courtesy the *Regina Leader-Post*).

triumph, Pederson certainly believed that a significant transfer could follow, although the party's history in Saskatchewan didn't guarantee this. Tory party fortunes, federal and provincial, had never been rich in the province. Before the Diefenbaker sweep in 1958, significant numbers of Saskatchewan Conservatives had been sent to Ottawa in only two federal elections. Tories partnered with others in Saskatchewan and served in Robert Borden's 1917 wartime Unionist administration. In 1930, eight of Saskatchewan's 21 seats were won by Conservatives who joined R.B. Bennett's frazzled Depression-stricken government. In other years Liberals, Progressives and CCFers dominated the Saskatchewan federal scene. Provincially, outside of early respectable showings in 1905 and 1908, the party waited helplessly until 1929 to form government and then elected no members in the six provincial elections that followed. From boom to bust to bust.

Whatever the real prospects for Pederson in 1960, there was some expectation of growth. This time he was able to field a full slate of candidates. All

55 seats would be contested. No more nine-candidate famine! T.C. Douglas called a provincial election for June 8, 1960. Both Douglas and his government remained popular and confident. They proposed a Medicare plan for the province, an exciting extension of their social reform package which would give the provincial government new powers the medical profession would view with alarm. Saskatchewan doctors would sound "battle stations"! There were already a number of private and voluntary medical insurance plans operating in the province. These existing plans did not cover every Saskatchewan citizen and charged premiums unrelated to family income or ability to pay. Douglas believed in "universal coverage, affordable premiums and financing from general progressive tax revenues."[5] The Liberals had a brand new leader. Ross Thatcher, a renegade CCF Member of Parliament, Moose Jaw merchant and hard-edged, defiant free enterpriser, was a man to watch, perhaps to fear. Social Credit also had a new leader, Martin Kelln, who with some Alberta financial support and encouragement from Premier Manning would nominate and fight in all 55 ridings. Four parties with four full slates of candidates should provide an interesting contest. With the anti-CCF forces thus divided, the outcome of the election would be difficult to predict. Would this, at last, be the Tories' chance to break into the two-party game?

The 1960 provincial election campaign was a significant contest for the Saskatchewan Progressive Conservative Party. For Tories the 1960 campaign was much more than just the beginning of a continuing story of conflict between Saskatchewan doctors and the CCF as the Douglas government struggled to establish a compulsory medical care program in Saskatchewan. At first, for Saskatchewan PCs it seemed an opportunity to enhance Tory party fortunes and become a real player in the province's traditional competitive two-party system. Things could only get better for the party. In the last five Saskatchewan elections, not only had the Tories been shut out of the legislature, they had drawn only small, starved popular vote counts ranging from 12% to 2%. In these elections Progressive Conservatives had fought for survival. In 1960 they would fight for revival under Martin Pederson, their 39-year-old, energetic and personable new leader, who gave them a measure of new confidence. As well, the federal political landscape had changed for Tories, and the provincials looked more hopefully to the future.

Federal and provincial Progressive Conservatives faced different realities and had differing strategies and goals in the Saskatchewan election in 1960. In Saskatchewan the agricultural industry suffered serious economic difficulty in 1959, as grain producers were caught in a cost-price squeeze with the costs of fertilizer, farm machinery and fuel increased and the price of a bushel of wheat stalled at a near-Depression level. The result was a serious reduction in net cash incomes. To make conditions worse in 1959, drought and an early snowfall reduced the amount of grain harvested in the province and further lowered farm incomes. In the autumn of 1959 the Saskatchewan Farmers' Union and the western Wheat Pools called for deficiency payments from Ottawa for grain producers to raise the level of farm incomes. Diefenbaker's government turned a deaf ear to these calls for help. Instead, in March 1960, the Tory federal government promised farmers a substantially less-popular helping hand, an Acreage Payment Program. This promise, to the consternation and frustration of Martin Pederson—who made farm issues the core of his 1960 campaign—was not kept until August 1960 after the provincial election. Pederson had wanted to appeal to farmers with a federal-provincial Acreage Payment Program in order to win rural support. Voters in the rural seats Pederson hoped to win were generally supportive of the Diefenbaker government but angered by his refusal to provide deficiency payments. Now they looked to Ottawa for the promised acreage payment relief and expected Pederson to use his influence with federal Tories to get it for them.[6]

The federal Tories had economic problems of their own. An economic slowdown faced the Diefenbaker government soon after its decisive majority victory in 1958. This surprised and perplexed Diefenbaker, who had "taken for granted that the period of Canadian post-war expansion would continue indefinitely."[7] Unemployment in Canada rose to almost 8% in 1958 and continued to increase until February 1960, when there were 500,000 persons registered as unemployed. On March 3, Diefenbaker told a national television audience, "No one will suffer from unemployment while I am prime minister."[8] The ghost of R.B. Bennett haunted him. The national economy became the federal Tory government's major preoccupation. Future deficit budgets appeared inevitable.

Diefenbaker knew that the accelerating economic slowdown had made him politically vulnerable nationally, and given those troubles was not at all certain how much assistance federal Tories could offer their provincial fellows. Nor was it at all clear how much help they really wanted to give. Allan Briens, in his comprehensive study of the 1960 provincial election in Saskatchewan, makes a persuasive case for the existence of a federal Tory strategy to avoid a provincial Liberal victory in Saskatchewan by undermining Martin Pederson's efforts to build Tory party strength.[9] Diefenbaker and his supporters believed a strong PC appeal might draw sufficient numbers from the CCF to allow the Thatcher Liberals to seize a victory in Diefenbaker's home province, a Grit win that would be both a personal humiliation for the "Chief" and a huge encouragement for Saskatchewan federal Liberals in the 1962 federal election just ahead.

In 1962, in the west, Diefenbaker would need to keep all of his 16 Saskatchewan federal seats in order to offset possible losses in eastern Canada. With no serious expectation of significant PC provincial gains in Saskatchewan in 1960, and certainly no possibility of the election of a Pederson government, Diefenbaker and his supporters were content to leave things as they were in Saskatchewan rather than risk a provincial Liberal win. Ross Thatcher's attempts to lure Tories into anti-socialist "saw-offs" with his

Liberals to defeat the CCF were frustrated by Diefenbaker's encouragement of efforts to recruit PC candidates in all of Saskatchewan's 55 ridings. Obviously, in 1960 many of the PC candidates were hurriedly selected, often by unenthusiastic local executives, and were themselves relatively inconsequential players. Their essential role was not to get elected but rather, along with the full slate of Social Credit candidates nominated in 1960, to provide four-way races in all 55 Saskatchewan ridings. This would prevent the creation of a Liberal-led coalition of anti-socialist forces and guarantee the governing CCF the advantages of a divided opposition in the upcoming election battle. The vote-splitting among the anti-socialist parties, encouraged by Diefenbaker, was instrumental in keeping the CCF in power. To what degree Pederson and his provincial Tories were aware of Diefenbaker's federal self-interest and apparent acceptance of the political status-quo in his home province we cannot be sure, but clearly it was a federal Tory game plan that was in play in Saskatchewan in 1960.[10] Liberal federal self-interest was also evident in the Saskatchewan provincial election of 1960, when Ross Thatcher's request for assistance from his federal counterparts went largely unheeded. Lester Pearson's Liberals saw all PCs, federal and provincial, as antagonists, and were reluctant to play an active role in Thatcher's provincial campaign because it involved attempts at collusion with enemy Tories.[11]

An older but still energetic CCF waged a steady, well-calibrated campaign, balancing nicely between reforming zeal and quiet trumpeting of its past record. The CCF was "Tried and Trusted," their advertising boasted. Medical care was the outstanding issue of the campaign. Douglas argued that his party and his government were the people's friends, ideologically best suited to bring about compassionate reform in health services. The Liberals, he charged, particularly the Thatcher Liberals, were not to be trusted. They were tools of big business and special interests, more apt to prey upon the little guy than to champion him.

Early in the campaign Douglas and the CCF found themselves fighting the Saskatchewan College of Physicians and Surgeons (SCPS), which for a time functioned more like a fourth opposition political party than a collegial body of Saskatchewan doctors. The SCPS unleashed a savage, sustained public campaign against the government's health care initiative. The College levied its own membership for funding, solicited donations from the Canadian Medical Association, and built a war chest to finance radio and newspaper advertisements, the hiring of public relations personnel, the printing and distribution of information brochures, and the rental of accommodations for public meetings. All of this was in the name of a "non-partisan," "non-political" effort by the College to educate the public about the evils of the Douglas program and the coercive power of the state. This enlightenment, of course, was not to be interpreted as an attack on the CCF.[12]

The intervention of the SCPS made Medicare the towering, dominant issue of the 1960 election campaign. The College feared "socialized medicine." It opposed the compulsory nature of the scheme and its direction by a government administrative body that would reduce the medical profession to civil servitude and jeopardize the freedoms of doctors and patients. The "doctor-patient" relationship, said the doctors, was a Canadian core value and, of course, the definition thereof would be their own. SCPS intimations of tyranny and communism hovering over the province, and a threat that the medical profession would boycott any plan with which they disagreed, made the doctors' campaign genuinely frightening to many. The only political party that flatly rejected the concept of comprehensive government medical insurance was the Social Credit. Social Credit advocated more government assistance through subsidies to encourage Saskatchewan residents to join existing medical care plans. Martin Pederson and the PCs accepted the principle of prepaid medical insurance. The Tory program, "21 Points for Progress," stated:

> Every citizen is entitled to adequate medical aid in all circumstances regardless of ability to pay. A Conservative government would establish an impartial royal commission to investigate the medical needs of the people of the province and to determine the price of a medical plan that would provide the maximum of assistance with the minimum cost. The commission would then recommend specific legislation to the government to achieve this objective.

Pederson, while positive about the concept of state involvement in health care, was a cautious player in the Medicare game. He stayed clear of any offensive rhetoric on either side of the heated doctor-government quarrel and committed himself to no specifics beyond the promise of a Royal Commission study.

The Liberal Party wholeheartedly took up the SCPS's cause. They attacked the government's proposed health reforms, calling them premature and lacking needed consensus. The Liberal proposal was for a free-enterprise, non-profit plan administered by existing private plans and implemented in cooperation with the medical profession. Once elected, a Thatcher government would establish an independent body to determine the costs of the various plans and let the public decide by plebiscite. Martin Pederson publicly questioned Thatcher's political convictions and credibility, calling him "a political turncoat leader of a party hungry for power at any cost."[13] Pederson's personal disdain for "turncoats" in politics was well known in his own party ranks.

If the conflicting programs for health-care reform offered up by politicians caused consternation in the public mind, there was also some confusion in the ranks of the doctors themselves. Among doctors there was desire for health-care reform of some kind and at least guarded appreciation, even sympathy, for the government's efforts to bring about change. It would be close to impossible to gauge with any accuracy and fidelity the extent and various degrees of support for the government plan held by individual doctors, particularly near the end of the Medicare dispute and especially in rural areas and smaller Saskatchewan communities across the province where many doctors may have been less controlled by the College and more sympathetic to, and influenced by, the needs and fears of their neighbours and patients. How many family physicians were made uneasy by the extreme nature of the furious SCPS attacks on the government medical-care proposals? How many doctors, along with an increasingly skeptical public, thought the demons and dragons sighted by the SCPS were for the most part only windmills? There were University of Saskatchewan administration and academic voices raised in support of the principles of the CCF's health care program. Dr. Alexander Robertson, Head of the Social and Preventative Medicine Department and Dr. Wendell Macleod, Dean of Medicine, spoke out clearly and publicly in support of the government's health reform package.[14] These prestigious endorsements were good news for the busy operatives toiling in CCF election war rooms. They could only have spread some consternation among Tory and Liberal Party planners.

There were issues other than Medicare for Martin Pederson in the 1960 campaign. One of these was of secondary importance and the rest were minor. In the 1958 federal election, which produced a massive Diefenbaker majority, the CCF was reduced from 25 federal seats to eight. Even M.J. Coldwell, the CCF federal leader, was defeated in his Rosetown-Biggar riding. In an effort to rebuild and survive, the CCF engaged in negotiations with organized labour to build a new leftist federal political party. The Canadian Labour Congress, created in 1956 by the union of two great Canadian labour groups, the Canadian Congress of Labour and the Canadian Trades and Labour Congress, joined with the CCF and created this new party which, in July 1961 at a founding convention in Ottawa, became the New Democratic Party (NDP). Organized labour would bring desperately needed money, manpower and political "know how" to the union. Labour's influence in the new party would be sizeable. Some Saskatchewan folk worried about this.

This CCF-CLC merger became a secondary issue in the 1960 provincial election in Saskatchewan. The CCF's marriage with organized labour might have become a weightier weapon in the hands of the opposition if the impassioned Medicare debate, especially after the intervention of the medical profession, hadn't dominated the 1960 campaign. Two major concerns over the proposed CCF-CLC merger were voiced by opposition parties. Saskatchewan Tories were particularly exercised and vocal in their opposition to the nuptials. They did not "forever hold their peace."

Pederson's 1960 election hopes were based on winning rural ridings. In order to do this he needed to focus on rural concerns and push for economic support for farmers. Both he and Ross Thatcher expressed doubt that

Saskatchewan farmers would be well served by voting for the CCF, a party that would be replaced by a new labour-dominated party that addressed eastern labour issues and traded in class strife. A CCF-CLC merger that would surely marginalize the rural agenda could hardly prove beneficial to western farmers. Pederson warned farm voters against voting for the CCF, a party soon to be gobbled up by eastern big labour with a range of perspectives still strange in the rural west. The new party, Pederson warned, would be an organization directed by "CCF brass and labour bosses in the east." Pederson argued that the Saskatchewan CCF, in joining with organized labour, would no longer be a grass-roots movement. The new CCF-CLC party would be much more left-wing than the CCF and would be indifferent to western agriculture.[15] Pederson urged Saskatchewan voters to anticipate the undesirable changes that would overtake the CCF after its merger with the Canadian Labour Congress. He appealed to Saskatchewan CCFers, particularly to the party's rural members, to be wary of the dangers of a labour-based leftist takeover of their party. He urged them to find a new home in the Progressive Conservative Party. Dennis Gruending, in his excellent biography of Allan Blakeney, describes unease about the merger even in the leadership ranks of the CCF:

> There was a resistance to seeing the party change from a Saskatchewan-style CCF dominated by farmers and the legacy of the Social Gospel to a largely urban-based labour party.[16]

The party doubters were re-assured by Premier Douglas himself that such a merger was a known and safe way in Saskatchewan. He reminded them that the CCF had begun in 1932 as the Farmer-Labour Party, a party dedicated to advancing the interests and welfare of farmers and workers. The CCF-CLC merger proposal of 1960, therefore, had something of a "back to the future" quality to it.

Beyond the commanding, central Medicare dispute and attempts to make a serious wedge issue of the proposed CCF-CLC amalgamation, only a handful of minor election issues were added to the debate in the 1960 campaign. Throughout the campaign Pederson charged the Douglas government with responsibility for slow industrial growth and economic stagnation. He argued that the province would be better served by the election of a free-enterprise government that would open Saskatchewan to new wealth and investment opportunities. There was some lively to-and-fro over a largely bogus issue of socialist threats to local government freedoms. In June 1957, the CCF government had called for a study of possible restructuring of local governments in the province. The committee studying the local government scene reported in March 1960 that there were in fact too many ineffective and inefficient local governments, and recommended amalgamation into larger school and local government units. These would be implemented only with the cooperation of local governments.[17] From the first announcement of the study

Pederson expressed doubts that the reason for the committee's examination of local government was to correct inefficiencies. Rather, he asserted, it was the result of the CCF government's desire to further concentrate its own power.[18] Rural voters beware. Pederson wanted rural voters to be given a vote on the issue in the June 8 provincial election. He challenged the Douglas government to reveal its "hidden" agenda. It's doubtful that he really believed such a hidden agenda existed. Whereas Martin Pederson may have felt some genuine discomfort with suggestions for the enlargement of municipal administrative units because of residual Tory populist trust in smaller government operating close to the people, it is probable that he framed the issue solely to suit his own political needs. Publicly, in order to lure CCF rural voters and secure his Tory rural base, he characterized the proposed changes as seriously threatening to local autonomy. In any event, the question of larger units of school and government administration, like all other issues in the 1960 campaign, was overshadowed by the impassioned battle over Medicare and gained Pederson little, if any, attention.

The Liberals fussed over the perceived plight of small farms, small towns, the Métis and the Indian. They warned against pernicious "big labour" influence in the CCF. The Liberals called their 1960 platform "The Key to Progress." It offered an appetizing menu of private-enterprise investment, efficiency in government, and tasty new social programs.

Martin Pederson's first warning sign of impending trouble was the nomination by Social Credit of a full slate of candidates. Having won three seats in 1956, the Socreds were expected to defend them and nominate some others, but a full slate of candidates was both unexpected and worrisome. Pederson saw every Social Credit vote as a small-c conservative vote that his PCs should have won. No one knew how much of a spoiler Kelln and the Socreds might prove to be in June.

In 1960 the Progressive Conservatives called their platform "21 Points For Progress." It was an ambitious, far-ranging document. As noted earlier, the PCs accepted the principle of a government-sponsored universal comprehensive medical care plan, but they offered little detail of their choice of plan. They called for further study of health-care needs in Saskatchewan before a plan was devised. There was no hurry for a Tory government to act on the health file. That could safely come later. The 1960 Tory platform was all about rural Saskatchewan. It focused primarily on agricultural initiatives. Other Tory policies addressed the promotion of municipal development, particularly in rural areas, the enhancement of the role of the provincial government in education, the enrichment of the life of senior citizens, the need for promotion of free-enterprise, and the resultant entrepreneurial savvy and energy that new initiatives and new freedoms would bring. But the big pitch was to towns, villages and farmgates. In 1960 Pederson knew that Tory resuscitation, if it were to come, and party recovery if it were to begin, depended almost solely on his and John Diefenbaker's rural friends.

The platform promised legislation to allow the use of purple gas in farm trucks, an acreage payment of $1 per acre to a maximum of $100 per farm, a lower rate of interest on farm loans (to 4%), and the establishment of a Farm Credit Agency. Pederson pledged to introduce a more comprehensive crop insurance plan. He promised a $5 million grant to municipalities to ease rural property taxes and grants to rural snow plow clubs. The platform included provision of free vocational training for young farmers. It promised the appointment of sales representatives to develop and promote new markets for grain. The PC policy statement included the establishment of a water and soil conservation program and the provision of unemployment insurance for farm workers. Pederson's Tories promised to improve the province's infrastructure by having the government assume the full cost of constructing grid roads and maintaining sections of the provincial highways within town and village limits. Progressive Conservatives would establish an effective Department of Industrial Development to inaugurate a rural development rehabilitation program to provide loans to new industries located in rural communities.

Programs for education and human betterment were offered. The education section of the Tory platform promised that a Progressive Conservative government would assume at least 50% of the operational costs of the provincial education system and provide additional scholarships and bursaries. The platform promised to establish a veterinary college at the University of Saskatchewan and expand other provincial post-secondary education and vocational training facilities. The PC program included a pledge to immediately provide an increase of $10 a month to Saskatchewan seniors to supplement the $55 they received from Ottawa. Pederson would raise the minimum level of the supplementary pension from $2.50 to $10 and augment the incomes of those receiving disability and mother's allowances.[19]

As stressed earlier, Tory planners knew from the outset of the campaign that they must win in the country to get back into the legislature. While the Liberal and Social Credit parties offered attractive policies of their own to win rural support, promising new agricultural programs and enhanced prosperity and security on the farms, the farmer-targeted, coherent, wide-ranging Tory appeal was more than competitive in the quest for the rural vote. Pederson would have his answer on June 8.

The 1960 election campaign was a tug-a-war between government and official opposition. The PCs attracted more public and media attention than they had in 1956 because Progressive Conservative federal victories had made voting Tory in Saskatchewan a little less eccentric. But the Douglas-Thatcher fight was the main bout. They were the real contenders. They defined the issues, argued them, ignored and marginalized the Tories and Socreds, and returned to the legislature each with slight gains. The CCF won the election. It was their fifth win with the redoubtable Tommy Douglas. It was to be his last provincial campaign. The government won 38 seats. This was an increase of two seats in the Assembly, but the CCF popular vote dropped by 4%. Even so, Douglas considered the outcome an endorsement of his Medicare scheme, a conclusion contested by the Liberal Party and the Liberal press.[20] Thatcher's Liberals increased their numbers from 14 to 17 legislative seats with a 3% increase in popular vote.

Social Credit lost the three seats they held and dropped from 22% of the popular vote won in 1956 to 12% this time. Pederson's Tories were again shut out of the legislature although their popular vote moved from the 2% won in 1956 to a more robust 14% in this election. The Tories gained votes from the faltering Social Credit but it was of little help. Obviously any transfer of federal PC strength to Pederson's provincial candidates had proved minimal. The Progressive Conservative vote was distributed relatively uniformly among all regions and voter groups across the province. It was a wide and thin distribution which failed to register a single win.

The PC defeat on June 8, 1960, could not have surprised anyone. Martin Pederson, who from the beginning of the campaign identified the rural vote as crucial to any hope of Tory success, assigned considerable blame to unpopular federal farm policies. Diefenbaker's refusal to provide deficiency payments and the government's delays in acreage payments and final Wheat Board payments until after the election were especially galling to Pederson. Pederson was also critical of Saskatchewan Tory Members of Parliament for not forcefully entering the provincial election contest and selling beneficial Diefenbaker farm legislation to the farmers of their home province. A combination of these factors, he thought, "resulted in a defeat that should have been, at the very least, a minor victory for the Saskatchewan Progressive Conservative Party."[21] Whereas Pederson at first thought medical care would be a minor campaign issue, it became the overarching issue of the 1960 election; and with only vague, non-committal proposals, Pederson and the Tories had little substance to contribute to the discussion. It soon became apparent that both Pederson and Social Credit leader Kelln were irrelevant in the Medicare debate and, as such, they were largely ignored. Pederson more so than Kelln. You can't score points if you are not suited-up and in the game.

Provincial newspapers printed various interpretations of the CCF victory and the dismal Tory showing on June 8. One newspaper, the *Yorkton Enterprise*, cited the splitting of the free-enterprise vote as one of the factors leading to the re-election of the CCF and maintenance of the political status quo in the province, a condition which John Diefenbaker and his federal strategists apparently would find tolerable. The newspaper congratulated Martin Pederson for his success in increasing the PC's share of the popular vote, despite the "general disappointment at Prime Minister Diefenbaker's failure to provide the benefits he promised our farmers."[22]

Pederson knew federal Tory power had to be tapped. He knew that between them Social Credit and his Tories had garnered 26% of the 1960 vote. He hoped to capture all of it and more next election. Social Credit voters were just Tories gone astray were they not? With Social Credit moving on and leaving little in its wake, surely there was new opportunity on the Saskatchewan right for Pederson's Tories.

Pederson saw the Medicare war clouds gathering in Saskatchewan and, like Diefenbaker, he hoped to stay safely out of harm's way. Even though the next provincial election was four years away, he knew he had to gear up for it. The four years leading to the 1964 provincial election were turbulent ones in Saskatchewan. The guns of political warfare were never silent. The Medicare dispute between the government and Saskatchewan doctors exploded into frightening pyrotechnics. In the convulsions that followed, Martin Pederson avoided identification with any lobby group. He did not attend or address any pro- or anti-Medicare rallies. Like Diefenbaker, he knew that the Medicare debate was dangerous and that a little judicious shilly-shally would serve the Tories well federally and provincially. Pederson suggested that the Progressive Conservatives, with no members in the legislature, might be able to play the role of "independent arbitrator" in the dispute.[23] This was either naïveté or pretty ornamental stuff that impressed nobody. For months a doctors' strike, petitions, appeals, cavalcades, and wildly partisan committees on both sides of the question cast an appalling shadow over the province. "Citizens for Medicare" supported the government while provincial "Keep Our Doctors" and "Save Our Saskatchewan" committees opposed the government plan. During May, June and July 1962, three cavalcades of pumped-up protesters converged on the Legislative Buildings in Regina demanding the withdrawal of the Medicare legislation. There was much impassioned rhetoric and juiced-up theatrics from zealots on the anti-government side. There were sustained appeals for rational debate and compromise from pro-Medicare advocates, encouraged by what they sensed was a growing desire for settlement by an exhausted public.[24]

The Tory "no show" in the battles over Medicare was characterized by Liberals and by some PCs as a "cop-out," but it was much more strategic than the critics recognized. Diefenbaker and Pederson believed neutrality and appeasement in the health-care war would pay dividends for Diefenbaker in the upcoming 1962 federal election and for Pederson in the later 1964 provincial election. Diefenbaker knew he would enter the 1962 election on the defensive. The nation's unemployment numbers were mounting, the economy was sagging and deficits were threatening. He needed a sweep of Saskatchewan seats to offset expected losses in eastern Canada. He had no intention of disturbing his western coalition, which included Liberal and CCF-NDP Diefenbaker supporters. As mentioned earlier, Pederson believed he had something to gain by neutrality. By refusing to take sides in the fracas, he might enter the 1964 provincial election campaign having lost no friends and perhaps gained some reputation for discretion and composure, qualities the times obviously required. While the two Tory leaders both personally favoured the concept of prepaid medical care, they knew that Saskatchewan

Progressive Conservatives were divided and could be found in both pro- and anti-Medicare camps. Leave well enough alone! Sleeping dogs? Diefenbaker urged restraint and cautioned the party to wait for the compromise in Saskatchewan he knew would come. The hot Medicare dispute cooled, and on July 23, 1962, the Saskatchewan College of Physicians and Surgeons finally reached an agreement with the provincial government.

Saskatchewan had changed premiers as the CCF became the CCF-NDP, and T.C. Douglas headed off to Ottawa to lead the New Democratic Party, leaving Woodrow Lloyd, the new leader in Saskatchewan, to midwife the Medicare birthing and face the Liberals in the provincial election ahead. In the weeks leading up to the July 23 truce between Saskatchewan doctors and the province, Woodrow Lloyd served his most difficult and perhaps his finest hours in government. In late November 1961, Lloyd had been sworn into office as the new premier, succeeding T.C. Douglas, who had served luminously in that office for 17 years. Woodrow Lloyd, an educator from Biggar, Saskatchewan, was no Tommy Douglas, but he was an authentic, stout-hearted social democrat. Lloyd had served for 16 years as Minister of Education in the Douglas government. At first some political toughies in Liberal ranks thought Lloyd soft. They underestimated him. His belief in the government's Medicare program and resolve to see it established was based on a profound social and political faith that governments exist to serve human needs and can do so. It was in many respects utopian and idealistic, but it served him and the government well.[25] Woodrow Lloyd led the government with resolve and courage through the final weeks of the struggle and earned his place as a hero of the Saskatchewan Medicare wars.

When the hostilities ended, an exhausted population was left anxious that such a convulsion not be repeated. A note of optimism was sounded by Saskatchewan writer Edwin Tollefson in his timely analysis, *Bitter Medicine: The Saskatchewan Medicare Feud*. Tollefson was hopeful that the bitter medicine of the controversy might, over time, prove curative, reminding Saskatchewan of the distress of the Medicare upheaval and warning against the extremism in both leadership and debate that provoked it.[26] Perhaps a lesson had been learned in Saskatchewan.

With health care battles apparently over, Ross Thatcher and the Liberals were excited and defiant as they prepared for the next election. They would win in 1964. The recklessness of the Medicare debate with all its disproportionate, high-octane hokum on both sides gave them hopes of toppling the Lloyd government. Martin Pederson, ever the Resistance Fighter, battled on to sustain his provincial party, hoping to build on spin-off from the continuing federal PC strength in the province. He was dismayed that such help seemed so meagre and reluctant to come.

10

Singing the Blues

With the 1964 election approaching, Martin Pederson was desperate to build on the 14% of popular vote won in 1960. He knew Ross Thatcher was courting PC voters with urgent calls to unite the right. "Don't split the anti-CCF vote!" was the appeal, an appeal that would become a refrain in Saskatchewan politics in years to come. Pederson wanted and needed a helping hand from Alvin Hamilton. Unlike Diefenbaker, who did not cosy with the provincials while he was prime minister, Hamilton had always favoured a strong provincial arm and had kept in touch with home. Hamilton had chosen Martin Pederson for the Saskatchewan leadership and felt some obligation to assist him. He had urged Pederson to seek and win a nomination in Arm River. Pederson did this.

After the defeat of the Diefenbaker government in 1963, Hamilton, no longer a federal cabinet minister, was urged to return to provincial politics and replace Pederson as leader. He would not do this. He stayed loyal to a friend. Hamilton knew how quickly Tory knives could flash. He would come home and do what he could to help Pederson in Arm River and perhaps visit a few other ridings.

All three parties prepared for an expected June 1964 election. Woodrow Lloyd had emerged as a gallant champion of Medicare. Medicare was in place now and gaining acceptance across the province. Lloyd was a big man, solid, unflappable and deeply conscientious. He was admired, if not loved. He would campaign with unremarkable but unflagging competence in a tough slugfest with Ross Thatcher's Grits. This time Medicare should not be a hot button issue. The "political potency" of Medicare had weakened rather quickly. Although delegates at the Saskatchewan College of Physicians and Surgeons convention in October 1962 had talked about exercising their influence at the next provincial election, the doctors played no great part in the 1964 contest.[1]

The Liberal Party was dizzy with excitement. After 20 years out of office they really wanted in. Maybe this time! Ross Thatcher and Dave Steuart, his provincial president, attack dog and Prince Albert by-election winner, were in constant motion. Months of banquets, membership drives and fundraising had filled both provincial office and local levies with a confidence not felt in the party since the James Gardiner heydays. Thatcher was a fighter. On the platform he was loud and bold, a performer who delighted Liberal audiences with partisan taunts and boasts. He shouted and strutted like a Louisiana strongman. At last, the Grits in Saskatchewan thought they had a winner.

Martin Pederson had some satisfactions as the 1964 campaign neared. In particular, he now found himself recognized and cautiously welcomed by federal PC officers around the province. Lester Pearson's 1963 win over Diefenbaker had not only tossed the Tories out of office in Ottawa, it had enraged the Saskatchewan Tories against Liberals, both federal and provincial, enough to strain any Liberal-Tory anti-CCF coalition sentiment that might have existed. It was far from certain that Saskatchewan Tories would help Thatcher's Liberals in 1964. There were strange stirrings in some ridings. Tories wanted candidates of their own. What did "The Chief" think? Diefenbaker, himself, after the Tory defeat in 1963, began to pay more and more attention to the provincial party.

Martin Pederson had developed into a good public speaker. He had gained confidence and was earnest and persuasive on the stage and even more so in one-on-one conversations or scrum interviews with media. He was as good a television performer as the other party leaders, possibly shaded by Ross Thatcher, who was then coached by Toronto's MacLaren Advertising media consultants. Pederson had a strategy of leaving the stage directly his meeting ended and bounding to the back of the hall to stand at the door shaking hands as his audience departed. "Thanks for coming tonight," he'd say to each person. He called this strategy a "courtesy" and advised his candidates to do the same. It was good advice.

Premier Woodrow Lloyd called the 1964 election for April 22, a little earlier than the more traditional June date many expected. The government's 1964 budget, called "A Budget for New Horizons," had been generous and upbeat, providing increased funding for education, vocational schools, highways and Saskatchewan Jubilee celebrations.

The government boasted about its completed highway construction programs, the extension of electricity and natural gas to farms and rural communities, and the Squaw Rapids hydroelectric installation. Medicare was not a visible pro or con issue. In the budget debate both John Brockelbank, the provincial Treasurer, and Premier Lloyd spoke of Saskatchewan's abundant crops, healthy economy, prosperity and high hopes. Lloyd and his ministers exuded confidence throughout a quiet last session of the legislature. There was no evidence of unease, certainly not of jitters in the caucus. The government would win again!

The tried and trusted CCF election machinery that had delivered winning numbers since 1944 swung into action. The Tommy Douglas "Humanity First" coalition of farmers, workers and teachers—battle-tested veterans and CCYM-youngsters—all were called to defend the emerging enlightened commonwealth. Tommy Douglas and M.J. Coldwell would come home to Saskatchewan to lend a hand. All should be well.

The Liberals would campaign for change. This aging government, they trumpeted, having lost contact with the people, must be thrown out if opportunity, freedom and enterprise were to come again to Saskatchewan!

New leadership was needed in these times, they argued. That new leadership could only be delivered by the Liberal Party. Liberal slogans—"Let's get things moving," "Win with the Liberals," "We can't afford to miss the boat again," and "Pull together with pride"—all suggested that happy days were just an election away if Saskatchewan folks at last would get it right and turn right!

MacLaren's Advertising of Toronto were helping to create fetching copy for Liberal election publications, and their media consultants were working hard to soften and sweeten Ross Thatcher's abrasive TV persona. A gentler, more positive Thatcher was seen and heard.[2] The Liberals conducted "a swinging campaign with lively mass meetings, a full slate of younger candidates and promises of tremendous economic developments."[3] Thatcher offered a soup-to-nuts selection of promises: tax free, cheaper purple gas use by farmers, agricultural credit, free school books, sales tax cuts and studies of Saskatchewan's Indian and Métis social conditions. Medicare would be kept, perhaps enhanced. Less government control and expanded services would follow a Liberal victory, and no one need fear a witch-hunt in the civil service.

The Progressive Conservative campaign of 1964 was the liveliest since the days of Haultain and Anderson. Martin Pederson led a slate of good candidates, respectably financed and offering arguably one of the best provincial programs of the last five elections. For the first time in years there were Tory candidates in Saskatchewan ridings who actually believed they might win.

The Tories ran 43 candidates for the 59-seat legislature and made a serious attempt to position themselves as an alternative to the government. To do this, they would have to push the Liberals aside. The fight for Social Credit and dissident CCF votes was on. Pederson, who proved a deliberative, grown-up leader, had held firmly to his promise not to join a Liberal-led anti-government coalition. From this he gained a reputation for resolve. Liberal strategists watched the signs of Tory recovery warily. They fretted that the Tories could be spoilers.

One development that gave Pederson hope was an apparent change in Diefenbaker's attitude toward the provincial Tory party. "The Chief" appeared to be growing more supportive. Alvin Hamilton would be in the province to campaign, and word coming out of Ottawa was that Diefenbaker too planned a visit to the province during the election. Another whisper was that "The Chief" was not averse to the fielding of a provincial candidate in Prince Albert, his home riding, in spite of unspoken understandings with local Grits that Liberal MLA, and former city mayor D.G. Steuart, would not be opposed.

Not since 1952 had John Diefenbaker entered a provincial election campaign in support of a Progressive Conservative candidate. In the 1952 provincial election Diefenbaker appeared with W.J. Bichan, the Tory candidate in Prince Albert, and presented a program for northern development.

Martin Pederson and John Diefenbaker (n.d.) (SAB S-B2647 Progressive Conservative Fonds). The two men had an uneasy relationship over the years.

He took no part in the 1956 and 1960 provincial elections that followed. Why would Diefenbaker interest himself in the 1964 campaign? Speculation at the time, particularly by Prince Albert Tories, was that "The Chief," then no longer Prime Minister after his 1963 defeat by the federal Grits, had no wish to see a provincial Liberal win in Saskatchewan which might somehow reflect favourbly on the minority federal Liberal administration in Ottawa, a government which he expected to see toppled in the House and hoped to defeat in the next election. In 1964 Diefenbaker's Progressive Conservatives held all 17 federal seats, and he wanted to hold them all whenever the next federal election was called. In 1964, a respectable provincial Tory showing in Saskatchewan certainly would do him no harm.

Apparently the locals agreed. On Thursday, February 27, 1964, the Prince Albert Provincial Constituency annual meeting passed a resolution calling on the party to nominate a candidate in the next provincial election. The annual meeting was held in the basement of the Lincoln Hotel, a favourite Diefenbaker committee room. The guest speaker was provincial Tory leader Martin Pederson, who previewed aspects of the PC's 1964 election program then in the making. Many of Diefenbaker's federal executive members were in attendance, and it seemed obvious that the Chief approved of a PC candidacy to oppose Liberal incumbent D.G. Steuart. Dr. Glen Green, prominent federal executive member, George Whitter, Jr., a Diefenbaker family friend, and Dick Spencer, a young city alderman, all addressed the annual meeting and called for the nomination of a PC candidate in Prince Albert. Dr. Green told the meeting, "People want a third force in the legislature. We can win this seat."[4]

How would a Tory challenge to D.G. Steuart affect the existing apparent Diefenbaker-Steuart entente? It's probable that even Prince Albert Grits and Tories, if they cared to hazard guesses, found it difficult to gauge the personal relationship between the two men. How much more than a truce between combatants would Davey Steuart's fierce Liberal Party partisanship and John Diefenbaker's relentless pursuit of personal destiny allow the two home-town politicians? The relationship could only have been further strained when Diefenbaker visited the riding on Friday, April 10, and attended a "P.C. Smorgasbord Dinner" in support of the provincial campaign. George Whitter, Jr., the Treasurer of the Prince Albert Provincial Progressive Conservative campaign, was convinced that Diefenbaker was eager for a local provincial candidacy and unconcerned about local Liberal reaction. Why else would "The Chief" agree to a transfer of $800 from his federal account to the provincial account once the provincial election was called?

Just how Steuart's last resounding 2,522 vote majority in a 1962 two-party by-election battle sat with Diefenbaker we can't be certain. But it's entirely possible that the wily old chieftain suspected Steuart's huge by-election win might turn federal Liberal heads and encourage them to mount a serious challenge to himself. A Tory provincial candidacy could well serve as a shot across the federal Liberal bow in Prince Albert.

The whispered rumour of Diefenbaker support for a provincial candidate in his Prince Albert home turf proved true. On March 23 Martin Pederson was on stage in Prince Albert at the Coronet Motor Hotel ballroom for a provincial convention that nominated Dick Spencer, 33-year-old city alderman and high school teacher, to run for the Tories.[5] Local Liberals were surprised and unhappy. They would be even more so on election night. Anyone doubting Diefenbaker's involvement in the decision to contest Prince Albert became a believer when they saw the provincial campaign conducted out of the Lincoln Hotel, Diefenbaker's old committee rooms, under the direction of a number of the Chief's own organizers, including Edward Jackson, Diefenbaker's chief country organizer. It was not by chance that one week before the April 22 vote Alvin Hamilton arrived in Prince Albert to address 600 happy Tories in the northern city's Union Centre. Diefenbaker's quiet encouragement of PC candidacies was not restricted to Prince Albert. He was also a mentor to Norval Horner in Shellbrook and Ray Hnatyshyn in Saskatoon.

Since their 1960 election defeat provincial PCs had been working to build the political infrastructure necessary for maintaining party continuity between elections. By 1964 they had an organization that, if not a machine, was at least a small engine. Tory membership numbers were climbing, constituency executives functioning, liaisons between provincial and federal personnel strengthening and YPC youth groups appearing where none had existed. A sense of pride in the party and a growing identification with the provincial leadership was heartening to Pederson. He had travelled the province meeting with handfuls of old Tory loyalists and potential new members. Always his message had been, "What we are federally in Saskatchewan we can be provincially."[6]

Martin Pederson was an experienced organizer with considerable skill in recruitment and personnel management. He knew the worth of poll captains, canvassers, scrutineers, car drivers, election headquarters officers and foot soldiers of all ranks. Although still far behind the other parties in high profile candidates and bulging bank accounts, it is probable that, 1929 aside, the PCs had never entered a provincial campaign with more or better manpower than in 1964.

In 1964 Saskatchewan Tories stepped out with a platform called "The Bold New Program." It was handsomely packaged in blue and white party colours, and under a distinguished photo portrait of Martin Pederson it proclaimed "Development's the Key" and "The Swing is to the P.C.s." The platform had echoes of both Alvin Hamilton's 1956 and Pederson's 1960 platforms, but it had new dash.

The Tory resource development program was showy, some thought risky. It called for the construction of a railway from Meadow Lake to the port of Churchill. Some surviving "True Blues" gasped at the declaration that the railway could be built by incentives to "the major railways" or by the provincial government itself. The program argued that the short railway haul would encourage exploration, mining and development in northern Saskatchewan. Pulp and paper, potash and dried fish harvested from northern lakes would be transported by rail to Churchill and shipped to European markets. Inventive stuff![7] Probably the chief value of this "Railway to the North" proposal was that it drew sustained attacks and gave both northern development in Saskatchewan and the entire PC platform much-needed attention. The critics called it a preposterous whimsy; its partisans saw it as a real, live, new idea worthy of serious attention. None would remember an earlier, similar Tory proposal made by Haultain in the 1908 provincial election.

The Tories pushed for more potash exploration and development of the "tourist" potential of the South Saskatchewan River Dam. A "Diefenbaker Park Commission" would be set up to plan the lake and beach areas around it. The PCs vowed to free municipal governments of the cost of education, eliminate the 5% sales tax on children's clothing and school text books, reduce the number of cabinet ministers and pass a Redistribution Bill that would cut the number of members of the Legislative Assembly from 59 to 40. A PC government would safeguard labour union members from involuntary check-off of union dues for political parties. All in all, a surprisingly challenging platform that surely told Saskatchewan that its Progressive Conservative Party was alive and eager to govern.

With each speech in support of "The Bold New Program," Pederson reiterated Alvin Hamilton's mantra, the call for more integrity and civility in political debate. He argued for a responsible third force in Saskatchewan politics. His Tories, of course! The Liberal-CCF Gingham Dog and Calico Cat duel must end. Pederson was also critical of the government's hurried introduction of legislation permitting public funding of Catholic high schools and its apparent intention to impose a form of county system in rural Saskatchewan. As the campaign entered its final days, Martin Pederson returned to his fight for the Arm River seat. His Liberal opponent, 81-year-old Herman Danielson who had held Arm River for 30 years, was now vulnerable. This old Scandinavian was the same Liberal who had defeated John Diefenbaker in Arm River by a slim 190 votes in 1938. Political battles here had always been close fought, and Pederson had high hopes for a personal win in Arm River. It would be his third try for a seat in the legislature. He'd played a lot of ball as a schoolboy, and he knew what strike three meant.

On election night, April 22, 1964, Martin Pederson won Arm River, but he was the only Tory winner in Saskatchewan. The long election night count, pending possible recounts and tabulation of hospital, absentee and advance ballots, put Ross Thatcher's Liberals out front with 33 seats to the CCF's 25 and the PC's one seat. These figures were confirmed in the final count, and Saskatchewan had a new government, the first Liberal government since 1944.

Although the CCF government lost five cabinet ministers and tumbled from 38 to 25 seats in the legislature, their popular vote held up well, declining by less than 1% from its 1960 level. This was only a fraction below the winning Liberals.

What seemed good news to the Tories was the 127,410 total votes they won this time. They garnered nearly 20% of the popular vote, up from 14% in 1960. It was their largest share of the popular vote since the election of the Anderson government in 1929. Some good news at last! With their leader now in the legislature, liaison with the federal party growing, and the CCF's 20-year stranglehold on government broken, Saskatchewan Progressive Conservatives felt a welling of optimism, even a tingle of pride in themselves. Good things were happening for them.

But were they? The Woodrow Lloyd government, however dedicated and competent it may have been, was old, used and a touch boring when it was ousted. "The Saskatchewan C.C.F. government died, above all, of old age."[8] People wanted change! Ross Thatcher, cocksure and relentless, seemed a man right for the times! He would "get things moving again." The province was prosperous, and a new government would make it more so! For now, at least, all eyes would be on this man and the building of "The New Saskatchewan" he had promised. The CCF was still very much alive and would provide a formidable, experienced opposition, hungry to return to power. Where in this continuing two-party theatre of war would Progressive Conservatives find themselves?

On election night in 1964 Woodrow Lloyd was in his Biggar constituency election headquarters cautioning patience and steadfastness until the final tallies were registered and his government's defeat confirmed. Premier-elect Thatcher drove to Regina from his Morse constituency headquarters to claim his prize at a wild provincial victory party.

Martin Pederson spent election day in the Arm River riding, returning in the evening to his Saskatoon provincial office to hear the returns. Beginning that night and over the next several days, he made phone calls to his defeated PC candidates, encouraging each of them. "It's a breakthrough," he told them. "We won't stop now!"[9] Pederson was always mindful of the need to cement his relations with his candidates, many of whom he had personally recruited. With him this was more than a sober political judgment; it was an expression of a comradeship he felt for his team. He was a team player himself.

We can't really know how genuinely sanguine Martin Pederson felt in the days following the party's improved performance in 1964. He sounded on top of the world. But if he had been less a believer and party loyalist and more objective and analytical, he might not have been hopeful about the prospects of the Saskatchewan Progressive Conservative Party. In reality that party's condition was still very uncertain.

The defeated CCF was soon on its feet and punching back. CCF strategists claimed the party had been too careless and complacent in the campaign, but having learned how to fight again it would win the next round. The resilient CCF rank and file did not blame Woodrow Lloyd. For now, Lloyd remained a respected Medicare hero. He would be better known and better presented in the next election. They hoped his solidity and composure would contrast favourably with the more unpredictable Ross Thatcher.

In office, Thatcher's Liberals were ebullient and eager to build the "New Saskatchewan" they genuinely believed their business-friendly government could deliver. At first, the sun was shining on the "New Saskatchewan." Wheat crops were good, potash mining was expanding, a new pulp mill was built in the north, the sales tax was reduced from 5% to 4% and farmers were allowed to use tax-free purple gas in farm trucks. Thatcher delivered small surplus budgets and new spending on highways and education. Even several cranky hassles over provincial labour legislation and Premier Thatcher's often abrasive, uncompromising behaviour failed to dim the surface sheen of the new government. But all of this starlight couldn't last. Thatcher, on the pretense of needing a stronger mandate but more likely because he sniffed an economic downturn ahead caused by falling wheat sales and a glut in potash markets, called a snap election for October 11, 1967, after only three-and-a-half years in office. He hoped to bury the CCF, now running as the New Democratic Party of Saskatchewan, and co-opt the PCs, who should now heed his call for coalition. Pederson's Tories were caught by surprise.

The early election date wasn't the only problem facing Martin Pederson. Changes in the fortunes of the federal party in the province and Pederson's own relations with John Diefenbaker were clouding hopes of Tory provincial gains. Diefenbaker cooled to Pederson's ambitions after Thatcher's win in 1964. Diefenbaker saw the new Liberal government's hold on power as long-ranged. He thought Thatcher secure in the premier's chair for another term or two. As well, Diefenbaker and many leading federal Tories were pleased with Thatcher's no-show in the federal Liberal campaign in 1965 and his ongoing battles with Ottawa, Pearson and the federal Liberals. Apparently "The Chief" now felt a bit of kinship with the rogue Grit Premier of Saskatchewan. There would be no encouragement of provincial PC efforts to defeat Ross Thatcher in 1967. "The Chief" gave clear direction to his Prince Albert organizers that unlike 1964, this time no PC candidate would be nominated in the Prince Albert provincial riding.[10] On Thursday, September 21, Martin Pederson had told the *Prince Albert Daily Herald* that he wanted candidates in the Prince Albert East-Cumberland and Prince Albert West constituencies: "I have been pressing as hard as I can to have candidates in both Prince Albert ridings. I hope there are a sufficient number of Conservatives to demand that their local committees hold conventions to nominate."[11] There wasn't a "sufficient number of Conservatives" with any such demand. John Diefenbaker and his federal executive had said no!

In 1966 Diefenbaker was busy fending off the manoeuvrings of Dalton Camp for a review of Diefenbaker's leadership of the party and Camp's own re-election as national PC president. Diefenbaker attended the October 14 Moose Jaw Provincial PC convention to shore up his own strength at home before the November 15, 1966, federal Tory annual meeting in Ottawa. While in Moose Jaw, he wanted to check the loyalty quotient of Martin Pederson, who was rumoured to be consorting with Camp in some sort of "dump Dief" conspiracy.[12] No evidence of this buzz was found, but "The Chief's" suspicions of Pederson never faded.[13]

From the outset, Thatcher's Liberals were cocky. Their leadership was dynamic, their local organizations honed and their foot soldiers eager. Toronto's MacLaren Advertising was again on hand for spin and glitz, and constituency redrawings and redistributions advantageous to the government were put in place. "Keep Things Moving in the New Saskatchewan" was the hearty Grit battle cry. The old red-and-white Liberal colours were changed to the Saskatchewan Roughriders- green and white to tap into provincial loyalties. There was still enough economic prosperity around to make people believe in the "New Saskatchewan."

NDP Leader Woodrow Lloyd, dubbed "A Man for All People," campaigned on a traditional "people before profits" platform, accusing the government of sellouts to corporate powers to entice foreign capital to the province. The NDP called for more government investment in housing, a dental care plan for Saskatchewan children and protection of labour.

Pederson's Tory platform was relatively thin. It featured four main areas of concern: agriculture, education, northern affairs and Indian affairs.

"Thatcher has sold out the farmers. Our wheat exports are declining and the Liberals in Ottawa do nothing about it. The floor prices offered by Ottawa are of no value if we sell the wheat," the PC publication charged. Progressive Conservatives called for an end to population flow from farms to urban centres. They argued that farming must be made a "lucrative business," and one way to do this would be to aid small farmers in the production of livestock. "Farmers must be encouraged to get into the livestock business." A PC government would help provide basic herds and help with construction of livestock facilities, buildings, hay shelters and feed banks throughout the province. Its government would

> challenge the concept of paying for education through property taxes, a worn-out concept which no longer works. The burden of paying for education would be taken from the local tax payer by financing education through a special tax which everyone would pay.

Education costs, Tories argued, could be lowered by using schools to better advantage by not letting them sit unused and idle for long periods of time. The Tories charged the Liberals with abandoning the roads-to-resources program of the Diefenbaker government and that the

> Thatcher Liberals have abandoned northern Saskatchewan. In so doing, they have opened the way to demands for annexation by Alberta of a large portion of northern Saskatchewan unless access to the north and services to northern Saskatchewan communities are provided.

Perhaps the most interesting, certainly the most unique plank of the 1967 platform was the Tory blueprint for change in Saskatchewan Indian affairs. Pederson advised Saskatchewan voters that

> we must stop being hypocritical and criticizing Indians as a drain on society, a role we have given them. Our attitude towards the Indian must be changed. The subject of their equality in our society has been pushed under the rug for too long. The Indian in our society is a part of our society worth saving.

Specifically, Progressive Conservatives proposed a plebiscite among Indians to see if they favoured representation by an "Indian Council system." If so, the province's Indians could elect a non-political member from each of several areas to sit on such a Council. The Council in turn would elect two of its members to sit in the Legislative Assembly on the government side regardless of which party was in power. This, the Tories argued, would take Indian problems out of the realm of politics and stop the buying of Indian votes. This Aboriginal policy was meant to distinguish it from other party platforms, but it turned no heads, Indian or others.

Lloyd and Thatcher both believed the Tory campaign was failing, and each predicted the Conservative vote would go his way. "I have news for them both," Pederson replied. "We're getting back the Tory vote."[14] But he knew the battle was solely between the Grits and New Democrats. On October 11, the results would prove it. As the provincial campaign entered its last week, Progressive Conservatives could see a meltdown coming. Tory audiences had never been large or noisy like those of the CCF and Liberal parties, but in the last weeks before polling day things got worse with only handfuls of Tory faithful turning out to hear Martin Pederson. In each of the Rosthern, Melville and Grenfell meetings his audiences numbered fewer than 50 persons. One Thursday, October 5, in the town of Grenfell a subdued audience of 30 men and woman heard a tired and distraught PC leader lash out at both opponents and delinquent fellow Tories. Pederson charged the Liberals with "brainwashing" his Conservative supporters into thinking their vote would be wasted if they voted Conservative:

> It is most surprising to me to think that some of this propaganda actually came from Conservatives! I'm tired of leading a party whose members vote to defeat another party but not to elect themselves.[15]

On election night, Saskatchewan's Tory party crashed and burned. All of its 41 candidates were beaten. Martin Pederson lost Arm River, the party's foothold. The party's improved 1964 percentage of popular vote was cut to 9% in 1967. Ross Thatcher's Liberals won re-election with 35 seats in the 59-seat Assembly and 46% of the total vote. They faced an NDP opposition of 24 members elected with 45% of the popular vote. Once again, the legislature was without a single Tory. They had been squeezed out of the game and out of sight.

The unhappy truth for Conservatives was that the Liberal Party continued to be the prime right-of-centre choice in 1967. Most chilling was the probability that Saskatchewan would remain an essentially right-of-centre/left-of-centre, two-party province, and Saskatchewan's PCs would continue as a third-party tag-along, throw-away until it gained ascendancy over the Liberals and the right to challenge the leftist NDP. In October 1967 this ascendancy seemed a faraway prospect, and the Tories were singing the blues. On election night, after seeing his party shut out of the legislature and suffering a personal defeat in Arm River, Martin Pederson told the media that he had hoped that five or six of his candidates might have been elected but, as with Diefenbaker and Rupert Ramsay before him:

> You can't run a successful campaign without heavy bankrolling. I had to do it with very little money and very little outside help. The Liberals and the C.C.F. had both! We didn't.[16]

Pederson said his entire campaign budget was only $15,000 while the

Liberals spent $250,000 and the CCF probably as much. The "very little money" and "very little outside help" lamented by Pederson could have been augmented in some measure by eastern Tory money and speakers coming to Pederson's rescue. There was little sign of such rescue attempts, however loud and urgent the Saskatchewan calls for them had been.

The election, and particularly his own loss in Arm River, left Martin Pederson disheartened. There was bitterness in his post-election reflections. He was disturbed by the shifting federal-provincial relations that followed John Diefenbaker's removal and Robert Stanfield's election as national leader at the September Tory convention. Now what supporting role, if any, would Diefenbaker play in Tory federal or provincial affairs and for how long? Would Diefenbaker be more helpful or less? Pederson had always fretted over Diefenbaker's ambivalence about building the provincial party, but now he wasn't sure it mattered anymore! Pederson knew he wouldn't lead the party into the next election. He didn't know how much Tory party there was for anyone to lead. In 1967 there was little left to build a dream on.

Martin Pederson waited six days until Tuesday, October 17, to make known his intentions about the party leadership. He called a press conference in Saskatoon and announced, "I'm not resigning at this time. We will look at that in due course." Then he lectured both his provincial Conservatives and the province's Progressive Conservative Members of Parliament, most all of whom he believed had abandoned the provincial party and himself in the 1967 election struggle just ended. This was a very public rebuke, startling in its edge and candour. Pederson struck out at the "laggards" in the provincial party:

> We must get rid of the deadwood in the party. I'm going to put the party through a rugged re-organization and if party members don't shape up, I will ship out! I'm not prepared to continue as leader unless the party fights with me. I'm not prepared to fight alone any longer.

He delivered an equally sharp attack on the Saskatchewan Members of Parliament whom he said "hid and did nothing to help the provincial party in the 1967 campaign." In 1967, all of Saskatchewan's 17 federal seats were held by Progressive Conservatives. Yet Pederson credited only Alvin Hamilton with any meaningful assistance during the election. "Federal members must understand that they are in danger if the party isn't re-organized and the provincial wing strengthened,"[17] Pederson stated. Bill Tufts, Provincial President of the Saskatchewan PC party, echoed his leader, saying, "Unless there is a beefing up of the provincial organization there will be some surprises in store for our Members of Parliament."[18]

Saskatchewan Liberals were content with their 1967 victory in spite of the loss of two cabinet ministers. They had battered the PCs into relapse and returned as government with three new seats and a 5% increase in total vote over 1964. Yet Liberals weren't running victory laps around the province. They had hoped for a bigger win, perhaps a blowout, and they didn't get it. While the NDP lost two seats and were numerically a weaker opposition, they actually gained 4% more of the total vote in 1967. The Tory 9% vote loss from 1964 was shared almost equally by New Democrats and Liberals. The Liberals had expected a bigger cut and puzzled over the swing of PC votes to the NDP. They should have known what Conservatives in Saskatchewan had always known, that such a transfer was more an anti-Liberal vote than an NDP conversion. This was a hangover from Tory-Grit battles fought long ago and not forgotten. The NDP remained spirited and self-possessed, confident that they would soon be back in charge.

By 1968, good economic times had stopped rolling in Saskatchewan and all Ross Thatcher's bluster and boosterism couldn't put the prosperity picture back up on the screen. The province was slipping into recession caused by conditions beyond the control of its government.[19] Ideological divisions and party doctrinal debate always give way to strategic and pragmatic voting in Saskatchewan. Highways, hospitals, jobs, schools, fair wages, good farm incomes and economic diversification, not red or blue "isms," are what have always counted in this largely "have-not" province.[20]

Thatcher no longer talked about economic expansion and the vitality of his business-friendly administration. Instead he talked about retrenchment and austerity, about economies and cutbacks. Sagging sales and falling wheat and potash prices slowed economic investment. Lower government revenues, inflation, rising public demands for more health and education dollars, labour-management tensions and population decrease all sounded alarms. What happened to the land of milk and honey?

The Liberal budget of 1968 was presented in the legislature on Friday, March 1. This was a day the NDP and some Liberals called "Black Friday" because of the cutbacks and restrictions the budget imposed and the shock it created. From this budget day until the deficit budget in 1970 to the 1971 provincial election, the province was fed an assortment of bitter pills prescribed to revive a stagnant economy. Cutbacks in government expenditures, an increase in the sales tax, a tax on farm fuel, the closure of some small hospitals and utilization fees for hospital and medical services were the most politically damaging to the Liberal government.

Martin Pederson knew he could not take advantage of the Liberal distress. He resigned the PC leadership in 1968 following the party's third defeat under his watch. He had been Tory leader for 10 years. The prospects of any early breakthrough in Saskatchewan were out of sight and he knew it. Probably Pederson took some satisfaction in knowing he had kept the Tories alive and untarnished. He left the party with a provincial membership considerably larger than he had found it. Subsequent developments in Saskatchewan would show that Pederson had laid more and better Tory building blocks than he knew when he bade it farewell.

Ed Nasserden speaking at the Bessborough Hotel in Saskatoon, 1970 (SAB S-SP-B6017-3 *Saskatoon StarPhoenix* Fonds).

Although he didn't win government or even come close to power, students of provincial politics can sift the archives of Saskatchewan print media, as they will, and never find Martin Pederson called a "loser"! The word didn't fit the man!

The party remained moribund and leaderless for more than a year after Pederson's departure. Then in March 1970, the provincial PCs met and elected Ed Nasserden, a Rosthern farmer and former Member of Parliament, as party leader. Nasserden's somewhat odd-ball convention was a small, distracted mix of federal and provincial Tories, Social Credit remnants and disaffected Liberals. The PCs were at a very low ebb in Saskatchewan with no real prospects of success in sight. At one point a Progressive Conservative-Social Credit merger to form a new political party seemed a possibility and Ed Nasserden reached for it. Nasserden and Lloyd Avram, president of the Saskatchewan Social Credit League, along with PC and Social Credit party officials met in Regina on Saturday, October 17, 1970, at a preliminary meeting to explore the possibility of an official merger of the two right-of-centre parties. A joint statement reporting on the Saturday meeting stated

> there was general agreement that because many of the aims and objectives of the two parties seek a common goal and purpose, it is now in the interests of both parties and the people of Saskatchewan to consider joining together as one political body.

Nasserden himself added,

> A combination of the two parties will give voters a choice between the new party, the Liberals and the NDP. I hope a merger of the two provincial parties might help bring about a similar realignment at the national level.[21]

The PC membership was slated to vote on the proposal at a meeting in Regina held on November 9–10, 1970, and Nasserden expected approval of the merger and the calling of a founding convention at which a leader would be chosen and future policies discussed. His expectation was that the new party would keep the Progressive Conservative name. These best-laid plans came to naught. The two parties were both so puny and dispirited that they couldn't put it together. The merger didn't happen and Nasserden soldiered on alone. An election was looming in the province, and the Tories would have to fight. But with what? Ed Nasserden was a tallish, bespectacled, uneasy man with little leadership experience. He was a ponderous public speaker, too drab to hold an audience for long. His meetings were wandering, uneventful affairs that drew small crowds and little media attention. Yet he had a genuine decency about him that was obvious and attractive in small group encounters.[22]

Ross Thatcher called the provincial election for June 23, 1971. He would fight the NDP and its new leader, Allan Blakeney. Blakeney had succeeded Woodrow Lloyd in June 1970. As the 28-day campaign dragged on, it became apparent that the Liberal government was in trouble and the premier himself in failing health.

The Liberal campaign was built around the premier and his favourite themes of the need for foreign investment and the crucial choice between socialism and private enterprise. Thatcher flew by government aircraft to major rallies around the province, defending his record of fiscal responsibility and "good business government." At his rallies, banners proclaimed "Saskatchewan is Proud of Ross Thatcher." Hecklers at his Prince Albert and Moose Jaw meetings loudly disagreed.

Allan Blakeney and the NDP could hardly wait to attack Thatcher's record in health care. They remembered the Medicare wars. Like a leering cat pouncing on an amazed little bird, the NDP savagely attacked the Liberals' utilization fees, first calling them deterrent fees and then "a tax on the sick." It was the most lethal weapon in their arsenal and they knew it. Blakeney's "New Deal for People" promised immediate removal of deterrent fees in Saskatchewan.

New Democrats fingered Thatcher as a nasty bully who, masquerading as an efficient steward and corporate manager, was, in fact, an incompetent thug who had mismanaged Saskatchewan into recession. The NDP promised expanded social programs and an end to "giveaways" to foreign business giants. They vowed to protect rural Saskatchewan, encourage small business and keep young people from leaving the province. Jobs, jobs, jobs! In short, it would soon be the best of all possible worlds if only "Little Allan" were Premier of Saskatchewan.[23]

In 1971 it wasn't at all clear what part, if any, the Tory party would play in this new best of all possible Saskatchewan worlds. Ed Nasserden travelled to a few sparsely attended Tory conventions and was able to field only 16 candidates for Saskatchewan's 60 legislative seats. The PC Party's 1971 program was reheated 1967 fare. Nothing new. It didn't matter. There was little to sell, and no one was buying. Nasserden was neither a fool nor a dreamer. He knew the realities of the Saskatchewan game. He knew he was just a caretaker. He knew if he succeeded in anything it could only be to keep the empty PC meeting hall heated and lighted, its doors locked, its windows secure until the Tories came back to gather there again.

On election night, June 23, all 16 PC candidates, including Ed Nasserden, were defeated. All ran last. The party lay cold and dead. The PCs registered less than 10,000 votes, or 2% of the total provincial vote. Nasserden told the Canadian Press, "This didn't break my heart. We are going out to pick up the pieces and rebuild."[24] Some pieces! Some rebuilding! After Ross Thatcher's death in 1971 a by-election was called to fill the vacancy in the late Liberal leader's Morse constituency. Ed Nasserden, in a strange, obviously token last wave of the banner, ran in the Morse by-election and lost badly. He resigned the PC leadership and left politics in 1972.[25]

The Conservative rout was inevitable. What was surprising and prophetic was the Liberal collapse. Allan Blakeney's NDP romped to a decisive win, leaving the Liberals so bruised and vulnerable their immediate prospects were doubtful. The NDP formed a new government with 45 seats, leaving only 15 of the 60 legislative seats to the Grits. Thatcher lost six cabinet ministers and 20 seats in a dizzying plummet. The Liberal Party, reduced to a bewildered rump in the Legislative Assembly, suffered another blow with the sudden death of Ross Thatcher a month after the election. The 54-year-old Liberal leader had been in poor health before the campaign began and exhausted himself fighting it.

Folks on the street corners and in the coffee shops of Saskatchewan talked more about the stunning defeat of the now-leaderless Grits than about the worsened condition of the Tories. Some Tories saw opportunity for themselves in the Liberal free-fall. They experienced an odd, forlorn hopefulness that now the PCs might have some chance of rebuilding and moving up into second place in the Saskatchewan race. A pipe-dream perhaps, a long shot probably! Certainly, in such a race, even with the Liberals faltering, the Tories would have to come from far behind. Only extraordinary circumstances would allow such a "catch-up." Yet in the roiling provincial affairs of the 1970s anything seemed possible.

What Saskatchewan Tories needed was a leader who was not a run-of-the mill guy. They needed a man with exceptional drive and ego, someone extraordinary, someone tough and ambitious with gall and dash and a little charisma thrown in. He didn't have to be a nice guy or even a good guy. Dick Collver seemed just right for the job!

11

The Collver File

A year separated Ed Nasserden's quiet exit from the PC leadership and the March 1973 election of Richard L. Collver as his successor. That interim year and the one to follow were crucial in deciding Tory chances for revival. Some questions needed answers. The big question was about the Liberal Party. How healthy was it, and what was its life expectancy? The Liberals were down but would they stay down? Had the Saskatchewan electorate lost faith in the Grits as the free-enterprise champion? Were the power brokers on the Saskatchewan right disillusioned by Thatcher's "New Saskatchewan" failures and now open to a new right-of-centre messenger? Could the PCs regroup and reorganize in time to be that messenger and, under new leadership, could they begin a long march to the uplands and to government?

Saskatchewan Tories were stirring in the months immediately before their leadership convention. In the federal constituencies PC members and operatives who, hitherto, had largely ignored the provincial scene now took notice of it. Saskatchewan, particularly rural Saskatchewan, remained cool to Pierre Trudeau and the Ottawa Liberals. Across the province champions of individual initiative, Chambers of Commerce, small-business advocates and even elements in the media looking for diversions slowly began cooling their once hot, provincial Liberal loyalties. They were no longer sure the Liberals could bell the NDP cat.

Some thought the 1971 choice of D.G. Steuart as new Liberal leader a serious miscue. Steuart was too closely identified with the mercurial, ham-fisted Ross Thatcher and the perceived sins of his bully-boy, one-man government. Many thought it probable that feisty, colloquial Davey Steuart would only bring more of the same at a time when Saskatchewan was looking for a lighter touch in party warfare. Even Ross Thatcher's quarrels with Ottawa and Liberal intra-party squabbles at home were likely to continue with Steuart in the top job. There was no reason to believe that the new premier, Allan Blakeney, who had humbled Ross Thatcher, would have trouble besting the battle-fatigued Liberals under their new leader, himself a little worn. Slowly, quietly at first, right-of-centre attentions in Saskatchewan began to turn to an emerging new Progressive Conservative Party. These attentions fastened particularly on its new leader and a handful of ambitious young acolytes hungering for personal advancement and helping him turn a ramshackle organization into a real political force. By 1975 fewer and fewer blue notes were being sounded by Saskatchewan Tories.

Dick Collver was born in Toronto in 1936. As a young man he moved west and earned a BA at the University of Alberta. He spent a year studying law but did not finish. His grades were "blah," so he said, and he went on to article in accountancy with Price Waterhouse, then took a job in Edmonton as manager of a medical clinic.[1] After five years in Edmonton he moved to Saskatoon, and started his own company, Management Associates Limited, a firm that managed investments and business affairs for professional clients. Their major contract was the Baltzan family medical clinic in Saskatoon. Four Baltzans, the father and three sons, all successful doctors, operated the clinic.

Management Associates Limited prospered and so did Collver. But Dick Collver hankered for the challenge and the rush of political games. Collver, an ambitious, restless young man, had left home at 17, married at 22, driven a truck, laid linoleum, and sold shoes and veterinary supplies along the way. He obviously had business and salesmanship in his bloodstream. His father, himself a salesman, had told his son, "If you're going to get into business, you've got to sell!" Dick Collver learned to sell![2] Soon he learned that selling was as much a political talent as a primary element of business.

In Saskatoon Collver attracted the attentions of a restless business community, wary of Allan Blakeney's left-leaning NDP. Collver's outspoken, unapologetic right-wing views, his "bring it on, let's roll" attitude pleased his clients and their friends. They liked him. He seemed a mix of street-fighter and the nice boy next door. Later, as his short Saskatchewan political career unfolded, both detractors and admirers found Collver a bit of a conundrum, a sort of paradox. There seemed to be a "good Collver" and a "bad Collver." The "good Collver" was sympathetic, upbeat and waggish. The "bad Collver" was impatient, explosive and sullen. Always there was a confidence and a panache about him that his supporters found reassuring and his adversaries found unsettling.

Collver had admired Alberta's PC chieftain Peter Lougheed, and after moving to Saskatoon professed admiration for Ross Thatcher. When Saskatoon's mayor, Sid Buckwold, a defeated federal Liberal, was named to the Senate in 1971 Collver, a stocky, sandy-haired young man, precocious and without any previous political experience except some fundraising for the Liberal Party, ran for mayor of Saskatoon on a breezy, pro-business, local autonomy platform. He primped as a dashing, can-do politician, part roustabout, part golden-boy. He lost.

This first cold dunking may have settled him for more considered efforts later. While many saw this mayoral candidacy as a showy fling by a brash young interloper with soaring testosterone levels, others were impressed by the kick-ass audacity of it. Collver drew plaudits from a group seeking the revival of the Tories in Saskatchewan. They saw him as a possible leader of that party. So did he. A Progressive Conservative leadership convention was slated for March 16–17, 1973. Richard L. Collver would be both a new and different Tory leader. Having come from Alberta in 1965, he was new in the province. He was also new to politics and new to the Progressive Conservative Party. He was an aggressive businessman and in that occupation he was different from the Saskatchewan Tory leaders who had served before him, reaching back to Haultain, all of whom had been lawyers, teachers or farmers. Three of the last of these, Rupert Ramsay, Alvin Hamilton and Martin Pederson, had followed each other in the party leadership and as friends and colleagues shared in the crafting of Tory platforms. They had fought elections they had limited or no hope of winning. These three had been sober, earnest, message-driven campaigners holding fast to a moderate right-wing populism that combined freedom of enterprise with government involvement when social needs required it.

Perhaps two conditions set Dick Collver apart from his immediate predecessors in the Tory leadership. The first of these was his own ego and personality, and the second was the changing political dynamics of Saskatchewan in the early 1970s that opened a narrow passage for him and gave him some hope of squeezing through and edging forward, pulling the party with him. Collver was a natural competitor, a fighter who had to win. There was a sense of adventure about him. He would throw himself totally into the competition whatever the game. This time the game was politics. Rick Swenson, a former Tory cabinet minister in the Devine government and later an interim leader of the party, remembered Collver as one "who smelled political power." This, Swenson said, "was a common problem with some politicians who should come to that business for the right reasons."[3] Roy Bailey, Tory Member of Parliament for Souris-Moose Mountain, who ran against Collver for the provincial leadership in 1973 and was elected to the legislature in 1975 was not impressed with Collver:

> I didn't understand Dick Collver! Collver didn't understand Saskatchewan politics or make much of an effort to gain background on issues important to the province. What seemed most important to him was his own personal ambition.[4]

As a young Tory who travelled and campaigned with Collver in the 1970s, Rick Swenson described the leader as "fun to be around because of his personality and drive." Swenson characterized Collver as "ruthless and unorthodox" but went on to say, "We should all thank him for the kick-start he gave the party in the 1970s."[5] The job of providing that "kick-start" required a leader with extraordinary desire and drive, but because of his aggressive nature Collver had both admirers and detractors in Tory party ranks, particularly near the end of his career. No less a veteran observer of Saskatchewan politics than John Diefenbaker thought Collver not only unlikely to become premier but grossly ill-suited for the job.[6]

Many in the party, this writer included, were ambiguous in their assessment of Collver's leadership style.[7] Yet, in the beginning at least, it worked.

"His ambition was to be premier. His vehicle was a moribund party which could easily be molded into a stage for his views and a captive to his style."[8] To revive the Saskatchewan Tory party Collver faced a daunting, upward climb beginning at near point zero. Yet with the decisive defeat of the Liberal government in 1971 and the death of Ross Thatcher one month after the election, Collver saw a changing political battleground in Saskatchewan and sensed the possibility of moving up from poor third-party rank and at least joining in a race for second place, a chance never given to his immediate predecessors in the Tory party leadership. The selection of Davey Steuart, Thatcher's well-worn deputy, to lead the Grits in what appeared would be a transitional leadership at best, along with apparent tensions and internal wrangling in Liberal Party ranks, perceived weariness in the province with familiar Liberal faces and agendas, and seeming desire in Saskatchewan to try someone and something new, gave Collver hope that the Liberal Party's hold on Saskatchewan's right-wing vote could at last be slipping. If anyone had the energy, organizational skills and ambition to speed this slippage, it was Dick Collver. He would lead a disciplined, "born again" Tory party to a remarkable revival in 1975.

Collver's announcement of his candidacy for the Tory leadership may have surprised another contender. Roy Bailey, a school superintendent from Rosetown, also wanted the job and was fast gathering support for a bid on it. Although both Liberals and New Democrats ignored the upcoming leadership convention, veteran political buffs and elements of the Regina and Saskatoon media took notice. They probably found a serious provincial Tory leadership contest extraordinary. The Dick Collver-Roy Bailey fight for the top in the PC Party might be fun to watch. Bailey had sound personal and professional credentials. Going into the convention he had a following of southwestern Saskatchewan town and country support and a thumbs-up from former PC leader Alvin Hamilton. Bailey was seen as an able administrator, a bit dry and school-teacherish in speaking style, no dazzler but competent enough. He seemed a straight-arrow guy in the mould of Alvin Hamilton and Martin Pederson, although ideologically to the right of them.[9] Bailey had been an unsuccessful provincial candidate in 1956 but would return to politics as a winning Tory under Collver in 1975. In 1973 Bailey was not the darling of the Regina and Saskatoon business communities or the choice of Saskatchewan Chambers of Commerce. However, his rural and small-town support was considerable and building in the countdown days to the leadership convention. He would have worn sensible shoes in the leadership had he won it.

The PC convention was held on March 16–17 at Regina's Vagabond Inn. For Tories, it was a big-scale event. The organizers were better financed than ever before with funding begged or borrowed, and they staged a grown-up affair. The convention not only chose a new leader, it elected provincial officers and activated the PC Women's and Youth federations. It began the planning of policy workshops, publicity strategies, membership drives and the co-ordination of provincial and federal organizations. It was a working convention. The first of its kind for the Tories. Federal support for this provincial revival was evident in the attendance of seven federal PC Members of Parliament, including Saskatchewan's Alvin Hamilton, Manitoba's Gordon Ritchie and Jack Horner from Alberta. Never had such federal attention been seen before. This was Big Blue stuff! Surprising. Encouraging. National leader Robert Stanfield and PC National Director Liam O'Brian came from Ottawa, and even John Diefenbaker had agreed, albeit reluctantly, to have his Prince Albert federal constituency president, Dick Spencer, attend and move the nomination of Dick Collver. The Diefenbaker-Collver relationship wouldn't always be this cosy. Far from it.

More than 400 energized Tories filled the Vagabond Inn convention centre under banners proclaiming "A New Beginning," "For a Better Saskatchewan" and "Blueprint for Tomorrow." They wore cowboy hats for Bailey, marched in the aisles behind Collver's Dixieland band, flashed badges and waved placards in demonstrations for their favoured leadership candidate. And behold the media! They were there big time! No one doubted the Progressive Conservative Party was coming alive and this convention well worth a story. Martin Pederson was in the audience. Perhaps his mind cast back to earlier Tory conventions not as bright and hopeful as this one. Pederson drew loud cheers when his presence was acknowledged by the convention chair. He was a popular figure at the two-day Tory affair. Undoubtedly there would be those at the convention who would remember, perhaps with a hint of guilt, the days of party defeat when Pederson was less celebrated.

When the votes were counted Richard L. Collver won the leadership with a comfortable majority. Roy Bailey made the choice unanimous. There were no losers in the convention centre that day. Both leadership camps seemed to agree that the PC provincial party was like an unconstructed model kit, a political model waiting to be put together and that Dick Collver had the energy, flair and hard edge to be the builder. They sensed that he ached to be premier, and they didn't care a rap whether it was personal ambition or an ideological calling that drove him. They all wanted to win, and they thought this might be their time. At least they knew the PC Party was on the radar in Saskatchewan. The convention elected a new, bulging executive of 29 members, with regional representatives from each of the federal constituencies, Women's Associations and Youth Federations. Five members at large, including former leader Martin Pederson, were added later.

Collver wasted no time taking charge. On Monday, March 19, 1973, his first marching orders as leader were issued by mail to every PC member in the province. "The immediate emphasis of our party is to vigorously organize and canvass for memberships," it read. Sell memberships, raise money now! Start this week! "Our appointment with destiny is now!" he announced with Rooseveltian flourish.[10] Organizing of riding structures and candidate searches for an election expected in 1975 were begun almost immediately. Collver, his wife Eleanor, and their three children began a summer tour of the province on June 30.[11] The purpose was to introduce himself to a province he hardly knew and show people how much he cared. He travelled Saskatchewan from Swift Current in the southwest over to Yorkton, westward to Rosetown, into the northeast to Nipawin, west and over to Meadow Lake, down to the Battlefords, then southeast to Fort Qu'Appelle. The tour lasted from July 1 to August 22.

At every stop, when Collver broke from folksy one-on-one encounters for little pep talks to knots of gathered voters, he expressed affection for his adopted province, explaining that he'd been moved to this new love by his late father who "rode the rails" to Saskatchewan to work in the harvest and had described the province to his son as "a vigorous and dynamic land, filled with individual opportunity." In the light of this somewhat dubious effusion, Collver's listeners were sure to know that the young Tory leader identified with rural life in Saskatchewan and would be a friend to the farmer. Dick Collver knew the need to massage the essential Tory rural base although he was never particularly good at it. Although the summer tour was almost totally ignored by the provincial media, it introduced Collver on the ground and encouraged local riding associations to sell memberships and begin candidate searches for an election then only months away. A big priority was establishing party policy. Plans for 18 policy workshops covering subjects from agriculture to the status of women and anything in between were announced. Dick Collver reminded everyone along the route that he had promised to nominate a full slate of Tory candidates against Allan Blakeney's NDP. "This promise must be kept," he told audiences.

Collver and a handful of his political "fixers," known by some as the "mafia," began an arduous hunt for candidates.[12] Martin Pederson had fielded a full slate in 1960, but because the party lacked a winning image there were few stars among them. This time it was easier, but just barely. The Tories reached the magic number with 61 candidates nominated and in the field before Allan Blakeney called the provincial election in 1975, an election the results of which would give the PCs a glimpse of a distant promised land. Later, remembering the grunt-work search for candidates, Collver told an interviewer: "It was virtually impossible. No one wanted to run for us… In the vast majority of areas there just weren't any PCs."[13] On January 26, 1974, only two Tory candidates had been nominated. By October 24 of that year, 18 candidates had been nominated and 10 other conventions called.[14] Finally, what the party newspaper, *Saskatchewan Horizons*, rather liberally described as a "diversified and talented" slate of candidates was fielded for the upcoming election and the Collver promise of a full slate of 61 candidates kept.

The choice of constituency for Tory leader Collver was crucial. He could have his pick of hometown Saskatoon seats, but he couldn't win any of them. His losing mayoral campaign in Saskatoon made him more than a little gun-shy of the city of bridges. The same warning signs were out in Regina, an NDP stronghold. Arm River, the seat once held by Martin Pederson, already had a Tory contender in popular farmer Ron McLelland. Where would Collver run? He wanted a town and country riding. He knew Tory chances were best in rural Saskatchewan. Collver and his strategists looked north to Diefenbaker country. Diefenbaker's Prince Albert federal constituency contained a number of provincial seats, most of which elected NDP members to the legislature while providing massive federal majorities for Diefenbaker. These Diefenbaker majorities were delivered by coalitions of PC, Liberal and NDP voters loyal to "Dief the Chief." Could Collver tap some of that Diefenbaker vote? He wanted Nipawin. Diefenbaker was slow to warm to Richard L. Collver, whom he thought a mere tourist in Saskatchewan politics. He remained unenthusiastic about Collver, even though his own federal constituency president would contest the Prince Albert provincial seat for the Collver Tories.[15] The Nipawin riding was northeast of the city of Prince Albert. It was a large urban-rural seat with the bustling town of Nipawin as its centre. What was particularly attractive about Nipawin was the size and dedication of its organization. The Nipawin provincial constituency was the Nipawin zone of the Prince Albert federal constituency. The chairman of the Nipawin zone, Clarke Brown, and his veteran, highly motivated executive were some of the best workers in the Diefenbaker campaigns. Brown and his executive took an early interest in a Collver candidacy in Nipawin.[16] The zone had a complete organization in place. Diefenbaker always held his last federal election rally in Nipawin. The courting began.

In early February 1974, Collver, PC Provincial President Morris Chernesky and key executive members Doug Barmby and Austin Beggs drove north to Nipawin to attend a "Leader's Introductory Banquet." It was Collver's birthday, and the town's school glee club sang "Happy Birthday" to him. Nipawin organizers had worked hard to turn out a good crowd for him. The PC ladies had baked a big cake and decorated it in Tory blue and white.

Clarke Brown spoke glowingly of Collver. Collver spoke glowingly of Diefenbaker. The new PC leader urged his "fellow Conservatives" to find him a winning provincial candidate for Nipawin. It didn't take a psychic to know that candidate would be Dick Collver himself. Although Diefenbaker would begrudgingly approve the Collver candidacy in the Nipawin riding, their relationship would never be warm or unqualified. He did not believe Collver could win Nipawin without an extraordinary effort.[17] Diefenbaker was wary of any intrusions on his Saskatchewan fiefdom and thought Collver a facile huckster. For his part Collver was not easily mentored even by the venerable "Chief." "He doesn't listen," Diefenbaker explained.[18] Both men were self-absorbed and suspicious by nature. Dick Collver's flirtations with perceived Diefenbaker-betrayers Robert Stanfield and later Joe Clark did not go unnoticed by Diefenbaker, who watched and was not amused. Hawks don't share.

When Collver became PC leader in March 1973 the party had only 390 registered members. That number grew steadily month by month for the next two years, driven by Collver who, like Ross Thatcher, personally directed membership campaigns and fundraising events across the province. Collver was in a hurry. New PC memberships were issued at $5 per family, $3 single membership and $1 for students and pensioners. Collver carried a membership booklet in his pocket and sold memberships everywhere he visited, often embarrassing party workers by demanding an on-the-spot accounting of their personal sales. He was obsessed with growing the membership and the party's bank account.

Allan Blakeney called a provincial election for June 11, 1975. The "new Tories," as they liked to call themselves, would now be tested. How far the PCs had come in the last two years and how much the political landscape had changed in Saskatchewan was not immediately apparent to anyone. Dave Steuart's Liberals wanted to ignore the Tories, and at first believed they could safely do so. Blakeney and the NDP could absorb a little shift to the PCs as long as it came at Liberal expense. They would not direct much fire at the Tories this time. The Tory leader toured the province in casual dress, often western garb complete with the required urban-cowboy boots. He travelled by car and van. He took his pitch for change to farm gates, main streets, cafés and Legion halls. He was a versatile speechmaker, shifting easily from feigned gravitas to folksy banter. His speeches were short, uncluttered and easily followed by those who came to hear him. Collver never had too much to say. He enjoyed campaigning and discovered he was reasonably good at it. The Tories played it safe. Collver, the nice guy, called for new civility in public debate, more amity in public life, advising his candidates that "Mud thrown is ground lost." Good, clean stuff!

The PC platform was broad, vague and moderate, left that way by design as Collver later suggested. Saskatchewan Progressive Conservatives believed that with new organization, funding and leadership they had only to strengthen their percentage vote and win a handful of seats to get out of the ditch, back on the road and into the race. Collver's goal in 1975 wasn't government. Too soon for that! His goal was relevance and credibility, positioning the party for power in 1978.[19] The PC platform, expressed in generalities, was not expected to excite or engage. The new Tories believed that a growing potential of swing, undecided and young voters, tired of the two "old parties" as many now called the Liberals and the NDP, would support a moderate, generic program and new, young leadership. They hoped Collver was viewed as a fresh face, a young voice for third-party reform. Among other messages, the PC platform pushed for decentralization of government and less government, more power to local governments, unconditional municipal grants, making parents the prime educators of their children, job opportunities, environmental protection and cooperative rapport among doctors, patients and government. The platform offered free passes on Saskatchewan

Transportation Company buses to seniors, removal of the 5% sales tax, legislation fair to both labour and management and "common sense" as the trademark of government. A key economic proposal had an innovative ring. Collver proposed a Saskatchewan Investment Opportunities Corporation. This would be an alternative to Crown corporations developing provincial natural resources. Under the plan all assets of all Saskatchewan Crown corporations would be transferred to the new company and citizens could buy shares in the venture, with 70% of those shares by law held by Saskatchewan residents. All shares would be guaranteed by the government. The platform was published and distributed across the province in the party's newspaper, *Saskatchewan Horizons*. There was little to distinguish PC promises from the Liberal platform except perhaps the stock Tory pledge to tighten up welfare abuse and calm law-and-order queasiness.

This time the PCs had all the paraphernalia, bells, whistles, glitz and schmooze of a modern campaign. A new red, white and blue PC logo featuring a gold wheat sheaf decorated party campaign headquarters. Handy nail files bearing the party logo were handed out and a catchy, western-style campaign song was featured at meetings. The party produced and distributed lawn signs, posters and leaflets for use in the constituencies. At candidates' schools, candidates were briefed on policy and radio and television presentations.[20] Collver, who had attended each of the 61 nominating conventions, was booked to visit many constituencies again for a campaign or media event. Provincewide radio and television advertising, although limited in 1975, signalled a grown-up, prime time Tory campaign. The price tag for all of this was considerable. Although local constituency expenses and costs of election material produced before the election writ was issued (and therefore not subject to accounting) would leave the PCs well behind the governing NDP and the opposition Liberals, the Tories' provincial spending out of the central office in Saskatoon was equal, dollar for dollar, with that of the Grits and the NDP.

The Liberals watched and worried as provincial media paid more and more attention to the Tories. These Tories were new. That fact alone drew attention to them. People were curious at first, then more and more supportive. Many asked, "What do I have to lose?" Opinion polls two weeks into the election began to show a clear Progressive Conservative presence.[21] Increasingly, there was speculation about a Tory race with Steuart's Liberals for second place. Official records of provincial spending by the three parties show the Liberals as the big spenders in 1975 with $169,714, followed by Collver's Tories spending $168,591 and the NDP $164,971, in the most expensive campaign ever waged in Saskatchewan to that date.[22] The Liberals had the money and set the spending pace. Ross Thatcher had left a tidy sum in the party account, and Dave Steuart's fundraisers had added generously to it. The Liberals needed to present a new Liberal look to distance themselves from Thatcher's tangled legacy and hold the NDP to at least a close-fought win. Steuart lacked popularity with much of the Saskatchewan public, who saw him as a Thatcherite gunslinger, too old and worn to lead them into the future. The Grits had to hustle this time. They had to spend.

Allan Blakeney's NDP had governed in relatively good times. They had maintained fair tax policies and funded desirable social programs. Saskatchewan's farm economy was healthy and the province's resource development growing. There were no scandals. The premier was a superb administrator, a lawyer, Rhodes Scholar, skillful debater in the legislature and a good field general in a campaign. The New Democrats' victory was never in doubt, but they would spend and defend their record. They would take no chances. For months Collver and the Tories had worked hard to grub together a respectable war chest. Now they would spend it. They had drawn from membership drives, fundraisers, backrooms, boardrooms and bank loans. They knew they must win seats this time, overtake the Liberals and grab second spot in the legislature. Before their 1975 campaign ended, they had a profound sense that they were doing just that.

June 11 was a warm and sunny election day, and 80% of Saskatchewan's 556,000 eligible voters cast their ballots. Dick Collver spent most of the day in Saskatoon. When enough of the vote was counted and reported to indicate an NDP provincial victory and his own comfortable win in Nipawin, he flew north to tell a wildly cheering Nipawin crowd, "We've just begun! Next time we will be government." Collver took Nipawin from the NDP, winning 56% of the vote and a 782-vote majority. Allan Blakeney and the NDP again won government. The premier was re-elected in Regina-Elphinstone with a 2,622-vote majority and 60% of the total vote. But it wasn't all good news for New Democrats. Blakeney's NDP dropped from 45 seats to 39 seats in the legislature, losing three cabinet ministers. They saw their provincial popular vote reduced from 55% to 40%. The Liberals again won 15 seats but saw their popular vote drop from 43% to 32%. Dave Steuart won Prince Albert-Duck Lake and returned as opposition leader. Soon, he would leave provincial politics for the relative quiet of the Canadian Senate.

The big winners on June 11 were the Progressive Conservatives, who elected seven members to the Legislative Assembly with 28% of the popular vote. The party took second place in 19 ridings. Progressive Conservatives remembered the election of 1971 when they could field only 16 candidates and tallied only 2% of the provincial vote, electing no one. This time there was a tide in Tory affairs and taken, it appeared, at the flood. Now what about fortune?

This time things were different. Very different. Something had changed in Saskatchewan that night. "Both the Liberals and the N.D.P. heard the tread of heavy footsteps behind them."[23] Dick Collver knew they were his.

12

Song Sung Blue

In Regina Allan Blakeney told New Democrats to rejoice at "a good working majority" and advised them that the party's losses were "perhaps a reflection on us in not explaining our programs."[1] Odd that the fabled NDP election machinery would fail to "explain" government programs. Perhaps some fault lay with the programs themselves. Davey Steuart in Prince Albert exclaimed, "The Conservatives defeated us, but they will have to get off their mother love themes and start to come up with specific, productive policy!" He told supporters, "Politicians are either made or broken in the legislature. It will be a testing grounds for them."[2] Steuart privately might have conceded that these "mother love themes" had done much to bring the Tories to within 4% of the Liberal opposition's vote in the last election.

Apparently the electorate also liked the Tory messenger, Dick Collver, and showed impatience with both Dave Steuart's relentless free-enterpriser bombast and Allan Blakeney's often dreary recitations of social democratic virtue. Voters turned to the new Tory player whose very newness they found inviting. Soon Collver would be tested in the legislature. Both Steuart and Blakeney were curious about him and wary as they watched him.

Some playful Liberal critics called the little Tory cadre the "seven dwarfs." None of the seven PC MLAs had experience in the legislature. Only Collver from Nipawin and Roy Bailey, Collver's leadership challenger elected from Rosetown-Elrose, were considered reasonably competent debaters. Eric Berntson, a Souris-Cannington farmer, Dennis Ham, a Swift Current businessman, Larry Birkbeck, a Moosomin dairy farmer, Ralph Katzman, a Rosthern farmer, and Bob Larter, a farmer-businessman from Estevan, made up the rest of a caucus that in the next four years would grow in size and comfort if not in lustre.

From the beginning Collver was more taken up with party matters outside the legislature than with government business in the Assembly. The Tory leader appeared excessively interested in party organization and winning elections. Although he was a salesman whose sales pitch sounded populist notes, he was first and foremost a natural competitor more driven by a need to win office than by any ideological passion to do public service. Dick Collver wanted to be premier. He knew that most of the work of rebuilding the party that could bring him to power had to be done on the ground in the constituencies. He didn't shine in the legislature, but he was a masterful organizer in the field. He was less an idea man than an organization man. He

Dick Collver, MLA for Nipawin, March 1979 (SAB 78-2518-23).

appeared to believe that one could do politics the way one could do business. In this he may have been mistaken.

Collver liked to recount that the provincial Tories had only 300 members when he became their leader. That puny membership had grown to 10,000 by the 1975 election. Following PC gains in 1975, constituency quotas were assigned in pursuit of a 30,500 membership goal.[3] In March 1978 this goal was raised to a hefty 40,000 member total in preparation for the upcoming election.[4] While such a towering membership was probably unobtainable, its ambitious reach was part of Collver's obsession with developing big, cohesive organizations with sustainable memberships. Until 1970 provincial Tory campaigns in Saskatchewan were largely directed and financed by federal officers. In 1970 the provincial and federal associations were separated, creating two levels of PC organization in Saskatchewan. Dick Collver favoured this division of authority and strengthened it. Collver wanted control of the provincial machinery. He was dismissive of old-generation, "has been" Diefenbaker federal operatives in Saskatchewan and uncomfortable with far-away Ottawa Tory blue-bloods whom he did not know. The Alberta boy, newly come to Saskatchewan, was building a party here, and he intended to run it his way.

Tory provincial annual meetings in 1974, 1975 and 1976, each generously advised by regional policy conferences and on-site seminars and workshops, provided PC policy but failed to attract much media attention leading up to the 1978 election. In 1977 the Tories sought an upswing in media coverage and changed the annual meeting format to allow debate of policy resolutions on the floor of the convention, and adopted policy that was then sent to the rank-and-file membership for approval.[5] The 1978 platform was essentially the old 1975 program with approving nods to a more gentlemanly politics, strong viable local government, individual rights and initiative, law and order, lower taxes and welfare reform. It was embellished this time with equal status for women, job equity in the civil service, protection of the environment, and scrutiny of grants and funding for pressure groups. Nothing really new, nothing that would puzzle or startle an electorate the Tories were increasingly sure just wanted change. A change of government!

Ever since the June 11, 1975 provincial election Saskatchewan Progressive Conservatives, notwithstanding their sometimes awkward performances in the legislature, had been gaining ground. They had also been gaining members of the Legislative Assembly. They had never taken their minds off the arithmetic that counted, the popular vote that had left them a bare four percentage points behind the Liberals. In June, Collver's Tories had registered 124,573 votes, winning seven seats to Steuart's 142,853 votes and 15 seats. These numbers showed a surging PC Party and declining Liberal fortunes.

Added to that were disturbing upheavals in Grit intraparty affairs. As Dave Steuart prepared to retire and sink comfortably into a Senate seat in Ottawa, ambitious "Young Turk" Liberals, eager for the leadership at home, were running off in several directions calling "follow me." Three Liberal MLAs—Regina-Wascana's Tony Merchant, Regina-Lakeview's Ted Malone and Qu'Appelle's Gary Lane—were thought to want the leadership. All three were lawyers, and as such, some waggish critics said, given to natural airs of self-worth and entitlement. Certainly, all three were ambitious and able enough to compete and survive in Saskatchewan politics. Lane was the most experienced and wily of the three. He had been elected in 1971. Malone had won his seat in a 1973 by-election and Merchant, the rookie, in 1975. A fourth unlikely but mooted contender for the Liberal leadership was the son of the late Liberal premier, Ross Thatcher. Colin Thatcher, MLA for Thunder Creek, was never serious about running for his father's old job and could never have won the leadership. Subsequent events might suggest that Thatcher, even at an early date, may have cast an approving eye on the rejuvenated Collver Tories, thinking them a better bet than the faltering Liberals for toppling the NDP.

Gary Lane, after testing Liberal waters and apparently finding them unsafe for a leadership bid, withdrew from the race to ponder his future. Six weeks before the December 11, 1976, convention at Regina's Centre of the Arts, Lane bolted the Liberal Party and defected to the Tories. In both Grit and Tory ranks there was distrust of Lane, a careerist seen by many in both camps as lean and hungry, a cagey operator fretful under the leadership of another and possessing little philosophy or principle. Colin Thatcher, who may have been the pot calling the kettle black, described Lane as a deserter, a man "who was whatever he felt he had to be on a given occasion"[6] Dick Collver wasn't overly fussy. He wanted an eighth MLA and with Lane he got one, and a bright six-year veteran, experienced organizer and debater to boot.

More good news for Tories followed. The Liberals replaced the veteran Davey Steuart with 39-year-old Ted Malone, a Regina establishment candidate whose control of party affairs was tenuous from the start and whose performance as team manager, organizer and campaign leader was unsteady and uninspiring throughout a short, sad leadership tenure. Dick Collver wasn't impressed with Ted Malone. He found the Liberal leader patrician and humourless, a man with little "hustle." He thought Malone's win at the Grit convention no home-run for that party. The Liberal Party had deep wounds after a divisive leadership campaign, and Collver believed Malone couldn't heal them. So much the better for his Tories.

Soon Malone had by-elections to fight in Prince Albert-Duck Lake, Dave Steuart's old riding, and Saskatoon-Sutherland, left vacant by the death of the Grit member, Evelyn Edwards. He had troubles ahead. If Malone lost the by-elections to the PCs, Collver's numbers, already jumped a notch by Gary Lane's defection, could be plumped to 10 members with the Grits reduced to 12. A dangerous situation for the Liberal opposition! The by-elections were called for March 2, 1977.

Dick Collver was a fierce competitor and a consumate organizer. He had a cocky, "just watch me," air. He personally directed both by-election campaigns, shuttlecocking between Prince Albert and Saskatoon for a month of electioneering. In each constituency, working with locals, he helped map campaign strategy, assisted in promotion and fundraising and spent hours with his candidates and MLAs in door-to-door canvassing. He supervised the establishment and coordination of poll organizations in both ridings. He drove the campaigns at a furious pace. Organizers and workers called him "the boss." And he was. He was also a winner, a double winner on election night. Two Liberal seats were won that night, not by the ruling NDP but by the fledgling Collver Tories. On March 2, Saskatoon-Sutherland celebrated the victory of Tory lawyer Harold Lane. Lane won by 500 votes over the Liberal candidate. Collver was cheered by the faithful when he came to Tory election headquarters to congratulate them. They introduced him as "the next Premier of Saskatchewan." He couldn't stay long with them because he had to drive north to Prince Albert to celebrate the second win, a PC victory in Prince Albert-Duck Lake. A big, well-primed, late-hour crowd had gathered in Prince Albert's Coronet Motor Inn, waiting patiently for Collver to arrive. Tory candidate Garnet Wipf had won the seat easily, pushing the Liberals back into third place. Dick Collver was again introduced as "the next Premier of Saskatchewan" and cheered to the rafters. How sweet it was! Collver was a happy man, a tired, happy warrior when he drove back to Saskatoon, "the next Premier of Saskatchewan" still ringing in his ears. He liked the sound of it. Tory strategists knew serious fault lines were showing in Liberal Party structures. Inevitably, the losses reflected badly on Malone who was becoming increasingly vulnerable.

Soon a third provincial by-election would again pit Tories and Grits against each other. The NDP called a by-election for June 8, 1977, in Pelly, an NDP stronghold, following the death of its popular sitting member, Leonard Larson. In the 1975 general election Larson had carried Pelly handily with 51% of the vote. The Liberals polled a solid second with 32%, and the PCs ran a poor third with 17% of the popular vote. In the by-election Blakeney's NDP were expected to retain Pelly easily with the real contest a Tory-Liberal battle for second place. Both the Liberals and the PCs sent their leaders, provincial officers, organizers and MLAs into the seat to fight an intense little war. Both Collver and Malone practically lived in the constituency for the three-week campaign. Some of Collver's ardent young workers trekked to Pelly and slept in their cars at night. Federal Liberal cabinet ministers Jack Horner and Warren Allmand travelled west to campaign side by side with Liberal locals. The Pelly by-election campaign was old-time slug-and-grunt politics fought door to door and face to face in towns, villages and farms. No house, store, hotel bar or coffee shop, no post office, ball diamond, grain elevator, retirement lodge or nursing home was spared the politician's visits and imploring solicitations. NDP canvassers urged voters to stick with the trusted Allan Blakeney. They said his tested land and resource policies and unquestioned intellect and probity put him up front. Collver, they said, was too erratic and shifty to be entrusted with office, and Malone too callow and preppy to be taken seriously. The NDP feared the Tories and dismissed the Grits.

The Liberals concentrated their assault on the PCs. In random surges of high-voltage rhetoric they charged Collver with superficiality, opportunism and right-wing extremism. They made shadowy references to the fitful Conservative J.T.M. Anderson government of the 1930s and that party's rumoured dalliance with the nasty Ku Klux Klan. It's probable that in 1977, Pelly voters, certainly the younger ones, had never heard of Anderson or the Ku Klux Klan. The Liberal battle was with the rising PCs whose advance they had to stop or at least slow. In Pelly the once invulnerable Liberal Party was now threatened and fighting not just for second place in a by-election race but to stay standing in provincial affairs.

A repeat win for the NDP in Pelly was indicated as early returns from big polls in Kamsack, Norquay, Pelly village and Veregin rurals were tabulated. Blakeney won Pelly with 50% of the total vote. This surprised no one. During the campaign, day-to-day scrutinizing of marked voters' lists and constant analysis by canvassers of all three parties had telegraphed an NDP victory and a hot race for second place. On election night the Pelly Liberals, although warned of a close battle with the PCs, were shocked to see their share of the vote drop to 21% from the 32% garnered in 1975 and the Tory vote rocket up from 17% in 1975 to 29% in the by-election. The Tory surge put them securely ahead of the third-place Liberals. What was most alarming for Malone was that the shift of Liberal votes all had been to Collver's Tories. What drove all this?

Much of the Liberal-Tory verbal jousting had become falderal to the ears of Pelly voters, who saw little or no ideological differences between the two opposition parties. What probably accounted for the truant Liberal vote wasn't core differences between a centrist Liberal and a centre-right Tory party, but rather outstanding differences in leadership and, most particularly, raw desire for change. Dick Collver was a fresh face, someone whose energy and infectious optimism had growing appeal. He looked and sounded like a winner, someone who could defeat Allan Blakeney and the NDP. Ted

Malone didn't. One wonders what implications, if any, the Liberal reverse in Pelly held for Malone. His razor-thin lead over Collver's PCs in the legislature and his hold on official opposition status were still intact. But perhaps he suspected that Collver was winning the race for the top.

Dick Collver relished the Tory showing in Pelly. Beyond the psychological lift it gave the faithful and the media attention it grabbed for the party, Pelly was a personal win for Collver in a one-on-one match with Ted Malone. The appearance of meltdown in the Liberal Party and Malone's apparent failure to control it underscored Collver's claim to leadership of the anti-NDP forces in the province.

Even before the Pelly by-election Collver had another disenchanted Grit in his sights for defection. It was Colin Thatcher, Liberal MLA for Thunder Creek. Thatcher, the son of the late Ross Thatcher, joined the Tories two weeks after the Liberal trashing in Pelly. The junior Thatcher, reportedly sullen and quirky in Liberal ranks and dismissed by many as a political lightweight, was nonetheless a big catch for Collver. He knew that adding one more body to the PC caucus drew him even with the Liberals in the legislature. Both parties now had 11 members and shared the official opposition's distinctions and perks. The next provincial election was expected for June 1979, if not sooner, and Collver knew if he could beg, borrow or steal more converts he would enter that campaign as leader of the official opposition, a step nearer the premiership.

Afoot in the corridors of the legislature were rumours of Dick Collver's hunting for Liberal and New Democrat converts and offering them money and political favours to join him. Unsavoury as his trolling for defectors might have seemed to some, it was not at all improbable to Collver's detractors. While the rumours were never substantiated, they were never entirely dismissed and probably did Collver's increasingly vulnerable image little good. Allan Blakeney, never given to personal political attack, privately spoke of Collver with suspicion and distaste. Bill Knight, NDP Secretary said, "Collver brought out the competitive edge in Blakeney. He found Collver smarmy, threatening and dangerous and was going to stop him."[7] For his part, Collver dismissed Blakeney as a prissy academic who "could be taken."[8]

After the 1975 provincial election and certainly after Pelly, it was obvious the next Saskatchewan general election would be an NDP-Tory head-to-head shoot out. If Allan Blakeney was "to stop" Collver, it would have to be soon. Just when a provincial election would be held was Blakeney's call. With the popularity of Joe Clark and the federal Progressive Conservatives on the rise, there were prospects of a 1979 federal PC victory and a Clark government in Ottawa with spillover onto Collver's provincial Tories. This made Blakeney cautious. But regardless of when the provincial writ was dropped, the parties had to be ready and Tory and NDP machines were set in motion with early candidate searches.

In 1978 Saskatchewan Tories still spoke of their 1975 fielding of 61 candidates as near miraculous, given the condition of the party at the time. That recruitment had been hard work. Theirs hadn't been a star-studded slate, but it had been a full slate, however assorted and limited. This time would be different! When the PCs began nominating candidates in late 1977 and on into 1978, the party had colour in its cheeks and a spring in its step. Its conventions were large, its nominations contested, most of its candidates known and able. Tory coffers, legions and spirits were brimming. Tories thought they could win this time.

On September 19, Allan Blakeney called an early election for October 18, 1978. His internal polling put the NDP at 45% of the popular vote to the PC's 35%. Malone's Liberals were at 20%—and falling.[9] Some voter uncertainty about Dick Collver registered in the polling, as did voter indifference to Ted Malone. Allan Blakeney appeared a comfortable personal favourite among the leaders. Bill Knight, NDP secretary and campaign director, said, "Let's go!" They already had 40 of their 61 candidates nominated and a bruising anti-Collver strategy secreted away and waiting under wraps.

The Tories were surprised but not blindsided by the early call. They had hoped to fight a provincial election after a federal PC victory which would have boosted them immensely, but they were not in bad shape. When the early election call came, they had 34 of their 61 candidates in the field.[10] Across the province where PC conventions were once lonesome gatherings of dispirited faithful come to acclaim a single contender as candidate, large, showy meetings were now held, contested by two or three energized aspirants battling for the Tory nod. In Radville, 650 people packed a hall to nominate Bob Pickering for Bengough-Milestone after a hard-fought contest. In Weyburn, 700 PC members nominated Glen Dods, winner of a spirited race with two other candidates. Hafford's population of 515 souls was more than doubled when 1,100 PC members chose John Gerich, a local farmer and former RCMP officer, from a field of four candidates. A close battle for the Saskatoon-Nutana nomination was won by University of Saskatchewan Professor of Agricultural Economics Grant Devine before 500 enthusiastic Tories with leader Dick Collver applauding from the front row. Grant Devine would be heard from later. The Meadow Lake convention drew 1,200 people to a high school auditorium for a hotly contested convention that elected George McLeod. Arm River's Gerry Muirhead was chosen by 800 delegates in Davidson. At the time, both Meadow Lake and Arm River were held by the NDP.[11] Collver returned from the large, noisy conventions flushed with confidence.

The Saskatchewan Progressive Conservative Party, building on the successes of 1975 and the by-elections, was now a formidable organization. In 1977, when it convened its annual meeting in Regina, the party was gearing for a provincial election. Policy resolutions were debated and approved for distribution to the membership, pep talks were delivered by Collver and new federal leader Joe Clark, and a new provincial president was installed.

Election talk was heard in every convention hotel room and corridor. The party was ready for prime time. The new president was George Hill, a lawyer-businessman from southern Saskatchewan. Hill was a competitor and a motivator. He was immensely personable and a superb fundraiser with contacts in Alberta, where petro dollars in deep pockets were found. To augment the work of the provincial office in Saskatoon a new regional office was opened in Regina, serving as a metro for the Regina city constituencies and for organizational activities in southern Saskatchewan.

When the election call came, David Tkachuk, a Collver acolyte and one-time party director, was named campaign chairman. This may have been a mistake. Tkachuk, an eager, darkhaired, whippet-lean seemingly humourless young man, untried in real politics, was unpopular with many candidates who found him more gunslinger than team leader. Tkachuk was no match for his good-humoured, ebullient NDP counterpart, Bill Knight. Knight, NDP Secretary and a former Member of Parliament, was a charmer, a shrewd human-resource manager and a trusted political advisor to Allan Blakeney. As campaign chairman, Knight, more than any other New Democratic strategist, was responsible for the direction of the NDP's 1978 campaign.

Like Collver, George Hill emphasized the paramount need for strong local organization. They wanted constituency organizations that, as Collver said, existed "in the flesh" and not "just on paper." They wanted organizations that held annual meetings, involved local memberships in fundraising and policy decisions, organizations that had year-round dynamics and permanence. These critical disciplines Collver had borrowed from Ross Thatcher, who had learned them from his own early years in the CCF before converting to the Grits.[12]

The Liberals, more than a little dazed by the early election call and still hurting from their 1975 rough-up, were slow to field a full slate of candidates and knock together some kind of respectable program. Their best hope was just to stay alive this time and be around to fight another day. Liberal planners worried about their party identify. "Look at us," they said, "We're Liberals and we're different from and better than the Tories!" But perhaps, to the voter, that was like choosing between Heinz and Libby's ketchups. Also, some Liberal tacticians wondered how able Ted Malone would prove in the engagements ahead. Was he ready for field command? Perhaps they recognized the danger of Malone's being ignored by both the other parties and by a jaded media looking for a performer with more colour and edge than the Grit leader could provide. Time would tell.

Tory strategists had no such trembles. They were almost giddy with prospects of winning in October. Tory candidates were summoned to Regina and Saskatoon to attend candidates' schools. They were introduced to the television camera and the radio microphone and experienced the excitements of mock interviews and the preparation of advertising clips. They were initiated and rehearsed by media types who offered helpful tips on image, grooming, breathing and voice modulation. Their pictures were taken. Samples of party brochures, placards and lawn signs were displayed with order forms and price lists for local purchase and use. Local campaign managers were schooled in office management, telephone and door-to-door canvassing and voter identification.[13] All in all, the 1978 campaign, building on the party's 1975 restructuring, was better financed and better organized than any in the past.

During the campaign, however, there were questions about how effectively the PC platform was being presented and debated. Criticisms were levelled at the PC central office for its failure to provide punch and variety in provincial advertising. Concerns were raised that Tory tracking and quick response strategies were inadequate for day-to-day warfare with the rapid-firing NDP. These concerns were heightened in the early days of the campaign by rumours reputedly spread by Grit and NDP operatives that Collver was an "outsider," whose business ethics and devotion to truth-telling were doubtful. After the election, with the benefit of hindsight, critics in the party faulted the Tory central office, first for not successfully selling Collver, then for ignoring early attacks on him and later, for failure to effectively defend him when these attacks intensified. For all the growing savvy in the party, it seemed Saskatchewan Progressive Conservatives in 1978 were not yet as sharp and quick as the more experienced plotters in New Democrat backrooms. Tories still had some tricks to learn.[14]

Although the NDP liked holding June elections, Blakeney's New Democrats moved confidently into the campaign under high blue September skies. They were energized by the good party polls, perceived advantages of an early election call, and evidence of unfolding personal business troubles for Collver. New Democrat polling showed Allan Blakeney sitting high in voter estimation while Collver's rise in popularity was stalled and Ted Malone was missing in action. In the game of leadership politics, traditional in Saskatchewan from Walter Scott through Jimmy Gardiner to Tommy Douglas, the leader's image, charisma and brokerage talents were extremely important, more so than any current-issue arguments or political ideology. This time the NDP would ditch their comfortable team approach of 1971 and 1975 and pit Blakeney, their tried and trusted paragon, against an apparently vulnerable Collver.

From the outset the NDP identified the Tories as their only threat. Their one interest in the struggling Liberals was a hope that the Grits could draw enough support to split the antigovernment vote. They feared a Liberal collapse. Both Ted Malone's failure to connect and the party's puzzling, late-born platform of referenda made such a rout possible. The NDP platform pledged continued, sound development and management of oil, potash and uranium resources. The platform offered a range of rebates and tax deductions, and urged voters to safeguard the labour, health and welfare gains of recent years under an enlightened NDP administration. Blakeney's superiority as premier, his experience, integrity and leadership, was the major theme of the campaign. New Democrats were eager to compare him to the Tory leader, particularly if a few dark touches could be added to the Collver image.

The Liberals fought gamely on with an unusual platform devised by a committee of party lawyers, themselves perhaps unsure whether they were seriously innovating or just playfully experimenting in a throw-away cause. The core of the platform was government downsizing, outlawing strikes in essential services, and the creation of run-off elections to prevent victory by anyone receiving less than 50% of the vote. These matters would be coded in proposals put to the voters in three referenda spread over the Liberals' first year in office, a period somewhat grandly called the "Year of Decision."[15] Party planners rationalized that the referenda plank would be a different idea and set Liberals apart from other parties. They were right. But how different did the Liberals want to be? Media, NDP and Tories either ignored the proposal, dismissing it as an undergraduate caper, or condemned the idea as a cynical manoeuvre doomed to fail. The term "referenda" was dead air to ordinary folk, and even Liberal candidates were puzzled by the mechanics of the process. What effect their platform had on Liberal fortunes in 1978 can only be guessed. The Grits campaigned under a slogan that promised "A Fresh Start for Saskatchewan." Both it and Ted Malone's leadership failed to excite. Malone marched off beating a toy drum with no one following behind.

"There is a Better Way, the Progressive Conservative Way" read the 1978 Tory slogan that was to map their way to power. The program for this "better way" was not much changed from the 1975 platform. Again, smaller government, enlargement of local government powers, and emphasis on individual initiative were basic. Civil servants would find no comfort in the PC pledge to get rid of political appointments and reduce the size of the provincial public service. A promise to examine welfare policies and a repeat of the law-and-order rhetoric from 1975 might gladden right-wing hearts. The party pledged more income for seniors and deductions for income tax purposes of a portion of mortgage or residential rental payments. Medicare would be protected from premiums or utilization fees. Tories reminded the electorate of Diefenbaker's earlier federal funding for provincial hospital insurance. More aggressively, the PCs promised to eliminate the provincial sales tax and reduce the provincial gas tax. And, of course, more jobs and hospital beds! The party argued that some private ownership of Crown resources should be permitted, and shares in these companies made available to Saskatchewan residents. It seemed a moderate, well-brokered populist right-of-centre platform which, if packaged and marketed properly, should sell well enough. The Tory platform, like the NDP platform, was light on ideological rant, and many of its practical bread-and-butter appeals could also be found in NDP publications.

But this election would not be decided by promise-of-the-day platform hawking. This election would be about leadership and stewardship in

Saskatchewan, and this time what people voted against would be more important than what they voted for.

The 1978 Progressive Conservative campaign wasn't planned as a contest of leaders. The Tories believed Dick Collver could at least hold his own with Allan Blakeney and that would be good enough. They thought Collver, still a relatively fresh face, would appeal to new voters and might even pull ahead of the premier if the electorate had grown tired of Blakeney after watching him in the legislature for 18 years. This time Blakeney would be fighting his sixth provincial campaign, his third as NDP leader. First elected in 1960, he had served in the Douglas and Lloyd cabinets as Minister of Health and Minister of Finance. He'd been on the trail awhile. At first the NDP feared Collver. He was appealing to New Democrats and Liberal supporters.[16]

With their platform in hand and a slate of candidates upscaled from 1975, the Tories would fight this election much as they had the last. There were no new grand strategies, and there would be no surprises. But in 1978 the NDP for the first time fought an electronic campaign guided by weekly polling. There would be surprises for Collver and the Tories. The 1978 campaign had just begun when they found themselves under heavy hostile fire. There would be no preliminary squaring off, no stalking the enemy and no "playing nice." This was war. The NDP war room had ordered a hard, first strike! In the opening week of the campaign NDP radio and television ads were loud at work creating a Medicare scare, warning with evangelical certainty that medical services in Saskatchewan could not be entrusted to a Tory government.

"The Tories will tax the sick," charged a radio voice. Tommy Douglas appeared on television imploring, "Don't let them take it away!" "Them" were the diabolical Saskatchewan Tories, poised to attack Jerusalem and dismantle the sainted Tommy's health-care system, close small hospitals and impose deterrent fees. Surely, it was suggested, if New Democrats were turfed from office, great woe would follow in Saskatchewan, with sickness and lamentation ranging o'er the land. This must not happen!

The attack on Collver and the Tories was starkly disingenuous. All right-wing provincial politicians were wary of disturbing Saskatchewan medicare. In the 1960s Ross Thatcher had dared only to tinker with the system. In 1978 Dick Collver understood better than Thatcher the seminal nature of health-care reform and the political risks of toying with it.[17] This astonishing nonsense was pure "mediscare," something the NDP was good at crafting. The "mediscare" campaign was to frighten folk, particularly old and needy folk, into believing their medical service benefits would be at risk with any government other than the NDP. Did anyone really believe this? Yes, they did!

The focussed campaign planners of the NDP knew something other party fixers were just beginning to notice. From American "fair is foul and foul is fair" professional political consultants, NDP operatives had learned the efficacy and potential of tracking polls, media management, television advertising and fear politics all in full play in the USA at the time. Down there they called fear politics "negative advertising." It could be dirty business, but it worked in the USA. Why not here? The NDP's "mediscare" developed in three stages. First, voters were reminded of the early CCF-NDP struggle for better hospital and medical care services in the province. The people's gratitude to the pioneers of Saskatchewan Medicare had to be rekindled. Remember Tommy Douglas! Then a bad guy who might endanger this health-care heritage had to be found and blamed. Collver was their man. Even though in truth it would be political suicide for any politician to meddle with Medicare, and no political party had any such plans in 1978, NDP propagandists slyly insinuated that Tories were disingenuous in their devotion to Medicare, and that PC leader Collver was eager to destroy the people's health-care program in favour of a private system run for profit. Shame on you, Dick Collver! The last stage was to find a trusted good guy to do battle with the bad guy and defend the people's cherished health-care system against private greed and privilege. Allan Blakeney, of course!

There's a lot of make-believe in politics; nods and winks and little white lies, even entertaining partisan whoppers told to be laughed off like fishermen's boasts. But there are also calculated strategies of deceit, fearmongering and smear, destructive to reputations and careers. Saskatchewan PCs were stunned by the NDP's early campaign "mediscare" blind-siding and personal attacks on Collver. They stumbled and never regained their balance. Tory momentum stalled.

Circumstances, some of his own doing, made it relatively easy to hand a "bad guy" rap to Dick Collver. He had come to Saskatchewan to do business but was soon, perhaps too soon, doing politics. He quickly reconstructed the Tory party apparatus, but by 1978 his own roots and reputation were only barely established. There was much about the PC leader that was unknown. And there were contradictions. Both Collver and his political image-makers struggled to define him. Was he really an accomplished "self-made man" who could bring business savvy and efficiency to government as his partisans boasted, or was he merely a flash-in-the-pan trader and huckster as his detractors insisted? Was he a populist or a hard core right-wing individualist, some convenient combination of the two, or just an ambitious young seeker with no particular ideological compass to follow? Perhaps he was a little like the hero or the villain in the old western cowboy flicks leaving town, with the townsfolk asking after him, "Who was that masked rider?" In politics it's always easy to ascribe qualities either good or bad to someone ill-defined.

Collver failed to establish much reputation in the legislature and didn't appear to be working on it. His spotty performance in debates, showy procedural quarrels with the Speaker, unsubstantiated charges of "filthy hospitals" in northern Saskatchewan, and smutty comments about homosexuals in government did him little good with an increasingly alert media and public.[18] He appeared unable to focus the energies of a spirited yet aimless Tory caucus, a caucus that had too much heigh-ho and too little grounding. Both before and during the 1978 election the NDP exploited Collver's personal business and legal battles with the Baltzans, a family who had been his early mentors and business partners in Saskatoon. The issue was property ownership and a lawsuit was threatened. Later Collver tangled in a court battle with Saskatchewan Government Insurance (SGI) over the bad debts of a failed construction company owner for whom Collver had signed loan guarantees. The NDP argued that SGI, on behalf of the government and people of Saskatchewan, naturally wanted to get its money back. It appeared unseemly that the Tory leader, a man who might be premier, should be squabbling with the province over bad debts. But that coin had another side. Were those debts really his? Collver argued that he had long since sold his shares in the construction company to Calgary businessmen and his personal guarantee was terminated with the sale. He said he was out of the picture and owed no one anything. Obviously a court battle with SGI in the midst of a provincial election campaign did him serious harm. To many it seemed this was a "blatant use of a Crown Corporation for outright political warfare."[19] The lawsuits called into question Collver's managerial competence, perhaps his probity. Both the Liberals and the NDP smiled. A man they had once feared now seemed vulnerable. Ralph Katzman, first elected in 1975 and re-elected in 1978, said, "The butchery done on Collver in 1978 was beyond belief! It caused two dozen Tory candidates to lose by a few votes."[20] Joan Duncan, who won Maple Creek in 1978, thought the Tories' failure to win government in 1978 devastating and blamed it directly on the NDP "Collver smear campaign."[21] Did the people trust Dick Collver? Could they respect him? An NDP 1978 election brochure, "A Solid Success," painted Collver as a platform performer given to off-colour jokes and sly diminutions of Saskatchewan's multicultural nature. The very mention of a Swiss bank account invites suspicion in prairie folk. Such a bank account across the mountains and the seas suggests intrigue and hidden wealth, secret loot stashed away from public view. Prodded by reporters, Dick Collver admitted he had a Swiss bank account. It was for the convenience of his daughter, who was travelling and studying in Europe, he explained. Maybe so, but why a Swiss bank account, the people asked! Collver himself had become an election issue!

From the beginning Blakeney wanted to fight the election on the issue of provincial control of natural resources. "The NDP believes the resources belong to the people of Saskatchewan," he told election audiences, echoing a dictum as old as the province itself. The development of oil, potash and uranium must be provincially controlled and the royalties earned to be spent funding Saskatchewan social democracy.[22] Federal resource policies threatened provincial rights. Who could stand up to Pierre Trudeau and the Ottawa Liberals? Who do you trust to best manage our resources? These were favourite NDP election challenges.[23]

By the last week of the campaign, Tory dreams of winning government had faded. The outcome had become obvious. People knew and trusted Allan Blakeney. They did not know and did not trust Dick Collver. They called him "tricky Dickie." To PC candidates everywhere it seemed as if Allan Blakeney was on all 61 ballots, and he was a hard man to beat. The message at the doors was that Collver was becoming dead weight. Collver himself was never outwardly disheartened but those around him, particularly in his Nipawin riding near the end of the campaign, found him apprehensive and moody as he saw his party's fortunes sink.[24]

During the long polling day, in PC committee rooms across the province there was anticipation of another failure to win power and talk of a "Collver effect." At first there was only anger about the NDP "mediscare" and the nastiness of the NDP treatment of Collver. Later, with ballots counted, more reflective party members concluded that their own campaign management and the Collver leadership had contributed substantially to the party's defeat. More and more attention was paid to this "Collver effect," and the blame game began. The PC executive director, Dave Tkachuk, seen as campaign chairman in 1978, became a lightning rod for the critics and came under attack from within his own party ranks. Some blamed Tkachuk for the party's failure to anticipate the devastating NDP Medicare commercials and respond to them. In particular, disaffected Tories faulted the party's television campaign, which appeared unable to change messages strategically and react quickly to NDP negative advertising. Colin Thatcher, Progressive Conservative candidate in Thunder Creek, in his account of the 1978 campaign was sharply critical of Tkachuk and the party's response to the attacks on Collver's credibility:

> Our advertising was bad and by the time we realized how badly we had been hurt and began our stumbling and fumbling to recover from it, it was too late. Our campaign headquarters was frozen and unable to react to the changing situations. There was no plan of attack or, for that matter, of defense.[25]

Allan Blakeney was a big winner in 1978. The NDP won the October 18 election with 48% of the vote and 44 of the 61 seats in the legislature. Their popular vote increased 8% over 1975. The Tories took 38% of the vote, an increase of 10% over 1975, and 17 seats, an increase of 10 seats over their 1975 total. Increases, yes, but Progressive Conservative hopes of forming government were dashed.

The Liberal Party was wiped out. It chalked up only 14% of the vote, an 18% plummet from its 1975 showing, losing all of its legislative seats, including leader Ted Malone's Regina-Lakeview. In 58 of the 61 ridings, Liberals ran third and most lost their deposits. It was a disaster. Across the province Liberal election headquarters closed up early that night and Grits went home to bed.

The much-hoped-for PC breakthrough in the cities didn't happen. New Democrats won all the Saskatoon, Moose Jaw and Prince Albert seats, and all but one of the Regina ridings. The NDP captured Prince Albert-Duck Lake and Saskatoon-Sutherland, seats taken by the Tories in recent by-elections. The PCs remained a town and country party with solid rural strength, but a party still awaiting the urban recruits that would give it victory. Next time.

Shortly after the election Tory candidates, winners and losers, gathered in Regina with Dick Collver and provincial campaign personnel to appraise the situation.[26] What had happened? Whose fault? The surface mood was one of disappointment. As for Collver, there was no blood-letting, but neither was there much talk of the considerable gains made by the party on October 18, or any loud "Three Cheers for the Leader" rung up in chorus. Underneath the meeting's calm there were smoulderings about the leader's credibility gap, public questionings everyone knew had hurt them badly. Dick Collver's days at the top were numbered. These would be moody, unsettling days for him.

What had the party expected of him? Miracles, maybe! He had provided some of these. But he had run out of magic. The NDP's adept exploitation of the Collver integrity issue had done its work. Collver's negotiating powers, his ability to bridge compromises and build coalitions, all essential functions of party leadership, were seriously weakened by his reputed scrambled ethics and perceived business mismanagement. The election reversal capped it for him. His resignation as leader and departure from electoral politics was assured.

For a year Collver stayed on as PC leader, seldom in the legislature, sometimes fundraising, often away in Arizona seeking personal investment opportunities. In the spring of 1979 he purchased property in Wickenburg, Arizona, and began to do business in land sales. He made no secret of his intention to serve out his term as MLA for Nipawin and then move south to permanent residence in the United States.

Collver's critics saw his move to Arizona as proof that his meteoric political career had been no more than a dalliance with public service. They said he was never a public servant. They thought him only a gamester who, through faults of his own, had lost the roll of the dice and left the table in a disgruntled huff. Collver's Progressive Conservatives were disturbed by his abrupt and distasteful departure from public life. What was the cause of it? His failure to win his goal of the premiership would understandably lead to dejection and a degree of world-weariness in the man, but what can be said of Collver's embarrassing descent from high party office to lost leader and renegade? He appears to have been overcome by shattered dreams, broken pride, and bitterness brewed by the personal attacks of his enemies in politics. Perhaps Dick Collver was more vulnerable and more easily wounded than his partisans knew.

His friends found it sad that so much energy and talent had wasted away to naught, that so much hope and promise had been dashed, that it had been "song sung blue." There was genuine fondness for Collver, more so on the exciting upscale of his career than on its decline, but there was affection. Among his inner circle of party associates there remained a steadfast loyalty. Yet, even they knew it was time for him to go. They knew he was no pilgrim in politics. They knew he was only a traveller and one with whom many Tories would not like to take another journey.

On November 10, 1979, the party elected a new leader. Dick Collver took little notice of the man who replaced him or of the newly installed PC provincial president and executive. He had something else on his mind.

When the legislature reconvened in early 1980, Collver announced that he would form a new political party in Saskatchewan. His career as a Saskatchewan Tory ended on an appalling note of frivolity and betrayal when he abruptly left the party to sit first as an Independent and then, joined by another PC MLA, as the leader of the "Unionest Party," a party dedicated to Saskatchewan leaving the Canadian federation and joining the United States of America. After his 1978 defeat Collver knew he would never be first man in the province. Yet he still burst with almost ungovernable ego and energy. He had to do something! He needed a new experience, a new adventure. Why not a new party? His successor as PC leader, Grant Devine, was "disappointed" by Collver's decision to leave Tory ranks but, perhaps better than anyone else, understood that Collver's was a "pent-up, personal drive for activity and expression that couldn't be denied."[27] Grant Devine was a kinder judge of Collver than most observers at the time. Collver would spend the remaining months of his legislative term in this bizarre advocacy, providing entertainment for leering NDP benches and embarrassment for erstwhile Tory colleagues watching an inglorious flame out.

In 1979, in an apparently "exhilarated state," to use Diefenbaker's euphemism, Collver fired a .357 magnum revolver into the air from the window of his Regina apartment. He was charged with illegal possession and improper use of a firearm.[28]

When all of this ended, it must have been with considerable relief that his former party and his adopted province bade him farewell.

13

An Emergent Champion

The year between Collver's defeat in 1978 and the November 10, 1979, Tory leadership convention was a muddled period for the party. With Collver away from the legislature most of the time, and not particularly focussed when he did attend, the party's legislative performance was unpredictable. Some adult supervision would have helped. The party was broke. Its grassroots morale was low, and local organizations everywhere were idling. Tory chances of shaping provincial affairs appeared to have dimmed.

No successor to Collver was in sight, nor was there any particularly eager search for one underway until the last few months before the convention call. Eric Berntson, MLA for Souris-Cannington, could have had the leadership but didn't want it. Gary Lane, not unexpectedly, was said to covet the job, as he had the Liberal leadership after Dave Steuart's exit but now, as then, he was neither loved enough nor trusted enough to be a real contender. The party wanted a white knight, a dream candidate, someone with Dick Collver's positives and none of his flaws.

In spite of the bands, bagpipes and other razzle-dazzle trimmings of American-style orchestration, the PC leadership convention in Saskatoon's Centennial Auditorium had an uncertainty about it. Was this leadership field strong enough? Did any of the three hopefuls have a little magic? Did a favourable political wind sit in the shoulder of the Tory sail? No one was sure.

The three candidates were: a Regina car dealer, Regina South MLA Paul Rousseau; a farmer and Wolesley school principal, Indian Head-Wolseley MLA Graham Taylor, by convention time considered the front runner; and 35-year-old Dr. Grant Devine, a University of Saskatchewan Professor of Agricultural Economics from Saskatoon. Devine had been defeated in Saskatoon-Nutana in the 1978 provincial election.

Each man was allotted 45 minutes for a demonstration and candidate's speech. Grant Devine delivered an earnest, philosophical declaration about family values, individual initiative and freedom of enterprise. He crowded the stage with supporters and was escorted to the podium by uniformed buglers. Devine was well received and was obviously an able platform performer. Paul Rousseau, using only a part of his allotted time, promised a business-like approach to government, suggesting that his experience running a car dealership would equip him to provide it. Used car salesmen jokes sniggered around him. His sales pitch won only quiet applause.[1] Graham Taylor's general appeal for change and economic diversification drew a somewhat warmer response, but not much. Devine's colourful convention demonstration and address lifted him into the lead.

Grant Devine won an easy first-ballot victory with 418 votes. No real surprise. Graham Taylor polled 201 votes and Paul Rousseau trailed with 74 votes. Although no particular effort had been made by convention planners to conjure stardust memories of the departed Dick Collver, some attending this convention may have suspected that a relatively low entry-level requirement had been attached to the race to succeed him. It hadn't been an exciting race, and the unseasoned and untried winner remained a stranger to many. They would have to get to know Dr. Grant Devine.

Devine was a surprise package. He was a home-grown farm boy with a PhD in Agricultural Economics from Ohio State University. He had been raised on a farm where his grandfather homesteaded near Moose Jaw and had gone on to gain a Master's degree in Business Administration and a Master's degree in Agricultural Economics from Alberta before earning his Doctorate from Ohio State. Devine's rural background was more important than his academic achievements to PC Party faithful. As a boy he had worked on the farm, played piano, excelled in baseball, ridden horseback and taken part in student government. He had been a keen and popular student at university and a religious, family-oriented young man when he came to Saskatoon to teach Agricultural Marketing and Consumer Economics at the University of Saskatchewan. Quite a package. Then came politics. He was attracted by Dick Collver's ambiguous mix of populism and right-of-centre enthusiasms and ran for the PCs in Saskatoon-Nutana in 1978. Like all Tory candidates in Saskatoon that year, he was badly beaten by the NDP.

Devine didn't feel defeated. From his boyhood he drew strong family and Christian beliefs that enriched his emerging trust in private enterprise and individual initiative. He was convinced that these values could be expressed in politics and applied in government. He became more than an observer of the new right in Saskatchewan; he became a fervent activist.

The convention that chose him as leader had yet to see him lead. His energy and appeal as a campaigner would surprise them and prove decisive for the party in its upcoming battle with the NDP. Devine liked a bit of show-biz in politics and was good at it. A favourite lively saying of his was, "Give 'er snoose Bruce!" Before becoming a player, Grant Devine had been a student of politics and knew that electoral politics in Saskatchewan has always been brokerage politics. Saskatchewan political parties have always hocked pragmatic solutions to perceived current problems in order to build coalitions and win government.[2] Saskatchewan parties, all essentially moderate and centrist, have not sought long-term fundamental changes and social rearrangement. They have not chased ideological goals nor been obsessed with the pursuit of abstractions. The ideological orientation and initial stable partisan support of the early CCF as a protest party in drought and depression years made them for a time some exception to this. But only until the protest cooled. Then, no longer a mission, a movement or a crusade, they became a political party like all the others, seeking to satisfy the voter as citizen and consumer.

In Saskatchewan there have always been emotive, philosophical slogans like the 1944 CCF "Humanity First" and the 1982 Tory "There's So Much More We Can Be," but it has been the concrete, bread-and-butter, everyday stuff that mattered. What have always sold are promises of tax review, low energy costs, farm security, more health and education dollars, new jobs, better roads, wider provincial rights, industrial growth and attractive leadership. These win elections. From the outset Devine seemed to understand this.

Grant Devine would have to wait two years and longer before fighting his first provincial election. The intervening months spent as a party and opposition leader without a seat in the legislature were painful, even dangerous for him. NDP wags sniped at him in the Assembly, calling the seatless and. absent Tory chieftain "Dr. Invisible." There were novices and malcontents in his own caucus, a caucus seen by critics as a pack of uncontrollables. Devine, untried, had yet to gain their confidence. Some were restless and uncertain about him. Colin Thatcher, Tory MLA for Thunder Creek, considered Devine "an inept Leader of the Opposition." He characterized Devine as "an insecure, indecisive person who found talk much easier than performance."[3] At the time, Thatcher was himself a troubled and hostile personality and was given little credence. A very different assessment of Devine in caucus is made by former Rosthern Tory MLA Ralph Katzman, who found Devine "a patient and skilled consensus builder, a leader highly regarded by our caucus."[4]

In the fall of 1980 three provincial by-elections were held, and Devine was nominated in Estevan, a safe southeastern riding opened especially for him by the resignation of Bob Larter, a popular local PC MLA. At last, it seemed, he could escape the public gallery and lead his Tory forces from the Assembly floor. This didn't happen. Devine lost the by-election. The PC campaign in Estevan was a loser from the beginning. Devine and his wife Chantal were a handsome, charming couple who campaigned tirelessly but didn't yet connect with Estevan folks. To them, Devine remained a Professor of Agricultural Economics parachuted into the seat from Saskatoon. His Tory campaign, ignoring locals and handled out of Regina, failed to transfer the PC vote to the new man. Ken Waschuk, a PC operative from Regina, described the campaign as a poorly conceived and managed affair conducted by amateurs. "It was a typical smart-guy election" he said. "We party guys from Regina went down there and didn't call in the locals. We paid the price."[5]

The entry of a credible Liberal candidate, a former Liberal Member of Parliament and future Liberal provincial leader, Ralph Goodale, sealed Devine's fate. Goodale divided the anti-government vote, and the seat returned to the NDP. Devine lost Estevan by 98 votes, a heart-breaking squeaker, a huge embarrassment to him and the party. That night he told a gloomy crowd at Tory election headquarters that he would not abandon Estevan. "I'll be back," he vowed. "Next time, we'll win!" He would have to wait many months for "next time" to roll around; but when it came, it was a time of Tory jubilation and startling consequences for Saskatchewan.

The defeat in Estevan was accompanied by a surprising Tory by-election win that same day in Kelsey-Tisdale, a seat that had been held by the NDP. A third by-election held in North Battleford was an easy NDP win in another of their strongholds. The numbers in the legislature were unchanged. The PCs had held their own but failed to elect their leader. The party's medical chart would have to read "listed in serious but stable condition." With a provincial election expected for June 1982, many Tories were testy and despairing about the party's readiness to fight a campaign. Not so, the party leader!

Grant Devine was busy in the field visiting communities, civic leaders, local newspaper offices, service clubs, introducing himself and searching for candidates. He was beginning to find his voice and his way in politics, beginning to enjoy the fight, gathering confidence in himself as audiences responded to the colour and vigour of his call for change. A powerful platform performer, a campaigner of rare energy and talent was emerging.

In 1982, as he headed into his third election campaign as premier, Allan Blakeney was aware that Saskatchewan was facing a recession. With declining potash markets, falling grain prices, inflation and high interest rates, the provincial economy was threatened. Yet NDP polling remained positive, and he was encouraged to call an election before things worsened. What NDP pollsters failed to discover was the depth of Saskatchewan voters' fears about their own household economies, seriously threatened by rising gas prices, soaring home mortgage interest rates and creeping unemployment. Saskatchewan voters worried about themselves and wondered what the "Tested and Trusted" people's consuls Blakeney and Romanow, the government House Leader, were doing to help them! Not much, they thought!

The Saskatchewan voter cared little about constitutional haggling, Crow Rate disputes or puzzling academic debates with Ottawa about provincial resource management. They cared about their own pocket books! Many of them thought Allan Blakeney and his government had been around a very long time and were all tired out. Time to go! With Liberals now an endangered species, the PCs were the only practical alternative to the governing New Democrats. If there was going to be a change, it would have to be to Grant Devine. Saskatchewan Tories were gaining momentum.

Blakeney made the election call at his own nominating convention in Regina-Elphinstone. He called it for April 26. This time there could be no NDP Collver-bashing or "mediscare" blindsiding. Blakeney would campaign on the record of his government, offering more of the same "good government." Saskatchewan voters were told that Blakeney's was a "Tested and Trusted" government brought to them by "The People Who Care." These caring people, the NDP advertising blitz announced, deserved re-election. They expected to get it! Their last budget was balanced. They had imposed no tax increases. Their "Family of Crown Corporations" was apparently doing good business under prudent management. The government promised new money for nursing homes, low-rental housing and a program to control mortgage rates to relieve lower-income families. Once again NDP strategists featured Premier Allan Blakeney as leader, an experienced, gifted statesman admired across the nation and respected at home. As a campaigner some may have thought him a tad smug and preachy, but who in the NDP lead team was otherwise? Their belief in their own personal stars and in the hegemonic right of Saskatchewan social democrats to govern the province made them too comfortable and too sure of the outcome of the 28-day campaign just begun.

From the start the Tories sensed that an uncertain electorate was shopping for change. The NDP political engineers were slow to gauge this or dared not admit it even to themselves. For a time they were blissfully unaware they were in a fight they might lose. Early in 1982 the Saskatchewan Progressive Conservatives had obtained a substantial line of bank credit. With that they were very much in the campaign advertising game. They also believed themselves only two percentage points of decided voters behind the NDP, with a whopping 35% of voters undecided and fretful.[6] For the first time ever the Progressive Conservative Party entered a provincial campaign armed by state-of-the-art polling information to plumb and analyze public attitudes and guide their attacks on the enemy. Decima, a first-rate polling firm, was hired for the job. Decima pollsters found that the Saskatchewan people were worried about inflation, interest rates and high taxes. Decima advised Tory strategists that voters were tiring of the government and found the NDP leadership arrogant and unresponsive, governing high above the heads of the people. Decima polling told Grant Devine that Allan Blakeney was vulnerable. Tory planners knew the political situation was fluid.[7] They had hopes of winning the 1982 election.

The lead Tory planner was the party's superb new campaign chairman, Bill McKnight, Member of Parliament for Kindersley-Lloydminster. McKnight had served as provincial president during the roller-coaster Dick Collver years. He was a natural for the campaign chairmanship. McKnight was bluff and personable, a skilled organizer and an experienced team leader. Unlike the sometimes uneven and troubled direction of Tkachuk and Collver in 1978, McKnight's campaign leadership proved smooth, relaxed and big-pictured. This guy was right out of a "Human Resource Management" manual! McKnight was an innovator. In 1982 he wanted no more of the traditional strategic saving of sexy platform highlights until near the end of a campaign. He wanted a jump start and directed an aggressive marketing of the Tory platform in the first few days of the campaign. "Do it now! Do it first!," he urged.[8] In this election the PCs did what the NDP had always done and brought into the province a slew of out-of-province Tory MPs, MLAs and professional campaign workers from across Canada to help out. And they did. In 1982 McKnight and his PC planners used aircraft as never before. The Tory campaign took to the air with workers and speakers flown to events around the province, gathering voter support and media attention. McKnight himself put in a lot of flight time, keeping a wary eye on an unfolding campaign that would surprise just about everyone.

Then there was the leader himself. Grant Devine had a mission to lead the province in a sharp turn to the right. "Profit has become a dirty word in Saskatchewan," he said. "We have to become proud of profit."[9] Once in office there would be no dawdling along trying to build consensus in a divided Saskatchewan. He would proceed in a straight line to overthrow what he called "socialist tyranny" and restore personal ambition, aspiration and competition—qualities the NDP had replaced with mediocrity.[10] To do this Devine was willing to polarize the province if necessary to get things done. He believed his Tory government could build a strong new pro-business, free-enterprise culture in Saskatchewan, and that once the people tasted these new freedoms, they would never look back. His was "conviction" politics. He was possessed by a rightist calling that was more urgent and genuine than that of Dick Collver, whose motivation was far more contingent and strategic. Collver did not have the passion and the zeal of the revolutionary. Grant Devine did. On the early campaign trail Grant Devine was shifting easily from straight talk, often in bursts of colloquial fragments, to crafted oratorical eloquence. His versatility as a public speaker was impressing Tory supporters and worrying Blakeney handlers, who found their own man somewhat reserved and academic by comparison. In Saskatchewan politics, at times of unrest and dissent, a little demagoguery has always been effective. Witness Gardiner, Diefenbaker and Tommy Douglas! Devine fought an aggressive campaign, taking the fight directly to the premier. He drew howls of laughter from partisan audiences when he mocked the NDP campaign slogan "Tested and Trusted," suggesting that "rusted and busted" would better describe the Blakeney government. Devine was contemptuous of the NDP's "Family of Crown Corporations" television advertising that boasted of excellence in management and public service. He'd ask, "What about the real flesh and blood Saskatchewan families struggling under a double yoke of inflation and taxation? If things are so good," Devine mocked, "where's the prosperity and where are our children?"[11]

"Devine's relentless, day-by-day campaign and rising Tory polls caught the NDP flat-footed and put Blakeney on the defensive for most of the campaign, looking desperate, out of touch and just plain bewildered at times."[12] An observer of past Saskatchewan political campaigns might have been more than a little reminded of a puckish Tommy Douglas tormenting his opponents in earlier years.

The Tory campaign opened with a sharp attack on the NDP claim that they were "the people who care." "Care about what?" Devine argued that New Democrats cared only about bigger government, larger Crown corporations, more bureaucracy and government planning. They didn't care about people! Devine's populist pitch in the first week of the campaign was that New

Grant Devine and his wife, Chantal, campaigning during the 1982 provincial election. Devine's Progressive Conservatives won a landslide victory (SAB 84-1494-R16-12).

Democrats were governing above the masses and out of touch with people. It was the PCs, their advertisements boasted, who really cared, and a PC government would prove they cared by eliminating the provincial gas tax, controlling mortgage interest rates, providing low interest loans to young farmers, and increasing natural gas and telephone service in rural Saskatchewan. A Devine government would set free the entrepreneurial spirit of the people, encouraging investment, enterprise and initiative. A Devine administration would value individual self-worth and moral responsibility. "There's So Much More We Can Be" was the party slogan in 1982, a mix of Chamber of Commerce boosterism and vapid high-school Graduation Day spiel. A second, more robust Tory slogan, "Open for Business," was resurrected from an old Ross Thatcher campaign.

The lavish PC promises of tax cuts and mortgage interest rate control announced in the first days of the campaign dazzled the NDP. Devine jumped into a lead which he never relinquished. The Tory campaign had excitement and momentum from the start. The NDP campaign was defensive and sluggish. It couldn't catch up. Grant Devine provided day-to-day razzle-dazzle performances before larger and larger crowds as he criss-crossed the province calling for a "coalition of common sense."

Blakeney's New Democrats fought back with their own promises of tax relief measures, home-ownership grants, assistance to young farmers and health-care improvements, but they had lost much of their audience. The voters weren't really listening. Saskatchewan wanted a change. People wanted to share in the benefits of the new economic vitality and wealth offered by the PCs and felt assured that their existing provincial services and social programs would be secure under new management in Regina. They had nothing to lose!

Even organized labour, always a strong NDP power base, providing money, manpower and votes, held back this time. Before the election call the Blakeney government had ended a 16-day provincial hospital workers' strike by legislating them back to work and prohibiting strike action in any essential service during an election campaign. This back-to-work legislation was seen by labour as an outrageous betrayal of workers by a government traditionally friendly to them. Labour sat on their hands. They stayed home on election day, doing significant damage to NDP candidates in urban ridings. The Tories publicly clucked and tut-tutted in feigned disapproval of the legislation, hoping to grab a piece of the disenchanted labour vote. Privately, they were overjoyed with the angry rift between the government and its erstwhile friends. Tories thought roughing up labour just before a provincial election an astounding NDP miscalculation. And it was!

In the last days of the campaign Grant Devine brought the PC campaign to enemy territory. He planned a last major rally in Regina, a heavy trade union and civil service centre and an NDP stronghold. Tory organizers had some apprehension about the success of the rally. They needn't have worried. Regina's Centre of the Arts filled quickly with the biggest rally of the campaign. That night 3,600 cheering, stomping, pumped-up Tory partisans gave the PCs a tumultuous demonstration not seen in Saskatchewan since the 1950s with the Douglas-Coldwell CCF rallies in the Regina Armories and the Trianon Ballroom. There was jubilation in the packed auditorium. The hall rocked like a revival meeting. On stage a glowing Grant Devine shouted above the uproar, "There's so much more we can be!" He believed this, and they believed him! Election day, Monday, April 26, was Blue Monday in Saskatchewan, but it wasn't the PCs singing the blues. That day they would paint the province's electoral map Tory blue as they registered an astonishing landslide victory and returned to power after more than 50 years in the wilderness. At last, they would prevail in the prairie socialist wonderland. They would reach their promised land.

Early on election night Progressive Conservative victories exploded across the province. Everywhere PC candidates grabbed quick, large leads and held them. In Estevan organizers moved their celebration from the PC Committee Rooms to the curling rink to house a huge election night victory rally. That night 700 noisy Tories packed the curling rink and joyfully welcomed Grant Devine to the stage to claim victory in Estevan and across the province. His glowing, boyish exuberance rolled out over a giddy partisan crowd that couldn't get enough of him and wouldn't let him go. They knew that Estevan that day had elected a Premier of Saskatchewan. "We're going to be number one," Devine shouted from the platform.[13]

Gone were the usual long election-night counts and teeter-totter races. The Tories won government with 54% of the vote and 55 seats in the 64-seat legislature. Former Tory leader Bill Boyd, in an August 2003 interview with the author, exclaimed, "If the 1982 campaign had lasted another 10 days, Devine might have won 60 of the 64 seats, if not them all."[14] Allan Blakeney and an incredulous NDP were hurled out of office, reduced to a rump opposition of nine shell-shocked members elected with 37% of the vote. Tory candidates swept to victories in urban Saskatchewan, defeating even the redoubtable Attorney General Roy Romanow in Saskatoon-Riversdale.

Grant Devine had sunshine on his shoulders. He was Premier of Saskatchewan. Thus began the "Devine years" as they would come to be known and remembered.

Grant Devine, shortly after being elected as Premier of Saskatchewan in 1982. After almost 50 years in the political wilderness, Saskatchewan Tories were back in power (SAB 82-773-0024).

14

Blue Skies Smiling?

The new government was sworn into office in an outdoor ceremony in front of the Legislative Building. Tory MLAs had trekked from across the province to the legislature and milled about the roadway and lawns with family, friends and assorted curious onlookers. Their chatter and exaggerated camaraderie was reminiscent of a high school reunion or a company picnic. The newly elected were salad-green and still all tuckered out from hometown victory celebrations. They looked more amazed than triumphant, perhaps asking themselves, "What happens now?" It was a big show. Before a large crowd and a provincial television audience the new premier shouted "People all across Canada are watching us." They were, perhaps with varying degrees of hope and apprehension.[1]

New cabinet members ranged from adventuring rookies to wide-eyed, right-wing reformers. The caucus was woefully inexperienced, a handful elected in 1975 and a few more in 1978. Devine himself had no legislative experience until his own 1982 win in Estevan. Devine's cabinet was made up of 17 members. It included two women—Joan Duncan, MLA for Maple Creek and Pat Smith, MLA for Swift Current—the first women ever to serve in a Saskatchewan cabinet. None of the members had ever served in a cabinet before. Twelve of the 17 new ministers represented rural constituencies. By occupation there were six farmers, four business operators, four teachers, two lawyers and a public relations manager.

Experience aside, together they were strong in a shared mission to free Saskatchewan from what they saw as stultifying NDP collectivist restraints. The sheer size of their victory gave them overweening confidence and a deceptive sense of a sweeping neo-conservative mandate. For them, this was showtime! Devine brought his two leadership opponents into the cabinet, Graham Taylor in Health and Paul Rousseau in Industry. Devine's two mentors in the earlier leadership race, farmer Eric Berntson and lawyer Bob Andrew were named Minister of Agriculture and Minister of Finance respectively. Berntson, from the beginning of the Devine years, was the leader of the band in all matters, second only to the premier. Devine's first cabinet was largely town and country. The big city members were new in politics and would have to season awhile before their later appointments to cabinet. After the long wait the Tory roller-coaster years in power began. These would be aggressive years, roiling years of trial and error, success and failure, years that would end in disillusion and scandal.

"Let's keep a good thing going" was one of the NDP's 1982 election slogans. The 11-year-old "good government" of Allan Blakeney had in many ways been a good government. Blakeney himself was recognized as an able veteran in the top job. The government had established Crowns in oil, potash and uranium, increasing provincial revenues. Blakeney had added to the province's health services with prescription drugs, chiropractic care and children's dental-care legislation. The province's minimum wages were among the highest in Canada, and its unemployment numbers were below the national average. The last Saskatchewan budget was balanced. Yet in 1982 the voters said "enough!" They wanted change. In particular, they wanted to share in the new prosperity promised in Devine's ebullient campaign.

The Tories were quick to keep their two key "bread-and-butter" promises of removing the gas tax and pegging the home mortgage interest rate at 13.5%. This cost the province $160 million. Reductions in oil royalties further drained provincial coffers, and failed the "open for business" test that suggested lowering the cost of doing business in Saskatchewan would stimulate private-sector investment and job creation, producing new prosperity in the province. This didn't happen. There was no sudden flow of investment dollars to the province or change in Saskatchewan's dreary investment climate. Regardless of who was in power, Saskatchewan was still the same small prairie island, a long way from outside markets and the attention of the east and corporate Canada.

The Tories' first year produced a startling budget deficit of $227 million, a flood of red ink after a succession of NDP balanced budgets. This, the government pronounced, was manageable, cyclical, even stimulative. Not to worry! But this, the Tories' first deficit, was followed by deficit after deficit, building to a massive accumulated provincial debt of $5 billion plus in 1991 when they were toppled from power. So much for supply-side economic magic and the comfort of Devine's promise to restore investor confidence and "personal ambition, aspiration and competition" in Saskatchewan.

Government strategists knew that publicly owned Crown corporations—both utility Crowns and resource Crowns—had become provincial institutions, part of the traditional private, public and cooperative mixed economy of the province with which the people were comfortable, if not entirely happy. Serious thoughts of selling off the Crowns would have to wait until more propitious times. In the meantime, the Tories believed there was a bloated government to shrink, a hostile civil service to purge, free-ranging labour unions to kennel, and patronage to dispense to safe, right-minded friends. There seemed an urgency, a touch of paranoia in each of these enthusiasms. Many Tories with small business and rural regular-folk backgrounds were spooked by an NDP professional, bureaucratic civil service they thought poised everywhere in government to sabotage the new Tory order of things in Regina.

Tories believed "Big Government" in Saskatchewan had been built systematically over time by CCF and NDP administrations, and now brimmed with socialist sympathizers. "Big Labour" supported the New Democrats and wanted bigger and bigger government and a bigger and bigger unionized civil service to provide labour with more jobs, bargaining power and political clout. Big government civil servants, the Tories argued, substituted a flaccid, ambiguous professionalism for the initiative, decisiveness and energy that leaner government and private-sector business would demand. The new PC government had changes to make.

The government disparaged unionism, weakened public-sector unions, attacked the right to strike and waged war on the civil service, seeking to reduce it, to tame it, even in many instances to replace it. Deputy ministers, chairmen of Crown corporations, Order-in-Council appointees, senior officials and a range of lesser personnel thought to be NDP partisans were fired, losing their jobs to Tory partisans as the provincial bureaucracy was painted blue. "The extent of the purge was unprecedented in post-war political history in Canada."[2] There was dismay and fear within the Saskatchewan public service. Civil servants looked over their shoulders into the eyes of Orwellian Big Brothers. The civil service expected some changes with a new government but nothing this brutal. For them, this seemed an ugly caricature of an orderly transition process. The little NDP opposition whimpered "foul" and there was some outcry from the media, but the lay-offs and firings drew surprisingly little general censure at the time. In the hinterland people didn't really like civil servants all that much anyway. Many warlike Tories cheered the government on, calling the purges cleansing and healthy. Business voices joined the clamour to "clean up the socialist public service." "Off with their heads!" "Down with the Reds!"

Before their first term ended the Tories' designs on the Crown corporations, their flirtation with privatization, began to show. A lively anti-Crown corporation lobby was active in Saskatchewan business and Tory party circles. It was particularly vocal after the PC landslide in 1982. The lobby's simple mantra read that private enterprise was more energized and efficient than publicly owned Crown corporations. The lobby insisted that the Crowns stifled economic growth by limiting opportunities for private investment. Saskatchewan, they argued, wasn't "open for business" as long as so much of its business was done by government. They disputed the socialist claim that the private-sector profit motive drove up costs. Whereas the older traditional utility Crowns dating back to the Tommy Douglas years were relatively safe in 1982, the resource Crowns—oil, potash and uranium—were not. The Tories weren't ready yet for wholesale marketing of the Crowns, but they were eager to restrain Crown growth and begin a piecemeal sale of many of them. Privatization of SaskOil, the Potash Corporation of Saskatchewan (PCS) and the Saskatchewan Mining Development Corporation's uranium industry all would be plotted in Devine's first term and continue in earnest during his second.

Premier Grant Devine addressing the "Open for Business" conference, November 1982 (SAB 82-2101-R4-5).

The PC government approached the end of its first term with a mixture of distraction and resolution. Things had not gone all that well for them in their first four years in office. A succession of deficits, growing interest payments on provincial debt, drought, and a developing farm income crisis beyond the control of government clearly posed electoral problems for Grant Devine. Still, the sheen of the landslide victors of 1982 hadn't entirely worn off and Tories, driven by neo-conservative ideology, optimistically believed that privatization with better public marketing in a second term would yield salutary results and stabilize the province's shaky economics.

Devine believed that the Saskatchewan economy would perform well once freed from socialist controls, and a vibrant new business spirit could be built. He called an "Open for Business" conference in Regina in November 1982 to attract international investors to the province. "Private business is welcome in Saskatchewan." Investor confidence had to be created. A new image was needed and old attitudes and perceptions changed. Devine in his first term believed that Crown corporations in the resource sector were a valuable part of the provincial economy. He believed that a balance between public sector and private sector could be achieved and that Crowns should "compliment rather than compete with Saskatchewan citizens."[3]

The Saskatchewan economy did not cooperate with the new Tory premier's plans to open Saskatchewan for business. High inventories and reduced production of potash in the early 1980s resulted from soft international markets, and 1,200 PCS workers had to be laid off. In the same period the provincial uranium industry suffered weak demand and low prices.

The provincial oil industry faced tumbling oil prices in 1986 and the loss of 5,000 jobs in the oil patch. The farm economy was weak during the 1980s. Poor growing conditions and rising costs of shipping grain to market caused the most grievous problems. Foremost of these was the collapse of commodity prices. In mid-decade the United States and the European Economic Community began a subsidy war to capture a larger share of the international market for their own producers. These huge farm subsidies resulted in an oversupply of grain, leaving Saskatchewan farmers with depressed grain prices and millions of bushels of unwanted grain. Loan payments on newly purchased farmland could not be met and farmer debt mounted. The value of farmland depreciated during the period.

In 1985 the Tories' provincial budget showed a $584 million deficit and the accumulated debt of Saskatchewan neared the $2 billion mark. With the province suffering drought and recession the government had to abandon its popular 1982 election pledges to eliminate the 5% sales tax and reduce the provincial income tax. Instead, they imposed a new 1% flat tax which would rise to 2% in 1988 and a tax on the people's transport, the used car. So much for "There's so much more we can be." It was obvious that fulfilling Tory election promises that had won government for them had now put Saskatchewan into deficit. The province would remain there trying to pay interest payments on a mounting provincial debt. Dr. Bill Waiser describes the Devine government in its first term as "continuously spending more than it took in like a losing gambler who did not know when to quit."[4]

Soon, very soon, there must be a provincial election. For this election the government would have to fight more than a little defensively, crafting a campaign that obscured the first-term alienations, forgotten promises, deficits and threatened treasury, a campaign that again must set out to woo the electorate with visions of a new entrepreneurial Saskatchewan, a land of commerce and opportunity. All of this Saskatchewan folk had been promised before. They would be told to wait a little longer! PC backrooms buzzed with Tory wizards at work mapping out a new election strategy. Maybe the old pocketbook magic would work again! Remember the gas tax nixing and the pegged mortgage interest rates of 1982? Play it again Sam! The Tory rural base with its decisive farm vote must be massaged and protected. Saskatchewan farm income needed propping up. Maybe federal Tory friends back east could help.

Premier Grant Devine called an election for October 20, 1986. In spite of deficits, growing provincial debt, the faltering "open for business" campaign, "iffy" polls and urban political drift back to the NDP, Devine was cautiously confident. From the start Tories knew their rural base, if it held, could re-elect them. The Tories were now the government. In 1982 the NDP had been in power, and spending public money had broadcast extravagant praise for their "Family of Crown Corporations." This NDP description of the Crowns as family had a comforting populist warmth that must have drawn an NDP vote or two. Now it was the Tories' time to advertise using public dollars, and government television advertisements called "Saskatchewan Builds" featured scenes of happy Saskatchewan folk of town and country together building their homeland province. Heigh-ho, heigh-ho! How could anyone resist the schmooze of it? It was a good campaign lure! If the voters' minds could be kept off the worsening financial state of things and away from tiring right-wing ideological rant, they might buy into the practical Tory message, "Keep on Building Saskatchewan," and find hope in the new tomorrow it promised. The sales pitch would be carried across the province by the premier, a superb campaigner and himself now Saskatchewan's Minister of Agriculture.

Devine had always scorned the NDP farmland ownership program. Once in office he threw out the NDP Land Bank and established a land ownership policy of his own. With the old, offending NDP Land Bank the government would buy farmland from older retiring farmers eager to sell the land, and lease it to younger farmers who couldn't afford to buy the land but wanted to get established in farming. The young lease-holders were given the right to buy the land they were renting from the government after a five-year period if they were able and wished to do so. Progressive Conservatives objected to the Land Bank. They saw the government, not individual farmers ending up with the title to the land. The Tories likened a concentration of farm lands in government hands to Russian-style "collective farms," with Saskatchewan farmers becoming "share croppers."[5] Devine's new Farm Purchase Program offered young farmers 10-year guaranteed loans at 8% for the first five years and 12% for the final five years. These low-interest loans to young farmers wanting to buy land played extremely well with Saskatchewan farm voters. It is no exaggeration to suggest that Grant Devine never took his eyes off the rural vote. He knew it was crucial to his securing and holding power. Besides, he genuinely cared about farmers. He thought of himself as one of them. Devine brought natural gas and telephone service to more and more farm homes, livestock cash advances and rebates on farm fuel were made available, and legislation passed protecting farmers from farm foreclosures. It had been a genuinely good performance by the Devine government. Town and country voters would remember this on polling day.

The March 1986 provincial budget had shown yet another deficit, at first estimated as $389 million, later proving three times greater. The government did not dwell on the deficit. Instead it hurried on to more spending. It introduced the Saskatchewan Pension Plan, providing farmers, homemakers and part-time employees with pension benefits. In the spring the government made low-interest farm production loans available to farmers. The scheme could cost the treasury a cool $1 billion with farmers rich and poor, big and small, borrowing $25 an acre at 6%, no questions asked. It was a bonanza for rural Saskatchewan and a big boon for the Tory party who made a lot of new down-on-the-farm friends. For the town and city folk a housing program was announced before the election call. Available were matching grants of $1,500 for home improvements, $10,000 home improvement loans at 6% and $3,000 grants for new home buyers. Home mortgage interest rates were pegged at 9.75% for 10 years. To many, "Keep on Building Saskatchewan" did not seem an empty cry.

The NDP hadn't forgotten that they had been ambushed by early PC give-away promises in 1982 when Devine jumped out in front and stayed there. This time New Democrats were quick off the mark shouting "Let's Get Saskatchewan Working Again," ready to outbid the Tories with their own gift-wrapped package of goodies. The New Democrats housing program was even more costly than the Tory plan. Blakeney promised $7,000 grants to first-time buyers of new homes, up to $7,000 matching home improvement grants for existing homes, and mortgage interest rates pegged at 7%. Blakeney offered small business loans of up to $250,000 at a guaranteed interest rate of 7% over seven years.[6] Like the Tories, they too paid the required attention to health and education funding and to the chronic Saskatchewan misery of bad highways. More money would be provided for all three. In 1986 New Democrats desperately wanted to win. They were off on a spending spree just like the high-bidding Tories. The voters were being bought. Some might rightly have asked what had happened to the storied NDP prudence and financial responsibility of old.

The campaign would be a leaders' struggle with Devine and Blakeney featured front and centre in day-to-day slug-fests. Devine relished campaigning. He was a natural. He was breezy, confident and ad hoc on the platform. At town hall and big city rallies he was in his element, entertaining, scornful and eloquent. Yet even his partisan audiences, now smaller and less celebratory than in 1982, held back a little, cooled by tough economic reality and growing doubts about Tory balance and accountability in office. Some thought Allan Blakeney rather studied and flat as a campaign performer, but his intellect and consistent control of subject in legislative, academic debate commanded genuine respect in the Assembly and across the province. He cared more about governance than about political war games. Blakeney considered Devine an effective politician but "a woefully inadequate administrator."[7]

Blakeney's leadership of the little eight-member NDP opposition rump from 1982–86 had been defiant and remarkable. By 1986 his New Democrats were back in play and in contention for a return to office. It would be a battle. While they had restored their hold on the major cities in the province, they had a fight on their hands to regain crucial rural seats lost in 1982. In Saskatchewan the old CCF, with its farmer-labour bonding and its heroes, M.J. Coldwell and T.C. Douglas, was fading from memory. Now the labour-born NDP, successor to the CCF, was seen as an urban party, a big-city party. Saskatchewan country folk didn't think they had much in common with workers singing "Solidarity Forever," and looked more and more to the PCs as their political home. Rural and small-town Saskatchewan seemed to

Premier Grant Devine and wife Chantal, with Prime Minister Brian Mulroney (left). Devine and Mulroney forged a strong political alliance that proved to be invaluable to Devine when, half way through the 1986 election campaign, the federal Tories announced a $1 billion deficiency payment for western grain farmers. Many political observers believe that this timely federal intervention enabled Devine to win the election (SAB 84-3656-R5-13).

belong to Devine and the Tories, who had assiduously wooed them since forming the government in 1982.

The provincial Tories got a big lift up onto the saddle when mid-way through the Saskatchewan election the federal PC government announced a much-desired $1 billion deficiency payment for western grain farmers to augment low grain prices. Grant Devine had asked his Ottawa Tory friends for help. He went to Ottawa to plead his case and brought back the bucks. Then, in open-necked plaid shirt and cowboy boots country costume, he stumped the province, taking credit for every dollar. Why not?

At last the nasty, promise-crammed 1986 campaign ended. Probably the voters had heard enough righteous people's party malarkey from the NDP and enough sententious, family-values sweet-talk from the Tories. They were tired of it all. It was time to vote. Every voter had a price, and both NDP and Tory leaders had been high bidders and eager buyers. They both expected to win.

The election night results proved a bit of a mixed grill. While the Devine government was returned to power, winning 38 of the 64 seats in the legislature to the NDP's 25 and the Liberals' lone seat, the Tories actually ran behind the NDP in the provincewide popular vote. Blakeney's New Democrats garnered 45.2% of the provincial popular vote to the government's 44.61%. The popular vote count was an embarrassment to Devine even though there was only a skiff of difference between the parties. They were still the government. That was all that really mattered. The NDP piled

Grant Devine's close ties to the farm community were instrumental in allowing him to hold on to power in the 1986 provincial election, where he lost the popular vote to the NDP, but won more seats, mainly those in rural areas (SAB 84-1494-R16-30A).

up big margins in the cities while Devine's PCs swept to victories in town and country. The NDP's advantage in provincial popular vote was explained by the hiving of New Democratic strength in Saskatchewan's four big cities. Whereas there were more rural constituencies, their voter populations were smaller than those of the NDP-dominated, big-city ridings. Perhaps a disturbing peculiarity of the election was the sharp division of the province along rural-urban lines, hardly a comfort to either Devine or Blakeney, both of whom would have liked a more even city-mouse/country-mouse mix in their caucus ranks. The Saskatchewan Tories lost 17 seats in the 1986 election. Their 1982 urban gains, albeit many of them won by very small margins, were largely wiped out in a Saskatchewan big-city sea change. In 1986 Devine was able to win only two of Saskatoon's 10 seats and only two of Regina's 10 seats, while losing all four of the Moose Jaw and Prince Albert ridings won by the party in 1982. Devine's 1986 cabinet losses included Gordon Dirks, MLA for Regina Rosemount, Rick Folk, MLA for Saskatoon University, Myles Morin, MLA for the Battlefords and Sid Dutchak, MLA for Prince Albert-Duck Lake. The NDP's hold on the province's big-city vote would not be seriously challenged until the 2003 provincial election, when the party would lose three Saskatoon seats to the new right-of-centre Saskatchewan Party.

    The glow of electoral victory faded quickly among Tories who knew some cold realities, only guessed at by the public. Government leaders knew the economy, much of it beyond their control, was in shambles, and that many of their high-priced promises could not be kept. They knew their deception about the 1986 budget deficit would be exposed and the provincial debt would continue to climb dangerously. Thus, the PCs began their second term knowing that funding cuts, lay-offs and shelving of programs would have to be imposed. They knew they were now being scrutinized by a wary public and a cranky media. They knew the business community was uneasy, the labour leadership hostile and the provincial civil service disoriented.

Yet, in desperation, perhaps in colossal naïveté, they pushed on to rescue the economy and themselves with neo-conservative schemes of privatization and experiments in decentralization that would not work. This administration did not hesitate to undertake reforms that it believed would bring about fundamental changes in the province.[8]

But these bold designs were bound to fail.

15

Rolling the Dice

The swearing in of the second Tory administration had none of the sunny show-biz qualities of the first inauguration. This time it was an edgy affair. Many of the familiar 1982 players were gone, sorry casualties of the recent provincial shoot-out and the inherent fragility of the caucus itself. Devine delayed calling the legislature while assorted Tory fixers huddled in basement offices in the Legislative Building plotting manoeuvers to deal with the economic mess and rescue the government from blame. If the government wasn't to blame for the shambles who, or what, was? What kind of voodoo could now be called to put things right? Devine had four years to turn things around. Would there be a real strategy or would the government, like excited young soccer rookies, simply chase madly after the ball wherever it went, without any thought of a game plan? Would it be all impulse with no design and little captaincy? Possibly.

With the election won, Devine turned and faced the real numbers of economic malaise in the province, something largely concealed until the ballots were marked and in the box. Now the government talked of recession, drought and grasshoppers, declining potash, oil and uranium revenues, and the fiscal restraint and money management that required painful cutbacks and layoffs. All legitimate concerns! But how come? What had happened to the good times rolling? What had happened to Grant Devine's lively optimism and lavish spending promises of the campaign just ended? What had happened to "Give 'er snoose Bruce"? Now it was all "Whoa, Nelly"!

Even before the hugely unpopular June 1987 budget with a startling $1.2 billion deficit and the increasing of the flat tax, the government was busy with the axe and chopping block, cutting funding to a variety of social programs, including legal aid, mental health, Voice of the Handicapped, human rights, student summer employment services and student aid programs in a new-found enthusiasm for fiscal restraint. The government attacked Allan Blakeney's prescription drug plan legislation, restricting it with deductibles and up-front costs. Then the government eliminated the school-based children's dental plan, tossing hundreds of dental therapists out of work. Of course there were those who thought the endangered social programs excessive and unsustainable in a largely "have not" province, but any change in established health-care services in Saskatchewan was seen as an attack on social democracy and had to be approached with craft by politicians wanting to survive. Saskatchewan people had, since Tommy Douglas's New Jerusalem visions, felt entitled to more—not less—social programming.

Saskatchewan's new-right hard-liners heartily disliked the word "entitlement." It was a bad word, a deceptive word, a fairy-dust concept that both enraged and frightened free enterprisers. True-blue Tories blamed soft-headed CCF and NDP social planners in a succession of Saskatchewan socialist governments for the sentimental persuasion that everyone had some inherent right to the same degree and quality of earthly goods and services. Surely, the Tory true-blues argued, these "rights" had to be earned by ambition and hard work. "Entitlement" smacked of free rides, free lunches, freeloaders, lead-swingers, give-aways, welfare abuse and all manner of weakness and drift. "Entitlement," argued the hard-liners, was egalitarian expectation run wild. Such dogma might have seemed a little out of step with the troubled times and with the earlier compassionate conservatism of Diefenbaker, Hamilton and Pederson. Yet the economies, cutbacks, restructuring and downsizing rolled relentlessly on in Saskatchewan. The civil service was reduced by forced early retirements, elimination of positions and firings. Urban municipal capital fund programs and infrastructure programs were cut back or cancelled. Provincial revenue-sharing funding was sharply reduced, forcing increases in municipal property taxes. School, hospital and university operating grants were frozen for two years and public-sector wages locked in place.

The Devine government's privatization campaign was renewed with gusto. Slick advertising bells and whistles touted a Tory version of the "Saskatchewan way" back to solvency. At first the public seemed to buy the pitch that an unburdening of public enterprises better managed by the private sector was healthy. They entertained the notion that the public purse was filling with profits from these sales, and taxpayers would soon benefit hugely from provincial debt reduction and family tax relief. The sale of SaskOil continued in stages, the Prince Albert Pulp Mill was sold to Weyerhaeuser in a deal pleasing to that American giant, the Saskatchewan Mining Development Corporation, Saskatchewan Government Printing Company, Saskatchewan Forest Products, the Potash Corporation of Saskatchewan and part of SaskTel and Saskatchewan Government Insurance were sold to private investors.[1] But when some government functions in parks management and road building were given over to private companies, and SaskEnergy, the profitable natural gas division of SaskPower (a favourite Saskatchewan public utility), was threatened with sale, Devine's privatization bubble burst. A combination of clever, tactical NDP opposition in the legislature, now led by Roy Romanow, and public demonstrations forced the government to pull back.[2] Continued Tory attacks on unionism and provincial welfare, failed investments and stumbling mega projects resulted in bad polls for the government. Saskatchewan's population was falling and its provincial debt rising. There was no good news! In 1990 Devine was forced to bring back the gasoline tax and cancel home improvement grants and loans, breaking major promises and extending his government's tenure into a fifth year. This is a province where four year terms are traditional! His own party polls were ominous. Devine played for time. He looked for deliverance. None was in sight!

As in the past, the Tories hoped rural Saskatchewan could save them. In 1990 the government extended its provincial sales tax by harmonizing it with the federal Goods and Services Tax. Rural Saskatchewan was told the extra dollars raised would be spent on farm programs. This didn't suit city taxpayers who shared the increased tax load. A final, extraordinary plan to salvage Tory rural strength was announced by the premier. Called the "Fair Share Program," it was a desperate roll of the dice. The plan called for a decentralization of government services, moving up to 2,000 jobs from Regina to rural centres across the province.[3] It was supposed to have populist appeal in struggling towns and small cities, adding to their populations and strengthening their economics. But they weren't impressed! What about the Regina civil service families who didn't want to move from their city homes to rural climes, particularly larger families with both husband and wife holding jobs and children in school? They would find no fairness whatsoever in an uprooting thrust upon them in the name of rural-urban amity and equity. The "Fair Share Program" to them and to a widespread provincial audience was just plain jelly-brained nonsense that had to be stopped. The Tories were now a neverland government floating free from the everyman realities of a troubled province. Leading up to the election, the polls reflected a massive public rejection of both Devine and his government. In the spring of 1990 an Angus Reid poll had the Tories well back in third place with only 11% of the vote. By June 1991, Angus Reid showed the NDP with an astounding 44% lead over the PCs with Devine himself running behind both Roy Romanow, the new NDP leader, and Lynda Haverstock, the new Liberal leader.[4] After nine years in office Tory time in Saskatchewan was about to be called.

Devine finally announced an election for October 21, 1991, and put a full slate of 66 candidates in the field. It would be hard to judge how many of these felt any real hope of election. Many would seriously fear the loss of their deposits in a humiliating rout. No so the New Democrats! NDP forces were scrappy and confident, happily kindling bonfires under a vulnerable government. They knew the political axiom: "The opposition doesn't defeat the government; governments defeat themselves!"

In 1991 the NDP didn't present a comprehensive outline of the policies it would implement once in power. The reason for the general nature of the platform was Romanow's unease about the economic state of things in the province and the real danger of his discovering, once in office, that the provincial cupboard was bare. The NDP platform, rather ambiguously called "The Saskatchewan Way," was short on specifics. It didn't need them. Roy Romanow, elected by acclamation to succeed Allan Blakeney as NDP leader at a November 1987 leadership convention, didn't need much message. Saskatchewan wanted change.

Roy Romanow was articulate and telegenic, and in 1991 he was the consumate messenger for change. Like Devine, he loved "doing politics" and had considerable star quality when doing it. He liked the game, and he liked to win. In 1991 he was fresh and eager to engage. In contrast, Devine, now in his third election battle, was fagged by the weight of government misadventure and spooked by gloomy polls and shrunken crowds. Devine was fighting for his political life and, at best, for a tangled legacy of neo-conservative experiments.

The NDP platform sold easily. It promised to end deficits and wipe out the provincial debt over a 15-year period. It attacked Tory mismanagement and preached fiscal conservatism. It complained about poverty and food banks and loss of population. Romanow promised to reverse the Devine government's decision to extend the PST by harmonizing it with the federal GST, enrich energy conservation, recognize environmental concerns and Aboriginal land claims. Portentously for Saskatchewan, the NDP introduced its "Wellness Model" for health-care change without dwelling overly on necessary hospital closures and centralization of administration.[5] NDP strategists thought these realities were best left for later.

The 1991 PC campaign was anxiously and unevenly fought across the province. Only in a handful of town and country ridings with popular incumbents seeking re-election was there any feel of confidence. In small-city Saskatchewan PC hopes were dicey. The Regina, Saskatoon, Moose Jaw and Prince Albert big city races were hopeless from the start. Devine fought the campaign the only way he could. He gave a spunky, hokey-optimistic performance. "No retreat!" He stayed close to the party's rural strongholds where he had friends. He could still lift them cheering to their feet. Michael McCafferty, former Diefenbaker aide and a Tory caucus researcher in 1991, followed the campaign eagerly and described Devine's performance as a "remarkable show of inner strength, outstanding in the face of heavy odds against him."[6]

The Progressive Conservative platform called for a balanced budget by 1993. It promised child tax credit and removal of the sales tax from farm operators, small business and co-ops. It ballyhooed the premier's valiant efforts to obtain federal aid for distressed Saskatchewan farmers and flogged the "Fair Share Program" as a boon to small-town growth. Rivalling the ambiguity of the NDP's "The Saskatchewan Way" was the mock-heroic 1991 Tory slogan, "The Courage and the Will." Much of the PC strategy was to get on and stay on the offensive, attacking the NDP platform as a wild spending spree that would cost $3 billion. Conservative advertising challenged, "How can an NDP government, pledged to eliminate the provincial sales tax and balance the budget, pay for all of this?" Tory literature warned that small communities "counting on new jobs will be told 'no'" if the NDP cancelled the "'Fair Share Program." They warned voters that the NDP intention to "buy back" privatized companies would rob small families who had invested their savings in privatization. This was a desperate, hollow campaign. It was bound to fail.

On Saturday, October 19, as campaign time ran out, the Tories played the "family values" card with newspaper spreads entitled, "The Real Issues." Real issues in the campaign, they said, were homosexuality, abortion and the taxing of church property. Devine was presented as the advocate of wholesome, straight living: "homosexuality is not a moral life." He was the protector of the unborn: "Dr. Morgantaler is not welcome in Saskatchewan." He was the defender of the faithful: "There have been attempts to make churches pay property taxes in Saskatchewan. The PCs will resist this." These advertisements, however meaningful they may have been to many, did not speak to "the real issues" in Saskatchewan in 1991. There was only one "real issue" in that campaign and that was to throw the Tories out.

In the last days of the campaign the PCs were surprised and alarmed to hear Liberal footfalls close behind them and sounded an urgent appeal for a united front against the NDP. "Don't split the free-enterprise vote," they cried. "Every Liberal vote is a vote for the New Democrats!" The Tories had reason to fear the Liberals and particularly their 43-year-old leader, Lynda Haverstock. On October 21, election day, a Canadian Press release announced that "Haverstock has been the biggest surprise in an otherwise ho-hum Saskatchewan election campaign." They were right. Haverstock shone in the leaders' forum, easily holding her own in debate with the more experienced Devine and Romanow. Throughout the campaign her meet-the-people tours were busy, folksy forays into small-town Saskatchewan coffee shops and grocery stores where, as an immensely likeable and articulate lady with an infectious optimism, she made friends for herself and for the often uncertain Liberal candidate following behind her. While hardly a media wizard's dream for modern electronic politics, the party's call to arms, "Facing Reality in Saskatchewan," seemed to fit Haverstock. Lynda Haverstock was the first woman ever to lead a Saskatchewan political party. This wasn't always a plus for her, where even in her own Liberal ranks gnarled old-guard Grits were reluctant to take direction from a young woman new on the political scene. Whether or not the Liberal party was ready for Haverstock, the province of Saskatchewan was certainly ready for change, a change of government!

On October 21, 1991, with freezing rain and snow in many parts of the province, Saskatchewan voters trudged to the polls and toppled the Tory government. From the beginning of the campaign Saskatchewan voters had known what they wanted to see done and on election day an impressive 81% of eligible voters turned out to do the job. A jubilant NDP swept into power. In the new Legislative Assembly 55 ebullient New Democrats would face an emaciated opposition of 10 Tories and one lone Liberal. Devine's

Conservatives had lost 28 seats and suffered a dizzying 20% plummet in their share of the popular vote. The NDP took 51% of the popular vote. The PC opposition garnered 26% and the Liberals, more than doubling their 1986 numbers, tallied 23%.

The ravaged Tories hung on as the official opposition and the handful of Tory MLAs, survivors of the NDP onslaught, were relieved and grateful to still have jobs. But in the party backrooms where Tory fixers and strategists toiled and morning-after election reality-checks were made, there was only foreboding. The backroom boys knew what had happened, and they knew what it meant!

The PC Party had posted poor third-place showings in 25 of the 26 big city ridings. Only in Saskatoon River Heights had the party held second place. Once secure PC big town-small city urban-rural seats such as Biggar, Weyburn, Yorkton, Swift Current, Nipawin, Melville and Melfort were lost to the NDP, some of them coughing up Tory cabinet ministers. In every one of the 10 seats won in 1991, 1986 Tory majorities were slashed, including Estevan, where Grant Devine's vote plunged by nearly 20%. The really bad news for Tories was about the Liberals.

The Liberal Party elected only one member, its leader Lynda Haverstock. Haverstock won easily in Saskatoon Greystone. She was the only holdout to an NDP grand slam in the 22 key seats in Regina and Saskatoon. While this one Liberal seat didn't even earn the Grits party status, their provincewide numbers were dangerously threatening to provincial Conservatives. The Liberal Party, with 23% of the popular vote balanced across rural and urban ridings, and gaining strong second-place positioning in 29 constituencies, was only a scant 3% behind Devine's flagging PCs and challenging them for provincial second place. Clearly, the Liberal Party had gained much from Saskatchewan voter distemper in 1991, and the province's traditional two-party see-saw politics suggested there would be little or no room for two perceived right-of-centre parties. One would have to go, unless, of course, the CCF-NDP hegemony was to take permanent root. How strong and competitive would Haverstock's Liberals prove to be? In particular, how toxic would the effect of Devine's controversial and often dysfunctional administrations be? Which party, in time, would grow strong enough to challenge the NDP for office and take it from them?

What had the short Devine tenure really been about? Obviously, many in the province had envisioned some sort of neo-conservative revolution which would build a brave new entrepreneurial Saskatchewan. This didn't happen. Such designs were frustrated by severe economic uncertainties and the hinterland nature of a provincial economy which didn't readily attract industry or follow market rules.[7] These realities were largely beyond the control of any government. What seems certain is that after a decade of Tory government and politics, the political culture of Saskatchewan has taken a sustained right-turn. The familiar idiom and dialogue of the political right is no longer strange and discordant as it once was to many in social democratic Saskatchewan. Devine himself has left an imprint as arguably the province's most notable and aggressive champion of the Saskatchewan right wing. It will be interesting to see how provincial history treats this man.

Devine was able to implement some parts of his rightist agenda. Large-scale privatization of Crown corporations was carried out. Labour union powers in Saskatchewan were weakened, and cutbacks in provincial welfare programs were initiated. Yet, "He did not take the government out of business, but instead offered incentives, subsidies, loan guarantees and other financial inducements to stimulate and support private enterprise."[8] Thus, his government assisted in the establishment of a pulp mill, paper mill, heavy oil upgraders, a bacon-processing plant and a fertilizer plant, new industries that experienced various degrees of success in ensuing years. The heavy upgraders in Regina and Lloydminster are still making profits and SaskFerco, the nitrogen fertilizer plant, is still paying dividends. Devine leaves a legacy of a stronger industrial base in Saskatchewan, something succeeding governments have built upon. The quality of the Devine legacy in Saskatchewan has not yet been fully or finally assessed.

In government Devine said he was a compassionate conservative in the tradition of John Diefenbaker. He claimed that he stood for a balance of compassion and competition. In 1984 in the legislature Devine advised the Assembly:

> Be progressive on the one hand and conservative on the other. Make sure you provide those kinds of programs that are needed by seniors, by young people, by handicapped or by those that are less fortunate. Look after health, after education, look after social programs, but make sure you do it right. And at the same time be very conservative when it comes to providing economic incentives to people who go to work, particularly with tax cuts and incentives.[9]

Devine was speaking less to the legislature than to the wider public audience which he constantly kept uppermost in mind:

> Devine was less interested in managing government than he was in marketing his ideas and attitudes to potential consumers, a salesman with a populist style and a neo-liberal message.[10]

What the Devine government could not escape was responsibility for its lavish 1982 and 1986 election promises and the costs incurred in keeping them. These excesses heavily freighted and crippled the government with mounting interest payments on accumulated provincial debt that tallied a staggering $500 million in their last year in office.[11] For many in

Saskatchewan it must have seemed a good thing that this was the Tories' last year in office.

Was the Tory experiment of the 1980s a good idea hung up on bad times and betrayed by poor engineering, or just a delusional episode to be endured by Saskatchewan and forgotten as soon as possible? At all events, for Tories, there was more bad news on the way.

16

Jailhouse Blues

In 1994, before sentencing PC caucus whip and Cut Knife-Lloydminster MLA Michael Hopfner to an 18-month jail sentence for making false claims of $57,348 on his communication allowance, Court of Queen's Bench Justice Ross Wimmer reminded the courtroom that

> Politics should be regarded as a worthy pursuit engaged in only by honourable men and women inspired by the opportunity for public service. Regrettably episodes of the sort we heard about in this case can only foster cynicism and distrust, and perhaps discourage the best among us from seeking public office.[1]

Hopfner was neither the first nor the last member of Grant Devine's Tory caucus to be charged with various abuses of public trust and brought to court in the years between 1994 and 1999. In those five years, 17 Tory MLAs and three caucus employees were charged and tried before an assortment of 17 learned Provincial Court and Queen's Bench Court judges. Four MLAs were acquitted and charges against one employee dismissed. The penalties to the others ranged from jail terms to conditional discharges, payments of restitution, fines and required performance of community service. One Senate career was destroyed and one young family man under investigation was driven to suicide. Clouds of suspicion hung over many heads and households for years.

This wasn't some wonky political brouhaha, a cheerfully witless trademark squabble in Tory ranks. This wasn't an accident or a nasty invention of low-rent supermarket tabloids. It wasn't a docket of naughty transgressions by badly behaved juveniles to be easily forgiven and forgotten. This was an historic full-blown scandal that shattered lives and destroyed a political party. For five long years the people of Saskatchewan watched a courtroom parade of notable Tory public figures facing conviction and disgrace. They were fascinated. For them, this wasn't the routine Saskatchewan knock-about politics. It was far too real and sinister.

Progressive Conservatives watched, appalled, as exquisite agonies were slowly inflicted on Tory bad guys by relentless RCMP investigations, court judgments and merciless media glare. All the while NDP operatives watched from the sidelines, smiling. Devout New Democrats, supposedly outraged by Tory wrongdoing, felt reassured of their own purity, a questionable but not unpleasant confirmation. They shed no tears for Grant Devine. The NDP knew their hold on office had been secured by the PC fall from grace and offered up no prayers for Tory redemption.

A nutshell account of this improbable tale of scam and folly begins with the system of carelessly regulated caucus grants and communication allowances available to MLAs before and during the Devine years in office. The caucus grants funded research and secretarial services for the MLAs in the legislature and clerical services, rent, furnishing and supplies in constituency offices. The communication allowances provided postage, speech writing, newsletters, announcements and a variety of handouts bearing the MLAs' names and greetings. These caucus grants and communication allowances were given on the honour system, without audit and accounting to the legislature. The amounts were calculated by the size of the caucus, the number of constituents to be reached and the cost of mailings.

It was understood that the grants and allowances were to facilitate MLA efficiency and services in the constituency and not for personal gain or partisan political promotions at election time. These were rules set by a committee of representatives of all parties in the legislature and published in the "Members Handbook." Understanding these rules, to a number of Tories, did not mean following them. It may be that those who devised and sanctioned such a loosely controlled system of public funding were naïve to believe that an honour system was capable of governing politicians of any stripe. Certainly, this would be a cynic's view.

The principal authors of the complex fraud scheme appeared to be John Scraba, Communication Director of the PC caucus, as ringleader, Lorne McLaren, MLA, cabinet minister and caucus chairman, Michael Hopfner, MLA and a caucus whip, and John Gerich, MLA, cabinet minister and also a caucus whip. All four were jailed for defrauding the public of tens of thousands of dollars. Senator Eric Berntson also drew jail time on one count of fraud; but the extent of his involvement in the planning and direction of the scam was never established, although his position as deputy premier and a veteran power in the party invited suspicion.

Briefly, this is how it worked. The scam began in the years between 1982 and the 1986 provincial election when the PC caucus account was bulging with caucus grant money allotted to their large 55-member caucus. There was more money than caucus officers needed for administration and research services for Tory MLAs In 1985, with an election looming, the account was emptied and $450,000 quietly transferred to a bank account in Martensville, Saskatchewan, a town in MLA Ralph Katzman's Rosthern constituency. Katzman, a loquacious, genial member of caucus, was the signing officer. Apparently, the plan was to squirrel away thousands of dollars as a war chest for the upcoming 1986 election, a blatant misuse of public funding. Caucus grants were provided for caucus administration, not for party promotion. But who would know or care?

By late 1986 there was only $69,139 left in the covert Martensville account. Katzman told investigators and the court that he had given $35,000 of the money to fellow MLA Lorne McLaren, who had personal financial problems, and smaller amounts to other unnamed MLAs. He admitted giving $250,000 to the Saskatchewan Progressive Conservative Party. Katzman couldn't account for withdrawals of $55,000 and $33,000 from the Martensville account, but he did acknowledge he had transferred the $69,139 to his personal Martensville bank accounts and didn't know what to do with it! There it sat until finally returned to the government by the PC Party.

With tens of thousands of dollars gone missing and with Katzman either less than forthcoming or simply overcome by events he didn't understand, the improbable Martensville account episode ended, leaving intriguing questions behind. There was much silence in Tory circles. Humphrey Bogart's celebrated motto, "Never rat on a rat," seemed to apply.

Tory scamming with MLA communication allowances began in 1987 and led eventually to a parade of courtroom dramas that titilated Saskatchewan from 1994 to 1999. This was the big show. In 1987, Tory caucus members decided to contribute 25% of their communication allowances to a central fund, supposedly for advertising caucus business. Such pooling was allowed to all parties in the legislature as long as the rules for its legitimate use were followed. The PC caucus didn't have legitimate use in mind. The Tory caucus leadership wanted to circumvent those rules with a scheme that would allow a pooled fund of communication allowance money to be used in a variety of illegal ways, reaching from personal use to partisan promotion of the party. Obviously, a means of drawing money from the government into a caucus central fund and safely spending it improperly had to be found and the abuse hidden. A tangled web was needed. We are talking fraud!

The Progressive Conservative caucus Director of Communications and a procession of caucus chairmen, whips and deputy whips set up four numbered dummy companies to receive the pooled fund from the communication allowances. MLAs wanting cash or ineligible goods or services would submit signed requests for payment forms to the numbered companies, which would attach phoney invoices for legitimate advertising services not rendered and submit them to the provincial Department of Finance for payment. The government cheques would then be deposited in the numbered companies' accounts and cheques written on these accounts, transferring the money to the PC caucus account. Large cash sums were then withdrawn from the caucus accounts and hidden in two Regina bank safety deposit boxes to be used as the plotters decided. Many of the cash payments to MLAs were made with $1,000 bills. The RCMP estimated that $517,000 in total had been stashed over time and that $277,000 was unaccounted for. The police suspected that much of the missing money had gone to Tory MLAs.[2]

How had these tens of thousands of communication allowance dollars been spent? The police investigation told the story, or as much of it as they knew. The expenditures included a parade of personal thefts ranging from hefty $114,200 and $57,000 big-catch swindles to smaller-fry thievery of $12,000 to $4,000 and less. The PC Party was given an illegal transfer of $125,000 for political promotion. There were illegal loans to MLAs and improper generous perks and salary topping-ups for caucus chairmen, whips and deputy whips. Then there was a smorgasbord of tasty dishes ineligible under communication allowance guidelines. Consider: a new Pontiac car, T-shirts and baseball caps, computers, video cameras, portable public address systems, a show horse saddle, a holiday in Hawaii, Saskatchewan Roughrider season tickets and a golf club membership. These goodies were all provided through false expense claims on the public purse. We are talking petty fraud!

Slowly, like a Chinese water torture, case after case came before the courts, the media and the public. Added to the sad play's principal actors mentioned earlier and to a handful of bit players, there were no fewer than eight one-time Devine cabinet ministers charged, convicted and sentenced. These were: The Honourable Grant Hodgins (Melfort), conditional discharge, $3,645 in restitution and 240 hours of community service; The Honourable Harold Martens (Morse), conditional discharge, $5,850 in restitution and 240 hours of community service; The Honourable Ray Meiklejohn (Saskatoon-River Heights), conditional discharge, $4,500 in restitution, 240 hours of community service; The Honourable Joan Duncan (Maple Creek), fined $5,000 with $12,405 in restitution and placed on probation for one year; The Honourable Bob Andrew (Kindersley), fined $5,000 with $4,224 in restitution; The Honourable Sherwin Petersen (Kelvington-Wadena), conditional discharge, $9,285 in restitution, three years of probation and 240 hours of community service; and The Honourable Beatty Martin (Regina-Wascana), who after a conditional discharge paid $2,900 in restitution, performed 200 hours of community service and was placed on probation for a year. Finally, in 2000, with only Ralph Katzman's sentencing on conspiracy charges outstanding, the proceedings ended with the conviction, appeals and denials of Senator Eric Berntson. And, of course, there followed and lingered some inevitable fantasies about others, thought culpable but still undiscovered; fantasies of $1,000 bills being counted and stacked in shadowed basement cells at midnight hours down in the bowels of the Legislative Building. What delicious fun indeed for Tory critics and Devine-haters!

At first, there was very little sense of resolution or closure anywhere. Protestations of innocence, accusations, questions and suspicions continued. Why did the process take so long? Had the investigation been an RCMP and NDP government witch hunt? What about perceived inconsistencies in sentencing by a mixed bag of judges? Were all who came before the courts treated fairly? Were all the bad guys caught or did others, particularly in the NDP caucus, go unpunished because they were never investigated? Was all this nasty public pilloring necessary? Was there a growing "Hang 'em first, try 'em later" rush to judgment? Could there not have been more seemly examinations by a legislative tribunal? Wasn't confusion invited by the very thin line separating caucus communications from party promotion? Perhaps former Tory cabinet minister Grant Schmidt was right when he lamented that many honest people were victimized by what happened in the caucus office. "If you are an honest politician doing an honest job" he said, "you get tainted by the dishonest."[3] And what about those who were dishonest? How did the bad guys justify themselves to themselves and to each other? Had their little brief authority in cabinet ranks and an added touch of personal greed carried off their better judgments? Had these mostly ordinary Saskatchewan folk who had come to Regina to be a part of government grown so grand that they saw themselves above the law and above their own sworn oaths of office that had pledged them to honourable public accounting? Could it be that they saw colleagues with hands in the public-funding honey pot and asked, "Why not me too? Stealing from the government isn't really stealing is it?" But it was and it is! Perhaps the miscreants learned that at the end. And perhaps not.

And what about Premier Grant Devine? Was he involved? What did the premier know and when did he know it? How could the head of government not know—something? Was Devine's head buried in the sand all those years, a "don't ask-don't tell" Clintonian evasion? Those who know Grant Devine remain rock solid in their conviction that the premier was never involved. What we do know is that not a jot of verified, published evidence linking Grant Devine to the fraud schemes has ever surfaced, and no public accusations of his involvement have ever been made. No blame game has been played either by injured Tory victims or by NDP headhunters indulging their bloodlust. Even those puritans in New Democratic ranks who believe racking and scourging good for political sinners have not chased Grant Devine. There has been no pursuit by the media, or tacky insinuations by know-all/tell-all pundits or columnists. It's probable they knew there was nothing to hang on the premier.

Devine himself has always categorically denied any complicity with the robbers or knowledge of their schemes. In 1996, during the Michael Hopfner trial, Devine issued the following wholesale disclaimer: "I have never been involved in, approved or condoned or been aware of any illegal activity in the Legislative Assembly of Saskatchewan."[4] At the end of the fraud trials, he expressed sympathy for PC Party members blamed for the shortcomings of a few and admitted his personal sense of betrayal by offending members of his own caucus.[5] Bill Boyd, who succeeded Devine as PC leader, said, "There were some bad apples in the barrel, but Grant Devine certainly wasn't one of them."[6]

Perhaps for some it's hard to believe that caucus officers' wrongdoings could go unnoticed by the premier. Maybe under ordinary circumstances, in more ordered times, that might have been so. But the years of scandal-making weren't ordinary times for Grant Devine. In the years between 1987 and the 1991 provincial election, the years when most of the frauds were committed, Devine wasn't the confident young 1982 generalissimo, pistol in hand leading his Tories to an extraordinary victory. Instead, by 1987 he was a troubled leader of a failing, delusional government, a besieged premier facing certain defeat when the election writ was dropped. He must have known that he would then be fighting, not for government but for survival. It's possible that during those troubled last years Devine wasn't tending the store carefully enough, and caucus office shenanigans weren't a big part of his watch. It's probable that he didn't know what was going on. Devine was a competitor. He liked the game of politics and played to win, but he played by the rules. He thought everybody else, at least his Tories, also played by the rules.

Even so, as party leader he could not escape some responsibility for the misconduct of others, and he never tried to. He knew that leaders, even when wronged and betrayed themselves, must carry the can for party colleagues, the good and the bad. It goes with the territory. He also knew that all across Saskatchewan innocent Progressive Conservative loyalists, who for years had manned polls, sold memberships and raised money to elect their candidates, were now deeply humiliated and wondering whether their party, trashed by a handful of thieves, would live or die.

17

Going, Going, Gone

Could Saskatchewan Conservatives survive their 1991 rout and the devastation of the fraud scandals? They were bankrupt of everything but a few dollars and a handful of good men willing to hang on. Surviving would be tough!

Grant Devine resigned the party leadership in 1992, although he continued to sit for Estevan until the 1995 provincial election when he left public life. The NDP never forgave Devine for the beating he had given them in the 1982 PC landslide and for denying them power in 1986. They began a demonization of him that continued in Saskatchewan for more than a decade. New Democrats were good at this! They had practised on Dick Collver.

The NDP no longer talked about Progressive Conservatives, they talked only about Devine Conservatives. Piously they decried what they called Devine years, Devine government, Devine deficits, Devine lies, Devine betrayals and scandals. The most agitated among them seemed to believe that at Grant Devine's approach, diligent Saskatchewan householders should sweep themselves and their belongings indoors, lock up their houses and sound neighbourhood-watch alarms. New Democrat spinners drew Devine as both the cause and consequence of all Saskatchewan distempers in the 1980s and beyond. They wanted to bury the man and the party with him. They knew, if they succeeded, they would have enough anti-Tory blame and scare ammunition for several electoral wars to come. New Democrats had learned that politics could be a dirty game, and they knew how to play.

In November 1992, the PCs threw a retirement bash for Grant Devine in Saskatoon. Outwardly, at least, it was a good party. There were no gnashings of teeth, only tributes to a still much-admired departing leader, some jokes, reflections and suitable gifts of a saddle, a shotgun and a rifle. There had been some criticism of Devine, as is often, if not always, the case following a defeat. These negatives are part of the war games of politics where egos and ambitions are inevitably involved and people get bruised. In Devine's case the negatives voiced were more of a sympathetic appraisal of the man than any serious "dumping" on the leader. For the most part, the criticisms seem to involve his cabinet and staff management style which some apparently deemed not "hands on" enough, "too loose," they said. These were not new assessments. There had been some party dissatisfaction and fault-finding with Devine's management style registered as early as the summer of 1981 at a caucus retreat. Colin Thatcher, a member of Devine's first cabinet, writing in 1985 described Devine as one "who did not demand enough from his immediate staff and surrounded himself with inept executive assistants." Thatcher suggested that Devine's inability to make up his mind and his habit of putting off decisions caused frustration among party faithful and with some caucus members.[1]

Other critics expressed similar views but tempered their censure by describing Devine's work days as whirlwinds of activity that left him with little time to manage his own government:

> Sometimes he failed to understand what his cabinet ministers were doing or trying to accomplish. Worse still, the staff he selected to manage his office and his government were often youthful and inexperienced when his greatest need was for maturity and judgment. Devine's staff faced a monumental job of managing a government beset with challenges requiring more than youthful enthusiasm.[2]

Whatever the post-mortems, it was clear that Grant Devine would leave office with a good measure of loyalty from his party, whose affection for him did not appear much shaken by the electoral disaster he left behind. Devine would soon return to the management of the family farm and to other professional pursuits. His interest in provincial conservatism and willingness to serve the cause of the right wing in Saskatchewan remained genuine and wholesome. He continued as a mentor to many young Tories. There was no obvious pushing and shoving to replace him. Apparently there was no heir apparent. Whatever his private feelings, Devine seemed cheerful enough the night of his farewell party. Justifiably, he felt he had given all he could to the job and had spared nothing of himself in the giving. Yet, it might not have surprised some attending the party if the retiree felt a touch relieved to be leaving a career that had blazed up bright and hot like a straw bonfire, and suddenly smouldered and died. It would be two years before a leadership convention would be called to replace him.

In the meantime, Thunder Creek MLA Rick Swenson would serve as interim leader and Leader of the Opposition in the legislature. Swenson was an earnest, well-spoken young farmer first elected in a 1985 by-election. He came from good Tory stock with solid party credentials. Swenson had held two cabinet posts in Devine governments. His father, Don Swenson (a past president of the Saskatchewan Progressive Conservative Party), had run unsuccessfully in Thunder Creek in 1975. In 1978 the senior Swenson again sought the PC nomination in Thunder Creek but lost it to Colin Thatcher, son of former Liberal Premier Ross Thatcher and himself a former Liberal MLA. The Swensons, although not exactly new frontier men, were solid defenders of much of the good in the old. Both men were trusted and valued in the party and beyond. The junior Swenson gave the party capable leadership in a short but seamless career as party boss and Leader of the Opposition in the Assembly. Many hoped he would seek the top post whenever a leadership convention was called. This didn't happen. Swenson didn't want the job:

> It became apparent to me that the tools to succeed and the drive it takes to make a party re-invent itself were totally lacking. I thought, why become leader if you couldn't help re-build the party, much less aspire to be Premier?[3]

He felt "bruised and beaten up" by the fraud scandal distempers and the unrelenting malice of the critics of his party.[4] He was tired of the battle zone and wanted to escape it. Later, more Tory talk would be heard from Swenson.

Two men wanted the leadership. Grant Schmidt, a former MLA for

Rick Swenson, photo taken the year he became Acting Leader of the Opposition (courtesy Rick Swenson).

Melville and Tory cabinet minister, announced his candidacy. So did Bill Boyd, the MLA for Kindersley. Boyd was a 38-year-old farmer-businessman with a diploma in welding and engineering technology, a promising newcomer and a favourite of the caucus. Boyd was unreserved in his praise of Grant Devine. "He encouraged me to enter politics, and his dynamic leadership was an inspiration to me."[5] Boyd's taking Devine as a role model was later evident in his own lively, hard-edged performances in Assembly debates. Schmidt, a Melville lawyer, was first elected in the 1982 Tory landslide, taking Melville from the NDP in a close-fought contest. He was easily re-elected in 1986 with 53% of the vote and narrowly defeated in 1991, the year that Bill Boyd entered the legislature. These men were very different contenders. It's probable neither of them knew just how much the survival of the Progressive Conservative Party in Saskatchewan depended on the outcome of their race for the top job.

Grant Schmidt had been a dogmatic, controversial cabinet minister in the Devine government. He was outspoken, often flying without tether in argument, sometimes snarly and not too fussy about the rules of engagement when in a fight. He made enemies easily. Opinions about Schmidt were mostly unequivocal and often negative. He was the "love him or hate him" type. Many thought he fit nicely the old Scottish saying, "He would start a fight in an empty house." That's the way he wanted it. Arguably, Schmidt had been the most provocative, perhaps the most unpopular of Devine's cabinet members. His selection as leader would have been a serious misjudgment by the party. Whereas the party badly wanted and needed colour and vigour in a new leadership, it did not want and dared not hazard extremism of any sort. Tory feet must now be firmly and safely planted in the centre-right. Grant Schmidt would not do! Schmidt was named to Grant Devine's cabinet in 1985 as Minister of Social Services. It was in his handling of the social services file that he built a reputation for insensitivity and confrontation. Schmidt had been raised on a farm near Melville. After graduating from Grade 12 he had worked as a labourer for the railway in order to finance studies at the University of Saskatchewan in the College of Law and had lived frugally during his lean university student years. It is likely that his attitudes towards work and welfare developed first in his early years working on the farm, then in later years pounding railway spikes and shovelling gravel for the railway, and finally in his tight budget years as a university student struggling to pay his bills. One can only speculate to what degree Schmidt was a passive victim of early experiences.

Certainly, by the time he entered politics he had stationed himself solidly in the ranks of the right wing. He believed past NDP welfare programs needed reforming. He was convinced that the leftist welfare philosophy kept the poor dependent and hopeless, and that they needed challenge and the opportunity to work if they were ever to find independence. Schmidt believed in social conservative "work ethic" values and disciplines. He said it wouldn't be easy to change a welfare culture that had been developed and layered over years of social democratic party rule in Saskatchewan. But he would try. There were those who thought he would succeed. "In the bureaucratic world of welfare, any effort at reform required iron and unrelenting will. Schmidt had that will."[6]

Grant Schmidt had a tough guy, "tough love" attitude toward social welfare recipients whom he regarded, in the aggregate at least, as lazy slackers who cheated the system when allowed. He was not alone in these attitudes and suspicions. They were found in both Tory party ranks and in social conservative elements in the general population at the time.[7] But Schmidt's constant personalizing of welfare issues and his insulting rhetoric when attacking social assistance programs and clients made him a "hit man" whose assignment, it appeared, was to expose wrongdoers and turn them, not always gently, away from their moral failure back to Grant Schmidt's conservative virtues.

Critics charged him with hectoring the welfare poor. In 1987 he started pilot programs to require "single, able-bodied" welfare recipients to attend at government offices to claim their cheques in person rather than receiving them in the mail. This, supposedly, was to instill a sense of responsibility in the recipient and prevent possible frauds. Another "discipline" imposed by the government was to have landlords co-sign rental cheques with welfare tenants in order to ensure that rent allowances were paid to the landlords for rent and not squandered on non-essentials.[8] Although these measures of control and later "workfare" programs would undoubtedly find favour with some of the voting public, the constraints on the disadvantaged poor imposed by Social Services would appear callous and punitive to others, and do nothing for Grant Schmidt's appeal as a future candidate to lead the party and the government.

Bill Boyd was seen as a "fresh face," someone carrying no baggage from the Devine years. Most importantly, he was an Eston district farmer who could talk the talk and be listened to at farm gates and in small-town coffee shops. The party's only hopes lay in a handful of rural seats where formidable PC incumbents were seeking re-election. Boyd was the right man to make that crucial rural appeal.

Saskatchewan's Progressive Conservative Party elected a new leader on Saturday, November 19, 1994. The party still had a membership of 9,000 eligible voters. This time their polling of that membership, or at least of those who cared enough to participate, would be by a computerized telephone vote. This somewhat refreshing phone-in system was a first in Saskatchewan. Party operatives, in a happy coinage of their own, called this "teledemocracy" and predicted a greater grassroots involvement in the future. When the phoned-in votes were tabulated, Bill Boyd was the winner. He celebrated his victory at a party function in Regina. Of the 3,300 votes cast, Boyd won 60% and defeated Grant Schmidt. With a country and western band providing lively entertainment, the young winner told the crowd, "For a farm boy like myself, to come up in the ranks to take this job, I can't tell you how proud I am of the party and of Saskatchewan."[9] As events would prove, the party had chosen well. Not only had Bill Boyd "come up in the ranks," however thin those ranks had become, he was well on his way to establishing himself as what *Regina Leader-Post* senior political columnist Murray Mandryk later called "arguably the best raw-talent politician in the Legislative Assembly."[10] Another highly regarded Saskatchewan political journalist, James Parker of the *Saskatoon StarPhoenix*, described Boyd as "an effective, often ruthless debater, a tough partisan politician."[11] Both Mandryk and Parker recognized Boyd as a forceful advocate for rural Saskatchewan.

Boyd knew he had little time to gear up for the Conservative struggle in an election soon to be called. It would be hard to put on a happy face with the Liberals looking good and a mounting docket of Tory fraud charges still concentrating the media and titillating the public. Could his worn out and bled white Tories win even a handful of seats, enough for party status in the legislature? He knew his greatest challenge wasn't Lynda Haverstock and the apparent revival of her Liberals, or even Roy Romanow's governing NDP. It was distancing himself from the real and perceived failures of the last Conservative government and escaping the demons of the fraud trials. For starters, he called his party the New PCs. Then he hit the road with an earnest message of rural survival. The New PCs would fight a limited, frugal campaign. Boyd travelled the province in a cramped and aging mini-van decorated with party colors and slogans. No comfortable bus or corporate-loaned aircraft for him. Boyd, by some sleight of hand, had produced a full slate of 58 candidates. Most all of them surely knew their best bets were for poor, third-place showings. Yet they ran. Only five of the 58 had ever run before. They must have believed in something or somebody.

Realistically, there were only 12 seats the New PCs had even faint hopes of winning. The Tories had won eight of these in 1991 and in another four, Tory candidates had come a respectable second in 1991. This time, without Grant Devine as a celebrity candidate, even Estevan was uncertain. Clearly, the New PC's strategy was to target these 12 hopefully winnable seats and in Grant Devine's cowboy colloquial tongue of earlier happy days, "Give 'er snoose Bruce" to win them. In 1995 Boyd had few notable candidates. Most were bottom-drawer material even from a constituency perspective. Others, who might have given the party some profile in local races, wouldn't run.

Premier Roy Romanow called the 1995 election for June 21. He faced a Progressive Conservative Party now calling itself the New PCs, although how in substance it differed from the old PCs one could only guess. Romanow would direct most of his attacks on the rising Haverstock Liberals. He knew they were positioned to become the next official opposition. Pre-election polling gave the NDP a commanding 51% of the decided vote. The Liberals held a comfortable second place in the polls, and the New PCs trailed far behind. The New Democrats' 1995 campaign slogan was "The Saskatchewan Way Is Working," and the polls seemed to reflect public agreement that this was so.

Boyd's New PCs fought strategic campaigns in selected rural ridings they had to win. Here, independent business-oriented young farmers were identifying less and less with the Tommy Douglas generation and the "social democratic political populism" of the past.[12] Here Boyd could preach social and economic conservatism to willing ears. Here he could defeat NDP "lefties" and outflank Liberals threatening him in the centre-right. These few country seats were winnable. Boyd spoke easily and persuasively on rural issues, and in these ridings his New PCs had nominated some of their best candidates. This was crunch time, and he knew it.

The NDP waged a cool leadership campaign around the savvy, telegenic Roy Romanow. From the beginning, Romanow's campaign was coming up aces. New Democrats touted "putting the house in order," reducing budget deficits with spending cuts and increased sales and personal income taxes. Romanow promised to stay the course with fiscal responsibility and continued massaging of his "Wellness Program" health model.

The Liberal campaign suffered some logistical glitches at first, but on the outside at least appeared a lively, leader-driven effort. The 1995 Grit slogan was "Restoring Health to Saskatchewan." The Liberals attacked the draconian cutbacks of Romanow's "Wellness Program," particularly the top-down decision-making in its implementation. As she did in the 1991 campaign, Haverstock held the spotlight as her party's chief campaigner and drew assorted mutterings from some Grit operatives wanting a little star dust for themselves. Some thought Haverstock over-managed party affairs and was too exclusive and controlling. Haverstock, herself, spoke of intimations of hot Liberal friends cooling, traces of hostility, even of disloyalty.[13] Perhaps she had not had the time or taken the time to build the essential bonds needed to withstand old guard complaints which, like faculty club gossip, can be aimless and mischievous or targeted and malignant. Time would tell. At all events, big election night wins for Haverstock could turn all sulks to cheers, knit up intra-party unravellings and establish her hold at the top.

No such rumblings upset Bill Boyd's party. The New PCs had one purpose, limited and clear: survival! Without Bill Boyd they knew this might not happen. The Tories sounded their signature call for personal accountability, good fiscal management, and moral responsibility in government. Boyd himself escaped the taint of the fraud scandals. He hadn't served in any Devine government. He maintained that the party itself should not be blamed. The "failings" were those of a few miscreants whose crimes had unfairly been charged against the innocent.[14] The New PC's platform was risk free with near zero content. It called for a cut in the sales tax to boost the economy, a 5% reduction in government spending and legislation that would require off-reserve Treaty Indians to pay all sales taxes. Boyd spent much of his time attacking the hugely unpopular federal Liberal government's proposed gun-control legislation and the provincial Liberal Party's flip-flopping on the issue. In rural Saskatchewan Haverstock was vulnerable on this issue.

Closer to home, some New PC candidates appeared to be winging it in local contests with promises to cut the size of the cabinet, reduce the premier's staff, and limit the number of ministerial assistants. Both NDP and Liberal spokespersons commented on the reluctance of many New PCs to identify with their party. They had quietly removed the PC logo from their advertising and featured a picture of their leader, Bill Boyd. Throughout polling day across the province election workers noted a slower, thinner voter turnout than in recent elections. This proved the case when all votes were tabulated. On June 21, only 66% of eligible voters cast ballots, whereas in the previous six provincial elections voter turnout had been 80% and upward. This time there was an evident sag in voter interest. Was this voter fatigue, cynicism or a genuine satisfaction with Romanow's centrist politics and slow march to business-smart spending restraints and balanced budgets?

The New PCs held their breath election night as they followed polling results on radio and television. Their attention was fastened on the 10 or 12 Tory country redoubts they hoped to hold. As expected, Romanow's New Democrats again won easily with Lynda Haverstock's Grits in second place.

The Romanow government returned with 43 seats and 47% of the popular vote. They were followed by the Liberals with a healthy 35% of the vote and 11 seats in the Assembly. The Grits were now the official opposition. In Tory headquarters there were smiles and high-fives all around as the New PCs registered solid wins in five rural seats and placed second in five others. The New PCs garnered 18% of the popular vote, down from their 1991 total of 26%. The party ran last in 48 ridings, and most of their badly beaten up candidates lost their election deposits. Yet with five members in the Assembly, four of whom had at least some legislative experience, Saskatchewan Tories were still standing and had enough to build a dream on.[15]

The down-sized, five-man Tory team, led by an energized and determined Bill Boyd, carried on with surprising vigour in the new legislature. But even they must have known that some sort of alliance with the Liberals, some joining of hands to reach for relevance, was in the cards. Boyd himself had proposed merger talks with Haverstock before the 1995 election. Not unexpectedly, with several former Tory MLAs and staff still under fraud investigation, Haverstock refused, saying, "The last colour the Liberals wanted to be painted was Tory blue."[16] Soon, however, to borrow the 1991 Liberal campaign slogan, both parties would be "Facing Reality in Saskatchewan." The dramatic 1995 upswing in Liberal fortunes and Haverstock's considerable achievements were never celebrated by her party. Instead, the party entered a peevish interlude of second guessing and complaint, with Grit gains squandered in internecine slagging that ended in a messy power takeover. A harried Lynda Haverstock resigned as Liberal leader and sat as an Independent. Perhaps a long-term shelf life in politics was never in Haverstock's cards.

Lynda Haverstock, who was described by a former Liberal colleague MLA Ken Krawetz as a "failed team builder and team player," possibly was not as much to blame for the party's misfortunes as her critics believed.[17] Certainly, distemper in the Liberal Party did not end with Haverstock's departure. Grit internal divisions and rivalries persisted, especially with an upcoming leadership race in sight to replace Haverstock. A new Liberal leader was chosen. He was Jim Melenchuk, a Saskatoon medical doctor who had run unsuccessfully for the legislature in 1995. "But soon it became apparent that he did not have the skills to unite the Liberal caucus."[18] The party remained fractious and confused, seemingly no longer a credible alternative to the governing NDP. Bill Boyd and the Tories, although a resolute little band firmly united behind their leader, remained demoralized by the recent Tory fraud scandals and by the 1991 Tory rout at the polls. Rumors circulated about ongoing Liberal-Conservative discussions of mergers or coalitions, adding uncertainty to uncertainties in both Tory and Grit camps.

These meetings began in the spring of 1997 when the five members of the PC caucus and three members of the Liberal caucus met, they said, by coincidence in a Regina restaurant and discussed the state of Saskatchewan politics. They agreed that the status quo, if left unchanged, could only result in a perpetual NDP government. Not a good idea! A second meeting of this group was held with Liberal House Leader Rod Gantefoer attending. It was decided that merging the caucuses would not succeed and that a new political party was essential. An initial meeting of the Liberal and Tory party leaders, Jim Melenchuk and Bill Boyd, was arranged. Melenchuk apparently gave some thought to supporting the scheme, but perhaps because he was not assured of the leadership of the new party he withdrew from the discussions. Boyd made it clear from the outset that he did not want to lead the new party. He believed that a new image for the right wing in Saskatchewan required a new face in the party's top job. The Liberal House Leader, Rod Gantefoer, who played a key leadership role in the creation of the new party, described the final negotiations:

> It became obvious that something needed to be done and myself, Draude and Bjornerod continued discussions with, at this time, Tories Boyd, Heppner, and D'Autremont and Toth. We convinced Krawetz to join us at the last moment, and the eight of us embarked on a new adventure, the creation of something new that would be a real alternative to the NDP.[19]

In Reform Party ranks, emboldened by their 1997 federal election successes in Saskatchewan, there was talk of forming a provincial wing of that party to contest the next provincial election. It was only a matter of time before elements in the troubled Liberal caucus and Boyd's handful of new PCs would unite in some kind of political coalition in the legislature. Reformers would be welcome to come to the party and would shelve any ideas of a provincial wing of their own. A new right-wing party would be born in Saskatchewan.

In August 1997, two short years after the provincial election, four of the five New PCs in the Legislative Assembly joined with four Liberals to form a legislative coalition of eight members. The New PC contribution to the coalition consisted of Tory leader Bill Boyd, MLA for Kindersley, Dan D'Autremont, MLA for Cannington, Ben Heppner, MLA for Rosthern, and Don Toth, MLA for Moosomin. The four Liberals were Bob Bjorerud, MLA for Saltcoats, June Draude, MLA for Kelvington-Wadena, Rod Gantefoer, MLA for Melfort, and Ken Krawetz, MLA for Canora-Pelly. Only six Liberals were left in the Grit caucus, and one New PC, Jack Gooshen, MLA for Cypress Hills, now sat as an Independent. Gooshen, with the outcome of legal charges against him pending, was not invited to join his fellow New PCs in the coalition. The Tory-Liberal legislative coalition then had more members than the Liberals and was named the official opposition in the province. In September 1997 the legislative coalition officially became a political party, calling itself the Saskatchewan Party. Bill Boyd resigned as leader of the Saskatchewan Progressive Conservative Party, and the party that had elected five members to the Assembly in 1955, garnering 18% of the popular vote, was left with no representation in the legislature.

The birthing of the Saskatchewan Party was witnessed with keen interest in the province. To many observers, particularly in the media, the cobbling together of a new political party must have seemed an audacious venture. The reaction of some wounded Progressive Conservatives, and of Liberals and New Democrats, was immediate and predictably hostile. Both Liberal loyalists and NDP opponents of the new party depicted Liberal defectors as wildly extreme right-wingers, and New PCs as unprincipled renegades who cared only for their personal ambitions and survival in Saskatchewan politics. Not so, maintained defenders of the new party! They argued that the Saskatchewan Party was a necessary strategy of the centre-right assembled to prevent continued NDP domination in the province.

The PC's Bill Boyd contended:

> No one was betraying conservative principles. There was no choice left to us if we intended to defend these principles. The new party was the province's only hope of overtaking and beating an entrenched NDP.[20]

Liberal Rod Gantefoer echoed Boyd's opinion:

> After witnessing the scandals of the PCs and the turmoil in Liberal ranks, this decision was absolutely necessary if there would ever be a hope of a free-enterprise alternative in this province.[21]

Boyd and Gantefoer's confidence that a new right-of-centre party could successfully compete with the NDP would prove well placed.

The political landscape was changing in the province with the creation of this new party. Just how "new" the new party was, of course, is a matter of definition. That aside, the big question remained, "What now is to be done with the Saskatchewan Progressive Conservative Party?" On November 9, a chilly Sunday in 1997, fewer than 200 PC delegates huddled behind closed doors in a Regina convention to debate a motion that, if passed, would disband the Progressive Conservative Party of Saskatchewan. Some of the delegates were angered by the fact that PC members holding Saskatchewan Party memberships as well as their own could vote on a motion engineering the demise of the Tory party. Yet Tom Lukiwski, the PC Executive Director, defended the holding of dual memberships, saying, "It's the right thing to do." He argued that Tories with a vision of how the province should be governed probably doubted that the PC Party, at that time weighted down with fraud scandal baggage, could deliver on their vision.[22]

The motion before the convention was to render the provincial PCs "inactive" for the next two provincial elections. Ten trustees were to be appointed to safeguard that 10 handpicked Tory candidates were fielded in each of the two elections to maintain the party's status as a registered political party. The candidates were to be "paper candidates" only. They had no platform or leadership and would not campaign for recognition or for votes.

Bill Boyd, Progressive Conservative Party leader from 1994–97 (Calvin Fehr Photography, Regina).

All PC provincial memberships would be nullified with the exception of the 10 trustees and a small group of Tories holding lifetime party memberships. The motion passed easily, with 130 delegates supporting and only 32 voting against.

Supporting the motion were two former Tory leaders, Bill Boyd and Rick Swenson, and the current Tory party president Nick Stooshinoff. Former leader Swenson cut to the quick, advising, "A lot of people have a deep love for their province, and they want to contribute but feel right now the PC Party in its present configuration is a hindrance to that."[23] Swenson described his own leave-taking of the Progressive Conservative Party as "gut wrenching."[24]

So, with 10 appointed trustees keeping watch, the party would now take a strange cryogenic snooze for seven or eight years. Then it would either be warmed, revived and awakened to new tasks or just left in cold storage. Perhaps some old Tories, thinking this not a pretty sight, scratched their heads and asked, "What kind of cock-a-doodle do we have here?" One man who was shocked by what he saw as a betrayal of the party was former PC leader Martin Pederson. The man who had led the Tories for 10 years wasn't even consulted about the change. Pederson did not approve of it![25] Kris Eggum, the man the November 1997 convention elected leader of the soon-to-be "put to sleep" Progressive Conservative Party, thought the decision to retire the party "a difficult but necessary choice." Eggum, a former provincial and federal PC candidate, did not rule out a future revival of the party.[26]

Nevertheless, for now it was a done deal and for the right wing in Saskatchewan possibly a good deal. The Progressive Conservative Party "mired in scandal and corruption could no longer maintain enough credibility with the public to carry the right wing banner."[27] Now the Saskatchewan Party, as the results of the 1999 election would show, could carry that banner and did so. Former PC leader Grant Devine gave the new party a "thumbs-up," a significant endorsement! Devine's assessment was a clear-eyed reality check on the state of politics in the province in 1997. If a conservative agenda was to be successfully pursued, "timidity and nostalgia could not be allowed to get in the way." Devine, like many others found the transformation difficult. "Of course this was not an easy decision for our party but it was in no way a betrayal of the past," he said.[28]

When the necessary papers were signed and filed with the appropriate officers and clerks, the Progressive Conservative Party of Saskatchewan was "put to sleep," as they said, and appeared to be sleeping soundly. No Prince Charming with an awakening kiss was expected.

The raw realities of the Saskatchewan political game and the egos, ambitions and survival instincts of its right-of-centre players had brought about an alliance of PC and Liberal MLAs who in quick time cobbled together a new political party they called the Saskatchewan Party. To somewhat bemused rank-and-file Tories and Grits, this must have seemed a cold and hurried closure ordered by some remote corporate strategic planning committee advising, "It's all for the best!" Apparently such planners agreed with the American journalist and writer E.B. White who said, "If the boat is sunk, it is time to stop rowing!"

At the end, there was no ceremony, no valediction, no requiem chorus, nor apparent last lingering looks back. Sad. Perhaps.

18

Saskatchewan Tories and Conservatism in Saskatchewan

What can be said about Conservatism in the province and the role and impact of the Tory party on the politics of Saskatchewan? Perhaps a necessary direction in any study of Saskatchewan Conservative politics would be first to go behind the party platforms, programs and leaderships of the day, and look for sets of principles and core values that might help explain and justify the conservatism under review. For us to have an understanding of provincial Conservative politics over the years from Frederick Haultain to Bill Boyd we need to have some sense of federal conservatism as it unfolded in the Macdonald to Mulroney years. This federal conservatism and the differing ranges of federal party sponsorship given their provincial wings has always had a significant influence on Tory politics in Saskatchewan. From the beginning, federal Conservatives and Saskatchewan Conservatives have in varying measures affected and reflected each other. They have in a sense been part of the same team.

Today the Conservative Party is often called the "Tory" party. The origin of the term "Tory" is British, and it was current in pre-Confederation Canada as a popular reference to an ideology that stressed the importance of the group in society rather than the individual. This early Toryism also described the primacy of the high-born and property holder over the common citizen. Thus, Toryism elevated collectivism and privilege above the importance of the individual and the necessity of personal freedoms espoused by liberal political thought known to us as liberalism. An element of Toryism was "Tory democracy," a paternalistic concern for the welfare of the ordinary people expressed by British Tory leaders in the late 19th century.

Sir John A. Macdonald, the first Conservative Prime Minister of Canada, "balanced the liberal and tory elements of his Conservative ideology."[1] While his belief in Canadian business enterprise and in the robust individualism of entrepreneurs pursuing it was an obvious expression of his liberalism, Macdonald encouraged such enterprise only when it did not interfere with his government's efforts to build and strengthen the young Canadian state. Macdonald's conservatism included a belief in a strong central government with the power to significantly direct the economy for the national good. His tariff policy exemplified this and was designed to protect Canadian enterprise. Conservative government intervention in economic matters in the name of nation building over the years bore witness to an enduring Tory collectivist strain in Conservative politics and was found later in John Diefenbaker's vision of development of the Canadian north. Macdonald, like early Conservative leaders who followed him, had an affection for the British monarchy and a reverence for British institutions. This was both a Tory nostalgic casting back to traditions and perceived stabilities of the past, and a rejection of the seemingly unfettered American liberal individualism seen by Macdonald as a threat to Canadian sovereignty. Perhaps Macdonald anticipated progressive Tory party leaders who came after him when he said, "I seek to enlarge the bounds of our party so as to embrace every person desirous of being counted as a progressive Conservative."[2]

After Macdonald, Canadian Conservatism continued in play with changes and shifts of emphasis in succeeding periods of leadership. With Robert Borden and Arthur Meighen, who believed that men were competitive by nature, the liberal element in the party took on more prominence in the 1920s. Yet Borden's and Meighen's opposition to reciprocity in trade with the United States and Meighen's belief in state intervention in railway development were both clearly traditional Tory nation-building policies.

In the 1930s R.B. Bennett declared that he would battle the nation's Depression woes with a wide-ranging program of government intervention, a new economic deal he called "reforms." In those uncertain times state action was required to control or at least mediate adverse economic events. Among other measures of relief for western Canada, Bennett advocated an extension of John A. Macdonald's old protectionist National Policy with the imposition of higher tariffs to "blast a way into markets that had been closed to us" in order to sell western agricultural products. Bennett sought to market these reforms with an odd combination of heated patriotic appeals for love of country and free-enterprise rhetoric extolling the competitive nature of the Tory-created Canadian National Railway.

In 1942 federal Conservatives chose John Bracken, the Liberal-Progressive Party Premier of Manitoba, as their leader. Bracken had been a Progressive before becoming premier of Manitoba, and his election as federal Conservative leader signalled an infusion of western progressive ideas and consequent significant changes in that party, including changing its name to the Progressive Conservative Party of Canada. The Bracken Progressive Conservatives brought about a dramatic departure from some Conservative Party traditions. The most dramatic of these was the adoption of the Progressives' hostility to tariffs. This was a repudiation of the traditional Tory protection policy begun by Macdonald. Bracken also believed in fewer state initiatives and that "government must be decentralized"[3] The new Tory leader believed, as Diefenbaker did later, in "unhyphenated Canadians" and the social individualism of the melting pot. He broke with the traditional conservative disposition to make slow and sure incremental progress in the improvement of social conditions rather than by initiating more radical and dramatic changes to bring about such improvements. George Drew, former Ontario premier, who followed Bracken, continued comfortably in Bracken's new paths preaching economic freedom, competitive enterprise and personal freedom.

Drew's successor, Saskatchewan's John Diefenbaker, gave expression to "a combination of traditional Conservative attitudes absorbed from the western Progressive tradition. His populism and advocacy of welfare state policies are in the "Tory democracy" tradition of paternalistic concern for the condition of the people."[4] What Diefenbaker stood for "incorporated the Tory progressive vision of his time with some old-fashioned values."[5] Diefenbaker championed the security of the common man, a fair deal for the "average citizen" under a system of private enterprise. He returned to the nation-building tradition of the party of Macdonald with a new National Policy that called for the development of Canada's northern lands. Diefenbaker combined a nostalgic loyalty to the British connection with a fierce pro-Canadianism. Like Bracken, Diefenbaker called for an "unhyphenated Canadianism," but Diefenbaker's unhyphenated Canadianism, his "One Canada" cry, was more an appeal for equality in Canadian society than for conformity. His was an expression of one of the liberal strains found in western Canadian Conservatism, a choice of Main Street, small-town free enterprise over Bay Street economic and social privilege.

In 1967 John Diefenbaker was succeeded in the Tory leadership by Robert Stanfield, premier of Nova Scotia. In 1968 Stanfield and his party rejected the rigorous social individualism of the melting-pot society and espoused a plural society, made up of groups of differing national and ethnic origins reaching out to each other and joined to each other in a common bond of shared Canadian citizenship. In a 1972 speech Stanfield declared:

> This is not a country that believes in the philosophy of the melting pot. This is not a country where it is necessary to submerge your national or ethnic origins nor forget the language of the country of your birth in order to be a good citizen.[6]

Canada, in Stanfield's view, was a collectivity of collectivities. He apparently believed these diversities could build a greater unity and a clearer Canadian nationality and collective purpose than any melting-pot assimilation of peoples could achieve.

Stanfield's successors in the leadership, Joe Clark and Brian Mulroney, also espoused a Canadian pluralism. Clark saw Canada as a "community of communities." Mulroney echoed this unity through diversity theme when he declared, "We have a dream of a great Canadian nationality, diverse and unique in the northern half of this continent. We are a country of different communities, a people of many cultures."[7] Mulroney's authorship of the Meech Lake and Charlottetown agreements signalled his recognition of

Quebec as a distinct society within the Canadian federation. His free-trade initiatives, hardly in the Canadian Tory tradition, indicated a clear and growing continentialist attitude in the Conservative Party. Arguably, no Canadian prime minister ever sought and won a closer personal relationship with American presidential and congressional leaders than Brian Mulroney. Mulroney left politics in 1993. This was followed by the essential collapse of the party until its transformation by Stephen Harper early in the new millennium.

Turning to the provincial scene we find that Saskatchewan's provincial Conservatism has been both a reflection of established Tory core values that began with Macdonald, and adaptations of these in a new egalitarian and liberal Canadian West. Writing in 2001, political scientist Howard Leeson, in a notable essay, "The Rich Soil of Saskatchewan Politics," suggests "rich soil" as a metaphor for politics in the province. He writes, "The fertile social soil of this province has provided us with a hundred years of unique and innovative political life."[8] This couldn't be better said. The Conservative Party has always been a part of that political life. The party began in the years of settlement; it saw the early days of ugly language and religious confrontation, the suffering of drought and Depression, the roil of agrarian protest, the heat of ideological clashes, the interchanges of recession and relative prosperity, the disquiet of the new right experiment, and finally the challenges and political transformations of a new-millennium Saskatchewan.

Provincial Conservatives, albeit some more than others, have always been populist and progressive by nature. A Tory collectivist instinct has been evident in the provincial party since it began with Frederick Haultain who, like Macdonald and Meighen, believed in government action when common goals and public needs were at stake. It was Haultain who advocated public ownership of telephones, legislation to protect farmers against powerful eastern combines of lumber and grain dealers, a government-constructed and operated railway to Hudson Bay to move prairie grain to market, and government ownership and control of grain elevators. The historian, L.H. Thomas, believed Haultain "adopted much of the philosophy of the later populist or democratic socialist."[9] Certainly, he never flinched from urging government intervention in economic matters.

After winning government in 1929, J.T.M. Anderson's Conservatives were faced with the economic and social disasters of drought and Depression. There was no time for ideological musings. Immediate practical assistance by government interventions and aid programs had to be provided, and it was. These government relief measures, widespread and social democratic in nature, were undertaken in the spirit of traditional "Tory democracy" by the Anderson administration. The Anderson government's remarkably caring and effective response to the Depression's ills and sufferings should have done much to soften the party's image as an establishment servant of Anglo-Saxon Protestant privilege. Its defeat in 1934, however, suggested that voters were unimpressed by the party's undoubted progressive nature and blamed it for their continuing troubled times.

With the participation of the Farmer-Labour Party in the 1934 election, Saskatchewan continued with an essentially two-party system but saw its politics increasingly polarized along more distinct left-right ideological lines. On the left, the Farmer-Labour Party, followed by the CCF and the NDP, were all supported by smaller, less prosperous farmers and urban workers who espoused social democratic principles. On the right, the Conservative and Liberal parties appealed to the more prosperous farmers, small business and higher income voters. Although Saskatchewan's partisan political divisions have often been along largely ideological and class lines, there has been resistance to radicalism by provincial voters. Political scientist Evelyn Eager characterized Saskatchewan electors as "largely pragmatic and conservative."[10]

This conservatism and pragmatism was clearly expressed in John Diefenbaker's 1938 provincial election platform. Diefenbaker followed in the progressive direction charted by Anderson and moved the Conservative Party leftward. Although he had no seats in the legislature, the party's 29% of the popular vote had garnered the Tories a respectable second-place showing in 1934. Now, four years later, Diefenbaker needed a platform appealing enough to draw votes from the ruling Liberals, and leftist enough to compete with the mildly socialist CCF if he was to keep the Tories in second place in Saskatchewan and have them remain a viable alternative to form government in the near future. The 1938 Conservative platform, in addition to core agrarian reforms, included progressive labour and medical services proposals with undoubted social democratic appeal. These proposals upset some Tories who bemoaned the "leftist control" of unwelcome progressive elements in the party. Diefenbaker himself described the 1938 platform as a "radical reform program."[11] Diefenbaker's Conservatives were soundly defeated for second place by the CCF in 1938.

The 1938 success of the CCF guaranteed that provincial politics in Saskatchewan would continue to be fought along the left-right ideological lines begun in 1934. The Conservative Party, renamed the Progressive Conservative Party in 1942, remained a party of the moderate right with distinctively progressive social policies and leaderships, but its immediate role in Saskatchewan politics changed after 1938. Following their 1938 electoral debacle, Saskatchewan's Progressive Conservatives spent the next 40 years fighting eight consecutive elections that garnered only third- and fourth-place finishes. Finally, after impressive signs of revival in 1975, the party entered the 1978 election campaign as a real alternative to the current governing party.

What was the Tory party's role in Saskatchewan affairs during the 40 years it lodged in the wilderness? It can be said here that even at its lowest ebb, when the party dipped to fourth-place positions and single digit percentages of popular vote, there was never a chance that provincial Progressive

Conservatives would fold and leave the political gaming table. However extreme its struggle in the past the party had always been sustained by essential, even heroic leaders and small cadres of surviving diehards who supported them. One of the reasons the provincial Progressive Conservative Party survived the lean years in Saskatchewan was the continuing strength and relevance of the party at the federal level and the mutually beneficial relationship between federal and provincial Tories that resulted. Over time the federal party both encouraged its provincial wing and drew strength from it. During the Diefenbaker, Stanfield, Clark and Mulroney federal leadership years when the Progressive Conservatives held the majority of Saskatchewan federal ridings, the relationship between federal and provincial Tories, although certainly not always cordial, did provide some limited funding for provincial Tories by the national office and allow some cross-over sharing of riding membership files, executive officers and campaign personnel at election times. As noted earlier it was undoubtedly to the financial and organizational advantage of the provincial party that both Rupert Ramsay and Alvin Hamilton, while serving as provincial leaders, drew salaries and funding as "Directors of Organization in Saskatchewan" for the federal Progressive Conservative Party. Without these stipends, meagre as they were, the Saskatchewan PC Party of the 1950s might have withered and died.[12] In the wilderness years between Diefenbaker and Collver, the role of the provincial party was reduced from that of real contenders for office to that of third- and fourth-place players with little left to offer except some good ideas and leaders with common sense, decency, patience and calm. With the multi-difficulties of few candidates, unreliable friends, poor organizations and shrunken, disheartened memberships all reinforcing each other, the Tories struggled for relevance in crowded three- and four-party races. They had to keep the Progressive Conservative Party in the political conversation in Saskatchewan. They had to define and design moderate, practical policies and programs for the centre-right and tell the people all about them! Tories couldn't just sit mum in a corner and be ignored!

No one understood this better than Alvin Hamilton. He became the Tories' foremost idea man and advocate. He was convinced that a lively program of education and outreach, beginning with the party membership itself, had to be undertaken:

> There is a real need in Saskatchewan for a party that believes in private enterprise and is willing to educate the people of the province to what is possible. Only if we continue to make our views known can there be increasing support for those views.[13]

Alvin Hamilton's "Development Programs" of 1952 and 1956, built from Rupert Ramsay's earlier platforms and added to later by Martin Pederson in the 1960s, all contained proposals that were not merely centre-right but "red

Tory" in nature, depending on the degree of government involvement and social programming required. These progressive documents did much to position the Conservatives as a competitive alternative to either the CCF or the Liberals, when shifting circumstances might allow the Tory party a change of role from a seemingly hopeless third-party aspirant to a serious challenger for power. After 1964 Social Credit all but disappeared in Saskatchewan, leaving only the Tories and. the Liberals to oppose the CCF. The defeat of the Thatcher Liberal government by the NDP in 1971 began a steady decline for Saskatchewan Liberals and a corresponding rise in the fortunes of the Progressive Conservative Party. Because of the capable presentation of PC programs by moderate and responsible leaders, the party steadily gained the public trust needed for it to take advantage of Liberal decline when it occurred.

In the provincial elections of 1975 and 1978, Dick Collver, the new Tory leader, appeared to nudge the party to the right with an ostensibly free-enterprise versus public-enterprise appeal reminiscent of the winning Thatcher Liberal anti-socialist campaign of 1964. Just how doctrinal or just plain tactical Collver was in 1975 and 1978 is difficult to judge. He may have been less interested in rightist ideology than in winning an election and restoring the party at long last to its former traditional role as a legitimate competitor for power in a two-party system.[14] Whatever the case, whether or not he knew it, Collver was a harbinger of neo-liberal times just ahead in Saskatchewan when a true conservative ideologue would win office.

Grant Devine led the Saskatchewan Tories in the 1980s. Under him the party took a sharp neo-liberal turn to the right in response to worldwide conditions and resulting economic distress in Saskatchewan. In the mid-1970s, an Arab oil boycott following an Arab-Israeli war led to dramatic rises in the price of oil which the industrial world had to pay, forcing governments and individuals to borrow to meet their needs. These international and national economic and political factors were beyond any provincial government's power to regulate. The resulting scourge of rising debt and borrowing caused soaring inflation, rising interest rates, economic stagnation and unemployment—for which Keynesian strategies of government control of interest rates, taxation and spending policies proved ineffective. Thus nations, significantly England and the United States, turned to neo-liberal ideological solutions. Saskatchewan was affected by all of this and suffered an economic crisis in 1982, to which newly elected Tory premier Grant Devine reacted.[15]

Neo-liberalism stresses freedom of enterprise and competition as the prime engines of economic growth and prosperity. The neo-liberal is hostile to government interference in business and private life. He believes in unfettered marketplace solutions to economic problems.[16] Although Grant Devine began tentatively in the 1982 election campaign emphasizing his populist appeal, he was eager to embrace neo-liberal principles and did so with increasing enthusiasm and clarity as he approached his 1986 re-election bid, and right-left divisions in political debate deepened. Devine's neo-liberalism, with its healthy infusion of social conservative gospel, was more often called "neo-conservatism." Certainly, as political scientists James Pitsula and Ken Rasmussen point out, Devine's new right movement wore a Saskatchewan brand and was adapted to the social democratic traditions and hinterland nature of the province.[17]

In 1991 Saskatchewan's Tory government was soundly defeated by the NDP in a landslide win. After nine years of racking up huge deficits and accumulating a crippling provincial debt, Grant Devine left office hounded by accusations of corruption and mismanagement. During the Devine years the economy had suffered from weak markets, low international prices, economic uncertainties and high government spending. The newly elected NDP government under Roy Romanow was expected to chart a better course for itself and the province. Romanow's better management required Draconian measures to reduce deficits and the provincial debt with spending cuts, tax increases and reduced funding for a range of care services. Romanow was both an analytical and intuitive politician, and he knew he would be trading present pain for future gain in 1995. He proved to be a pragmatic centrist in politics, surprising and disappointing some social democrats.

Bill Boyd, who succeeded Grant Devine as Tory leader, faced the NDP in the 1995 provincial election. While Boyd ostensibly maintained the social and economic conservatism of the party, he substantially moderated Devine's neo-liberal appeals and ran on a safe, essentially rural-friendly program aimed at the party's traditionally loyal farm and country base. In 1995 there was little ideological distinction separating Boyd's much-tamed Tory agenda and Romanow's "fiscal conservatism, moderate economic liberalism and social progressivism."[18] This transformation from ideological contest to more and more electorally oriented politics would become the hallmark of Saskatchewan affairs as the province entered the new millennium. With the legislative alliance of the wounded Progressive Conservatives and the fractured Liberal Party and the subsequent birth of the Saskatchewan Party, conservatism in Saskatchewan, albeit perhaps with less and less definition, no longer lodged in any one party so much as it found expression in them all. As well, with the arrival of the Saskatchewan Party in 1997 and the cobbled NDP-Liberal coalition in the legislature following the 1999 provincial election, class distinctions no longer seemed the most important determinant of partisan support. In a 2001 essay, Kevin Wishlow expresses the view that traditional bipolar explanations of Saskatchewan's party system are no longer adequate. Wishlow discusses the concept of the "citizen as consumer" in a political marketplace of competing brokerage parties. He questions the notion that Saskatchewan's contemporary political parties are polarized along defined left-right ideological lines as they once were, and sees the voter as a consumer shopping in a political marketplace for desired benefits and supporting the party which seemed best able to provide them. Wishlow tells us:

> The difference between Saskatchewan's two major parties [NDP and Saskatchewan Party] in the end is less a matter of ideology than of who speaks for whom.[19]

In the last two decades of the 20th century ideological differences among Saskatchewan parties may have narrowed but the parties themselves, once considered the most critical components of the political process, are still significant players in the province's political affairs. Although the role of a party in the formation and dissemination of policy and in the shaping and organizing of public opinion has become more and more shared with a range of lobby and interest groups, private institutes, coalitions, research councils, public institutions of learning, and print, electric and "on-line" opinion makers, the political party remains the lead contributor in the political communications process in Saskatchewan. While today Saskatchewan political parties are less sharply divided along right-left ideological demarcations, elements of traditional conservatism, liberalism and social democratic culture remain alive and part of the province's political conversation. Questions of how much or how little government involvement and control in the lives of citizens there should be are still debated. Questions about private enterprise and individual initiative and empowerment are still asked. Questions about the condition of the Saskatchewan welfare infrastructure and the changing definition of "progressive" politics in the province are still posed. These discussions may be less lofty and more pragmatic in nature than they once seemed and not abstract enough to justifiably be called ideological but they, along with the inevitable identity politics of provincial party warfare, are lively and ongoing today.

Apparently the Progressive Conservative Party has gone from the provincial scene, but conservatism is alive and well in Saskatchewan. Whereas it is true that all provincial parties have elements of conservatism in their make-ups, it is in the Saskatchewan Party, a party created by Progressive Conservatives, Liberals and federal Reformers, that Conservatives might now feel most at home. It should be noted that because of the close relationship between the Saskatchewan Party and the federal Conservative Party, formal affiliation of the two parties may follow in the future and the Saskatchewan Party become the Conservative Party of Saskatchewan.

However, it seems likely that such affiliation will have to wait until the Saskatchewan Party has established itself by winning government in the province and the new federal Conservative Party has matured and contended longer on the national stage.

19

A Summing Up

When Saskatchewan prepared for its 100th birthday party, its Centennial celebration in 2005, one of its charter political parties was missing. Naturally, there was some muted nostalgia, but there had been too many signs of the Tory party's irregular and failing health along the way for any real surprise at the end. Apparently Saskatchewan Tory Time had come and gone.

Years ago in 1955, Saskatchewan held an earlier birthday party—its Golden Jubilee celebration. On September 5, 1955, the province became 50 years old. That day provincial politicians of all parties must have looked back on their spent years and ahead, hopefully, to the future. On September 5, in Regina, a distinguished group of platform guests and speakers celebrated the province's Golden Jubilee. On this occasion Liberal Prime Minister Louis St. Laurent, who had journeyed from Ottawa, reminded those assembled of an earlier visit by another Liberal Prime Minister, Sir Wilfrid Laurier, in 1905, who had come west for the inauguration of the province, an inauguration to which the Conservative statesman Frederick Haultain had not been invited. Prime Minister St. Laurent told of Laurier's address that day, expressing his sunny ambition for the new province, all of which, according to St. Laurent, had been gloriously realized.

On the platform with Prime Minister St. Laurent sat four former Saskatchewan Liberal premiers, Martin, Dunning, Gardiner and Patterson, all beaming. And why not? They knew that for its first 50 years the province had been largely built by Liberal governments led by themselves. The host of this 1955 affair was the Honourable T.C. Douglas, current CCF Premier of Saskatchewan. He introduced two special guests, children of two deceased premiers of the province, Dorothy Scott, daughter of Liberal Walter Scott, Saskatchewan's first premier, and Byron Anderson, son of Conservative Dr. J.T.M. Anderson, until then Saskatchewan's one and only Conservative premier.[1] The junior Anderson looked lonely on the platform. In 50 years of predominantly Liberal rule only one Conservative government had ever been elected, and in 1955 no Tory government-in-waiting threatened the comfortable incumbent Tommy Douglas and the CCF, who had won three elections and would win two more. There weren't many Progressive Conservatives in the audience. What kind of Tory history had been made for them to ponder if they chose to look back? Theirs had not been a happy story. For years Saskatchewan Conservatives had been singing the blues, and that day they had little to celebrate at the half century nor, as it turned out, was a much brighter future ahead for them.

"Blues" in the entertainment world is sad, downbeat music, songs sung about hurt and things gone wrong. In Saskatchewan politics no one suffered the blues as did Conservatives beginning with Haultain's years of disappointment and ending in the wreckage of Grant Devine's neo-conservative dreams for the province 80 years later. Conservatives didn't just feel blue, they wore blue. Blue and white were Saskatchewan Tory party colours from 1905 with Haultain to the Collver campaigns in the 1970s, when a touch of red was added. Later, in the Devine years, the party sported a gaudier blue and orange badge. The Saskatchewan Tory story had no symmetry. It had no balance of wins and losses, no equation of success and failure, no finest hour! For the most part, it was a continuity of drift and frustration, of grim years battling to stay alive, an uphill struggle with little drama and only a few principal players. It seems remarkable that this struggle had never been abandoned. Why did Tories go on with it?

Surely one reason was that the Conservative Party of Saskatchewan was a very old party, as old as the province. Age alone gave it history, heroes and myth. These were hard to forget or discard. Even in the Territorial years of so called non-partisan relationships, federal Conservative and Liberal politics in far-away Ottawa coloured the affairs of the Territorial Assembly in Regina and seeded the young Tory and Grit parties that were to bloom and grow in the new province. These parties had federal heroes. Haultain, as a young man, was a John A. Macdonald Conservative and later a supporter of Robert Borden. Walter Scott was a devout Laurier Liberal. Although Haultain fought the first provincial election in 1905 as a "Provincial Rights" leader, that party was a thinly disguised provincial arm of the Conservative Party of Canada. The party remained a provincial arm, even if at times only a paper one through the Borden, Bennett, Meighen, Bracken, Drew, Diefenbaker, Stanfield, Clark and Mulroney national leadership years and beyond. Old habits are hard to kick.

The Tory party contested each of the 23 provincial elections held in the 90 years between 1905 and 1995, when it was swallowed up by the new Saskatchewan Party. In those 90 years and 23 provincial elections, Saskatchewan Conservatives won government only twice, were re-elected as government once, and served six terms as official opposition, three of these with single-digit memberships in the Assembly. For the party and a succession of leaders it was a staggered, off-again/on-again experience. There was no continuity of power, nothing was assured. Popular vote numbers dipped at times to single-digit percentages then rose to competitive, even winning levels only to plummet again. Yet, as discussed earlier, there has always been a conservative political party in Saskatchewan. Beginning with Provincial Rights and followed by the Conservative Party, the Progressive Conservative Party and the Saskatchewan Party, rightist or centre-right attitudes and principles have always been represented. Undoubtedly some of the party's most relevant and useful years were those following the disappearance of Social

Credit in Saskatchewan and the Liberal Party decline that began in 1975, when the Tories alone carried the right-wing banner against the dominant, left-leaning NDP.

There had always been enough tease and reason for the party to stay but never enough tenure for it to grow its reputation and establish its credentials. Yet Tory leaders—even the bland ones with little profile—hung in there, stubbornly refusing to walk away, always hoping for better luck next time. These leaders passed a torch, not always much flame but still a torch. Most of them had known each other and campaigned together as comrades. Each in turn reached out to the new leader and helped. Haultain, Anderson, Diefenbaker, Ramsay, Hamilton and Pederson had manfully held the Tory tent pole up in years of stormy weather, and certainly the flamboyant Dick Collver and the bantam, intrepid Grant Devine put a Tory stamp on Saskatchewan in the late 1970s and the 1980s.

Saskatchewan Conservatives, for the most part, had been well led throughout the life of the party. However, the potential of most Conservative leaders to govern was never tested, and their full capabilities remained undisclosed. What, for example, might John Diefenbaker or Alvin Hamilton have accomplished as Saskatchewan premiers had their provincial fortunes been different? Their later service to Saskatchewan and to Canada in federal Conservative governments suggests their contributions to provincial affairs would have been considerable. But they didn't have that chance. To win and hold government in Saskatchewan, political leaders need more than just basic party organization, adequate funding and a personal edge over contemporary adversaries. Above all, they need luck with the provincial economy. In Saskatchewan, economic prosperity trumps all other blessings. Good weather, good markets, stable agricultural prices, flowing resource revenues and generous federal transfers keep taxes controlled, deficits low and the electorate reasonably approving. Tory premiers Grant Devine and J.T.M. Anderson before him certainly learned this.

In government, parties, even those with little doctrinal glue to bind their partisans, can secure loyalty and ardour with patronage rewards of jobs, promotions, contracts, connections, influence and prestige, all devoutly to be wished by worthy party faithful. In opposition a party must appear to be positioned to win enough seats to challenge the government when it falters. It must be first in line when the "time for a change" cry is heard. But when that "time for a change" cry is not heard, and long, disheartening stretches in opposition reinforce weaknesses in the party, that party's struggle for relevance is bound to be desperate. Saskatchewan Tories certainly knew this. Repeated, demoralizing election defeats can contribute to intraparty conflicts and internal instabilities that make building the cohesion necessary to fight a common enemy difficult. The continued "True Blue" ideological spats during the Diefenbaker provincial leadership, and the Regina versus Saskatoon jealousies and minor frictions over provincial office location and staffing in the

Hamilton and Pederson years, can be cited as examples of internal squabbles that were not helpful. Certainly, they did nothing to provide winning conditions for the Tories.

Very few Saskatchewan Tory party leaders were ever favoured with winning conditions. What they did have, it seems, was an enduring loyalty to the party, a stubborn resolve to keep it alive and a persistent belief in tomorrow. They must have read and heeded American journalist Walter Lippmann's admonition, "The formal test of a leader is that he leaves behind in other men the conviction and the will to carry on."

What about the future? The Tory party is over now in Saskatchewan, but is it over just for now or forever more? It's likely that as long as the federal Conservative Party stays alive and active nationally, there will be rumours of a provincial PC revival and sightings of aging Tories gathering to rekindle old fires. It could be that for a time, relentless romantics, political junkies and hobbyists in Saskatchewan will chase after the past, refusing to allow perturbed Tory ghosts to rest. Perhaps. Yet, if the new Saskatchewan Party prospers, the conservative cause in Saskatchewan may be well enough served by it and a resurrection of the provincial PCs unnecessary, even impossible! Although ideological differences among Saskatchewan parties appear to be thinning in their pragmatic quests for broad-based support, a conservative impulse remains strong in Saskatchewan, and there will continue to be a significant body of right-of-centre attitude in the province and an association of partisans, a party, to express it in electoral politics. This right-wing party, whatever its name, will provide an agenda calling for limited government, wider private-sector initiatives and wealth creation, belief in the market, individualism and freedom of enterprise. Added to such a platform will be echoes of the Saskatchewan populist right, enduring charter articles of faith in hard work, personal responsibility, family values and the preservation of rural Saskatchewan to name the headliners. On the right we can also expect a variety of advocacy groups and agents ranging from chambers of commerce and right-wing institutes, coalitions and "think tanks" to Christian rights, evangelicals all voicing apprehension about what they deem excessive government involvement in the lives of the people. These critics will continue to be distrustful of growing "nanny state" social programs, judging them increasingly expensive, self-perpetuating and institutionalized as well as destructive of personal challenge and initiative.

As for the political left in the province, no one would doubt its survival. A devotion to leftist gospel, heroes and myth is a heritage value passed down from generation to generation in Saskatchewan. The social democratic liberal left in the province wearing some kind of party label will continue to be heard, and we can look for a growing variety of extra-legislative activist advocacy groups weighing in for the left on the side of more social programs, more government involvement and more government spending. Sententious leftist coalitions for "social and human justice," throbbing with mission and conviction, will be lobbying long and hard for more Aboriginal and Métis entitlements, more environmental safeguards, more anti-poverty funding and more union, worker, seniors, student, patient, inmate, animal, gay, lesbian, child and women's rights and benefits, all growing government and claiming public funding. Because societal norms are constantly changing it is difficult to chart the waters of the future, but inevitably there will be conflicting interpretations of Saskatchewan values and healthy, ongoing debate about them in the years ahead.

All Saskatchewan politicians, left and right, would do well to remember Marshall McLuhan's caution that "Politics offers yesterday's answers to today's problems." All of them will want to sift "yesterday's answers" carefully and consult past mistakes and dysfunctions before moving on.

Certainly, the Progressive Conservative collapse and the Liberal implosion that created the Saskatchewan Party in 1997 did not prologue a radical transformation of the political system in the province. The system is unaffected. The new party was simply the result of chance and changed circumstances, an adaptation to a new political landscape but not to a new climate. The role of government—what governments do and what governments do not do—may alter over time, affected by changes in our advancing electronic world, but the party system will live and continue to mediate the choosing of the governors.

How well the reshaped political right in the province will fare, only time will tell. We do believe there will continue to be a robust, two-party fight-bill in Saskatchewan, a province that has always enjoyed governing itself and living the best and the worst of an exuberant political life.

Like the fast flow of the great river after which Saskatchewan was named, this tradition will endure.

Epilogue

There is a PC postscript to consider. What about Saskatchewan's slumbering Progressive Conservative Party, apparently awakening in 2006 and fastening a lazy eye on the prospect of re-entry into provincial politics? Let's cast back to the events of 1997 when, six years after the crushing defeat of the Grant Devine government and the poisonous Tory fraud scandals, some 170 members of the PC Party gathered in a special meeting, amended the party's constitution and voted themselves into a state of hiatus, leaving the new Saskatchewan Party as the major right-wing challenger of the NDP. It was decided in 1997 that Saskatchewan Progressive Conservatives, although not contesting the elections, would remain officially registered as a political party for a period of two consecutive provincial elections. The party left itself with an executive committee to act in a caretaking role until some final—or at least some further—determination of the Tory status could he made.

The second of these two mandated consecutive elections was held in 2003, and the "to be or not to be" time for Tories had arrived. The caretaker executive committee announced that "the remaining members of the party and the executive committee had constitutionally taken over the operation of the PC Party."[1] Two years later, in June 2005, the executive committee, at a Saskatoon press conference, announced that a meeting of party members would be held at a date in 2006 to determine the future of the party, and in advance of that general meeting the party would take applications for new memberships. The executive committee further announced that at the 2006 meeting new and old party members would be given three choices: to revive the Saskatchewan Progressive Conservative Party, to disband the party permanently; or to continue the hiatus in some state. That meeting was held in Saskatoon at the Prairieland Exhibition Center on Saturday, May 27, 2006. Forty-two of the party's 75 paid-up members attended, and a decision to resurrect the PC Party of Saskatchewan was made.[2]

The party would attempt a comeback. Rick Swenson, a current executive committee member and former Devine government cabinet minister, would serve as interim leader of the newly reorganized Tory group. The Tories had found the will to live. Some asked, "why?" "We're back." "We're new." "We're needed," the Tories cried. Not everyone agreed!

The decision to revive the PC Party was immediately noted and questioned by provincial media, political journalists and, of course, by the Saskatchewan Party, which had an obvious interest in what appeared to be unfolding on the political right. Perhaps the widespread attention given the Tory revival plans is understandable. It is remembered that the Tory meeting in 1997 that put the PC Party into hiatus had been a confusing affair that ranked somewhere between a funeral and a christening. Many longtime PC members attending that gathering were deeply saddened by the apparent demise of their party while others, eager to leave the past behind, were excited by the challenge and confident the fledgling Saskatchewan Party would be a saviour and a winner for right-wing politics in the province. It is probable that no one was more conflicted at the time of the 1997 meeting than second-generation, lifelong Tory Rick Swenson, who had served as interim leader of the PC Party from January 1993, when Grant Devine resigned the leadership, to 1994, when Bill Boyd took over the reins. In 1997 it was Swenson who moved the motion to disband the PC Party for two elections. In a conversation and a later correspondence with the author in 2003, Swenson commented:

> I brought forward the motion that shut the PC Party down. I don't know whether that was right or wrong. I know there are those who believe the party was betrayed that day in 1997, but at the end of the day you have to keep trying to build this province. I believe removing the NDP from power is essential to that goal. Whether the Saskatchewan Party has the ability to do that effectively remains to be seen.[3]

Whatever misgivings Swenson and other advocates of a PC revival may have had about the Saskatchewan Party's ability to successfully challenge the NDP, their doubts were not confirmed by the results of the two provincial elections held during the Tory hiatus. In 1999 and again in 2003 the Saskatchewan Party mounted impressive campaigns, sounding strong right-wing appeals for tax cuts, job creation, elimination of government involvement in business investments, increased private-sector economic development, crime prevention, "workfare" programs and population growth. Led by former Reform Member of Parliament and Beechy, Saskatchewan farmer, Elwin Hermanson, the party proved itself a clear right-wing alternative to provincial New Democrats by winning 25 seats to the NDP's 29 seats, and the Liberals' 4 seats, in the 58-seat legislature in 1999, and increasing their numbers to 28 seats to the NDP's 30 seats in 2003.[4] The Saskatchewan Party appeared to have a commanding lead in rural Saskatchewan and needed only to increase its urban seat count in order to win government in the province. The new centre-right party, six years after its founding, was knocking on the doors of power. If the prime reason for pulling the PCs out of active politics in 1997 was to build a common front to defeat the NDP, putting the PCs back on the ballot in 2007 and splitting the anti-NDP vote in future elections would appear to make no sense. Former PC leader and premier Grant Devine, a 28-year veteran of PC politics in Saskatchewan, opposed reviving his old party. Devine expressed concern that an active Progressive Conservative Party would split the provincial right-wing vote and provide mixed messages from the right: "If you split the vote three or four ways in Saskatchewan, it's just that much more confusing."[5] Devine believed the principles of conservative politics in Saskatchewan were now represented and adequately expressed by the Saskatchewan Party.

The principal advocates of a PC revival appeared to be Rick Swenson and Grant Schmidt, two former cabinet ministers in the Devine government. Both men were members of the PC Party's executive committee and had served on that committee during the hiatus years. Swenson had played a relatively prominent role in Progressive Conservative affairs in the past but left politics in 1995 when he did not seek re-election in his Thunder Creek riding. Schmidt, elected in 1982 in Melville and re-elected in 1986, suffered defeat in 1991. He then sought the provincial leadership of his party in 1994 but was defeated by Bill Boyd. After the defeat Schmidt left politics but returned in 2003 when he sought and won a Saskatchewan Party nomination in the new Melville-Saltcoats seat only to have the nomination revoked by the party's executive council which fretted that his earlier flamboyant career and ties with the failures of the Devine years would make him a doubtful winner for them. Schmidt then ran as an independent but was easily defeated by the official Saskatchewan Party candidate. Here Schmidt's dalliance with the Saskatchewan Party ended.

With the success of the Saskatchewan Party and the sunny days apparently ahead for it, how does one explain the desire of some for a PC rebirth in the province? How do those who advocated that revival rationalize their enthusiasms? The Saskatchewan Tory revival engine seemed to be driven by long-time Progressive Conservatives. Did they, because of loyal personal or family affiliation, somehow feel entitled to right-of-centre leadership roles? Did they believe they occupied some hereditary office as right-wing champions in the province for which the Saskatchewan Party didn't qualify? Affection for party heroes and myth, attachments to tradition and known ways are never easily or painlessly discarded. Every longtime practitioner of electoral politics in Saskatchewan knows this. Certainly a reluctance to change what has been valued in extended political associations is natural and inevitable. But in the to-and-fro of the often heated debate over reviving the PC Party, one might ask of those on both sides of the question how much principle and ideology has been involved in the discussions, and how much nostalgia and personal ego has stood in the way of thoughtful adjudication.

At the heart of the debate about party status was a continuing dispute over money. This ugly money matter created enough heat and discord to make future reconciliation of the remaining provincial Tory remnant and the ascending Saskatchewan Party nearly impossible. At issue was a $2.9 million PC Party trust fund that both parties seemed eager to control. Like a messy sorting-out of marital spoils after a separation, the two parties issued claims and counter claims that it appeared only court judgments could settle. The to-and-fro of argument over trust financing and party designation for the Saskatchewan PCs continued unabated for months. The $2.9 million trust fund was money raised from contributions to the party during the Devine years. It had been set up in 1981 and grew.[6] Through the years of hibernation the Tory party annually had received limited funding from the trust fund to keep a Regina office and staff it. After the hiatus ended in 2003, Rick Swenson charged that the trustees had begun interfering in the operation of the PC Party in 2004 and stopped providing income for its day-to-day functioning by cutting funding in half in 2005 and refusing party funding altogether in 2006.[7] The trustees maintained that they had withheld money because they questioned that the PC Party at the time still existed in its original form. They argued that

> only people who were party members in 1997 when the party was put into hibernation for two elections should be allowed a say in the party's future and that the Progressive Conservative Party must go through a fair and unbiased process with the original membership determining its future.[8]

The Tory executive committee countered that

> the party's constitution gave them the right to set the process and that new and lifetime members should have a voice in deciding the future of the party.[9]

Swenson accused the trustees of withdrawing funding from the PCs because of a connection of three of the five trustees with the Saskatchewan Party, a party, he said, that obviously didn't want the Tories re-established and competing in provincial politics. Saskatchewan Party executive director Bob Mason dismissed this suggestion as baseless.[10] The trustees argued that the trust deed severely binds and restricts the dispensation of money out of the fund and legal opinions needed to be sought. The PC executive committee publicly stated they would take legal action seeking control of the trust money. Whereas the legal wrangle would go to the courts for adjudication, the political scrambles and squabbles continued in public, and relationships between the PC executive committee and the Saskatchewan Party leadership appeared to worsen.

Bill Boyd, the direct and plain-spoken former Progressive Conservative Party leader and one of the principal founders of the Saskatchewan Party, has had little patience with the PC's tale of woe. Boyd accepts that political times have changed in Saskatchewan. In the past, he says, the PC Party certainly played an important part in representing provincial conservatism, but the conservative messenger has changed in Saskatchewan. Boyd believes that

> The reality today is that the Saskatchewan Party is now the conservative party in Saskatchewan. Saskatchewan electors

have recognized this, and voters in two provincial elections have endorsed our conservative agenda in significant numbers. The next step is to form government.[11]

Boyd believes that a sincere effort has been made by Saskatchewan Party personnel to reconcile with the dissident PC group and to involve Swenson in Saskatchewan Party activities, but that Swenson and others have remained wounded and distant, seemingly uninterested in rapprochement: "Rick seems to feel some kind of personal entitlement and appears to have an agenda of his own."[12] Rod Gantefoer, MLA for Melfort, another principal founder of the Saskatchewan Party, agrees with Boyd's assessment that the new party has become the premier conservative voice in the province. Gantefoer is confident that the centre-right is strengthening in Saskatchewan and feels assured of the ascendency of the Saskatchewan Party: "We are a government in waiting!"[13]

Progressive Conservative spokesmen Rick Swenson and Grant Schmidt, undismayed it seems by the disappointing turnout of only 42 members at the May 27, 2006, Tory revival meeting, continue to maintain that they are leaders of a legitimate political party with a solid claim to $2.9 million in the Tory trust fund. Swenson favours a return to the hustings for the party. However, he says such a PC re-entry may be delayed until after the next provincial election in 2007 or early 2008, and until a proposed "policy convention" is held to provide the party with a platform. There is still water to flow under the bridge.

As one might have expected, Grant Schmidt was sharp in his criticisms of the Saskatchewan Party, his antipathy concentrated by that party's embarrassing rejection of him as a candidate in 2003. In a 2006 interview, Schmidt argued:

> The Progressive Conservative Party has always been a party that looks to its membership. The Saskatchewan Party does not have a history of looking to its membership. They are not a membership-based party. They don't allow debate and discussion.[14]

Later he despaired of both the NDP and the Saskatchewan Party: "The voters' choice in Saskatchewan right now is between a socialist party with no vision and a capitalist party with no vision."[15] Rick Swenson's "take" on what happened that day in 1997 when the PC Party was disbanded for a period of two years and his later reasons for re-establishing the Tories are described in a May 2006 interview published in the *Moose Jaw Times-Herald*. Swenson told the newspaper:

> The PC Party agreed to stand back when the Liberals and many PC supporters joined to form the Saskatchewan Party with the aim of overthrowing the NDP. But too many former Conservatives are now dissatisfied with the Saskatchewan

Party. The Saskatchewan Party is all about grabbing power, and that's it![16]

In public statements discussing policy Swenson has maintained that his desire to see a Tory revival is only partly driven by the trust fund dispute. Swenson also accuses the Saskatchewan Party of neglecting

> important issues not being dealt with in the province such as the need for electoral reform as a way to help bridge the urban-rural divide and improve the quality of politics in Saskatchewan. We must find some way of drawing people together, and a well-functioning political system is one way to make that happen. I think we've not been well served in the last dozen years or so with the way the Legislative Assembly has been so divided.[17]

Here Swenson, who left politics in 1995, was expressing dissatisfaction with divisions in the Assembly during 11 years of his absence from the legislature. Too soon he may have forgotten some of the scenes of political storm and stress he must have witnessed during the Devine years when government and opposition partisan clashes were loud and constant.

Swenson, the interim leader of the newly reorganized Progressive Conservative Party, unlike some others—including his former leader Grant Devine—was not concerned about dividing the anti-government vote and extending an NDP hegemony in the province. Swenson maintained, "The more choices people have, the better. I always compare politics to consumers. In politics the consumer is looking for the best product at the least cost. Consumers do best when there's lots of people going after the vote."[18] Obviously, the concept of the voter as consumer as expressed by Swenson is far too pat and fleet to be taken at full-faced value, and it would be unfair to Swenson himself to suggest that he intended it to be swallowed whole. We would need to hear more from the PCs on this notion of consumerism if in fact it is to be new PC thinking. Saskatchewan's long-established tradition of two main political parties contending often in a three-party field would make Swenson's multi-party, "the more choices the better" system improbable in the Land of Living Skies. As discussed earlier, unquestionably ideological differences among Saskatchewan political parties are narrowing. Provincial voters now choose from among parties much less ideologically sorted into left and right bodies than they once were. But political left and right concepts and values remain relevant and meaningful in the province. Swenson will find it difficult to escape blame from some Conservatives if he appears at best to compromise or at worst to betray the Saskatchewan political right by dividing it.

What will happen to the $2.9 million trust fund we cannot be sure. There are undoubtedly some legal somersaults yet to be turned before we know how the Tory money is to be spent and by whom.

The Progressive Conservative Party's self-designed disappearance has caused a rare but only a brief bewilderment in Saskatchewan. In Saskatchewan politics, the caravan moves on quickly. Whether the PCs will fade totally away like Social Credit in the past, or linger on in some yet unknown new form, we can only guess. But like the winds and the rains and the snowfalls of winter, Saskatchewan politics has been difficult to predict, and second guessing remains a very dicey pursuit. Politics, after all, unlike science, does not have established order and coherent systems. As Dalton Camp, the outstanding Conservative author and journalist, notes, "political systems and theories collapse under the weight of exceptions."

It is the continual confounding of assumptions that makes political study in Saskatchewan so enduringly fascinating.

Appendix:
Provincial Rights Party, Conservative Party
and Progressive Conservative Party Leaders in Saskatchewan
1905–1997

Frederick W.G. Haultain	1905–1912
Wellington Willoughby	1912–1918
Donald Maclean	1918–1921
J.T.M. Anderson	1924–1936
John G. Diefenbaker	1936–1940
Bert Keown	1940–1944
Rupert Ramsay	1944–1948
Alvin Hamilton	1949–1957
Martin Pederson	1958–1968
Edward Nasserden	1970–1972
Dick Collver	1973–1979
Grant Devine	1979–1994
Bill Boyd	1994–1997

Endnotes

For a summary of all Saskatchewan provincial election results, see Howard Leeson (ed.), *Saskatchewan Politics: Into the Twenty-First Century* (Regina: Canadian Plains Research Center, 2001), Appendix A, "Provincial Electoral Results, 1905–1999," 407–10.

Chapter 1
1. John Diefenbaker was well aware of the Haultain grave and, himself a former provincial Conservative leader and Chancellor of the University of Saskatchewan, would also be buried on the campus.
2. L.H. Thomas, "The Political and Private Life of F.W.G. Haultain," *Saskatchewan History* 23, no. 2 (1970): 1.
3. W. Christian and Colin Campbell, *Political Parties and Ideologies in Canada* (Toronto: McGraw-Hill Ryerson, 1974), 86.
4. Earl G. Drake, *Regina, The Queen City* (Toronto: McClelland and Stewart, 1955), 51.
5. As later events would attest, he did not envisage a two province division of the Territories.
6. Evelyn Eager, *Saskatchewan Government: Politics and Pragmatism* (Saskatoon: Western Producer Prairie Books, 1980), 23.
7. Ibid., 4–5.
8. L.H. Thomas, *The Struggle for Responsible Government in the North-West Territories* (Toronto: University of Toronto Press, 1978), 158.
9. Norman Fergus Black, *A History of Saskatchewan and the Old North West* (Regina: Saskatchewan Historical Company, 1913), 431.
10. Grant MacEwan, *Frontier Statesman of the Canadian Northwest: Frederick Haultain* (Saskatoon: Western Producer Prairie Books, 1985), 4.
11. Thomas, *The Struggle for Responsible Government*, 258.
12. Bill Waiser, *Saskatchewan: A New History* (Calgary: Fifth House, 2005), 479
13. Black, *A History of Saskatchewan*, 453.
14. Ibid., 454.
15. Ibid.
16. Black, 455.
17. Laurier letter quoted in Black, *A History of Saskatchewan*, 456.
18. Hugh G. Thornburn (ed.), *Party Politics in Canada* (Scarborough: Prentice-Hall of Canada Ltd., 1979, "1904 Election total," Appendix, 315.
19. Stanley Gordon, "F.W.G. Haultain, Territorial Politics and the Quasi-Party System," *Prairie Forum* 6, no. 1, (1981): 8–9.
20. David E. Smith, *Prairie Liberalism: The Liberal Party in Saskatchewan 1905–1971* (Toronto: University of Toronto Press, 1975), 8.
21. C.E.S. Franks, "The Legislature and Responsible Government" in Norman Ward and Duff Spafford (eds.), *Politics in Saskatchewan* (Don Mills, ON: Longmans Canada Ltd., 1968), 21.
22. Thomas, "The Political and Private Life of F.W.G. Haultain," 52.

23. Stanley Gordon, "F.W.G. Haultain," 2.
24. John T. Saywell, "Liberal Politics, Federal Policies and the Lieutenant-Governor in Saskatchewan and Alberta," *Saskatchewan History* 8, no. 3, (1955): 83.
25. MacEwan, *Frontier Statesman*, 140.
26. Ibid., 156.
27. Drake, *Regina: The Queen City*, 128.
28. The festivities had been largely paid for by generous federal funding. Why not! Ottawa also wanted a good show.
29. MacEwan, *Frontier Statesman*, 153.
30. Gordon L. Barnhart, *Peace, Progress and Prosperity: A Biography of Saskatchewan's First Premier, T. Walter Scott* (Regina: Canadian Plains Research Center, 2000), 45.
31. C.C. Lingard, *Territorial Government in Canada: The Autonomy Question in the Old North-West Territories* (Toronto: University of Toronto Press, 1946), 250.
32. Saywell, "Liberal Politics," 85.
33. Gordon, "F.W.G. Haultain" 10.

Chapter 2
1. Thomas, *The Struggle For Responsible Government in the North-West Territories*, 182.
2. Smith, *Prairie Liberalism*, 6.
3. Barnhart, *Peace, Progress and Prosperity*, 58.
4. MacEwan, *Frontier Statesman*, 140.
5. Smith, *Prairie Liberalism*, 22.
6. D.H. Bocking, "Saskatchewan's First Provincial Election," *Saskatchewan History* 17 (1964): 4–5.
7. Thomas, "The Political and Private Life of F.W.G. Haultain," 51.
8. McEwen, *Frontier Statesman*, 85.
9. Archer, *Saskatchewan: A History* (Saskatoon: Western Producer Prairie Books, 1980), 137.
10. Bocking, Saskatchewan's First Provincial Election," 47.
11. Ibid., 50.
12. Saywell, "Liberal Politics, Federal Policies and the Lieutenant Governor," 87.
13. Bocking, "Saskatchewan's First Provincial Election," 51.
14. Archer, *Saskatchewan: A History*, 138 and Bocking, "Saskatchewan's First Provincial Election," 52.
15. Barnhart, *Peace, Progress and Prosperity*, 45.
16. Smith, *Prairie Liberalism*, 39.
17. Bocking, "Saskatchewan's First Provincial Election," 50.
18. Barnhart, *Peace, Progress and Prosperity*, 128.
19. Smith, *Prairie Liberalism*, 37.
20. Ibid., 28.
21. Thomas, "The Political and Private Life of F.W.G. Haultain," 54.
22. Barnhardt, *Peace, Progress and Prosperity*, 95.
23. Waiser, *Saskatchewan: A New History*, 138.
24. Gordon L. Barnhardt (ed.) *Saskatchewan Premiers of the Twentieth Century* (Regina: Canadian Plains Research Center, 2004), 35.
25. MacEwen, *Frontier Statesman*, 169.
26. Ibid.
27. Drake, *Regina: The Queen City*, 144–48.
28. Ibid.
29. Archer, *Saskatchewan: A History*, 164.
30. Barnhart, *Peace, Progress and Prosperity*, 163.

31. Smith, *Prairie Liberalism*, 57.
32. MacEwen, *Frontier Statesman*, 185.
33. Remarks by Premier Lorne Calvert at the Millennium Celebration.

Chapter 3
1. Michael Cottrell, "Willoughby, W.B." in Brett Quiring (ed.), *Saskatchewan Politicians, Lives Past and Present* (Regina: Canadian Plains Research Center, 2004), 244.
2. Smith, *Prairie Liberalism*, 52.
3. Barnhart (ed.), *Saskatchewan Premiers of the Twentieth Century*, 26.
4. J. William Brennan, "A Political History of Saskatchewan, 1905–1929" (PhD dissertation, University of Alberta, 1976), 327.
5. Smith, *Prairie Liberalism*, 51.
6. Scott's struggle with mental disability at the end of his career is described in Gordon Barnhart's *Peace, Progress and Prosperity*.
7. Waiser, *Saskatchewan: A New History*, 139.
8. Smith, *Prairie Liberalism*, 57.
9. Keith McLeod, "Politics, Schools And The French Language, 1881-1931" in Ward and Spafford (eds.), *Politics in Saskatchewan*, 136.
10. Ibid., 135.
11. Ibid.
12. Smith, *Prairie Liberalism*, 116.
13. Archer, *Saskatchewan: A History*, 181.
14. Drake, *Regina, The Queen City*, 167.
15. Raymond Huel, "The French-Canadians and the Language Question, 1918," *Saskatchewan History* 23 (1970): 1–15.
16. McLeod, "Politics, Schools and The French Language, 1881-1931," 140.
17. Smith, *Prairie Liberalism*, 123.
18. Archer, *Saskatchewan: A History*, 191.
19. Brennan, "A Political History of Saskatchewan 1905–1929," 587.
20. J.W. Brennan, "C.A. Dunning and the Challenge of the Progressives," in D.H. Bocking (ed.), *Pages from the Past: Essays on Saskatchewan History* (Saskatoon: Western Producer Prairie Books, 1979), 205.
21. See J.W. Brennan, "Press and Party in Saskatchewan, 1914–1929," *Saskatchewan History* 27, no. 3 (1974): 81–89.

Chapter 4
1. Smith, *Prairie Liberalism*, 127.
2. Denis Smith, *Rogue Tory: The Life and Legend of John G. Diefenbaker* (Toronto: Macfarlane, Walter and Ross, 1997), 77.
3. Eager, *Saskatchewan Government*, 8.
4. Smith, *Prairie Liberalism*, 130.
5. J.F.C. Wright, *Saskatchewan: The History of a Province* (Toronto: McClelland & Stewart, 1955), 212–15.
6. Patrick Kyba, "Ballots and Burning Crosses" in Ward and Spafford (eds.), *Politics in Saskatchewan*, 116.
7. Martin Robin, *Shades of Right: Nativist and Fascist Politics in Canada* (Toronto: University of Toronto Press, 1992), p. 71.
8. P.A. Russell, "The Saskatchewan Conservatives, Separate Schools and the 1929 Election," *Prairie Forum* 8, no. 2 (1983): 211.
9. Robin, *Shades of Right*, 68–69.
10. Patrick Kyba, "Ballots and Burning Crosses," 108.
11. Robin, *Shades of Right*, 43–44.

12. Calderwood, "Rise and Fall of the Ku Klux Klan" (MA thesis, University of Saskatchewan, 1968), 213.
13. See Brennan, "Press and Party in Saskatchewan, 1914-1929," 81–89.
14. Smith, *Rogue Tory*, 57.
15. Calderwood, "Rise and Fall of the Ku Klux Klan," 218.
16 Smith, *Rogue Tory*, 55.
17. Kyba, "Ballots and Burning Crosses" 114.
18. Russell, "The Saskatchewan Conservatives, Separate Schools and the 1929 Election," 220.
19. Robin, *Shades of Right*, 70.
20. Ibid., 84.
21. Smith, *Prairie Liberalism*, 191.
22. Russell, "The Saskatchewan Conservatives, Separate Schools and the 1929 Election," 221–22.
23. Eager, *Saskatchewan Government*, 53.
24. *Prince Albert Daily Herald*, June 7, 1929.
25. Norman Ward and David Smith, *Jimmy Gardiner: Relentless Liberal* (Toronto: University of Toronto Press, 1990), 121.

Chapter 5

1. Reminiscing in later years with Prince Albert associates, Diefenbaker expressed no regrets for his 1929 defeat, believing that he would have been swept away with the rest of Anderson's cabinet in the 1934 collapse, certainly adding no lustre to his 1938 party leadership.
2. Smith, *Prairie Liberalism*, 204.
3. Patrick Kyba, "J.T.M. Anderson, 1929–1934" in Barnhart (ed.), *Saskatchewan Premiers of the Twentieth Century*, 121.
4. Smith, *Prairie Liberalism*, 206.
5. Wright, *Saskatchewan: History of a Province*, 214.
6. Smith, *Prairie Liberalism*, 185.
7. Eager, *Saskatchewan Government*, 41.
8. Wright, *Saskatchewan: History of a Province*, 218.
9. Ibid.
10. Alma Newman, "Relief Administration in Saskatoon During the Depression" in Bocking (ed.), *Pages from the Past*, 240.
11. H.B. Neatby, "The Saskatchewan Relief Commission, 1931–1934," *Saskatchewan History* 3, no. 2, (Spring 1950): 48–53.
12. Ibid, p.56.
13. P.A. Russell, "The Co-operative Government's Response to the Depression," *Saskatchewan History* 24, no. 3, (Autumn 1971): 84.
14. Ibid., 86.
15. Ibid., 94.
16. Ibid., 93.
17. Ibid., 87–88.
18. Ibid., 92.
19. Ken Andrews, "Progressive Counterparts of the C.C.F.: Social Credit and the Conservative Party in Saskatchewan, 1935–1938," *Journal of Canadian Studies* 17, no. 3, (1982): 68.
20. Brennan, *Regina: An Illustrated History* (Toronto: James Lorimer, 1989), 136.
21. Glen Makahonuk, "The Saskatoon Relief Camp Workers' Riot of May 1933," *Saskatchewan History* 37, no. 2, (1948): 59.

22. *Saskatoon StarPhoenix*, May 11, 1933, p. 3.
23. See Glen Makahonuk's excellent analysis, "The Saskatoon Relief Camp Workers' Riot of May 1933," 55–69.
24. John G. Diefenbaker, *One Canada: Memoirs of The Right Honourable John G. Diefenbaker, volume 1: The Crusading Years* (Toronto: MacMillan of Canada, 1975), 172.
25. Smith, *Prairie Liberalism*, 127.
26. Ibid., 127.
27. Wright, *Saskatchewan: The History of a Province*, 212.
28. Russell, "The Saskatchewan Conservatives, Separate Schools and the 1929 Election," 214.
29. Eager, *Saskatchewan Government*, 75.
30. George Hoffman, "The 1934 Saskatchewan Provincial Election Campaign," *Saskatchewan History* 36, no. 2, (1983): 43.
31. Ward and Smith, *Jimmy Gardiner*, 165.
32. Hoffman, "The 1934 Provincial Election Campaign," 54.
33. Ibid., 47.
34. Waiser, *Saskatchewan: A New History*, 317.
35. Garrett Wilson and Kevin Wilson, *Diefenbaker for the Defence* (Toronto: James Lorimer, 1988), 158.
36. Hoffman, "The 1934 Saskatchewan Provincial Election," 49.
37. Kyba, "J.T.M. Anderson," 132.
38. Ward and Smith, *Jimmy Gardiner*, 168.
39. Wright, *Saskatchewan: The History of a Province*, 230.
40. *Moose Jaw Times*, June 20, 1934.
41. Ibid.
42. Christopher Ondaatje and Donald Swainson, *The Prime Ministers of Canada: 1867–1968* (Toronto: Pagurian Press Ltd., 1968), 91.

Chapter 6
1. Smith, *Rogue Tory*, 15.
2. Ibid., 55.
3. Gary Abrams, *Prince Albert: The First Century 1866–1966* (Saskatoon: Modern Press, 1976), 317.
4. Diefenbaker, *The Crusading Years*, 166.
5. Wilson and Wilson, *Diefenbaker for the Defence*, 209.
6. Diefenbaker, *The Crusading Years*, 149.
7. Ibid., 148.
8. Ibid., 145.
9. Smith, *Rogue Tory*, 96.
10. Ibid., 95.
11. The Farmer-Labour Party had now become the Co-operative Commonwealth Federation (CCF) and was aggressively led by George Williams.
12. Diefenbaker, *The Crusading Years*, 167.
13. Smith, *Rogue Tory*, 97.
14. Smith, *Prairie Liberalism*, 230.
15. Hoffman, "The 1934 Provincial Election Campaign," 51.
16. Smith, *Rogue Tory*, 80.
17. Andrew Milnor, "The New Politics and Ethnic Revolt, 1929–1938," in Ward and Spafford (eds.), *Politics in Saskatchewan*, 162.
18. Dick Spencer, *Trumpets and Drums: John Diefenbaker on the Campaign Trail* (Vancouver: Douglas & McIntyre, 1994), 21.

19. Andrews, "Progressive Counterparts of the C.C.F.," 66.
20. Wilson and Wilson, *Diefenbaker for the Defence*, 218.
21. Patrick Kyba, "From Contender to Also-Ran: John Diefenbaker and the Saskatchewan Conservative Party In the election of 1938," *Saskatchewan History* 44, no. 3, (1992): 113.
22. Ibid., 116.
23. Andrews, "Progressive Counterparts of the C.C.F.," 69.
24. Kyba, "From Contender to Also-Ran," 109.
25. Ibid., 111.
26. Andrews, "Progressive Counterparts of the C.C.F.," 65.
27. Diefenbaker, *The Crusading Years*, 178.
28. Ibid., 164.
29. Smith, *Rogue Tory*, 97.
30. Kyba, "From Contender to Also-Ran," 106.
31. Ibid., 107.
32. Ibid., 108.
33. Ibid.
34. Smith, *Rogue Tory*, 97.
35. Andrews, "Progressive Counterparts of the C.C.F.," 70.
36. *Regina Leader-Post*, March 3, 1938.
37. Kyba, "From Contender to Also-Ran," 107.
38. Peter C. Newman, "Foreword" to Spencer, *Trumpets and Drums*, vi.
39. Andrews, "Progressive Counterparts of the C.C.F.," 58.
40. Simma Holt, *The Other Mrs. Diefenbaker* (Toronto: Doubleday Canada, 1982), 162.
41. Diefenbaker, *The Crusading Years*, 174.
42. Many of his political friends in later years, this writer among them, were convinced this was the case.
43. George Williams's letter to Diefenbaker quoted in Kyba, "From Contender to Also-Ran," 112.
44. *Prince Albert Daily Herald*, June 9, 1938.
45. Holt, *The Other Mrs. Diefenbaker*, 173.
46. Smith, *Prairie Liberalism*, 241–42.

Chapter 7

1. The author was born in Melfort. For some years he and his parents were neighbours and friends of the Keown family, Bert, Scottie and their son.
2. Correspondence from D.E.L. Keown, son of Bert Keown, January 2, 2003.
3. Diefenbaker acknowledged this to the author on several occasions during election visits to Melfort during his last federal campaign.
4. Duff Spafford, "The Left Wing, 1921–1939," in Ward and Spafford (eds.), *Politics in Saskatchewan*, 44–56.
5. L.H. Thomas, "The C.C.F. Victory in Saskatchewan, 1944," *Saskatchewan History* 14, no. 1, (1981): 7.
6. Canadian Press, Tuesday, February 15, 1944.
7. Kay Pederson, widow of former PC leader Martin Pederson, knew Ramsay and admired his "decency and sincerity." Interview with author, July 12, 2003.
8. Patrick Kyba, *Alvin: A Biography of The Honourable Alvin Hamilton, P.C.* (Regina: Canadian Plains Research Center, 1989), 51.
9. 1944 Progressive Conservative Party Platform published in the *Prince Albert Daily Herald*, June 10, 1944.
10. Thomas, "The C.C.F. Victory in Saskatchewan, 1944," 9–10.

11. Walter Stewart, *The Life and Political Times of Tommy Douglas* (Toronto: McArthur & Co., 2003), 160–61.
12. Thomas, "The C.C.F. Victory In Saskatchewan, 1944," 10.
13. Ibid.
14. Havelock Ellis, *The Dance of Life*, (1923; Westport, CT: Greenwood Press Reprint, 1973), 225.
15. Smith, *Prairie Liberalism*, 258–59.
16. Thomas McLeod and Ian McLeod, *Tommy Douglas: The Road to Jerusalem* (Edmonton: Hurtig Publishers, 1987), 186.
17. Kyba, *Alvin*, 48.
18. Ibid., 47–48.
19. Diefenbaker named Hamilton Minister of Northern Affairs and National Resources in 1957 and he was the author of the "Vision" of national development begun in 1958.
20. Kyba, *Alvin*, 45.
21. Patrick Kyba, "Third Party Leadership in a Competitive Two Party Province," *Saskatchewan History* 36, no. 1, (1983): 18.
22. Kyba, *Alvin*, 51.
23. Ibid., 60.
24. Provincial PC advertisement printed in the *Prince Albert Daily Herald*, February 11, 1944.

Chapter 8

1. Hamilton's 1968 defeat was largely attributed to Saskatchewan resentment over Diefenbaker's removal as party leader in 1967. Hamilton remained active in the party and won re-election to Parliament in 1972.
2. Diefenbaker's Memoirs say little about Hamilton and the 1938 election.
3. Kyba, *Alvin*, 33.
4. This platform formed the basis of the PC "Ten Point Program of Development" Hamilton as leader would carry into the 1952 and 1956 elections.
5. In 1938 Hamilton supported Diefenbaker's opposition to "saw-offs" with the CCF to defeat the Liberals. He was always troubled by these arrangements which he saw as an assault on Conservative Party integrity. To ensure the party did not join in such coalitions was one reason for his decision to run for the top job.
6. Kyba, *Alvin*, 59.
7. A few weeks before the Tory leadership convention, in an August 5, 1949 letter to Hamilton, Bert Keown told him "If you are elected I will give you all the support I can." Keown remained a man of some influence in the party.
8. Hamilton's decision to keep the party provincial headquarters in Saskatoon upset Regina Tories who fussed that the party's central office should be in the Queen City. Hamilton's relationship, especially with "old family" Regina Tories, was always difficult.
9. Kyba, "Third Party Leadership in a Competitive Two Party Province," 13.
10. McLeod and McLeod, *Tommy Douglas*, 144.
11. It was not the impression of those of us who knew him that he lamented this role or felt diminished by it.
12. Smith, *Prairie Liberalism*, 263, and Archer, *Saskatchewan: A History*, 284.
13. Alex Jupp, a former President of the Young Progressive Conservatives in Saskatchewan refused to run as a straight Tory candidate under Hamilton and ran in Regina as a Tory Independent. In 1956 he ran as a Liberal and was again soundly defeated.
14. Kyba, "Third Party Leadership in a Competitive Two Party Province," 17.

244 | SINGING THE BLUES: THE CONSERVATIVES IN SASKATCHEWAN

15. The Tory campaigns of Dick Collver and Grant Devine echoed this cry in later elections, and in 2003 the "conservative" Saskatchewan Party made job and population growth a paramount election call, decrying Saskatchewan's youth trekking west to Alberta and British Columbia.
16. Smith, *Rogue Tory*, 191.
17. Brett Quiring, "Robert Kohaly," in Quiring (ed.), *Saskatchewan Politicians*, 124.
18. Ibid., 124.
19. Kyba, *Alvin*, 77. There can be little doubt that Robert Kohaly was Hamilton's first choice to succeed him in the leadership. He spoke of Kohaly as a replacement for provincial leader as early as 1955. Kohaly told Hamilton that he did not want the leadership.
20. Kyba, "Third Party Leadership in a Competitive Two Party Province," 7.
21. *Saskatoon StarPhoenix* editorial, June 18, 1956.
22. Kyba, *Alvin*, 86.
23. Ibid., 85.
24. Allister Grossart, the new National Director of the party, took the Tory party logo out of the advertising and put Diefenbaker and the need for change of government in its place. This proved a highly effective rallying cry as it appealed to independents.

Chapter 9

1. The author knew and campaigned with and for both men in provincial and federal Tory politics.
2. Dale Eisler, *Rumours of Glory: Saskatchewan and the Thatcher Years* (Edmonton: Hurtig Publishers, 1987), 64.
3. Kyba, Alvin, 90.
4. As in 1957, the Progressive Conservative Party logo was again printed in small letters with the leader featured and the electorate urged to "Follow John" rather than "Vote Tory."
5. J.L. Granatstein, *Canada 1957–1967: The Years of Uncertainty and Innovation* (Toronto: McClelland and Stewart, 1987), 172–73.
6. Allan M. Briens, "The 1960 Saskatchewan Provincial Election" (MA thesis, University of Regina, 2004), 79.
7. Smith, *Rogue Tory*, 309.
8. Ibid.
9. Briens, 87–89.
10. Ibid., 88.
11. Barry Wilson, *Politics of Defeat: The Decline of the Liberal Party in Saskatchewan* (Saskatoon: Western Producer Prairie Books, 1980), 14.
12. Briens, 70.
13. *Saskatoon StarPhoenix*, May 24, 1960.
14. Briens, 74–75.
15. *Regina Leader-Post*, March 3, 1960.
16. Dennis Gruending, *Promises to Keep: A Political Biography of Allan Blakeney* (Saskatoon: Western Producer Prairie Books, 1990), 35.
17. *Regina Leader-Post*, March 9, 1960.
18. Ibid., December 9, 1959.
19. Briens, 39–41.
20. The *Regina Leader-Post* editorial of June 15, 1962, supported the argument that the legislature should not be allowed to make the law in this case. Apparently the election results didn't count as an expression of the people's will.
21. Brien, 115.

22. *The Yorkton Enterprise*, June 9, 1960.
23. *Regina Leader-Post*, July 5, 1962, 3.
24. For an excellent account of the dispute see Edwin Tollefson, "The Medicare Dispute," in Ward and Spafford (eds.), *Politics in Saskatchewan*, 238–67.
25. Brett Quiring, "The Social and Political Philosophy of Woodrow Lloyd," *Saskatchewan History* 56, No. 1, (2004): 17.
26. Edwin A. Tollefson, *Bitter Medicine: The Saskatchewan Medicare Feud* (Saskatoon: Modern Press, 1963), 146–50.

Chapter 10
1. Granatstein, *Canada, 1957–1967*, 192.
2. Eisler, *Rumours of Glory*, 122.
3. Edwin Tollefson, "The Medicate Dispute," in Ward and Spafford (eds.), *Politics in Saskatchewan*, 267.
4. *Prince Albert Daily Herald*, Friday February 28, 1964.
5. The participation and strong showing of the Conservative candidate in 1964 brought Steuart close to defeat in a three-way flight for Prince Albert. His 1962 by-election majority of 2,522 votes was slashed to a thin 78-vote win over the CCF. His defeat in Prince Albert would have been a huge embarrassment. On election night in Prince Albert it was obvious that a significant shift of voter support from Liberal to PC columns had taken place.
6. Like his friend and mentor Alvin Hamilton, Pederson believed in strong ties with the federal party and, when possible, a sharing of office staff, organizers and policy wonks.
7. Many Tory candidates found the northern railway plank too "inventive" and ignored it.
8. McLeod and McLeod, *Tommy Douglas: The Road to Jerusalem*, 203.
9. In Prince Albert the defeated Tory candidate smiled and told a late night CKBI Television audience, "With one seat won, we're 100 percent stronger than we were yesterday."
10. Dick Spencer, President of the Prince Albert PC Federal Association was told to "discourage" talk of a provincial nomination. Diefenbaker did not assist Pederson in the 1967 campaign nor did Robert Stanfield, then the new PC federal leader.
11. Prince Albert *Daily Herald*, Thursday, September 21, 1967.
12. Peter Stursberg, Diefenbaker: *Leadership Lost, 1962–67* (Toronto: University of Toronto Press, 1976), 168.
13. Spencer, *Trumpets and Drums*, 117.
14. Eisler, *Rumours of Glory*, 202.
15. *Saskatoon StarPhoenix*, Friday, October 6, 1967.
16. Canadian Press, October 11, 1967.
17. Ibid., October 17, 1967.
18. Ibid.
19. Smith, *Prairie Liberalism*, 314.
20. Eager, *Saskatchewan Government*, 66–67.
21. *Regina Leader-Post*, Monday, October 19, 1970.
22. The author, as a young Tory, campaigned with Nasserden in the 1965 federal election.
23. "Little Allan" was a Liberal Party sobriquet for the New Democrat leader.
24. *Moose Jaw Times-Herald*, Thursday, June 24, 1971.
25. Trent Evanisk, "Edward Nasserden" in Quiring (ed.), *Saskatchewan Politicians*, 177.

Chapter 11
1. Collver interview in PC newspaper, *Saskatchewan Horizons*, June 1978.
2. Ibid.

3. Correspondence with the author, August 20, 2003.
4. Correspondence with the author, February 29, 2002.
5. Correspondence with the author, August 20, 2003.
6. Assessment expressed by Diefenbaker to the author when he advised the author not to seek the PC provincial nomination in 1978.
7. Although the author nominated Collver for the party leadership in 1973 and ran for the party in 1975 and 1978, he was never entirely comfortable serving under him.
8. Wilson, *Politics of Defeat*, 83.
9. Bailey ran as a provincial Social Credit candidate in 1956. He was elected federally for the Reform Party in 1997 and re-elected in 2000.
10. Leader's newsletter to membership, March 19, 1973.
11. Leader's newsletter to membership, June 19, 1973.
12. Ken Waschuk and Dave Tkachuk were two of the most active recruiters. Many considered them furtive and collusive, but they were devoted to Collver and eager to rise with his tide.
13. Collver interview in *Saskatchewan Horizons*.
14. Minutes of PC Provincial Executive Committee meeting, January 26, 1974.
15. In an August 8, 1973 correspondence to the author, Diefenbaker warned: "There is no possibility of a Progressive Conservative nominated provincially in Prince Albert winning or even saving his deposit in 1975." Diefenbaker changed his assessment as that campaign progressed. In 1975 in Prince Albert the PCs won a strong second place trailing the NDP by only 258 votes.
16. Correspondence from Clarke Brown to the author, May 6, 1973.
17. Diefenbaker correspondence to the author, Ottawa, August 8, 1973.
18. One of Diefenbaker's softer negatives about Collver often repeated to the author.
19. Privately Collver spoke openly to his candidates about a 1978 goal for forming government.
20. The author attended one of these schools and was greatly impressed with the instruction provided in workshops by professionals.
21. Polling by "Decision-Making Information, Canada" in Wilson, *Politics of Defeat*, 92.
22. Wilson, *Politics of Defeat*, 93.
23. Gruending, *Promises to Keep*, 135.

Chapter 12
1. *Saskatoon StarPhoenix*, Thursday, June 12, 1975.
2. *Prince Albert Daily Herald*, Thursday, June 12, 1975.
3. Morris Chernesky, PC President's Memo, August 23, 1975.
4. *Saskatchewan Horizons*, Director's Report, March 1978.
5. Provincial PC.Annual Meeting, Regina, 1977; Eager, Saskatchewan Government, 78.
6. Colin Thatcher, *Backrooms: A Story of Politics* (Saskatoon: Western Producer Prairie Books, 1985), 31.
7. Gruending, *Promises to Keep*, 173.
8. Collver's disdain for Blakeney was often expressed to the author and to other Tory candidates in language more robust than that quoted above.
9. Wilson, *Politics of Defeat*, 139.
10. *Saskatchewan Horizons*, June 8, 1978.
11. Ibid.
12. Bill McKnight, Campaign Chairman of the remarkable 1982 campaign which produced a Tory victory, stated emphatically that if it hadn't been for Collver's earlier organizing talents, that 1982 landslide might not have happened! July 2003 interview with author.

13. The author, nominated in Prince Albert, attended the candidates' school held in Regina.
14. In fairness to the PC Central Office accused of not selling Collver or not defending him in the heat of battle, it may be that Dick Collver, who was known for micro-managing his campaigns, would not allow these defenses for fear of becoming personally featured and drawing unfavourable attention to himself. He may have thought ignoring his personal critics wiser and more strategic than engaging them.
15. Wilson, *Politics of Defeat*, 143.
16. Gruending, *Promises to Keep*, 173.
17. James Laxer, *In Search of a New Left: Canadian Politics after the Neoconservative Assault* (Toronto: Penguin Books, 1997), 103.
18. Gruending, *Promises to Keep*, 173.
19. Thatcher, *Backrooms*, 123.
20. Don Baron and Paul Jackson, *Battleground: The Socialist Assault on Grant Devine's Canadian Dream* (Toronto: Bedford House Publishing, 1991), 14.
21. Ibid.
22. Wilson, *Politics of Defeat*, 145.
23. Gruending, *Promises to Keep*, 175; Eager, *Saskatchewan Government*, 186.
24. In 1978 as the campaign ended the author represented Collver in an all-candidate forum on education held for the Nipawin riding. At best the mood in the PC Committee Rooms was subdued, perhaps in anticipation of disappointing election night results in Nipawin which saw Collver's own 1975 plurality of 782 reduced to 487 votes in 1978.
25. Thatcher, *Backrooms*, 130.
26. The author attended this gathering.
27. August 2003 interview with author.
28. Rand Dyck, *Provincial Politics in Canada: Towards the Turn of the Century* (Scarborough, ON: Prentice-Hall Canada Inc., 1985), 492, n. 76.

Chapter 13
1. Rousseau was considered a close friend of the departing Dick Collver. This may have been more a minus than a plus for him.
2. Eager, *Saskatchewan Government*, 66.
3. Thatcher, *Backrooms*, 188–221.
4. July 2003 interview with author.
5. Baron and Jackson, *Battleground*, 16.
6. Thatcher, *Backrooms*; Pioneer Trust Survey, 177.
7. James M. Pitsula and Ken Rasmussen, *Privatizing a Province: The New Right in Saskatchewan* (Vancouver: New Star Books, 1990), 34.
8. July 2003 interview with author.
9. James M. Pitsula, "Grant Devine, in Barnhart (ed.), *Saskatchewan Premiers*, 322.
10. Ibid.
11. Waiser, *Saskatchewan: A New History*, 435.
12. Ibid.
13. Ibid., 436.
14. Interview with author, August 2003.

Chapter 14
1. Waiser, *Saskatchewan: A New History*, 436.
2. Pitsula and Rasmussen, *Privatizing a Province*, 41.
3. Pitsula, "Grant Devine," 324.

4. For an excellent discussion of the financial difficulties of the Devine government in its first term see Waiser, *Saskatchewan: A New History*, 438–42.
5. Pitsula and Rasmussen, 44–45.
6. Ibid., 106.
7. Gruending, *Promises to Keep*, 235.
8. Baron and Jackson, *Battleground*, 22.

Chapter 15
1. Lorne A. Brown, Joseph K. Roberts and John W. Warnock, *Saskatchewan Politics from Left to Right, 1944–1999* (Regina: Hinterland Publishing, 1999), 40.
2. Pitsula and Rasmussen, *Privatizing a Province*, 196.
3. Gerry Jones, *SaskScandal: The Death of Political Idealism in Saskatchewan* (Calgary: Fifth House Ltd.), 9.
4. Pitsula, "Grant Devine," 346–47.
5. Brown, Roberts, Warnock, 53.
6. August 2003 interview with author.
7. Pitsula and Rasmussen, *Privatizing a Province*, 3.
8. Pitsula, "Grant Devine," 319.
9. Ibid., 322.
10. Brown, Roberts, Warnock, 44.
11. Pitsula, "Grant Devine," 330.

Chapter 16
1. Jones, *SaskScandal*, 124.
2. Ibid., 30.
3. Ibid., 185.
4. Ibid., 121.
5. July 2003 interview with Devine. It was the author's impression that years later the premier's concern for colleagues wronged by the fraud scandals remained deep.
6. July 2003 interview with author.

Chapter 17
1. Thatcher, *Backrooms*, 168.
2. Baron and Jackson, *Battleground*, 315.
3. Correspondence to author, August 20, 2003.
4. April 2003 interview with author.
5. July 2003 interview with author.
6. Baron and Jackson, *Battleground*, 141.
7. At a 1989 Tory party fundraising dinner Premier Devine, to loud applause, introduced Schmidt as "the fellow who says what other people think." *Regina Leader-Post*, July 6, 1989.
8. Baron and Jackson, *Battleground*, 144–45.
9. Canadian Press, November 21, 1994.
10. *Regina Leader-Post*, April 6, 2002.
11. *Saskatoon StarPhoenix*, April 5, 2002.
12. Leeson (ed.), *Saskatchewan Politics*, 7.
13. Lynda Haverstock, "Saskatchewan Liberal Party, in Leeson, (ed.), *Saskatchewan Politics*, 234.
14. Jones, *SaskScandal*, 180.
15. Boyd was optimistic about a Tory revival and considered the party's 1995 score of 18% of popular vote a good beginning. He was right. Conversation with the author on May 27, 2006.

16. Haverstock, "Saskatchewan Liberal Party," 231.
17. *Saskatoon StarPhoenix*, March 1, 2006.
18. Rod Gantefoer, Saskatchewan Party MLA, correspondence to the author, January 6, 2006.
19. Gantefoer, correspondence with the author, January 6, 2006.
20. July 2003 interview with author.
21. Gantefoer correspondence.
22. Mark Wyatt, Sterling News Service, *Regina Leader-Post*, Saturday, November 8, 1997.
23. *Regina Leader-Post*, Monday, November 10, 1997.
24. May 2003 interview with author.
25. Kay Pederson, widow of former PC leader Martin Pederson, interview with author July 12, 2003.
26. July 2003 interview with author.
27. Kevin Wishlow, "Saskatchewan Party," in Leeson (ed.), *Saskatchewan Politics*, 177.
28. August 2003 interview with author.

Chapter 18
1. Christian and Campbell, *Political Parties and Ideologies in Canada*, 86.
2. Donald Creighton, *John A. Macdonald*, vol. 1 (Toronto: Macmillan, 1966), 199.
3. Christian and Campbell, *Political Parties and Ideologies in Canada*, 98.
4. G. Horowitz, "Conservatism, Liberalism and Socialism in Canada" in Thornburn (ed.), *Party Politics in Canada*, 60–61.
5. Smith, *Rogue Tory*, 133.
6. Christian and Campbell, *Political Parties and Ideologies in Canada*, 109.
7. John Sawatsky, *Mulroney: The Politics of Ambition* (Toronto: Macfarlane, Walter and Ross, 1991), 300.
8. Leeson (ed.), *Saskatchewan Politics*, 3.
9. Thomas, "The Political and Private Life of F.W.G. Haultain," 54.
10. Evelyn Eager, "The Conservatism of the Saskatchewan Electorate," in Eager (ed.), *Politics in Saskatchewan*, 1.
11. Ken Andrews, "Progressive Counterparts...," *Journal of Canadian Studies* 17, no. 3, (1982): 69.
12. Kyba, "Third Party Leadership in a Competitive Two Party Province," 17.
13. Hamilton message to the membership, *Saskatchewan PC Newsletter*, July 12, 1952.
14. The author, who nominated Collver for the provincial leadership in 1973, ran under him as a PC candidate in 1975 and again in 1978, remains convinced that Dick Collver's only ideology was the getting and keeping of political power. To Collver, political power was like some shiny new thing that caught his eye and he had to possess.
15. Leeson (ed.), *Saskatchewan Politics*, 5.
16. Brown, Roberts, Warnock, *Saskatchewan Politics from Left to Right*, 30.
17. Pitsula and Rasmussen, *Privatizing a Province*, 8–11.
18. Jocelyne Praud and Sarah McQuarrie, "The Saskatchewan CCF-NDP," in Leeson (ed.), Saskatchewan Politics, 162.
19. Wishlow, "Saskatchewan Party," 197.

Chapter 19
1. Nathaniel A. Benson, *None of It Came Easy: The Story of James Garfield Gardiner* (Toronto: Burns and MacEachern, 1955), 271.

Epilogue
1. *Regina Leader-Post*, Friday, June 9, 2006.

2. *Saskatoon StarPhoenix*, Monday, May 29, 2006.
3. Correspondence with the author, August 20, 2003.
4. Winter Fedyk, "Elwin Hermanson," in Quiring (ed.), *Saskatchewan Politicians*, 107.
5. *Saskatoon StarPhoenix*, Friday, May 26, 2006.
6. *Regina Leader-Post*, June 9, 2006.
7. Ibid.
8. Ibid., Friday, February 3, 2006.
9. James Wood, *Saskatoon StarPhoenix*, Friday, February 3, 2006.
10. Ibid.
11. Boyd interview with author, May 27, 2006.
12. Ibid.
13. Correspondence with author, January 6, 2006.
14. Wood, *Saskatoon StarPhoenix*, Friday, February 3, 2006.
15. Murray Mandryk, *Regina Leader-Post*, Wednesday, May 31, 2006.
16. *Moose Jaw Times-Herald*, Wednesday, May 31, 2006.
17. Wood, *Saskatoon StarPhoenix*, Friday, May 26, 2006.
18. *Moose Jaw Times-Herald*, Wednesday, May 31, 2006.

Index

Aberhart, William, 76-77, 85, 108
Aboriginal entitlements, 226
Aboriginal land claims, 190
Acreage Payment Program, 115
Adrian, Stuart, 47, 73
Advisory Economic Council, 68
agrarian protests, 35, 216
agrarian reforms, 79, 83, 217
Agricultural Extension Department (U of SK), 91
Agricultural Field Man Service, 91
agriculture, as industry, 22, 24, 38, 91-93, 96, 108, 133
Albert Street Memorial bridge (Regina), 60, 69
Alberta Conservative Party, 14
Alberta Social Credit League, 76
Allen, Ralph, 70
Allmand, Warren, 155
Anderson, Byron, 223
Anderson Cart, 63
Anderson, James Thomas Milton, Dr., 46, 73-74, 85, 127, 223, 225
   and conservatism, 216-217
   as Conservative leader, 38-42, 44, 47, 51, 66-72, 78, 236
   as critic of immigrant education policy, 44-45, 48-50
   Education of the New Canadian, The, 43
   government of, 51, 57-61, 64-65, 67, 69, 84, 89, 92, 101, 131, 155, 216
   as premier, ix, 52-56, 58, 60, 62-63, 225
Andrew, Bob, 177, 198
Angus Reid poll (1990), 189
Arm River, by-election in, 46-49, 51-52, 72-73, 75
Assiniboia, provisional district of, 4
Athabasca, provisional district of, 4
autonomy, for territories, 2, 5-7, 9, 11, 18, 22, 28-29
Avram, Lloyd, 138

back-to-work legislation, 174
bacon-processing plant, 193
Bailey, Roy, 143-145, 151
Balfour, R.M., 82
Baltzan family medical clinic, Saskatoon, 142, 163
Barmby, Doug, 147

Barnhart, Gordon L., 19
Beggs, Austin, 147
Bennett, Bill (BC), 108
Bennett Buggies, 63
Bennett, R.B., 47, 56, 63, 67, 71-73, 81, 84, 113, 115, 214, 224
Berntson, Eric, 151, 167, 177, 196, 198
Bessborough Hotel, Saskatoon, 138
Bichan, W.J., 127
Birkbeck, Larry, 151
Bitter Medicine: The Saskatchewan Medicare Feud, 124
Blakeney, Allan, 119, 154-156, 158, 183, 185, 187
   government of, 172, 174, 178
   as leader of NDP, 139, 142, 146, 151, 159, 161-164, 173, 175, 183-184, 189
   as premier, 140-141, 148, 150, 157, 170-171
Blue Monday, April 6, 1982, 174
BNA Act, 81
Borden, Robert, Sir, 214, 224
   as federal Conservative, 5-6, 22, 24-25, 70, 113
   as prime minister, 25, 27, 35
   Unionist administration of, 113
Boyd, Bill, 175, 203, 208-210, 213, 231-233
   election of 1995, 207-208
   as New PC leader, 206, 209, 230, 236
   as PC leader, 199, 205-206, 211, 220
Bracken, John, 73, 89, 214-215, 224
Bradshaw allegations, 32-33
Bradshaw, John Ernest, 32
Briens, Allan, 115
Broadway bridge (Saskatoon), 60
Brockelbank, John, 126
Brown, Clarke, 147
Brown Elwood Commission, 33
Bryant, J.F., 46, 47, 50-52, 55-56, 67
Bryant Park (Prince Albert), 60
Buckle, W.C., 52
Buckwold, Sid, 142
budget deficit, during Devine years, 178, 181, 184, 186

Calder, James A., 20-21
Calgary Herald, 7
Calvert, Lorne, Premier, 28
Camp, Dalton, 133

Canadian Bar Review, 27
Canadian Congress of Labour, 118
Canadian Labour Congress, 118-119
Canadian Medical Association, 116
Canadian National Railway, 214
Canadian Pacific Railway, 18-19, 52
Canadian Trades and Labour Congress, 118
Canadianization, of foreigners, 42-43, 48-49
Cancer Commission, 68
Catholic schools, 15, 131
Catholic voters in 1905, 17-19, 26
caucus fraud scandals, 195-201, 203, 205, 2007-208, 210-211, 229
CCF, *see* Co-operative Commonwealth Federation
Centennial Auditorium, Saskatoon, 167
Centennial, provincial, 223
Centre of the Arts, Regina, 153, 174
Chambers of Commerce, 141, 173, 226
Charlottetown agreement, 215
Chernesky, Morris, 147
child tax credit, 190
churches, property taxes for, 191
Churchill, Winston, 71
civil service, 53-54, 92, 179, 186, 188
Civil Service Commission, 49, 92
Clark, Joe, 147, 156, 157, 215, 218, 224
Co-operative Commonwealth Federation, 28, 53-54, 76-77, 70-80, 82-84, 96-97, 110-113, 115, 127, 131-132, 135-136, 158, 169, 174, 179, 188, 219
  becomes NDP, 124, 192
  federal party of, 66, 101, 118
  government of, 102, 108, 114, 116, 119-120
  merger with CLC, 118-119
  rise of, 85, 87-88
  as protest movement, 75, 78, 168, 179, 217
  with T. Douglas as leader, 90, 94-95, 104, 109, 121-122, 126, 183, 223
  with G. Williams as leader, 74, 100
Co-operative Government, 78
coal freight subsidy, federal, 61
coal miners' strike, 61
coal mining, 61, 82
Coldwell, M. James, 77, 126, 174, 183
  as CCF federal leader, 53, 101-103, 118
  as Farmer-Labourer leader, 69-70, 76, 88
collective bargaining, 92-93
Collver, Richard, L. (Dick), 149, 158-160, 162-163, 170, 172, 201, 218, 224-225
  defeat of, 166-168
  and 1975 election, 148, 150, 153, 155
  and 1978 election, 157, 161
  as PC leader, x, 140-148, 151-152, 154, 156, 164-165, 171, 219, 236
Collver, Eleanor, 146

communication allowances, to PC MLAs, 196-199
communism, 117
Communist Party, 61-62, 95
compassionate conservatism, of Diefenbaker, 188, 193
Confederation, 2, 4, 55-56, 166, 213, 216
conscription, 35
conservatism
  federal, 213
  fiscal, Romanow, 220
  provincial, 2, 82, 213, 215-217, 221, 232
  social and economic, 206, 220
Conservative ideology, 213
Conservative Party of Canada, 89, 221, 224-226
  and Anderson, 56, 70
  and Bennett, 67
  and Bracken as leader, 104, 214
  and Diefenbaker, 83
  and Hamilton, 104
  and Haultain, 9-10, 24, 29
  and immigration, 20
  and Territories, 2, 5-6, 20
cooperative enterprises, 59, 109
Cooperative Government, of Anderson, 51-53, 55-56, 58, 64-65
Coronet Motor Hotel, Prince Albert, 129, 154
Crescent Park (Moose Jaw), 60
crop failures, 58, 65
crop insurance plan, 121
Crow Rate disputes, 170
Crown Corporations, 149, 163, 170, 172, 178-179
  privatization of, 178-180, 188, 191, 193
  publicly owned, 179
  in resource sectors, 178-180
  utility, 179
Crown lands, control of, 5, 13, 15, 18, 25, 49, 53-55, 68, 160

D'Autremont, Dan, 209
Dance of Life, The, 94
Danielson, Herman, 131
Davis, T.C., 66, 72, 84
Debt Adjustment Act, 59, 68
Debt Adjustment Board, 59
Delisle United Church Sunday School, 100
democratic socialism, 216
dental care legislation for children, 178, 187
Department of Agriculture, 91
Department of Education, 15, 41, 43
Department of Highways, 33
Department of Immigration, 49
Department of Industrial Development, 121
Department of Telephones, 32

Department of Women's Work (U of SK), 91
Depression, 52, 61-62, 69, 74, 77, 79, 82-84, 216
  and Anderson government, 51, 59-60, 65-67, 70
  and Bennett government, 113, 214
  and CCF, 75, 93, 168
  and economics, 56-57, 80-81
  and falling grain prices, 58, 114
Devine, Chantal, 169, 173, 184
Devine, Grant, 157, 167, 202-203,
  and caucus fraud scandal, 195-196, 199-200
  and family values, 191
  government of, x, 143, 173, 180-182, 188-190, 193, 198, 201-204, 207, 229, 231
  as leader of PC party, ix, x, 168-171, 183, 206, 225
  and neo-conservatism, 190, 192-193, 219
  and neo-liberalism, 219-220
  and 1982 election, 173-174, 219
  and 1986 election, 184, 219
  and 1991 election, 189-192
  as PC leader, 166, 168, 172, 185, 219, 236
  as premier, 175, 177, 180-182, 184, 187, 199-200, 225
  resigned as PC leader, 201, 230
  years of, 196, 205, 220, 231-232, 234
Diefenbaker, Edna, 74, 82-85, 101
Diefenbaker, John G., 1, 28, 63, 67, 71-72, 104, 106, 108, 113, 116, 120, 123-124, 129, 131, 133, 135-136, 145, 147, 152, 160, 166, 172
  compassionate conservatism of, 188, 193
  and conservatism, 214-215, 217-218
  as federal candidate, 103, 105, 118
  government of, 115, 125-126, 134
  as PC national leader, 73-74, 74, 76-87, 107, 110, 112, 122, 127-128, 224
  as provincial candidate, 41, 47-48, 51, 66, 70, 99, 101
  as provincial PC leader, 100, 111, 225, 236
Diefenbaker Park Commission, 130
Dirks, Gordon, 185
Dirty Thirties, 56, 63, 78
doctors' strike, 123; see also mediscare
Dods, Glen, 157
Douglas, T.C., 159, 172-174, 179, 183, 187, 206
  as CCF leader, 28, 88, 90, 93
  as CCF MP, 77, 126
  as CCF MLA, 102
  election of 1956, 107-109
  election of 1960, 114, 121
  as federal NDP leader, 124
  government of, 54, 89, 94, 97, 114, 119-120
  and medicare, 116, 122, 161-162
  as premier, 95, 104, 119, 223

Draude, June, 209
Drew, George, 102, 103, 215, 224
drought, 50, 56-57, 69, 104, 114, 168, 180-181, 187, 216
drug plan, prescription, legislation, 187
Duncan, Joan, 163, 177, 198
Dunn, C.M., 77
Dunning, C.A., 37, 39, 41, 43-44, 75, 223
Dutchak, Sid, 185

Eager, Evelyn, 217
education, 93, 96, 121, 133, 183, 193
Education of the New Canadian, The, 43
Edwards, Evelyn, 154
Eggum, Kris, 211
electric power, development of, 82
electrification of rural areas, 126
elevators, see grain elevators
Ellis, Havelock
  The Dance of Life, 94
English, as sole language of school instruction, 35
European Economic Community, farm subsidies by, 181

Fair Share Program, 189-190
family farm, 76, 93, 202
  debt of, 56, 58, 81-82, 181
  depreciation of, 181
  foreclosures of, 56
  income of, 181
  ownership program, 182
family values, 191
Farm Credit Agency, 121
farm fuel, tax on, 137
Farm Purchase Program, 182
Farmer-Labour movement, 85, 100
Farmer-Labour Party, 66, 68-69, 75-76, 119, 217
  1934 edition, 75
  land policy of, 76
farmers' revolt, 33
farmers, political action of, 37
Folk, Rick, 185
forest conservation, 92
Forget, A.E., 7-9, 19
Fraser, Hal, 72
fraud scandal (Tories), 195-201, 203, 205, 207-208, 210-211, 229
free trade initiatives, 216
freight tariff, 24

Gantefoer, Rod, 209-210, 233
Gardiner, James G., 77, 96, 125, 223
  cabinet of, 51
  government of, 45, 50, 54, 74
  as Liberal leader, 48-49, 52, 63, 65-69

as politician, 39, 41, 73, 75, 159, 172
as premier, 44, 46, 55
Gardiner machine, 39, 47, 53, 75, 82, 84, 96, 99-100
gas pipeline monopolies, 105
gasoline tax, 178, 188
Gerich, John, 157, 196
Given, Nathaniel, 99-100
Golden Jubilee, provincial, 223
Goldwater, Barry, 42
Goodale, Ralph, 169
Goods and Services Tax, 189-190
Gooshen, Jack, 209
Government Party, 38
grain elevators
  government ownership & control of, 22-23, 26, 216
grain handling and marketing, 23
Gravel Plains (later Runeberg) School, 43
Green, Dr. Glen, 128
Grey, A.H.G., Earl, 8
grid roads, construction of, 121
Gruending, Dennis, 119
gun-control legislation, 207

H.E. Keown and Co., 87
Ham, Dennis, 151
Hamilton, Alvin, 72, 74, 89, 96, 125, 127, 129, 144, 188, 218
  as leader of PC Party, ix, 87, 97, 99-104, 107-110, 112, 130, 143, 225-226, 236
  and Diefenbaker, 82-83
  as MP, 145
Hanbidge, Robert Leith (Dinny), 52, 72, 103
Harper, Stephen, 216

Haultain, Frederick William Gordon, 13, 21, 32, 48, 69, 109, 127, 130, 143, 224, 225
  as Chancellor of U of SK, 27
  as Chief Justice of SK, 27-28
  and conservatism, 22, 213, 216
  and 1905 election, 14, 17- 20
  and 1912 election, 26
  and ownership of elevators, 23
  as party leader, 25, 31, 87, 236
  as populist, 24
  as premier of North-West Territories, 1-3, 5-10, 28-29
  and school settlement, 15-16
  as statesman, 1, 7, 28, 223
  and trade reciprocity with US, 24
  and "two-province" provision, 11
Haverstock, Lynda, 192, 208
  as Liberal leader, 189, 191, 205-206
  as Lieutenant-Governor, 28
health care services, 75, 92-93, 96, 139, 161-162, 178, 187, 193
  funding of, 183
  improvements for, 173
  insurance for, 68, 81
  national plan for, 96
  reform of, 116-118, 161
Health Service Board, 68
heavy oil upgraders, 193
Heppner, Ben, 209
Hermanson, Elwin, 230
highways
  construction of, 75, 81, 93, 96, 126
Hill, George, 158
Hnatyshyn, Ray, 129
Hodgins, Grant, 198
home improvement loans, 183, 188
home ownership grants, 173
homesteaders, 3, 52, 76, 168
homosexuality, as immoral, 191
Hopfner, Michael, 195, 196, 199
Horner, Jack, 145-155
Horner, Norval, 129
hospital workers' strike, 174
hospitals
  closure of, 190
  insurance for, 81
  utilization fees for, 137, 139, 160
Hotel Saskatchewan, 103
Hudson Bay Railway, 22, 39
  government owned, 216
Hudson's Bay, 21
hydroelectric power facility, 82

immigrants, 3-4, 13, 20, 35-36, 40, 42-43, 53, 68, 82
  assimilation of, 43, 45, 54
  European, 3, 19, 31, 34, 42-45
  as voters, 14, 18, 48
immigration policy, selective entry, 45
immigration, unrestricted, 47
inauguration of province (1905), 223
Independent Labour Party, 66, 84
Independent Progressive Conservative, 105
Independents, 36, 38, 46, 48-50, 64, 67, 78, 84, 95, 97, 101, 166, 208-209
Indian affairs, 133-134
Indian Council system, 134
Indians, Treaty, off-reserve
  and sales taxes, 207
influenza epidemic (1918-20), 36

Jackson, Edward, 129
Johnson, Rev. T.W., 44, 65
Johnstone, Dr. D.S., 64, 78

Katzman, Ralph, 151, 163, 169, 196-198

Kelln, Martin, 120
  as Social Credit leader, 114, 122
Keown, H.E. Bert, 72-81, 83, 85, 87-89, 103-104
  as leader of Conservative Party, 87, 236
King coupes, 63
Knight, Bill, 156-158
Kohaly, Robert, 107, 109
Krawetz, Ken, 208-209
Ku Klux Klan, 45-49
Kyba, Patrick, 81

Labour Progressives, 84
labour relations, 92
labour unions, 178, 193
land policy, 76
land, nationalization of, 76
Lane, Gary, 153-154, 167
Lane, Harold, 154
Langevin, Adélard, Archbishop, 16-17
Langley, George, 37
Larson, Leonard, 154
Larter, Bob, 151, 169
Laurier, Wilfrid, Sir, 4-9, 11, 18-23, 223-224
  as builder of Liberal Party, 13
  and education clause in SK Act, 15
  and reciprocity with US, 27
  trade agreement of, 24
Leeson, Howard, 216
Liberal-Conservative coalition (1948), 97
Liberal-Conservative coalition (1997), 209, 212
Liberal Party of Canada, 2, 8, 13, 37, 115-116, 134, 142
  and gun control, 207
  and King, 111
  and Laurier, 21, 24
  and patronage, 20
  and St. Laurent, 110
  and Trudeau, 141, 163
Liberal Party of Saskatchewan, *see* Saskatchewan Liberal Party
liberalism, 2, 213, 221
Lincoln Hotel, 129
Lincoln, Abraham, 71, 128
Lingard, C.C., 7
Lippmann, Walter, 226
Lloyd, Woodrow, 131-132, 135, 139, 161
  government of, 124, 131
  as NDP leader, 133
  and 1964 election, 125-126, 128
  as premier, 124
Loucks, William, 100
Lougheed, Peter, 142
Lukiwski, Tom, 210

Macdonald, John A., 1-2, 18, 20, 71, 89, 224
  conservatism of, 2, 213-214, 216
MacEwan, Grant, 4, 25
Mackenzie King, William Lyon, 56, 63, 71, 74, 111
Mackintosh, Charles, Lieutenant-Governor, 3
MacLaren Advertising media consultants, Toronto, 126-127, 133
Maclean, Donald, 35-38, 236
Maclean's magazine, 70
Macleod, Dr. Wendell, 118
MacPherson, M.A., 51, 52, 55-56, 67, 72, 74, 89
Maharg, J.A., 37
Making of the President, 1964, The, ix
Malone, Ted, 153-158, 160, 164
Management Associates Limited, 142
Mandryk, Murray, 205
Manning, Ernest, 108, 114
Martens, Harold, 198
Martin, W.M., 33-39, 41, 75, 223
Mason, Bob, 232
McCafferty, Michael, 190
McConnell, Howard, 52, 68
McCulloch, Arthur J., 43
McDonald, A.H., 95, 97, 108-109
  as candidate of Conservative-Liberal coalition, 108
McKnight, Bill, 171-172
McLaren, Lorne, 196-197
McLelland, Ron, 147
McLeod, George, 157
McLuhan, Marshall, 227
medical care, 116, 122, 162
  compulsory, 114
  universal, comprehensive, 114, 120
medical insurance
  comprehensive, government, 117
  voluntary plans, 114
medicare, 28, 114, 116, 118, 122, 124-127, 132, 160-162, 164
  debate on, 118-120, 122, 124, 139
mediscare, 161-162, 164, 170
Meech Lake agreement, 215
Meighen, Arthur, 214, 216, 224
Meiklejohn, Ray, 198
Melenchuk, Jim, 208-209
melting pot society, 214-215
Merchant, Tony, 153
Merkley, J.A., 52
Metis entitlements, 227
Metis people, 3
Mine Workers Union of Canada, 61
Mines Act, amendments to, 61
Minimum Wage Act, 68, 81
Moose Jaw Times-Herald, 233

Morin, Myles, 185
mortgage interest rate control, 173, 178, 181, 183
Motherwell, W.R., 37
Muirhead, Gerry, 157
Mulroney, Brian, 184, 224
  and conservatism, 213, 218
  and pluralism, 215
municipal work programs, 58
Munroe, Dr. Frederick, 52

Nasserden, Ed, 138-139, 141, 236
  and 1971 election, 140
National Policy, protectionist, 214-215
nationalized school system, 16; *see also* schools
Native people, 3, 8; *see also* Aboriginal, Indians, Métis
natural gas, 105, 109, 182, 188
natural resources, 92, 96, 149, 170
  control of, 3, 5, 7, 13, 15, 24-25, 49, 53-55, 68, 160, 163
NDP Land Bank, 182
neo-conservatism, 220
neo-liberal ideology, 219
New Democratic Party (NDP) of Saskatchewan, x, 135, 137, 144, 147, 149, 154, 160, 165, 168-170, 179, 181-182, 192, 195, 198-199, 201, 209-210, 219, 221, 225, 229-230, 233
  and Blakeney, 139, 141-142, 146, 148, 150-151, 155-159, 161, 163, 171-175, 178, 183-184
  rise of, 118, 124, 132, 217
  and Romanow, 188, 190-191, 205-207, 220
  and welfare programs, 204
New Progressive Conservatives, 206-208
North Battleford asylum, 32
North-West Territories, 1, 3-6, 8, 14-15, 19, 28, 34
  non-partisanship in, 10, 29
  see also autonomy
North-West Territories Act of 1875, 2, 14
North-West Territories Act of 1888, 3
North-West Territories Act of 1891, 3
northern development, 96, 130

O'Brian, Liam, 145
oil industry, 181
oil policy, provincial, 105
oil revenues, 187
old age benefits, 92, 96
Orange Lodges, 34, 46
Orange Order, Protestant, 45
Orangemen, 47

paper mill, establishment of, 193

Parker, James, 205
Patrick, J.A.M., 72
patriotism, after WWI, 36, 45
patronage, ix, 9, 13, 19, 21, 48, 53-54, 65, 80, 82, 92, 178
  by Liberal Party, 64, 93, 100
Patterson, W.J., 74-76, 84-85, 87, 90, 93-95, 111, 223
  government of, 77-78, 83
Pearson, Lester, 116, 126
Pederson, Martin, 112, 119-131, 134-136, 138, 143-145, 147, 188, 211, 218, 225-226
  early years of, 111
  as federal Director of Organization in SK, 106
  and Hamilton, 107
  and health care, 117-118
  as PC leader, 113-116, 236
Perley, Ernest, 101
Petersen, Sherwin, 198
Pickering, Bob, 157
Pitsula, James, 220
pluralism, 215
populism, western, 22, 24, 39, 143, 151, 160, 168, 181, 193, 206, 215-216
Potash Corporation of Saskatchewan (PCS)
  privatization of, 179-180, 188
potash mining, 132, 163
potash revenues, 187
Prairieland Exhibition Center, Saskatoon, 229
Price Waterhouse, 142
Prince Albert Daily Herald, 50, 133
Prince Albert Penitentiary, 33
Prince Albert Provincial Progressive Conservative campaign, 129
Prince Albert Pulp Mill, 188
private enterprise, 193, 215
Progressive Conservative Association, 112
Progressive Conservative Party of Canada, 39, 89, 101, 103, 114-115, 121, 124, 211
  and Hamilton, 111, 112
  and Clark, 156, 218
  and Mulroney, 184, 218
Progressive Conservative Party of Saskatchewan, ix, 94-95, 134, 138, 141, 167, 171, 202, 205, 209-210, 217-220, 236
  caucus fraud scandal of, 195-201, 203, 205, 207-208, 210-211, 229
  collapse of, 210-212, 226-227, 235
  and Collver, 143, 145-146, 152-157, 160, 162
  and Devine, 168-170, 172, 179-180, 182, 184, 190-191
  and Diefenbaker, 85, 112, 128-129
  future of, 226
  and Hamilton, 103, 106-107, 111
  manifesto of (1944), 89-90, 92
  as neo-conservatist experiment, 194

as New PC Party, 206-208
  and 1960 election, 120-122
  and 1964 election, 127, 130-133, 137
  and 1982 election, 173-175
  and Pederson, 113, 119, 123, 126, 135, 147
  and Ramsay, 96-97
  revival of, 114, 229-231, 233-234
  trust fund dispute of, 231-234
Progressives, in SK, 36, 38, 41, 46-50, 64, 67, 88-89, 101, 133
prohibition legislation, 35
Protestant school administration, 15
Protestant voters, 17-18, 26, 31
Provincial Rights Party, 13, 17-22, 24, 29, 94, 224, 236
public schools, see schools
Public Service Act, 53
Public Service Commission, 53-54, 68
public trust, abuses of, 195
public utilities, 188
pulp and lumber industry, 82, 130
pulp mill, establishment of, 193

Quebec, as distinct society, 216

racial antagonism, 35, 42
railways, 3, 21, 22, 204, 214, 216
Ramsay, Rupert David, 87, 89-91, 94-97, 100, 102-104, 135, 143, 218, 225
  as PC leader, 96-98, 236
Rasmussen, Ken, 220
recession, 187, 216
Redistribution Bill, 130
reforestation and afforestation policies, 82
Reform Party, federal, 209, 221, 230
Regina Conservative Association, 82
Regina Daily Star, 47, 74
Regina General Hospital, 68
Regina Leader, 25-26
Regina Leader-Post, 98, 205
relief, rural and urban, 60
Riel, Louis, 18, 20
Riel uprising, 20
Ritchie, Gordon, 145
Robertson, Dr. Alexander, 118
Robson, H.A., 28
Rogue Tory, 73
Roman Catholic Church, 16, 34, 44, 76, 93
  see also Catholic voters
Romanow, Roy, 170, 175
  fiscal conservatism of, 220
  government of, 208, 220
  as NDP leader, 188-189
  and 1991 election, 190-191
  and 1995 election, 206-207
  as premier, 205

Ross, J.H., 4
Rousseau, Paul, 167-168, 177
Royal Canadian Mounted Police (RCMP), 8, 62
  investigations of Tory fraud, 195, 197-198
Royal Commissions (1931), 68
Royal Commission on bribes over liquor legislation, 33
Royal Commission on elevator ownership, 23
Royal Commission on immigration, 45, 54
Royal Commission on road construction contracts, 32
Rural Municipalities' Association, 34
rural Saskatchewan, 77, 98, 141, 146, 183, 205, 230
  county system in, 131
  electrification system in, 91, 126
  government assistance to, 57, 189
  and gun control, 207
  jobs for, 139
  loans to, 121, 182
  telephones, roads for, 21-22, 173
  way of life in, 76, 226

sales tax, provincial, 189, 190, 207
Salvation Army band, Regina, 36
Saskatchewan
  automony of, 13
  provisional district of, 4
  as welfare state, 215
Saskatchewan Act, 7, 14, 17
  education clause in, 15
Saskatchewan Chamber of Commerce, 144
  see also Chambers of Commerce
Saskatchewan College of Physicians and Surgeons (SCPS), 116-118, 124-125
Saskatchewan Conservative Association, 46
Saskatchewan Conservative Party, ix, x, 1, 10, 34, 36-38, 47-50, 66-68, 88, 94, 213, 224-225, 236
  and Anderson, 45, 62, 70-71, 155
  and Diefenbaker, 72-81, 84, 86, 217
  and Dunning, 39, 42
  and Hamilton, 82, 99-102, 105, 109-110
  and Haultain, 13, 18-19, 21, 24, 26-29, 31
  and 1929 platform, 53, 56, 64
  and 1938 defeat, 85
Saskatchewan Co-operative Elevator Company, 23, 37, 39
Saskatchewan Farmer-Labour Party, 88
Saskatchewan Farmers' Union, 114
Saskatchewan Forest Products
  privatization of, 188
Saskatchewan Government Insurance (SGI), 163, 188

Saskatchewan Grain Growers Association (SGGA), 23, 33-35, 37-39
Saskatchewan Horizons, 146, 149
Saskatchewan Investment Opportunities Corporation, 149
Saskatchewan Liberal Party, 8-9, 230
  decline of, 88, 138, 140-141, 144, 148, 151, 164, 209, 219-220, 225, 227
  and Dunning, 40, 43
  and farmers, 37, 117, 120-121, 217
  and Gardiner, 42, 46, 48-54, 65-67, 69, 74-75, 77, 99-100
  and Goodale, 169, 184
  and Haultain, 14-15, 19
  and Haverstock, 191-192, 205, 207-208
  and Malone, 156-161, 163, 167
  and Martin, 35, 38
  on medicare, 123
  and patronage, 64, 93, 100
  and Patterson, 80-81, 83-85, 87, 111
  scandal in, 33
  and school act, 68
  and Scott, 13-14, 16, 18, 20-21, 24-26
  and Steuart, 142, 147, 150, 154
  and Thatcher, 114-116, 122, 124-127, 131, 133, 135-137, 153
  and Tucker, 95, 97-98, 102, 104, 106-109
Saskatchewan Mining Development Corporation, privatization of, 179, 188
Saskatchewan Orange Association, 47
Saskatchewan Party, x, 185, 209-212, 220-221, 224, 227, 229-230, 232-234
Saskatchewan Pension Plan, 182
Saskatchewan Progressive Conservative Party, *see* Progressive Conservative Party of Saskatchewan
Saskatchewan Provincial Progressive Association, 39
Saskatchewan Relief Commission, 57-58, 68, 81
Saskatchewan Roughriders, 133, 198
Saskatchewan School Trustees Association, 34
Saskatchewan Social Credit League, 138
Saskatchewan Social Credit Party, 107
Saskatchewan Transportation Company, 149
Saskatchewan, University of, 1, 27, 71, 89-90, 98-99, 108, 118, 121, 157, 167-168, 204
Saskatchewan Valley Authority, 105
Saskatchewan Wheat Pool, 58-59, 114
Saskatoon StarPhoenix, 205
SaskEnergy, 188
SaskFerco, 193
SaskOil, privatization of, 179, 188
SaskPower, 188
SaskTel, 188
scandal, *see* caucus fraud scandal (Tories)

Schmidt, Grant, 199, 203-205, 231, 233
  and revival of PC party, 231
School Act of 1892, 15-16
School Act, amendment to, 37, 45, 53, 68
School for the Deaf, 68
schools, public, 34, 36-37, 40, 53, 68
  language debate for, 35
  sectarianism in, 44-45, 47-48, 53, 68
schools, separate, 13-17, 36, 45, 49, 64
Scott, Dorothy, 223
Scott, Walter, 13-14, 16-17, 27, 37, 39, 109, 159, 223-224
  government of, 20, 22-24, 26, 31-32
  as interim premier, 19-20
  as Liberal leader, 7, 18-20, 33
  liberalism of, 23
  and 1912 election, 24-26
  and 1916 scandals, 32
  and ownership of elevators, 23
  as premier, 9, 11, 19-21, 28, 31, 33, 54
  and trade reciprocity with US, 24
Scraba, John, 196
Sifton, Clifford, 5
small business loans, 183
Smith, David E., 21, 35
Smith, Denis
  Rogue Tory, 73
Smith, Pat, 177
social assistance, *see* social programs
Social Credit Party, 74-80, 83-85, 95, 97, 100-101, 106, 138, 235
  disappearance of, 219, 225, 235
  and Kelln, 114, 122
  and medicare, 117
  and 1960 election, 121-123
  and 1964 election, 127
  provincial rise of, 107, 109-110, 116, 120
  Saskatchewan Social Credit Party, 107
  see also Social Credit Party
social democracy, 93, 124, 151, 163, 187, 193, 204, 206, 220-221, 226
social gospel, 93, 119
social individualism, 214-215
social programs, 97, 120, 139, 150, 174, 187, 193, 204, 226
  see also welfare programs
social reform package, 114
socialism, 69, 93, 95, 102, 119, 139, 188
socialized medicine, see medicare
Soil Conservation and Utilization Program, 105, 108
South Saskatchewan River dam, 96, 105, 130
Spencer, Dick, 128-129, 145
Squaw Rapids hydroelectric installation, 126
St. Laurent, Louis, 110, 223
Stanfield, Robert, 136, 145, 215, 218, 224

Steuart, D.G., 125, 127-129, 141, 144, 148-151, 153-154, 167
Stewart, A.C., 52
Stipe, Reginald, 52
stock market crash, 50
Stooshinoff, Nick, 211
Stowers (Fair Land) School, 43
Swenson, Rick, 143, 202, 230, 232
  and caucus fraud scandal, 203
  as former PC leader, 211
  as interim PC leader, 229-230, 234
  and revival of PC party, 231, 234

tariff protection of wheat, 23
tax relief measures, 173
Taylor, Graham, 167, 168, 177
teledemocracy, phone-in system to elect leader, 205
telephone service (increased), 21-22, 182
telephones, public ownership of, 22, 216
Territorial conservatives, 10
 non-partisan relationships, 224
Territorial government, 4, 7, 15
 autonomy of, 4
Territorial Grain Growers, 37
Territorial Independents, 10
Territorial liberals, 4, 7, 10
Thatcher, Colin, 153, 156, 164, 169, 201-202
Thatcher, Ross, 118, 134-135, 141-142, 148, 150, 156, 158, 173
  death of, 140, 144
  government of, 114, 132, 161, 219
  as Liberal leader, 114-116, 121-122, 124-125, 149
  and 1964 election, 126, 131, 133
  and 1971 election, 139
  as premier, 137, 153, 202
Thomas, L.H., 216
Tkachuk, David, 158, 164, 171
Tollefson, Edwin
  Bitter Medicine: The Saskatchewan Medicare Feud, 124
Toronto Saturday Night, 8
Toronto, University of, 17
Tory collectivism, 22, 214, 216
Tory democracy, 213, 215-216
Toryism, 2, 65, 213
Toth, Don, 209
trade reciprocity with US, 23-24, 26
trade stagnation, 56
trade union, 174
Trianon Ballroom, 174
Trudeau, Pierre, 141, 163
True Blue Tories, 64-65, 67, 78, 89, 130, 188, 225
Tucker, Walter A., 95, 104, 108

Tufts, Bill, 136
Turnbull, F.W., 100

unemployment, 56-58, 65, 68
Unemployment and Farm Relief Acts, 57
unemployment insurance for farm workers, 121
Union Government, 35, 113
unionism, 188
United Farmers of Canada, 66, 88
uranium industry, 163, 180, 187
use-lease land policy, 75, 76

Vagabond Inn, Regina, 144, 145
Voice of the Handicapped, 187

Waiser, Dr. Bill, 34, 181
Wascana Lake, enhancement, 60
Waschuk, Ken, 169
water and soil conservation program, 68, 121
Weir, Robert, 56, 74, 81
welfare programs, provincial, 152, 188, 193, 204, 221; *see also* social programs
Wetmore, Edward, Judge, 32
Weyerhaeuser, 188
Wheat Board, 81
wheat crops, 34, 45, 132
wheat stabilization fund, 96
wheat tariff, 23
White, E.B., 212
White, Theodore, H.
  The Making of the President, 1964, ix
Whitter, George, Jr., 128-129
Williams, George, 74, 77, 84, 88, 100
Willoughby, Wellington Bartley
  as Conservative Party leader, 31-35, 236
Wimmer, Ross, Justice, 195
Wipf, Garnet, 154
Wishlow, Kevin, 220-221
women's rights, 32, 35
work ethic values, 204
Workers' Unity League, 61, 62
workfare programs, 205, 230
Workmen's Compensation Act, 68
World War I, 36, 70
World War II, 87, 90, 99, 107, 111

Yorkton Enterprise, 122
Young PC Association, 111